Developing a Comprehensive Faculty Evaluation System

Developing a Comprehensive Faculty Evaluation System

A Guide to Designing, Building, and Operating
Large-Scale Faculty Evaluation Systems

THIRD EDITION

Raoul A. Arreola
The University of Tennessee Health Science Center

ANKER PUBLISHING COMPANY, INC.

Published by Jossey-Bass
A Wiley Imprint
989 Market Street, San Francisco, CA 94103-1741   www.josseybass.com

Jossey-Bass books and products are available through most bookstores. To contact Jossey-Bass directly call our Customer Care Department within the U.S. at 800-956-7739, outside the U.S. at 317-572-3986, or fax 317-572-4002.

Jossey-Bass also publishes its books in a variety of electronic formats. Some content that appears in print may not be available in electronic books.

Library of Congress Cataloging-in-Publication Data

Arreola, Raoul A. (Raoul Albert), 1943-
  Developing a comprehensive faculty evaluation system : a guide
  to designing, building, and operating large-scale faculty evaluation
  systems / Raoul A. Arreola.—3rd ed.
     p. cm.
  Includes bibliographical references and index.
  ISBN-13: 978-1-933371-11-5
  ISBN-10: 1-933371-11-0
  1. College teachers—Rating of—United States. 2. College teaching—
United States—Evaluation. I. Title.
LB2333.A77 2007
378.1'22—dc22   2006025793

Printed in the United States of America
THIRD EDITION
PB Printing   10 9 8 7 6 5 4 3 2 1

Dedicated to

Russell P. Kropp

Mentor, Colleague, Friend

Table of Contents

List of Figures and Tables

Figures

Tables

About the Author

Raoul A. Arreola received his Ph.D. in educational psychology from Arizona State University in 1969, specializing in educational research and measurement. He has taught in the areas of statistics, educational psychology, personnel evaluation, and educational leadership, and has held a number of faculty and administrative positions involving assessment, strategic planning, faculty evaluation, and faculty development. These positions include director of the Office of Evaluation Services, associate director of the Learning Systems Institute, and associate professor of educational research and measurement at Florida State University; director of the Center for Instructional Services and Research and professor of educational psychology at the University of Memphis; and professor and chair of the Department of Education, assistant dean for assessment and planning, director of educational technology, and director of institutional research, assessment, and planning at the University of Tennessee Health Science Center. Dr. Arreola currently serves as director of assessment and professor of pharmaceutical sciences in the College of Pharmacy at the University of Tennessee Health Science Center.

Dr. Arreola has worked and published in the field of faculty evaluation and development for 36 years and has served as a consultant nationally and internationally to more than 250 colleges and universities in designing and operating faculty evaluation and development programs. He has also served as a consultant to the U.S. Department of Labor and the Florida House of Representatives on designing and evaluating professional and occupational licensing examination procedures. He is president of his own consulting firm, the Center for Educational Development and Evaluation (CEDA), which offers consulting and national workshops on developing and assessing faculty performance. These workshops have been attended by thousands of faculty and administrators from more than 500 colleges and universities.

In 2004 Dr. Arreola was presented with the McKeachie Career Achievement Award by the Special Interest Group on Faculty Teaching, Evaluation, and Development of the American Educational Research Association for his contributions to the field of assessing and developing faculty performance. In 2005 the American Educational Research Association presented him with the prestigious Interpretive Scholarship Award in recognition for his work in developing the *meta-profession* model of the professoriate, which underpins the processes described in this volume.

Raoul Arreola is married to Dr. Mona J. Arreola, associate director of the cancer center of St. Jude Children's Research hospital. They have four grown children and nine grandchildren (so far).

Preface to the Third Edition

More than halfway through the first decade of the 21st century it is clear that there has been a major shift in the social and economic paradigm within which higher education must operate. To the public demands for accountability, expressed as legislative mandates, has been added an emphasis on outcomes by accrediting bodies and a systematic shrinking of public funding. More and more colleges and universities are expected to fund their own operations rather than rely completely on public support.

> Although the major goal of the U.S. universities is the advancement and dissemination of knowledge, universities also need funding to support their activities. A university must seek revenue from a variety of sources and more and more, faculty members are encouraged to generate income. (Burroughs Wellcome Fund & Howard Hughes Medical Institute, 2004, pp. 27)

In addition, the value of a college degree itself has come under serious question (Hersh & Merrow, 2005). High among the issues of interest resulting from this increasing demand for accountability has been the performance of college and university faculty. The prestige and general high esteem in which faculty have traditionally been held, and which has tended to insulate them from normal societal standards of accountability, melted away in the bright light of the ubiquitous media and the "dot com" critics of the Internet. Market forces, responding to society's perception of the failure of traditional higher education, have brought forth the rapid emergence and success of private online educational institutions, as well as corporate universities.

In 1994 Stan Davis and Jim Botkin authored a particularly insightful book, *The Monster Under the Bed: How Business is Mastering the Opportunity of Knowledge for Profit.* The monster under the bed was seen as the paradigm shift being brought about by the impact of technology on all segments of American society—especially education. While chronicling the various social, political, economic, and religious forces that impact education, the authors make one major point that is of particular interest here: namely, that education, as a social enterprise, has historically been supported by different segments of society and that a shift in that support is once again occurring—perhaps to the detriment of the traditional higher education structures we have known.

> Through successive periods of history, different institutions have borne the major responsibility for education. Changes in education take a very long time to evolve. They are a consequence of greater transformations, often social, political, economic, or religious, and therefore are always a few steps behind the demands of the society they are designed to serve. But today schools are more than a few steps behind, and many feel they are on the wrong path altogether. (Davis & Botkin, 1994, pp. 23)

Davis and Botkin point out that from an historical perspective, organized educational efforts originated as a function of the church. Later, especially in America, the responsibility for supporting education moved to the government (when an educated populace was seen as necessary for the successful functioning of a free, democratic society). Now, with the ubiquity of the computer, the Internet, and the resultant "knowledge explosion" and global economy, the underlying support for education is in the process of moving from the government to the marketplace. The social paradigm under which higher education has successfully functioned and been supported for generations is undergoing a significant change.

A critical feature of this paradigm shift is the expectation of the public relative to admission to college. In August 2000 the Council on Higher Education Accreditation (CHEA), the umbrella organization for higher education accrediting agencies, issued an Occasional Paper prepared by the National Center for Higher Education Management Systems titled *The Competency Standards Project: Another Approach to Accreditation Review*. At its most fundamental level, this report proposed shifting the accreditation process from evaluating processes to evaluating outcomes. The question asked of higher education was about to change from "What resources do you have and what are you doing with them?" to "How much have your students learned and what can they actually do as a result of the experience you gave them?" This change constitutes a critical element of the paradigm shift.

Under the old paradigm, the college or university was expected to serve a "filtering" function. Each faculty member, in each course, each year, would flunk a certain percentage of students, so that by the senior year, the students that were left were the "survivors." That is, they constituted that segment of the population that could learn no matter what obstacles and challenges were put before them. A college graduate, then, was known by society to be the best and the brightest that could be produced. College graduates were valued and, mostly, paid appropriately.

This type of filtering contract higher education had with American society even extended down into high school where students were sorted, on the basis of standardized tests, into one of three tracks: the college preparatory track, the general education track, or the vocational education track (students were responsible for their own self-esteem in those days). The college prep students were those destined to go to college (although not necessarily survive); the general education track students would go to work upon graduation (they could go to college if they wanted but were not expected to survive); and the vocational education track students became electricians, mechanics, plumbers, secretaries, et cetera. It was a matter of common knowledge, as well as some research, that college graduates would make a lot more money during their lifetime than those that did not finish or never went to college.

The new paradigm moves higher education from a filtering function to, ironically, a true instructional/teaching function. Instead of sorting the bright from the not-so-bright, the talented from the not-so-talented, the persistent from the not-so-persistent, society is now demanding that colleges and universities accept virtually anyone who comes in the door and take them from whatever level of ignorance and ability they possess upon entrance up to some *specified level of employable competence.*

In this new paradigm college faculty, rather than being the primary, if not sole, repository of information, knowledge, and educational opportunity, now find themselves in competition not only with colleagues on more remote campuses, but with commercial enterprises as well. The tradition of tenure is being seriously challenged and in many institutions of higher learning it is being phased out. It is becoming more and more common to find colleges, especially community colleges, where as much as 80% of the curriculum is taught by adjunct or part-time faculty. All of these factors have led to not only a demand for rigorous evaluation of faculty performance, but also a reconceptualization of what it means to be a college professor in the first place.

The result of all these changes has been an increasing demand throughout higher education for a systematic, practical procedure for building and operating a comprehensive faculty evaluation system based on sound administrative principles and research evidence. In this context, the word *comprehensive* is used to denote the evaluation of the full spectrum of complex professional performances in which faculty must engage, including, of course, teaching. The first edition of this book, published in 1995, as well as the subsequent updating of that work published in 2000, were in response to the demand for such systems. The purpose of those works, as well as this one, is to provide a practical, proven procedure for developing and using a comprehensive faculty evaluation system. Based on 36 years of research and experience in building and operating large-scale faculty evaluation systems, as well as consulting experience with more than 250 colleges and universities, this new edition includes not only more detailed information about the process of building and operating a comprehensive faculty evaluation system, but a new model for conceptualizing the full complexity of faculty performance itself.

▥ THE EIGHT-STEP PROCESS FOR DESIGNING A SYSTEM

The heart of this new edition remains the same proven, reliable eight-step process for building a comprehensive faculty evaluation system. As has been shown repeatedly with many different types of institutions, following these eight steps will result in the development of a customized faculty evaluation system that reflects the mission, priorities, culture, traditions, and values of the institution and also responds to the specific needs and concerns of the institution's faculty and administration. These eight steps are detailed in Chapters 1 through 8.

1) Determine the Faculty Role Model

Determine the roles faculty play within the institution in terms of their specific duties, responsibilities, and activities.

2) Determine the Faculty Role Model Parameter Values

Begin the process of codifying the priorities and values of the faculty and administration relative to the roles faculty play.

3) Define the Roles in the Faculty Role Model

Develop clear definitions of each role in terms of specific activities to permit later measurement of those faculty performances in those roles.

4) Determine Role Component Weights

Continue the process of codifying the values of the faculty and administration relative to specific performances that define each role.

5) Determine Appropriate Sources of Information

Logically ascertain where information concerning various aspects of faculty performance may be obtained.

6) Determine Information Source Weights

Continue the process of codifying the values of the faculty and administration relative to the importance of certain information from various sources.

7) Determine How Information Should Be Gathered

Logically determine what types of forms or data-gathering procedures would be most appropriate for each type of information to be gathered.

8) Complete the System

Actually select and/or design and build the various tools (forms, checklists, etc.) necessary to gather the information needed to conduct the evaluation.

The explanation of each step in the process has been expanded and enhanced to provide more detailed guidance in building a faculty evaluation system. Much of the additional information provided is derived from the experiences of many institutions that followed the procedure as described in this book. Also, more specific definitions of the various roles to be evaluated (including Teaching and Scholarly/Creative Activities) are provided than in the previous edition.

Chapters 9 through 16 focus on implementing and operating the faculty evaluation system. Chapters 9 and 10 present methods for generating an overall composite rating (OCR) and using it for promotion, continuation or tenure, merit pay, and post-tenure review decisions. Chapter 11 discusses peer review issues within the faculty evaluation system, and Chapters 12 through 15 present a wide range of information about, and samples of, student rating forms, including legal issues, administration procedures, the interpretation of results, a catalog of items, and a checklist for identifying and selecting published forms. Chapter 16 includes several case studies of institutions that designed their faculty evaluation systems using the eight-step process described in this book.

■ CHANGES TO THE THIRD EDITION

In addition to expanding and updating the presentation of the eight steps, several other revisions characterize the third edition.

Updated Forms and Procedures for Steps 1–3

Experience with institutions wishing to develop their faculty evaluation system in an accelerated fashion has resulted in enhanced forms for use in the first three steps of the eight-step procedure and an alternate strategy for carrying out the first three steps more quickly. This new edition includes new forms and a description of an alternate accelerated strategy for carrying out the first three steps of the process of building a comprehensive faculty evaluation system.

New Research

As always, research in the field has progressed. Although no new or different significant findings concerning faculty evaluation have emerged in the literature since the publication of the second edition, there has been a general updating of the references throughout, especially in the chapters on student ratings.

New Case Study

A new case study has been added to the case studies included in the previous editions of this book. The new case study has been included as an exemplar of an institution that developed a web-enabled or electronic, computer-supported comprehensive faculty evaluation systems using the eight-step process described herein. This new case study includes descriptions and graphical representations of innovative techniques used to place much of the record-keeping functions of the faculty evaluation system online.

The Professoriate as Meta-Profession

Finally, and perhaps most significantly, this edition contains a new body of work that defines the professoriate as a *meta-profession*. That is, the college professor is conceptualized as practicing a profession requiring a high level of expertise in a number of skills *beyond* their traditional content expertise and research skills. A new rubric (the meta-professional model) for defining the more than 20 skill sets is presented with an indication of the extent to which each skill set is called into play as faculty pursue their responsibilities in teaching, scholarly/creative activities, service, and administration. The meta-profession model greatly facilitates both the specification of what aspects of faculty performance should be measured and provides a ready and meaningful link to professional growth (faculty development) activities. The meta-profession model also provides a much more detailed definition of the performance components of the teaching and scholarly/creative activities roles, thus facilitating the design and development of various forms and procedures for measuring that performance. The meta-profession model is included as a central part of the introduction section that follows.

As before, it must be emphasized that revising or building from scratch a comprehensive faculty evaluation system is a difficult and time-consuming process. However, since the evaluation of faculty performance impacts lives and careers, it is well worth the effort to construct evaluation systems to meet the highest standards of fairness and accuracy possible. Experience has shown time and time again that the successful completion of such a project depends upon the strong commitment of the administration. In the case of unionized institutions, it also requires the commitment by union leadership to fully engage in the collaborative process necessary to build the system. The steps described in this book, along with the many examples and forms, do not make the process easy, but they do provide a guide that many institutions have followed with successful results. Please keep in mind that the eight-step process cannot be carried out on the cheap. You must make a commitment of resources since time and money will be needed. So, if you are about to undertake the task of revising or building your institution's faculty evaluation system, I strongly recommend three things in addition to a budget and this book: patience, persistence, and, above all, a good sense of humor.

Raoul A. Arreola
April 2006

■ REFERENCES

Burroughs Wellcome Fund, & Howard Hughes Medical Institute. (2004). *Making the right moves: A practical guide to scientific management for postdocs and new faculty.* Chevy Chase, MD: Howard Hughes Medical Institute.

Davis, S. M., & Botkin, J. W. (1994). The monster under the bed: How business is mastering the opportunity of knowledge for profit. New York, NY: Simon & Schuster.

Hersh, R. H., & Merrow, J. (2005). *Declining by degrees: Higher education at risk.* New York, NY: Palgrave Macmillan.

National Center for Higher Education Management Systems. (2000). *The competency standards project: Another approach to accreditation review.* Washington, DC: Council for Higher Education Accreditation.

Acknowledgements

I want to acknowledge the contributions to this work by my good friends and colleagues—Dr. Lawrence M. Aleamoni, professor and head of the Department of Special Education and Rehabilitation Services at the University of Arizona, and Dr. Michael Theall, director of the Center for the Advancement of Teaching and Learning at Youngstown State University. I am grateful to both of these scholars for their collaboration in developing the *meta-profession* model of the professoriate (described in the Introduction), as well as their advice and suggestions in the development of several procedures and models involving peer and student ratings described herein. I am especially indebted to Larry for allowing me to excerpt material from the Aleamoni Course/Instructor Evaluation Questionnaire (CIEQ) and CIEQ Optional Item Catalog, and to Mike for his work in developing the scholarship of teaching and learning (SOTL) aspect of the meta-profession model in Chapter 3. I am also grateful for their guidance, based on their own large bodies of published work, in enabling me to present what I hope is a reasonable summary of the research on student ratings.

I also wish to acknowledge the contributions of Dr. Rebecca Schaupp, dean of the School of Business at Fairmont State University, and Dr. Tracie Dobson, also of Fairmont State University, in providing the new case study materials that describe their institution's work in developing a web-based automated comprehensive faculty evaluation system based on the procedure described in this book. Of course, I continue to be grateful to Dr. Thomas F. Hawk of Frostburg State University and Dr. Margo Eden-Camen of Georgia Perimeter College for their excellent original case studies that have been retained from the second edition.

Finally, I wish to express my profound gratitude to Dr. Russell P. Kropp who, as director of the Division of Instructional Research and Service at Florida State University 36 years ago, told a fledgling "baby Ph.D." to "Get up to speed on faculty evaluation—it's the wave of the future." This book is dedicated to him.

Developing a Comprehensive Faculty Evaluation System

Introduction: Preliminary Issues in Planning for the Development of a Comprehensive Faculty Evaluation System

■ THE NEW PARADIGM

When one examines higher education as a social enterprise within the larger context of the American culture and economy of the first post–9/11 years of the 21st century, it is clear that our colleges and universities are experiencing a significant shift in the paradigm within which they must operate. A clear indicator of this change is a decline in an organization's ability to obtain resources despite its best efforts. The significant decrease in public (state) funding for higher education that has occurred since the first edition of this book was published in 1995 has become painfully obvious. Hardly a month goes by without a report appearing in the *Chronicle of Higher Education* of a college going bankrupt and closing, or of two or more colleges merging to try to stay afloat economically. The recent demise of the American Association for Higher Education (AAHE) due to economic difficulties, as well as the evisceration of the 2005 Fund for the Improvement of Post Secondary Education (FIPSE), provides profound evidence of the paradigm shift. Increasingly, society is questioning the value it is receiving from its investment in institutions of higher learning (Hersh & Merrow, 2005). In response, colleges and universities are increasing their use of part-time, adjunct, and nontenure-track faculty, with some institutions using adjunct faculty to teach more than 80% of their entire curricular offerings. In fact, the concept of tenure itself is being challenged and the practice of post-tenure review has been adopted by a growing number of institutions. Arguably, the concept of tenure itself may prove no longer viable under the new cultural/economic paradigm (Arreola, 2005).

Under the old paradigm higher education was expected to serve a filtering function, sorting students into various levels—from the most able to the least able. Students were placed in situations where they were expected to collaborate *and* compete, where they were expected to act honorably but placed under sufficient pressure to guarantee that some would succumb to the urge to cheat (Cox, 2003). The practice of grading on the curve was the keystone of the old paradigm. The amount of time to learn was held constant, but the amount of learning by students was allowed to vary from "A" to "F." Only those who could learn regardless of the type and quality of teaching could become college graduates.

Under the new paradigm, society expects that colleges accept virtually anyone who wants to come, regardless of their aptitude, and that it is up to the colleges to bring those students to some specified level of employable competence. Evidence of this shift in paradigm can be clearly seen in accrediting agencies' adoption of an outcomes assessment model—especially in the evaluation of teaching effectiveness as evidence by student learning outcomes and measures of faculty performance. The new mastery-learning or competency-based curricular programs being implemented, especially by new, successful online universities, recognize the requirements of the new paradigm to allow time to learn to vary while keeping the expected learning outcome constant. More and more we are hearing from college and university leaders the expression, "I'm less interested in equality of opportunity and more interested in equality of outcomes." This thought is often expressed in the context of discussions concerning gender and racial disparities in education.

As another expression of the demand by society for accountability, we are also seeing more and more pay-for-performance models in faculty reward systems where raises and rates of pay are contingent on evidence of satisfactory or exemplary performance (Healy, 1999; Leatherman, 1999). Under the new paradigm the requirement of evidence of the quality of faculty performance has become a key expression of this demand for accountability. Although not always explicitly stated, more and more faculty evaluation systems are being predicated on the assumption that faculty are expected to be effective teachers *in addition* to being knowledgeable scholars. Implicit in many institutional policies and procedures relative to the assessment of faculty performance is the assumption that teaching, in and of itself, is a professional activity that extends beyond traditional scholarship (Arreola, 2000; Arreola, Aleamoni & Theall, 2001, 2003). In fact, the new paradigm requires a reconceptualization of the profession of college teacher as being a *meta-profession,* that is, a profession in which the practitioner must play a variety of roles that require expertise and skill in one or more professional areas beyond that of the faculty member's primary or *base* profession.

This shift in the paradigm has intensified the pressure on colleges and universities to build new or revise old faculty evaluation systems. More and more governing boards and/or state legislatures are mandating that higher education institutions implement comprehensive faculty evaluation systems that promote effective teaching and tie faculty pay more directly to demonstrated performance. These mandates rarely provide sufficient time for institutions to research, design, develop, and implement valid and reliable faculty evaluation tools and procedures. Thus as institutions move to implement faculty evaluation systems that respond to board and/or legislative mandates, inevitably questions of fairness, validity, objectivity, and reliability of the evaluation systems arise. This book provides a practical, proven model for the *development and use* of a comprehensive faculty evaluation system that responds to these issues. Chapter 16 contains several case studies of different types of colleges that used the process described in this book to design and build their comprehensive faculty evaluation systems. However, before moving into the steps involved in building a comprehensive faculty evaluation system, several preliminary issues should be addressed in orienting ourselves to the scope of the task at hand.

■ FACULTY EVALUATION: FAST, FAIR, CHEAP (PICK ANY TWO)

In many ways the design and implementation of a successful faculty evaluation program is as much a political process as it is a technical or psychometric one. The development of a comprehensive faculty evaluation system is a challenging and time-consuming process. There is no shortcut that will lead to a valid, fair, and useful system although new procedures have been developed during the last few years that have been successful in accelerating the process somewhat (see Chapter 3). However, the process of developing a fair and valid faculty evaluation system requires that the administration be committed to the project and be willing to provide the necessary support for the work that needs to be done. Experience has shown that following the steps described in this book for *developing* a faculty evaluation system greatly facilitates the process. The faculty evaluation system, developed using the steps described herein, will have the greatest probability of acceptance and successful use by your faculty and administrators, because both constituencies will have had early and ample input to its design and construction.

■ THE TRAP OF BEST PRACTICES

The strategy of studying what other institutions have done relative to a certain common endeavor and then adopting those elements that work well at those institutions, undergirds the best practices movement popular among higher educators today. However, in the realm of developing faculty evaluation systems, the strategy of adopting best practices can become a trap that may ultimately derail your institution's efforts to design and build its own successful faculty evaluation system. In faculty evaluation, what works well at one institution may not work at all at another. The reason for this is that the design of any successful faculty evaluation system must be predicated upon and reflect the values, priorities, traditions, culture, and mission of the institution. Unless the faculty evaluation system adequately reflects and includes these issues in its design, it is unlikely to be accepted by the faculty or function appropriately from an administrative perspective. Simply adapting or adopting the forms and procedures developed by another institution does not guarantee those forms and procedures will work at your institution.

Thus the *process for developing* a comprehensive faculty evaluation described in this book is not a best practice in the sense that it provides a final set of forms, policies, and procedures for a complete evaluation system that could simply be adopted by, or adapted for use with, any college or university. However, the *process* described in this book has repeatedly been shown to be successful in guiding and facilitating the design and development of a customized faculty evaluation system that works best for the institution using it. This is clearly demonstrated in Chapter 16 in which case studies demonstrate how different institutions using the *process* have developed different systems that best meet their unique needs and characteristics. The *process* for developing a faculty evaluation system described herein assumes that there is no one best faculty evaluation system that could be successfully applied to any and all colleges and universities. To that extent, then, the steps for developing a comprehensive faculty evaluation system described herein may be considered a *proven process* for developing a customized faculty evaluation system rather than a best practice.

■ SYSTEMATIC FACULTY INVOLVEMENT

Experience has shown that a necessary part of the process of developing a successful faculty evaluation system is the planned and systematic inclusion of the faculty. In this regard the best approach to developing a faculty evaluation system is to appoint a committee composed primarily of faculty, a few key administrators, and perhaps even a student or two (depending upon your institution's culture and traditions), which is responsible for gathering the information and following the steps outlined in subsequent chapters. Thus, various steps in the process described in the following chapters refer to the *Committee* as the operational entity carrying out the process. If the process is carried out primarily, or exclusively, by a single administrator or by an administrative group, the probability of a successful outcome is greatly reduced. This issue is examined more closely later in terms of the factors affecting faculty resistance. Thus an essential component of the process described herein involves systematic faculty input. It is important that the faculty see their input being used as an integral part of the design and construction of the system from the outset. Step 1 in the process therefore begins with direct inclusion of and collaboration with the faculty.

■ FUNDAMENTAL DEFINITIONS AND ASSUMPTIONS

Before examining in detail the steps in developing a comprehensive faculty evaluation system, it is important to clarify several underlying definitions and assumptions on which the system will rest. Primary among these are the definitions of the terms *measurement* and *evaluation*. The relationship between measurement and evaluation as well as the other terms and assumptions must be clearly understood before proceeding with the development of a comprehensive faculty evaluation system.

Measurement

An essential element of any faculty evaluation system is the measurement of various aspects of faculty performance. Therefore, it is good to begin by clarifying the definition:

> Measurement is the process of systematically assigning numbers to the individual members of a set of objects or persons for the purpose of indicating differences among them in the degree to which they possess the characteristic being measured. (Ebel, 1965, pp. 454–455)

Thus, the result of any measurement is a *number* by definition. It is important to deal with this issue early on. That is, since any faculty evaluation system will involve the measurement of some aspects of faculty performance, numbers will be unavoidable. There are those who may have an aversion to the use of numbers in faculty evaluation. However, if our evaluation system is going to be based on measurements of some sort (i.e., student ratings, peer ratings, department chair checklists, etc.), we must accept the fact that numbers will be involved in the process and begin dealing with their *appropriate* use from the beginning.

Evaluation

The relationship between measurement and evaluation must also be clarified since confusion on this issue has been found to be a major source of difficulty in developing a faculty evaluation system:

> *Evaluation* is the process of interpreting measurement data by means of a specific value construct to determine the degree to which the data represents a desirable condition.

Thus, the result of an evaluation is a *judgment* as to the degree to which the measurement data represents a desirable condition. Judgments may be expressed as words such as "excellent," "unsatisfactory," "good," or "poor." The main point to be grasped here is the *relationship* between measurement and evaluation. Measurements can, and should be obtained as objectively and reliably as possible. However, the process of evaluation will always be subjective (by definition).

In exploring this relationship between measurement and evaluation it is useful to take a closer look at the actual process of making an evaluation. Any evaluation rests upon a base of an implicitly assumed value or set of values. Basically, in conducting an evaluation, an observation is made of the performance of interest and then a judgment is made on whether that performance conforms to the set of values held by those making the observations. If there is a good match between observed performance and values held, such performance is judged to be desirable and generally given a positive or "good" evaluation. If there is a discrepancy between what is observed and what is held to be of value, such performance is judged to be undesirable and is generally given a negative or "poor" evaluation.

For example, suppose one was asked to evaluate the following measurement:

birth weight = 13 pounds

Would the evaluation be positive or "good" (indicative of a desirable condition)? Or would the evaluation be negative or "poor" (indicative of an undesirable condition)? The answer, of course, is "it depends." What the evaluation depends upon is the value system or context within which the measurement is interpreted. If the measurement of 13 pounds is interpreted from the perspective of a 115 pound human female, then the evaluation would likely be negative or "poor" since giving birth to a 15 pound infant is generally not a desirable situation for a human female. However, if the measurement were interpreted from the perspective of a 250 pound mountain goat, then the evaluation would likely be positive or "good" since this weight falls within the normal range of birth weights for an animal that size. The important principle to note here is that the evaluation of the measurement (i.e., judgment as to whether the measurement represents a desirable or undesirable condition) depends on the context and the value system brought to the interpretation. Notice that the measurement (birth weight = 13 pounds) did not change, but the evaluation went from "poor" to "good" depending upon which value construct or system of values was applied.

Clearly then, the evaluation process implies the existence and use of a contextual system or structure of values associated with the characteristic(s) being measured. Thus, before any evaluation system can be built, the values of those who intend to use it must be determined. In order to develop a faculty evaluation system that correctly reflects the values of the institution, we must not only determine those values and have them clearly in mind, but we must also express them in such a way that they may be applied consistently in our evaluation process. The model described in this book enables us to do just that.

Objectivity

Another major issue is the objectivity of the faculty evaluation system. Often, when embarking upon developing a faculty evaluation system, the goal of the institution's administration or Committee charged with the task is to devise an objective system. We must deal with this issue head on and recognize that total objectivity in a faculty evaluation system is an illusion. The very definition of evaluation makes it clear that subjectivity is an integral component of the evaluative process. In fact, the term *objective evaluation* is an oxymoron. The measurement tools used in the faculty evaluation system (e.g., student rating forms, peer observational checklists, etc.) may and should achieve high levels of objectivity, but the evaluation process is, by definition, subjective.

The appeal of the ephemeral and oxymoronic objective faculty evaluation system is that it would produce the same evaluative outcome regardless of who evaluated the performance in question. Since objective evaluation is impossible, it is important to determine how to arrive at the goal of consistent evaluative outcomes in a necessarily subjective process. We must determine how we can design an evaluation process that will provide the same evaluative judgment based on a set of data, regardless of who is considering the data. This can be done through a process called *controlled subjectivity.*

Controlled Subjectivity

Objectivity in a faculty evaluation system can be found in the measurement of faculty performance. The tools used to measure faculty performance such as observation checklists and student and peer rating forms may produce objective data (measurements). However, as noted earlier, although measurements can and should be as objective as possible, the evaluation process is subjective by definition.

The value in objectivity is in the consistency of outcome it provides regardless of who is involved. If a truly objective faculty evaluation system were possible, any two individuals evaluating a faculty member by examining exactly the same data would come to exactly the same evaluative judgment. However, since subjectivity in a faculty evaluation system is unavoidable, the goal should be to control its impact. The process for doing so may be called *controlled subjectivity.*

For example, consider the earlier given objective measurement of "birth weight = 13 pounds." If it were previously agreed that the measurement would be interpreted in terms of a 115 pound human female, then everyone interpreting the measurement would most likely have judged it to be "poor" or representative of an undesirable condition. Subjectivity in an evaluation system is controlled when there is an a priori agreement on what context and (subjective) value system will be applied in the interpretation of the objective data. Even though the evaluation process involves subjectivity, the consistency in judgment outcome that would derive from a hypothetical (and oxymoronic) objective evaluation system is approximated. Thus for our purposes:

> *Controlled subjectivity* is the consistent application of a predetermined set of values in the interpretation of measurement data.

A Comprehensive Faculty Evaluation System

The process of developing a faculty evaluation system involves attending to the technical requirements of good measurement and the political process of gaining the confidence of the faculty. Thus, a well-designed comprehensive faculty evaluation program may be defined as one which involves the

> systematic observation (measurement) of relevant faculty performance to determine the degree to which that performance is consonant with the values the academic unit.

By design, any faculty evaluation system developed using the model described in this book interprets all measurement data by means of a predetermined, consensus-based value system to produce consistent evaluative outcomes.

■ COLLEGE TEACHING AS META-PROFESSION

In considering the development of a comprehensive faculty evaluation system it is critical to define and understand the full complexity of the duties and responsibilities of the college teacher. Faculty engage in a variety of activities necessary for the successful achievement of the mission and goals of their department and institution as well as their personal professional goals and objectives. These activities may require not only expertise in a given content area but also skills and expertise in a host of other sophisticated psychological, technical, organizational, and group processes that are not necessarily related to their content field. Thus, the profession of college teacher or college professor is seen as a *meta-profession*: a profession that assumes content expertise as a foundation but requires professional-level performance in areas outside a faculty member's recognized area of expertise. In short, college faculty are expected to assume a variety of roles and to perform at a high professional level in each role.

Many of the roles faculty play do not necessarily depend on the faculty member's formally recognized area of expertise. Some roles, such as advising, serving on curriculum committees, or managing complex projects, may require expertise in areas outside the faculty member's own field. In short, in order for a department, college, or university to function properly, faculty play a variety of roles. Thus, in designing and developing a comprehensive faculty evaluation system in which faculty performances in all their roles are to be evaluated, it is critical to define those performances and identify their requisite skills.

In developing comprehensive faculty evaluation systems, it has been found that the conventional conceptualization and definitions of faculty roles as involving teaching, research, and service are almost universally insufficient (Arreola, 1979, 1986, 2000; Arreola, Aleamoni, & Theall, 2001, 2003). The process of developing a comprehensive faculty evaluation system inevitably points to the need to define a broader range of roles in order to accommodate the scope and complexity of faculty performance (Aleamoni, 1987).

When an individual is hired as a faculty member for the first time he or she usually comes to the position with advanced degrees and/or significant experience that qualify him or her as a professional in a specific content area or field. The profession represented by these degrees and/or experiences constitute what may be called the faculty member's *base* profession. The specific skill sets involved in a faculty member's base profession may be characterized as follows:

- *Content expertise.* The formally recognized knowledge, skills, and abilities a faculty member possesses in a chosen field by virtue of advanced training, education, and/or experience.

- *Practice/clinical skills.* Those skills in translating content expertise into actions to carry out a process, produce a product, and/or provide a service.

- *Research techniques.* Those skills in acquiring existing knowledge and/or creating or discovering new knowledge within one's area of content expertise.

The knowledge and skills which characterize a faculty member's base profession have traditionally been assumed to be sufficient to enable the individual to be an effective teacher. Current selection and hiring processes for college and university faculty positions are often predicated on this assumption. However, research in the field of the evaluation of faculty teaching performance has shown this assumption to be incorrect (Aleamoni, 1999; Hattie & Marsh, 1996; Marsh & Hattie, 2002).

Thus although the skills and knowledge associated with a faculty member's base profession are necessary for effective college teaching, they are insufficient. That is, faculty must, of course, be experts in the field that they are teaching. However, the act of practicing one's base profession, whether it is architecture, biochemistry, dentistry, or engineering, is substantially different from that of interacting with learners in such a way that they, too, gain the skills, knowledge, and practice skills of that profession. Faculty must be able to design and deliver a set of experiences to the learner such that, if the learner engages the experiences, there is a high probability that learning will occur. In addition, the faculty member must validly and reliably assess the learner's progress to enhance the learning process and, ultimately, certify that learning has in fact occurred.

Outside the classroom the college professor may also be expected to advise students, manage projects involving personnel and budgets, chair departments, serve on important committees and task forces, raise funds, recruit students, and more. Clearly, a faculty member may be expected to perform at a professional level in a multiplicity of areas outside their recognized area of expertise. Experience in developing large-scale faculty evaluation systems in colleges and universities of all types and sizes has resulted in identifying the following skill sets, characterized as the *meta-profession skill sets*, as being involved to one degree or another in the successful performance of the fundamental faculty roles of *teaching, scholarly and creative activities, service,* and *administration*:

- *Instructional design.* Those technical skills in designing, sequencing, and presenting experiences which induce learning. Requires knowledge and skill in task analysis, the psychology of learning, the conditions of learning, and the development of performance objectives.

- *Instructional delivery.* Those human interactive skills that promote or facilitate learning in face-to-face instruction, as well as those skills in using various forms of instructional delivery mechanisms.

- *Instructional assessment.* Those skills in developing and using tools and procedures for assessing student learning (including test construction, questionnaire and survey construction, grading practices, and grading procedures).

- *Course management.* Those organizational and bureaucratic skills involved in maintaining and operating a course.

- *Instructional research.* Those technical skills and techniques associated with the scholarly inquiry into all aspects of instruction, teaching, and education.

- *Psychometrics/statistics.* Psychometrics/statistics is concerned with the measurement of human characteristics and the design and analysis of research based on those measurements.

- *Epistemology.* That branch of philosophy that studies the nature and limits of knowledge as well as examines the structure, origin, and criteria of knowledge. Its application can often be seen in course or curriculum design in which the structure of the knowledge to be acquired by the student is taken into account in the design of instructional events or experiences.

- *Learning theory.* Learning theory deals with various models to explain how learning takes place and to provide a frame of reference for designing, developing, and delivering instruction.

- *Human development.* Theories and models of human intellectual, ethical, social, cultural, and physical development. Knowledge and expertise in the theories of human development are often required in the design and development of the entire educational experience.

- *Information technology.* Information technology (IT) is a term that encompasses all forms of technology used to create, store, exchange, and use information in its various forms (e.g., business data, voice conversations, still images, motion pictures, multimedia presentations, etc.). It is a convenient term for including telephony and computer technology in the same word.

- *Technical writing.* The delivery of technical information to readers (or listeners or viewers) in a manner that is adapted to their needs, level of understanding, and background. The primary skill is to write about highly technical subjects in such a way that a beginner (learner) or a nonspecialist can understand.

- *Graphic design.* Graphic design is the process and art of combining text and graphics to produce an efficient and effective means of visually communicating information or concepts.

- *Public speaking.* Public speaking is generally defined as speaking to large group of individuals, in a formal setting, for the purpose of imparting information and/or persuading others to a particular point of view.

- *Communication styles.* Individuals have various preferences for communicating with others and interpreting the communications from others. Numerous models have been developed which describe how to recognize an individual's preferred style of communicating and what strategy to use in communicating most effectively with him or her.

- *Conflict management.* The practice of identifying and handling conflict in a sensible, fair, and efficient manner. Conflict management requires such skills as effective communicating, problem solving, and negotiating with a focus on interests.

- *Group process/team building.* Groups of individuals gathered together to achieve a goal or objective, either as a committee or some other grouping, go through several predictable stages before useful work can be done.

- *Resource management.* The management of material resources to ensure their effective and efficient use in meeting specific purposes. Involves skills associated with inventory control procedures, replacement and maintenance scheduling, cost control, etc.

- *Personnel Management.* Skills in communicating effectively, developing teams, managing diversity, managing conflict, delegating responsibility, coaching and training, giving and receiving constructive feedback, and motivating and guiding either individuals or groups to achieve specific goals.

- *Financial/budget development.* Requires an understanding of a variety of economic and monetary concepts including cash flow, direct and indirect costs, debt management, depreciation, etc.; the ability to read and understand financial reports; and the ability to interpret and respond appropriately to federal, state, and/or local regulations and policies affecting the expenditure of funds.

- *Policy analysis and development.* Those skills necessary for understanding the political constraints faced by policy makers, assessing the performance of alternative approaches to policy implementation, evaluating the effectiveness of policies, and the role conflicts in values have on the development of policies.

Thus the professoriate may more appropriately be conceptualized as a meta-profession: a profession that is built upon the foundation of a base profession by combining elements from a variety of several other different profes-

sional arenas. This conceptualization makes possible a much more realistic and comprehensive view of the multiple roles played by the faculty member to facilitate faculty evaluation and faculty development practices and procedures. Table A shows an approximation of the frequency with which base and meta-profession skill sets are called into play in the traditional faculty roles of teaching, scholarly and creative activities, service, and administration. The approximate frequency of use of each skill set indicated in Table A is based on experience with large-scale faculty evaluation and faculty development programs, as well as preliminary (unpublished) research conducted with a sampling of faculty development officers from throughout the country (Arreola, Aleamoni, & Theall, 2001, 2003). For more information concerning this work see www.cedanet.com/meta.

By acknowledging the professoriate as a meta-profession that builds upon and extends beyond each faculty member's content expertise, the various skill and performance elements required in teaching, scholarship, and service as described earlier can be more clearly identified as shown in Table A. The careful identification and definition of the meta-profession role components provide the basis for more objective, performance-based assessment and evaluation procedures that result in the design of fairer faculty evaluation systems.

Also, by conceptualizing college faculty as meta-professionals they can more easily be seen as belonging to a broad unified set of professionals whose practice extends beyond their specific content expertise or base profession. The generalized meta-professional paradigm shown in Table A derives from the author's experience of designing, developing, and implementing large-scale faculty evaluation and faculty development programs (Arreola, Aleamoni, & Theall, 2001, 2003; Theall & Arreola, 2001).

■ LINKING FACULTY EVALUATION AND FACULTY DEVELOPMENT

Although the term *faculty development* is commonly used throughout the professional literature and the popular press, recognizing the professoriate as a meta-profession calls for the use of a more appropriate term for faculty efforts to enhance their professional skills repertoire. Therefore, for the remainder of this edition, the more appropriate term *professional enrichment* will be used instead of *faculty development.*

It should be noted that faculty evaluation and professional enrichment are really two sides of the same coin. Ideally, faculty evaluation programs and professional enrichment programs should work hand-in-hand.

If some aspect of faculty performance is to be evaluated, then there should exist resources or opportunities that enable faculty to gain or enhance their skills necessary for that performance. For maximal self-improvement effect, faculty evaluation systems must be linked to professional enrichment programs.

The meta-professional paradigm expands the possibilities in designing faculty evaluation systems. However, the impact on professional enrichment programs is direct and obvious (Aleamoni, 1997). The simple rule of thumb is that if a specific faculty performance is to be evaluated, there must be some resource available to enable the faculty member to gain expertise and proficiency in the skills required by that performance—especially if that performance area falls outside his or her recognized area of content expertise. Professional enrichment programs encompassing such topics as educational psychology, instructional technology, conflict management, public speaking, and organizational management, for example, may be required to assist faculty with the full range of their meta-professional performance.

Faculty evaluation systems—no matter how well designed—which are implemented without reference to professional enrichment opportunities or programs, are inevitably viewed by faculty as being primarily punitive in intent. Such faculty evaluation systems tend to be interpreted as sending the message, "We're going to find out what you're doing wrong and get you for it!"

On the other hand, professional enrichment programs that are implemented without clear reference to the information generated by faculty evaluation systems tend to be disappointing in their effect no matter how well the programs may be designed and funded. The reason for this is simple, if not always obvious. Without reference to a faculty evaluation system, professional enrichment programs tend to attract primarily those faculty who are already motivated to seek out resources and opportunities to add to and enhance their skill set repertoire. In short, the "good" seek out ways to get better—which is what tends to make them good in the first place. However, those individuals who are not thus motivated, and who, accordingly, are probably in greatest need of professional enrichment opportunities, generally tend to be the last to seek them out. Only when the elements of a faculty evaluation program are carefully integrated into a professional enrichment program does the institution obtain the greatest benefit from both. Thus, if an instructor's skill in assessing student learning is going to be evaluated, somewhere there should be resources and training opportunities to become proficient in that skill. If a faculty member's ability to deliver a well-organized and ex-

citing lecture is going to be evaluated, somewhere in the institution there should be resources available to learn and become proficient in the requisite public speaking and presentation skills.

It should never be forgotten that most college and university faculty have had little or no formal training in the complex and highly technical meta-professional skills involved in designing and delivering instruction or assessing student learning outcomes. Most faculty tend to teach in the same way they were taught and test the way they were tested. Thus, if faculty performance is to be evaluated, especially performance in teaching, the institution should provide the resources to develop, support, and enhance that performance. The meta-profession components of teaching performance are discussed in greater detail in Chapter 3.

A successful faculty evaluation system must provide 1) meaningful feedback information to guide professional growth and enrichment and 2) evaluative information on which to base personnel decisions. These two purposes can be well served by one system. The key to constructing a system that serves these differing purposes is in the policies determining the distribution of the information gathered. The general principle to be followed is that detailed information from questionnaires or other forms should be given exclusively to the faculty member for use in professional enrichment and growth efforts. However, aggregate data that summarize and reflect the overall pattern of performance over time of an individual can and should be used for such personnel decisions as promotion, tenure, continuation, and merit raise determination. Later chapters in this book discuss in greater detail the design of the elements of the faculty evaluation system that relate to these two purposes as well as the relationship between them.

It is important to acknowledge that faculty evaluation data will be used to provide faculty with diagnostic information to assist in their professional growth *and* provide administrators with evidence for use in personnel decisions (promotion, tenure, pay raises, etc.) An institution may choose to emphasize one use over another, but it is a mistake to pretend that the faculty evaluation data will be used only for professional enrichment purposes. Careful thought must be given to the appropriate design of the elements that may be used for personnel decisions even though the primary intent is to use the system for professional enrichment. Interestingly, it is often the faculty themselves who begin using faculty evaluation data in support of their applications for promotion and tenure, even though the formal system may not require it. Accordingly, the steps of the process described herein consider both uses of faculty evaluation data.

Table A. Approximate frequency of the required application of various skill sets in the performance of the Teaching, Scholarly/Creative Activities, Service, and Administration roles

SKILL SETS		Faculty Roles			
		Teaching	Scholarly/Creative Activities	Service	Administration
Base Profession Skill Sets	Content Expertise	●●●●	●●●●	●●●◉	●●◉◉
	Practice/Clinical Skills	●●●◉	●●●◉	●●●◉	●●●◉
	Research Skills	●●◉◉	●●●●	●●●◉◉	●●●●
Additional META-PROFESSION Skill Sets Required by Various Faculty Roles	Instructional Design	●●●●	●●◉	●●●◉	●●◉
	Instructional Delivery	●●●●	●●◉	●●●◉	●●◉
	Instructional Assessment	●●●●	●●●◉	●●●◉	●●◉
	Instructional Research	●◉◉	●●●◉	●●●◉	●●◉
	Psychometrics/Statistics	●●◉	●●◉	●●●◉	●●◉
	Epistemology	●●◉	●●◉	●●●◉	●●◉
	Learning Theory	●●●●	●●◉	●●●◉	●●◉
	Human Development	●●◉	●●◉	●●●◉	●●●◉
	Information Technology	●●◉	●●●◉	●●●◉	●●●◉
	Technical/Scientific Writing	●●◉	●●●◉	●●●◉	●●●◉
	Graphic Design	●●◉	●●●◉	●●●◉	●●●◉
	Public Speaking	●●●●	●●●●	●●●◉	●●●●
	Communication Styles	●●●●	●●◉	●●●◉	●●●●
	Conflict Management	●●◉	●●◉	●●●◉	●●●●
	Group Process/Team Building	●●◉	●●◉	●●●◉	●●●●
	Resource Management	●●◉	●●◉	●●●◉	●●●●
	Personnel Management	●◉◉	●●◉	●●◉	●●●●
	Financial/Budget Development	●◉◉	●●◉	●●●◉	●●●●
	Policy Analysis/Development	●◉◉	●●◉	●●●◉	●●●◉

Legend

- Almost Always ●●●●
- Frequently ●●●◉
- Occasionally ●●◉
- Almost Never ●◉◉

Arreola, R. A. (2007). *Developing a Comprehensive Faculty Evaluation System* (3rd ed.). Bolton, MA: Anker.

■ OBSTACLES TO ESTABLISHING SUCCESSFUL PROGRAMS

A successful faculty evaluation program can be defined as one that provides information which faculty, administrators, and, where appropriate, students consider important and useful. Note that by this definition, no particular set of elements, forms, questionnaires, workshops, or procedures is being suggested.

Taking this same orientation to faculty development programs, a successful professional enrichment program is perceived by the faculty as a valuable resource or tool in assisting them to gain or enhance skills, solve problems, or achieve goals that they and the administration consider to be important. From this perspective, the problem of establishing successful faculty evaluation and professional enrichment programs does not lie so much in not knowing what procedures to follow in evaluating faculty or not knowing how to gain new skills or enhance old ones. The problem lies in getting faculty and administrators to change their behavior in important and fundamental ways.

The primary difficulty in establishing successful faculty evaluation and professional enrichment programs is not so much a technical one of developing the right questionnaires or procedures. Rather, the real problem lies in getting large numbers of intelligent, highly educated, and independent people to change their behavior. If we recognize this fact and deal with it openly from the beginning we have a much greater chance of establishing a successful program.

Faculty evaluation and development programs can fail primarily for two reasons: 1) The administration is not interested in whether it succeeds, and 2) the faculty are against it. The first reason will be referred to as *administrator apathy* and the second as *faculty resistance.* A close look at these two obstacles to establishing successful faculty evaluation and development programs can provide us with insights into how to overcome them.

Administrator Apathy

Of the two threats to success—administrator apathy and faculty resistance—administrator apathy is the more deadly. If the administration is apathetic toward or actively against the whole program, it will not succeed. Anyone who has encountered a successful faculty evaluation and development program can point to one or two top administrators with a strong commitment to establishing and maintaining the program. Having a top administrator strongly committed to the program is a necessary but insufficient condition for success. The reasons for this will become obvious as we examine the issue.

One of the more common situations found in colleges and universities is where a second-level administrator, say a vice president or academic dean, is strongly committed to establishing a faculty evaluation and development program. The top-level administrator of the institution may be in favor of the program, apathetic toward it, or resistant to it. In the case of apathy, it is necessary to demonstrate to the top administrator the potential benefits of the program in terms of improved accountability evidence, as well as the improvement of faculty performance and student learning.

Resistance by the top-level administrator creates a different and more difficult problem to address. Such resistance tends to revolve around two issues: fear of loss of control in the personnel decision-making process and concern about dealing with faculty resistance. The issue of dealing with faculty resistance is explored in some detail in the next section. While the fear of loss of control or threat to authority is serious, several approaches have been found to be helpful.

Establishing the program on a purely experimental basis for a period of two years enables administrators to use the results of the program as they see fit. A consultant from another institution where a successful faculty evaluation and development program is already in place can present a more objective view to the administration on how such a program can benefit the institution as a whole.

Another good strategy is to entice the resistant top administrator to attend one of the national conferences on faculty evaluation and development that are held annually. In this way he or she can interact with individuals from other institutions involved in the process and perhaps gain a better perspective on what is involved. In any case, it is helpful for administrators to see that their fears and concerns do not have to be realized. The key is to gain the support of at least a second-level administrator so that some resources can be allocated for an experimental trial of some part of the proposed program.

Administrator apathy diminishes the chances of implementing a successful faculty evaluation and development program, but outright resistance drops the chances of implementing a successful program practically to zero.

Faculty Resistance

Administrative commitment is a necessary but insufficient condition for establishing a successful faculty evaluation and development program. Faculty acceptance is also necessary. Faculty resistance to establishing faculty evaluation and development programs stems from numerous sources. Most of the resistance, however, reflects two or three major concerns.

In examining these concerns, let's begin, once again, by stating the obvious: No one enjoys being evaluated. Few people enjoy being told that they need to improve, or, worse, need to be developed—especially people who have spent six to eight years in college being evaluated and developed to the point where they have been awarded advanced degrees. Thus, the overall phenomenon of faculty resistance is composed of two reactions: resistance to being evaluated and apathy toward being developed. Faculty resistance to being evaluated appears to grow out of three basic concerns:

- Resentment of the implied assumption that they may not be competent in their subject area

- Suspicion that they will be evaluated by unqualified people

- Anxiety that they will be held accountable for performance in an area in which they have little or no training or interest

This last anxiety is not unusual or unexpected, even though most faculty may attribute most of their concern to the second factor. Milton and Shoben (1968) point out the basis for this anxiety when they state that "college teaching is probably the only profession in the world for which no specific training is required. The profession of scholarship is rich in prerequisites for entry, but not that of instruction" (p. xvii).

This statement holds the key to faculty resistance to establishing faculty evaluation and development programs. Faculty understandably resent being tacitly questioned on their competence in an area "rich in prerequisites" for which they have been well trained. They are, not surprisingly, apathetic toward the idea of receiving further training, although, ironically, professional seminars in one's content area are generally held in high esteem. Faculty also view with some concern and trepidation the prospect of being evaluated in an area in which they may have little or no training or interest—namely, the design, development, and delivery of instruction.

Several publications have addressed the issue of overcoming faculty resistance to evaluation programs (Grasha, 1977; O'Connell & Smartt, 1979; Seldin, 1980; Arreola, 1979). The underlying premise for developing a comprehensive faculty evaluation system described in this handbook is the careful and deliberate preclusion or reduction of faculty resistance. It is useful, therefore, to examine some of the common errors leading to faculty resistance that may not be immediately apparent.

■ COMMON ERRORS

Several errors are commonly made when establishing faculty evaluation and development programs. The first and most common error is committed when a faculty evaluation program is implemented without reference or clear relation to a professional enrichment program. As noted earlier, when this is done, the faculty tend to assume that its purpose is to gather evidence for disciplinary purposes. However, by developing an integrated faculty evaluation and development program, it is easier for the faculty to see the relationship between the assessment of their strengths and weaknesses and programs to assist in their continued professional development. An integrated faculty evaluation and development program also serves to endorse the principle of continuous improvement within the institution.

Unfortunately, most often only a faculty evaluation program is implemented. Even then the form of its implementation almost guarantees faculty resistance. Generally, a faculty evaluation program begins by a committee constructing or adopting a questionnaire that is administered to students. These questionnaires usually contain questions that faculty perceive as boiling down to, "Was this instructor entertaining?" "Does this instructor know his or her stuff?" and "What grade would you give this instructor—A, B, C, D, or F?" The questionnaires are usually analyzed by computer and the results sent to the department head, college dean, or, in some instances, directly to the president. This action triggers all the concerns and anxieties that result in full-blown faculty resistance. Couple this, as occasionally happens, with a student publication that lists the best and worst teachers—perceived as job-threatening by the untenured—and hostile and negative reactions from the faculty are guaranteed.

On the other side of the coin, when professional enrichment programs are installed without reference to an evaluation system, apathy tends to run rampant among the faculty. This is not to say that the programs may not be innovative, creative, and effective for those who do participate. But what commonly occurs in the absence of a tie to an evaluation system is that only those faculty who are already committed to the concept of self-improvement will be the ones who seek out the program. Thus, the faculty who need the least improvement will tend to be the ones who use the program the most. Those faculty who don't have that commitment and who genuinely need assistance tend to avoid it. If a professional enrichment program is mandatory, based on the referral of the dean or department head, it is very easy for the program to take on the aura of being for losers only—a place where faculty are sentenced to several weeks of development when they are caught with a poor syllabus, bad student ratings, or declining enrollments.

How do we overcome these not inconsiderable obstacles? There is no easy answer to this question. However, the following suggestions, cautions, and strategies gleaned from the experiences of those establishing faculty evaluation and development programs may prove useful.

■ GUIDELINES FOR OVERCOMING OBSTACLES AND AVOIDING ERRORS

Seek Administrative Assistance

Identify and enlist the aid of a higher level administrator committed to establishing an integrated faculty evaluation and development program. The administrator must be prepared to overcome a year to 18 months of faculty resistance, some of which can become quite vocal.

Expect Faculty to Resist

Experience has shown that faculty resistance undergoes five predictable stages.

Stage 1: disdainful denial. During this stage, faculty generally take the attitude that "It'll never work" or, in the case of old-timers, "We tried something like that 10 years ago. It didn't work then, and it's not going to work this time either."

Stage 2: hostile resistance. During this stage, faculty begin to realize that the administration is going ahead with developing and implementing what they consider an overly complex and unwanted faculty evaluation system. Faculty senate meetings are hot and heavy. Special subcommittees are appointed. Complaints flow into the various levels of administration.

Stage 3: apparent acquiescence. Faculty seem to resign themselves to the fact that the new faculty evaluation system is going to be implemented despite their objections. Most faculty hope that if they ignore it the evaluation system will go away. A few voices of support are heard at this stage, however.

Stage 4: attempt to scuttle. At this stage, certain elements of the faculty and perhaps some department heads or deans greatly exaggerate the impact of the problems caused by the faculty evaluation system. Some isolated incidents of outright misuse may be perpetrated in an effort to get the system to collapse. Pressure on the sponsoring administrator to resign is intensified.

Stage 5: grudging acceptance. After 18 months to two years of operation, the faculty find that the system can actually be of some value. When all faculty are equally, but minimally, unhappy with the system, the faculty resistance barrier will have been successfully overcome. This is as good as it gets! There is no subsequent stage where faculty are happy with the system.

It should be apparent at this point why administrator commitment is so critical to the success of any faculty evaluation and development program. Only that commitment can get the institution through the first few stages of faculty resistance. If the administrator responsible for implementing the program is a second-level administrator and has to fight apathy or resistance from the top-level administrator, the probability of success is smaller, and the probability of that administrator's departure from the institution is greater.

Be Prepared to Respond to Common Faculty Concerns

Some of those concerns and the responses that have been found helpful include the following.

"Students aren't competent to evaluate me!" It needs to be made clear that most well-designed faculty evaluation systems do not ask students to actually evaluate faculty in the sense that students make any final decisions. Opinions, perceptions, and reactions are solicited from students. This information is considered along with other information from other sources when the evaluation is carried out by the appropriate person or committee.

"Teaching is too complex an activity to be evaluated validly!" The best response to this concern is to point out that faculty are being evaluated in their teaching all the time by their colleagues and administrators. A formal system can make that evaluation fairer and more reliable and valid.

"You can't reduce something as complex as an evaluation of my performance to a number—some things just can't be measured!" In responding to this and similar concerns, it is best to point out that faculty are already being evaluated all the time. These evaluations, however determined, are translated into a number every time a list of applicants for promotion or tenure is placed in some priority order or a decision about merit raises is made. Comprehensive faculty evaluation systems attempt to improve on existing informal and perhaps unstructured procedures by developing a systematic and fair set of criteria using numerical values based on controlled subjectivity. It should also be noted that faculty consistently reduce the evaluation of complex student learning achievement to numbers (out to three decimal places), and, based on those numbers, colleges award credit and degrees. As a profession, we are not inexperienced in the process of summarizing evaluations of complex human behaviors as numerical values.

Developing a Comprehensive Faculty Evaluation System

Establish a Center or Office

This center or office should preferably not be located in the office of the vice president or dean. It should not only operate the faculty evaluation system but also offer a carefully integrated set of professional enrichment opportunities and resources. One efficient and cost-effective way to do this is to combine the media center, test scoring office and any other instructional development and support office into one organizationally integrated unit. This unit should be directed by someone trained in evaluation and instructional development or educational psychology, and, most importantly, be someone who has an affable, non-threatening manner that inspires confidence. Remember that the objective is to facilitate the self-directed change in the behavior of faculty and administrators. The person in charge of the faculty evaluation/professional enrichment facility should be able to grasp and deal with this concept in a positive manner.

Establish a Faculty Advisory Board

Although the faculty evaluation/professional enrichment unit will ultimately report to a dean or vice president, it helps to have a faculty advisory board. The board can be elected by the faculty or faculty senate or appointed by an appropriate administrator. In any case, there should be some mechanism for faculty to have input into the policy development affecting the operation of the center and the programs offered, even if that input is only advisory.

Consider Using a Consultant

An outside consultant can play an important role in the process of overcoming faculty and administrative resistance. For example, in Chapter 16 the case study of the work done by Fairmont State University in developing their comprehensive faculty evaluation system describes a situation in which they used a consultant from another university that had successfully used the process described in this book to develop their faculty evaluation system. A consultant can serve as a valuable conduit between faculty and administration by communicating concerns, suspicions, and fears expressed by the faculty to the administration. The consultant can also assure administrators that other institutions have been able to implement successful programs. The function of serving as a conduit between faculty and administrators is often critical in the early stages of faculty resistance. The consultant can act as a lighting rod for all complaints, criticism, and confessions that might not ordinarily be expressed to a local colleague.

One of the most effective means of using a consultant for this purpose is to hold an open faulty meeting where, with the appropriate administrators present, the consultant presents an outline of the proposed faculty evaluation and development program and then responds to questions and comments. In this forum, the faculty can feel free to criticize the ideas presented by the consultant, or criticize the planned program, as if the consultant were solely responsible for the entire effort. What is really being communicated in this setting is a concern or an expression of opposition to the administration's proposals or practices without a direct confrontation with the administration. Breakthroughs in faculty resistance often occur in such forums. This approach also gives the administration the opportunity to present proposals that can receive perhaps a more honest appraisal by the faculty than they ordinarily might, with little risk being taken by either the faculty or the administration.

Integrate Faculty Evaluation and Professional Enrichment Programs

Make certain that for every element of the faculty evaluation program there is a corresponding and concomitant element in the professional enrichment program. For example, if an instructor's syllabus is going to be evaluated as part of the overall evaluation of teaching, make sure that workshops, seminars, or materials are available in the professional enrichment program designed to provide the instructor with the knowledge and skills needed to construct a good syllabus. This approach ensures that faculty have institutionally supported recourse when the evaluation system detects a weakness in their performance.

Use a Variety of Sources in the Evaluation System

Make certain that the faculty evaluation system includes and uses input from such sources as peers, self, and administrators, as well as students. It is important to specify the impact each of these various sources of information has on the total evaluation. The following sections in this book describe in detail the process for doing this.

Make Every Effort to Ensure That the Faculty Evaluation Program Is Functionally Valid

The aspects of faculty performance being evaluated should be ones that the faculty and the administration believe ought to be evaluated. In establishing the program's functional validity, it is important to remember that the process of evaluation requires that a set of data be weighed against a set of values. If the data show that the performance of an individual corresponds to the values being used or assumed by the evaluation system, that individual is evaluated favorably. If the faculty member's performance is at odds with the evaluation system's assumed values, an unfavorable evaluation results. The issue of the importance in determining values in the development of a faculty evaluation system is discussed in greater detail in Chapter 2.

To the extent that faculty are either unsure of or disagree with the assumed value structure of the faculty evaluation program, they will consider the program not to be valid and will thus resist it. Functional validity, or the extent to which the faculty believe in the fairness and utility of the faculty evaluation program is, in large measure, a function of the degree to which they are aware of and agree with the assumed values in the evaluation system. A number of specific and effective steps can be taken to establish the functional validity of a faculty evaluation program and these are described in detail in the following chapters.

Provide Detailed Faculty Evaluation Information— Primarily and Exclusively—to the Instructor

Policies may be established that call for mandatory periodic review of the evaluation information by an administrator. However, the issue of the initial control of the information must be resolved early so that the faculty evaluation/professional enrichment unit does not come to be seen as a watchdog agency for the administration. If this occurs, the effectiveness of the professional enrichment program will be severely diminished. The faculty evaluation and professional enrichment programs must be correctly seen as confidential resources for faculty to use in improving and documenting the quality of their own performance.

Establish a Facilitative Reward Structure

Establish policies that treat documented professional growth and enrichment efforts in a fashion similar to those of publication and research efforts. Successful professional growth and the acquisition and/or enhancement of the skills required by the various roles faculty must play should contribute meaningfully to promotion, tenure, and, where possible, merit pay decisions.

Tie Promotion, Tenure, and Merit Pay Decision-Making Procedures as Directly as Possible to the Faculty Evaluation and Professional Enrichment Program

This last suggestion is critical if the program is to succeed. A primary objection often heard to the idea of linking promotion, tenure, and pay to the evaluation of perform-

ance is that tying performance to money or other non-intrinsic rewards cheapens the academic enterprise. It is argued that faculty should teach for the love of teaching and conduct research simply as an expression of their scholarly commitment to the discovery of truth.

There may be some faculty who teach for the sheer love of teaching and would do so even if they were not paid. There may be some faculty who have a passionate drive for discovering truth through research regardless of personal cost. There may be some faculty who are committed to a continual quest for self-improvement regardless of how they are viewed by others. However, the great majority of faculty are profoundly influenced in their professional performance by those aspects of job security, prestige, colleague respect, and monetary reward that their institution controls. If faculty perceive that decisions concerning their careers are still going to be carried out by an administrator who may or may not use faculty evaluation and professional enrichment data in a systematic, fair, and predictable manner, the program will ultimately fail. This is true no matter how benevolent the administration may be.

The faculty evaluation program will only have a chance of success if faculty see that 1) obtaining the rewards their profession and institution have to offer is a function of their performance and thus under their control, and 2) the faculty evaluation and professional enrichment programs are valuable tools in helping them identify and overcome the obstacles standing between them and these rewards.

■ PRACTICAL CONSIDERATIONS IN PLANNING THE DEVELOPMENT OF YOUR FACULTY EVALUATION SYSTEM

The literature in the field of faculty evaluation contains an abundance of research concerning the theoretical and psychometric underpinnings of a variety of forms, questionnaires, and procedures for use in a faculty evaluation system, especially student rating forms (see Chapters 12 and 13). However, less attention has been paid to the fundamental, practical, everyday issues and problems that face those responsible for actually operating a fully functioning faculty evaluation program.

Clarify the Purpose Your Faculty Evaluation System Is to Serve

From a practical standpoint, any faculty evaluation system must ultimately serve a formative and a summative purpose. The system must provide the rich diagnostic information for improving or enhancing faculty performance, as well as for providing accurate, reliable, and relevant data on which to base personnel decisions. Faculty evaluation systems that start out ostensibly as formative (i.e., designed to provide feedback to facilitate professional growth and development) almost always end up serving a summative purpose as well. Sooner or later, a faculty member will submit evaluation data as part of the evidence in support of a promotion, tenure, or merit pay decision. Or, conversely, an administrator will ask for certain evaluative data to assist in making a difficult personnel decision concerning a faculty member.

In practice, a singular faculty evaluation system can be made to serve both formative and summative purposes. The key to developing and operating such a system is to carefully determine and prescribe the type of data to be gathered and what is to be done with it. The faculty evaluation system should be constructed in such a way that detailed, frequently gathered data are provided in confidence only to the faculty member for diagnostic and feedback purposes. Specified formats for summarizing the detailed data should be developed. See the case studies in the Chapter 16 for several examples. These formats, which will be used for administrative purposes, should reflect only aggregated data that provide a clear picture of the faculty member's pattern of performance over time. In no case should any particular term's detailed evaluative information concerning a faculty member be used for administrative decision-making. The detailed data should provide the basis for professional growth or skill enhancement efforts only. The principle to be followed in preparing summative data for administrative purposes is to make certain that the summative data convey a sense of a faculty member's overall performance across time as noted in Chapter 10 and not just a single term's performance, whether that performance was good or bad.

▪ DATA STORAGE AND CONFIDENTIALITY

Virtually any faculty evaluation system will gather information from students, peers, and administrators, as well as various other sources, depending upon the specific design of the system. From a practical standpoint, a way must be developed for maintaining confidentiality while the data are stored. There are basically three approaches to this: the centralized department file, the individualized portfolio, and web-based storage.

Centralized Department Files

A number of institutions place the responsibility of gathering and storing faculty evaluation data on the departmen-

tal or division head. In this system, a centralized file location is specified, and the department head controls access to the files. This approach places the responsibility for security and confidentiality on a limited number of people.

The advantage to this approach is that it is relatively unlikely that anyone will systematically violate the integrity of the information stored for a given faculty member. However, there are a number of disadvantages. First and foremost, it creates a great deal of work for the department head, especially if the department is relatively large. Second, if faculty perceive the central files as the primary evidence on which the administration will make decisions, there is a pronounced tendency for them to put voluminous amounts of material in their files, just to be safe. Finally, faculty may feel that the confidentiality of the information has already been compromised because the department head, as an administrator, will have already seen it. However, if the department head is serving as the chief faculty development officer, as is sometimes the case, this approach can be very effective, especially in relatively small departments.

The Portfolio System

A system for accumulating and storing faculty evaluation information which has gathered some popularity is the so-called portfolio system. Under such a system, faculty members themselves are responsible for assembling and maintaining their own files in a specified style and format to create their faculty evaluation portfolio.

The faculty evaluation portfolio may take many forms. Institutions using the procedure described in this book to develop their faculty evaluation systems generally produce manuals containing clear, step-by-step instructions concerning gathering the faculty evaluation data into a portfolio type format. In some instances, the institution has special three-ring binders produced for the portfolio. Sometimes special file pockets are provided within which to store certain types of documentation, such as published articles, syllabi, and examples of tests. Various summary and data recording sheets are provided so that the faculty member may assemble, in a consistent standardized fashion, the aggregate statistical data which are to be used for personnel decisions. See Chapter 16 for a case study of Georgia Perimeter College's work in developing a comprehensive faculty evaluation system using the steps described in this book, which includes a variation of the portfolio approach in assembling faculty evaluation data.

The advantage of the portfolio approach is that individual faculty members are responsible for assembling and maintaining their own evaluation data. No one person must assemble the data for all faculty, as is the case in the centralized filing system. However, this approach assumes a high level of trust between the faculty and the administration, because personnel decisions may rely heavily on the summary or aggregate data assembled in the portfolio. Peter Seldin (2004) has charted the growth of the portfolio approach to evaluating teaching and has developed a concise and highly effective procedure for assembling and using teaching portfolios to improve faculty performance and provide data for personnel decisions.

Web-Based Storage

Several institutions have developed electronic data storage systems that combine the best aspects of both the centralized and portfolio systems. Such systems generally create a secure, web-based site for each faculty member. Each faculty member is responsible for entering appropriate data onto web-based forms or screens and ensuring its completeness. Usually a key administrator such as a department chair or dean has the authority to view and perhaps update faculty web-based files. See Chapter 16 for the case study of Fairmont State University that describes its web-based data storage system.

▌ USING THIS BOOK

If you have purchased this book expecting to find a fully developed faculty evaluation system with forms and policies all worked out and ready to be implemented in a couple of weeks, you will be disappointed. Although it would certainly be possible to prepare such a package, it would not work on your campus for the simple reason that each campus has unique needs and characteristics to which any faculty evaluation system must respond. No "canned" faculty evaluation system, no matter how technically correct or how well it works on some other campus, will automatically succeed on yours. What this book *does* provide is a systematic, *proven* approach for developing a fair and consistent faculty evaluation system that responds to the unique values, needs, missions, traditions, and overall culture of your institution.

Many decision points in this book can lead to significantly different evaluation systems. However, any system developed by the process described herein will result in a faculty evaluation program that will have the maximum probability of being successfully implemented. The process described herein has been used successfully by many types and sizes of colleges (including liberal arts colleges, community colleges, technical colleges, and research universities) to create customized faculty evaluation systems that work best for them. No two institutions using this process may necessarily come up with the same system, although similarities will exist, of course, at least to the extent that the assumptions implicit in the process are accepted.

The following suggested schedule of key events is effective in using the model described herein for successfully developing a comprehensive faculty evaluation system. The events described generally take 18–24 months to complete. A more specific calendar for the steps in developing a comprehensive faculty evaluation system is in Chapter 8.

Event 1

Appoint a Committee or task force to coordinate the development of the faculty evaluation system. The Committee should include faculty members representing the various faculty constituencies, union representatives (if any), and one or two senior administrators. Student representatives may also be appointed to the committee, depending upon the culture and tradition of the institution.

Event 2

The Committee becomes familiar with the steps in the process for developing a comprehensive faculty evaluation system described herein.

Event 3

A presentation is made to the administration concerning the approach to be taken. Administration becomes acquainted with the steps of the process.

Event 4

A presentation is made to the general faculty concerning the process to be followed in developing the faculty evaluation system. *This event is critical.* The faculty should be given the opportunity to become acquainted with the steps to be followed by the Committee in developing the faculty evaluation system.

Event 5

The Committee begins the process of gathering the information and data specified by the various steps in the process.

Event 6

A preliminary trial of the new faculty evaluation system is implemented.

Developing a Comprehensive Faculty Evaluation System

Event 7

Any problems detected during the preliminary trial are corrected.

Event 8

The full system is implemented.

▪ REFERENCES

Aleamoni, L. M. (1999). Student rating myths versus research facts from 1924 to 1998. *Journal of Personnel Evaluation in Education, 13*(2), 153–166.

Aleamoni, L. M. (1997). Issues in linking instructional-improvement research to faculty development in higher education. *Journal of Personnel Evaluation in Education, 11*(1), 31–37.

Aleamoni, L. M. (1987). *New directions for teaching and learning: No. 31. Techniques for evaluating and improving instruction.* San Francisco, CA: Jossey-Bass.

Arreola, R. A. (1979). Strategy for Developing a Comprehensive Faculty Evaluation System. *Engineering Education, 70*(3), 239–244.

Arreola, R. A. (1986). Evaluating the Dimensions of Teaching. *Instructional Evaluation, 8*(2), 4–14.

Arreola, R. A. (2000). Higher education's meta-profession [Interview]. *The Department Chair, 11*(2), 4–5.

Arreola, R. A. (2005). Monster at the foot of the bed: Surviving the challenge of marketplace forces on higher education. In S. Chadwick-Blossey & D. R. Robertson (Eds.), *To Improve the Academy: Vol 24. Resources for faculty, instructional, and organizational development* (15–28). Bolton, MA: Anker.

Arreola, R. A., Aleamoni, L. M., & Theall, M. (2001, February). *College teaching as meta-profession: Reconceptualizing the scholarship of teaching and learning.* Paper presented at the annual American Association for Higher Education conference on Faculty Roles and Rewards, Tampa, FL.

Arreola, R. A., Aleamoni, L. M., & Theall, M. (2003, April). *Beyond Scholarship: Recognizing the multiple roles of the professoriate.* Paper presented at the annual meeting of the American Educational Research Association, Chicago, IL.

Cox, D. H. (2003, Winter). Academic integrity: Cheating 101—A literature review. *The News About Teaching and Learning at Memorial: Newsletter of the Instructional Development Office, 6*(2), 1–4.

Ebel, R. L. (1965*). Measuring educational achievement.* Englewood Cliffs, NJ: Prentice Hall.

Grasha, A. F. (1977). *Assessing and developing faculty performance: Principles and models.* Cincinnati, OH: Communication and Education Associates.

Hattie, J., & Marsh, H. W. (1996). The relationship between research and teaching—A meta-analysis. *Review of Educational Research, 66*(4), 507–542.

Healy, P. (1999, March 26). Mass. governor seeks to free some colleges from tenure and most regulations. *The Chronicle of Higher Education,* p. A43.

Hersh, R. H., & Merrow, J. (2005). *Declining by degrees: Higher education at risk.* New York, NY: Palgrave Macmillan.

Leatherman, C. (1999, April 9). Growth in positions off the tenure track is a trend that's here to stay, study finds. *The Chronicle of Higher Education,* p. A14.

Marsh, H. W., & Hattie, J. (2002). The relationship between research productivity and teaching effectiveness. *The Journal of Higher Education, 73*(5), 603–641.

Milton, O., & Shoben, E. J., Jr., (1968). *Learning and the professor.* Athens, OH: Ohio University Press.

O'Connell, W. R., & Smartt, S. H. (1979). *Improving faculty evaluation: A trial strategy; a report of the SREB faculty evaluation project.* Atlanta, GA: Southern Regional Education Board.

Seldin, P. (1980). *Successful faculty evaluation programs: A practical guide to improve faculty performance and promotion/tenure decisions.* Cruger, NY: Coventry Press.

Seldin, P. (2004). *The teaching portfolio: A practical guide to improved performance and promotion/tenure decisions* (3rd ed.). Bolton, MA: Anker

Theall, M., & Arreola, R. A. (2001, April). *Beyond the scholarship of teaching: Searching for a unifying metaphor for the college teaching profession.* Paper presented at the annual meeting of the American Educational Research Association, Seattle, WA.

Step 1: Determining the Faculty Role Model

Evaluation is process of interpreting data through the lens of a specific value or set of values to determine whether that data indicates a desirable or undesirable condition. If a faculty evaluation system is ultimately to be perceived as fair, it is necessary to begin its development by first ascertaining the values or value construct to be used in the evaluation process. Thus, the design and implementation of a successful faculty evaluation system is as much a political process as it is a technical or psychometric one. This is an important issue that is often overlooked by those involved in designing questionnaires, forms, or procedures for faculty evaluation systems. Much time and effort can be spent examining and discussing the reliability and validity of student ratings, peer evaluations, department chair evaluations, and the entire evaluation process. The literature abounds with research efforts to validate one form or another. Ultimately, however, the validity of any form is a function of the degree to which the form measures those aspects of faculty performance that faculty believe to be important to measure in the first place. Even if the forms or procedures in a faculty evaluation system have been determined to be valid and reliable from a technical psychometric perspective, if faculty perceive the forms as reflecting values with which they do not agree, they will not accept them. If the faculty perceive the forms and procedures as measuring things they don't believe should be measured, or if they simply don't like the sound of some of the questions, then the forms and procedures will be of little positive use. Gaining faculty confidence in the design of the faculty evaluation system and all of its components is the key to establishing a successful faculty evaluation system.

Once the faculty feel that the evaluation system is designed to measure the "right" things (i.e., the system reflects the faculty's values and priorities), then the issue of the technical validity of its various components can be tackled with accepted psychometric and statistical techniques. If we take these steps in reverse order, as is often the case, we stand a very good chance of becoming bogged down by technical arguments that can defeat the complex political process of developing a faculty evaluation system in which the faculty have confidence. Thus, we begin the development of the faculty evaluation system by engaging the faculty in determining what aspects of their performance *should* be evaluated in a faculty evaluation system.

The development of a successful, valid, and reliable faculty evaluation is a complex and time-consuming process that requires careful coordination. Thus, in all that follows it is assumed that a specific *committee* or *task force* has been appointed to coordinate and carry out the process of developing the comprehensive faculty evaluation system. It is recommended that the committee's membership include representation from the faculty and the administration. If possible the membership of the committee should also include faculty with expertise in psychometrics. From this point forward the committee or task force coordinating the project will be referred to simply as the Committee.

In addition, it is recommended that the activities described herein that involve faculty in the development of the faculty evaluation system, be carried out by the basic academic unit of the institution. Please note that for the purpose of our discussion here and throughout the remainder of the book, the basic academic unit will simply be referred to as the department—the term *department* will be used to indicate the basic academic unit. The basic academic unit may be either a subset of discipline-specific faculty within a larger unit, a department, or a division. It is recognized that, depending upon the precise organizational structure of your institution, it may be more appropriate to use "division", "section", or even "discipline-group" in place of the word "department." For example, a college division may include the disciplines of mathematics, physics, and chemistry, but not have any specific mathematics department, physics department, or chemistry department. In this situation the completion of Step 1 should involve the faculty within each discipline (mathematics, physics, and chemistry) meeting separately rather than grouping all faculty within the division together (unless, of course, there are only one or two faculty members in each discipline). It is also recognized that in certain very small colleges the procedures described herein may need to be carried out with the participation of the faculty as a whole. In any case the intent at this point is that the faculty within each appropriate basic academic unit be involved in the activities in Step 1.

The objective of Step 1 is to have each department identify and define the roles faculty play in the department. This is determined by taking an inventory of the actual activities in which the faculty engage in pursing their professional responsibilities. In this step faculty can generally easily identify the activities that, for them, define the traditional roles of teaching, scholarly and creative activities, service, and administration or management. Experience has shown that faculty may also identify other important roles that must be included in the design of the faculty evaluation system.

In carrying out Step 1 department faculty meetings, coordinated by the Committee, should be held so that faculty can complete FORM 1A and FORM 1B. These forms ask the faculty to 1) list all the activities in which they engage in carrying out their daily professional responsibilities, and 2) group these activities so that the activities associated with specific roles (e.g., teaching) are clearly identified. This procedure is critical for two reasons. First, it serves to fully engage the faculty in the development of the faculty evaluation system from the outset, which begins the process of building confidence in and faculty acceptance of the final product. Second, it provides an organized method for reflecting disciplinary differences in the design of the faculty evaluation system. For example, faculty in a physics department may define teaching as including such activities as "demonstrating the proper calibration procedure for a mass spectrometer" or "giving a lecture," while faculty in an agricultural outreach department may define teaching as including such activities as "consulting with the farmer on proper irrigation techniques during breaks in planting." Thus, although the faculty within an institution may all be responsible for carrying out the roles of teaching, scholarly and creative activities, and service, the specific activities that constitute the performance of those roles will vary significantly according to the faculty member's discipline. In order to ensure that the final faculty evaluation system is seen as fair, it must be recognized at the outset that the specific faculty performances that will ultimately be measured and evaluated may differ significantly from department to department, discipline to discipline. Step 1 provides us with the fundamental information that will later be required in the design of the various forms or other measurement tools and procedures that will be used in the evaluation system. Since the development of these forms will be based on the activity descriptions the faculty themselves provide, they will have a more immediately recognizable validity.

In completing Step 1 faculty within each department are tasked with producing a singular listing for the department that specifies the agreed-upon activities that define each role. In carrying out Step 1 the Committee may suggest the roles in advance and ask faculty to develop lists of activities that define each role. The Committee may also specify roles that *must* be defined. The specification of such roles, however, should take place *only* if an administrative mandate exists. An example of an administrative mandate would be a board policy specifying that any faculty evaluation system must include the evaluation of "instruction and service." If any such administrative mandates exist that limit or otherwise proscribe the design and operation of any faculty evaluation system, these mandates should be made clear to the faculty *before* starting Step 1. To engage in the processes involved in Steps 1, 2, and 3, and then retroactively deconstruct or modify the work of the faculty in order to match an administrative mandate will damage, if not derail, the entire process. If no such mandate exists, it is best to give faculty the opportunity to simply list all their activities, and by going through the process of identifying like activities and grouping them, determine the actual roles in which they are engaged. For example, by looking at a long combined list of activities from all the faculty in a department and logically grouping them by like activity, it may be found that faculty are engaged in the role of "professional growth and development" or "administration and management" in addition to the common roles of teaching, scholarly and creative activities, and service.

In this first step faculty are asked to list each activity in which they individually engage when carrying out their various professional responsibilities. Figures 1.3 and 1.4 show examples of the worksheets that faculty can use in developing their lists of activities. Figure 1.3 shows FORM 1A in which faculty list all their activities. Once each faculty member has developed his or her individual list of activities, the department must develop a consolidated list that defines specific roles for the faculty within that department. Once the department has developed its combined list of faculty activities, it must produce a singular document (using FORM 1B) that 1) identifies the roles faculty play within their department, 2) briefly defines each role, and 3) specifies the activities involved in the execution of each role. Figure 1.4 shows an example of FORM 1B which asks faculty to group their activities into broad categories or roles and to provide a preliminary name and brief definition for the role. At this point, in completing FORM 1A and FORM 1B, faculty should be assured that they are simply to describe what they do without being concerned about how these activities will be measured or evaluated. The specification of the measurement tools and the criteria and standards for evaluating performance can come only *after* it has been determined what professional activities should be considered in the design of the faculty evaluation system.

The determination of the broad categories (roles) faculty play, as defined by the consolidated list of activities entered on FORM 1B, begins the process of defining an institutional faculty role model for the new faculty evaluation system. Many institutions assume the traditional faculty role model of teaching, research, and service; however, faculty must engage in a wide variety of activities in response to their varied professional assignments that, when examined closely, often represent a variety of other roles as well. In addition to teaching and performing various service activities, faculty also advise students, publish articles and books, give presentations, consult, serve on committees, administer programs, and perform many other professional activities. Thus, a simple teaching, research, and service role model may be insufficient to adequately encompass the full range of legitimate faculty activities. Figure 1.1 shows a more comprehensive, expanded set of roles and brief examples of some of the activities that may define those roles. Other discussions concerning the description of faculty work can be found in Boyer (1990), Bowen and Schuster (1986), Braskamp and Ory (1994), Diamond and Adam (1993), Miller (1972), Rhodes (1990), and Rice (1991).

By starting with the listing of activities in which faculty actually engage in pursuit of their professional assignments, the institution's true operational faculty role model may be determined. The operational institutional faculty role model becomes the foundation upon which the entire faculty evaluation system will be built. That is, instead of simply defaulting to the traditional teaching, research, and service faculty role model, beginning with actual faculty performances provides us with a more accurate and complete definition of the roles faculty play as they pursue their various professional responsibilities within the institution. In addition, faculty are able to see their input being considered in the development of the evaluation system from the very beginning. Constructing this foundation with the detailed input of the faculty begins the political process of gaining faculty acceptance of the final design of the faculty evaluation system and the technical process of designing the measurement tools to be used.

Figure 1.2 is an action checklist suggesting several activities that have been found to be useful in carrying out Step 1. It is important that all faculty have an organized, structured, and institutionally supported opportunity to provide their input into this first activity in building the comprehensive faculty evaluation system. The completion of Step 1 can take several weeks depending upon the initiative of the Committee and the cooperation of the department chairs. However, as an option Steps 1, 2, and 3, may be completed in an accelerated fashion using the strategy of holding large-scale, day-long faculty workshops (this procedure is described in detail in the action checklist at the end of Step 3).

Figure 1.1. Partial List of Possible Faculty Roles With Examples of Defining Activities

TEACHING

Instructional Design
1. Developing course materials (e.g., handouts, slide presentations)
2. Developing computer simulations or exercises
3. Designing strategies for experiential learning events

Instructional Delivery
1. Delivering lectures
2. Operating chat room for online course
3. Facilitating small-group experiential learning events

Instructional Assessment
1. Developing written examinations
2. Grading examinations
3. Judging music recitals

SCHOLARLY & CREATIVE ACTIVITIES

Proficiency
1. Attending advanced workshops in your discipline
2. Acquiring advanced certification in your discipline
3. Pursuing postdoctoral work
4. Continuing Education credits in your field

Discovery/Creative Activities
1. Conducting basic research in your field
2. Writing a play, opera, or novel (if your field is theater, music, or English Literature, respectively)

Dissemination (of information in your discipline)
1. Books, monographs, etc.
2. Journal and magazine articles
3. Presenting recitals and exhibitions
4. Staging, directing, or acting in musical, theatrical, and dance productions
5. Exhibiting paintings, sculptures, and other creative arts
6. Writing Reviews, critiques
7. Popular press/media presentations (television, audio broadcasts, etc.)
8. Professional/keynote addresses, delivery of papers, poster sessions

Translation
1. Conducting applied research to produce a practical, useable, product, procedure, or service
2. Inventing and patenting a new product based on previous research (either your own or others')
3. Developing a clinic protocol for treatment of a specific disease based on the use of newly developed drugs or medical technology

PROFESSIONAL RECOGNITION
1. Awards, honors
2. Invited presentations/keynote addresses
3. Consulting activities

SERVICE

To the Institution
1. Serving on department, college, or university committees
2. Serving on the faculty senate
3. Chairing any committee (student, faculty, etc.)
4. Serving as a sponsor for student activities/groups
5. Advising students on programs of study
6. Sponsoring or advising student groups
7. Chairing master's or doctoral supervisory committees
8. Serving on master's or doctoral supervisory committees

To the Profession
1. Holding office in professional organization (president, secretary, treasurer, etc.)
2. Serving as journal reviewer, editor
3. Coordinating national conferences or meetings of the organization

To the General Community
Applying academic expertise in the local, state, or national community without pay or profit

Arreola, R. A. (2007). *Developing a comprehensive faculty evaluation system* (3rd ed.). Bolton, MA: Anker.

Figure 1.2. Action Checklist for Completing Step 1

Action Checklist for Completing Step 1*

Expected Outcome: Each department will complete and submit to the Committee copies of FORM 1B that represent its faculty's consensus on the identification of the various roles they play within the institution. Each role identified on FORM 1B will also include an agreed-upon departmental listing of the specific activities that define each role.

____ The Committee meets with the department chairs to familiarize them with the process of gathering the data specified on FORM 1A from individual faculty and developing a departmental summary or synthesis to be recorded on FORM 1B.

____ Prepare packets of FORM 1A for each department chair with sufficient copies so that each faculty member within the department will have at least three copies to serve as worksheets. Have department chairs distribute the forms to their faculty with a cover letter asking them to complete FORM 1A in preparation for a special department faculty meeting.

____ Although faculty will not be asked to complete FORM 1B individually, chairs may wish to distribute copies of FORM 1B to faculty to familiarize them with the process that will be needed to complete Step 1. (An alternative is to email the forms to faculty so they may print out as many as needed).

____ Each department must hold a faculty meeting in which all individual data listed on FORM 1A by each faculty member is consolidated, summarized, and synthesized and recorded on a single FORM 1B for the department. A completed FORM 1B must be submitted to the Committee by each department.

____ Committee members must be prepared to serve as facilitators for department meetings. Suggest to the department chairs that members of the Committee will be available to serve as meeting facilitators. When serving as a facilitator, the Committee member must be careful not to impose, or appear to impose, any particular definition or structure to the work being done by the department's faculty. The faculty must see the faculty role model being produced as result of their own thinking and their input. The only exception to this is in the event of the existence of external mandates as mentioned earlier.

* See action checklist for Step 3 for an alternate procedure for completing this step in conjunction with the completion of Steps 2 and 3.

Arreola, R. A. (2007). *Developing a comprehensive faculty evaluation system* (3rd ed.). Bolton, MA: Anker.

Figure 1.3: Copies of this form (FORM 1A) are used to gather preliminary information from individual faculty to begin the process of defining specific roles in terms of the actual activities in which faculty engage.

FORM 1A: Individual Activities List

Use this form to list the activities in which you engage in your various roles as a faculty member. Do not write narratives but, rather, write two-, three-, or four-word short descriptions of your activities. For example:

   1. *Grade exams*
   2. *Serve on admissions committee*
   3. *Develop PowerPoint presentations*
   4. *Advise student chess club*

1. _____	26. _____
2. _____	27. _____
3. _____	28. _____
4. _____	29. _____
5. _____	30. _____
6. _____	31. _____
7. _____	32. _____
8. _____	33. _____
9. _____	34. _____
10. _____	35. _____
11. _____	36. _____
12. _____	37. _____
13. _____	38. _____
14. _____	39. _____
15. _____	40. _____
16. _____	41. _____
17. _____	42. _____
18. _____	43. _____
19. _____	44. _____
20. _____	45. _____
21. _____	46. _____
22. _____	47. _____
23. _____	48. _____
24. _____	49. _____
25. _____	50. _____

Arreola, R. A. (2007). *Developing a comprehensive faculty evaluation system* (3rd ed.). Bolton, MA: Anker.

Figure 1.4: Copies of this form (FORM 1B) are used to consolidate the listings of the activities (provided by faculty on FORM 1A) into discrete sets of activities that define the performances within the various professional faculty roles (e.g., teaching, scholarly and creative activities, service, etc.) for the department.

FORM 1B: Role Names With Brief Definitions and Defining Activities

Department:_____

Directions: In the spaces below indicate the name(s) of the role(s) the department has identified based on the lists provided by individual faculty on FORM 1A. Provide a short definition/description of the role in the space provided below the role name. Below each role name list the activities and/or professional performances that further define and specify the role. Each department must submit a final FORM 1B that represents the faculty's consensus.

Role Name	Role Name
*Brief definition:*_____	*Brief definition:*_____
_____	_____
_____	_____
_____	_____

Activities Defining this Role

1. _____
2. _____
3. _____
4. _____
5. _____
6. _____
7. _____
8. _____
9. _____
10. _____
11. _____
12. _____
13. _____
14. _____
15. _____
16. _____
17. _____
18. _____
19. _____
20. _____

Activities Defining this Role

1. _____
2. _____
3. _____
4. _____
5. _____
6. _____
7. _____
8. _____
9. _____
10. _____
11. _____
12. _____
13. _____
14. _____
15. _____
16. _____
17. _____
18. _____
19. _____
20. _____

Arreola, R. A. (2007). *Developing a comprehensive faculty evaluation system* (3rd ed.). Bolton, MA: Anker.

▪ REFERENCES

Bowen, H. R., & Schuster, J. H. (1986). *American professors: A national resource imperiled.* New York, NY: Oxford University Press.

Boyer, E. L. (1990). *Scholarship reconsidered: Priorities of the professoriate.* Princeton, NJ: The Carnegie Foundation for the Advancement of Teaching.

Braskamp, L.A., & Ory, J. C. (1994). *Assessing faculty work: Enhancing individual and institutional performance.* San Francisco, CA: Jossey-Bass.

Diamond, R. M, & Adam, B. E. (1993). *New directions for higher education: No. 81. Recognizing faculty work: Reward systems for the year 2000.* San Francisco, CA: Jossey-Bass.

Miller, R. I. (1972). *Evaluating faculty performance.* San Francisco, CA: Jossey-Bass.

Rhodes, F. H. T. (1990). *The new American university.* Urbana, IL: University of Illinois.

Rice, R. E. (1991). Toward a broader conception of scholarship: The American context. In T. G. Whiston & R. C. Geiger (Eds.), *Research and Higher Education: The United Kingdom and the United States* (pp. 117–129). Lancaster, England: Society for Research into Higher Education and Open University Press.

2

Step 2: Determining Faculty Role Model Parameter Values

At the completion of Step 1, each department will have recommended which faculty roles they believe ought to be evaluated. In addition, by completing FORM 1B (Figure 1.4) each department will have also provided a brief definition of each role and an indication of the specific activities that operationally define it. The objective of Step 2 is to begin the process of defining the value structure on which the evaluation system will ultimately be based. In this step the institution begins to establish and specify the relative importance of each role to the institution. Here faculty are asked to determine how much value or weight they believe should be placed on each role in the faculty role model that resulted from their work in Step 1. For example, assume that teaching, scholarly and creative activities, and service are the three roles of the faculty role model for a given institution. Which of these roles is valued the most? Which the least? What is the priority order of this set of roles for the institution? Generally, teaching is said to be the most valued role. However, in reality, when it comes time for promotion, tenure, and other personnel decisions, we often find that research (just one expression of scholarly and creative activities) is valued more than teaching—or at least more than was originally thought or intended. Therefore, it is important to establish, in some more rigorous and specific fashion, the relative values of these different roles.

■ ESTABLISHING PARAMETER VALUES

Faculty role models can take one of two forms relative to their use in a faculty evaluation system—static or dynamic. Figure 2.1 is an example of a traditional static faculty role model.

Figure 2.1   Sample Static Faculty Role Model

Teaching	40%
Research	40%
Service	20%

In a traditional static faculty role model not only is the scholarly and creative activities role expressed as only one specific activity (research), performance in each role carries the same specified proportion of weight or impact on the total evaluation for every faculty member. That is, in the example above, 40% of every faculty member's overall evaluation will be based on their teaching performance, 40% on their research performance, and 20% on their service performance.

Colleges and universities have tended to use traditional static faculty role models such as the one in Figure 2.1. However, static faculty role models are inherently unfair when used in defining a faculty evaluation system. Static faculty role models have as their underlying premise that all faculty will be held accountable in the same degree for performance in all three major faculty roles. This assumption would be appropriate if all faculty had precisely the same set of professional responsibilities, duties, and resources. Realistically, however, we know that some faculty have professional responsibilities that concentrate heavily on teaching, while others may have substantial assignments and commitments to various service activities. Still others may have substantial amounts of their time, energy, and resources tied up in various scholarly and creative activities, including research. In addition, within any institution, a wide variety of opinions concerning the relative value of the roles which faculty play exists among the faculty and administration. Some hold teaching to be of primary importance, some hold research to be of greatest importance, and others (especially faculty with large advising or committee responsibilities) maintain that service is the most important faculty role.

Static faculty role models derive from a desire by every academic institution to achieve excellence in their primary missions of teaching, scholarship, and service. This desire has generally been translated into faculty evaluation systems that require every faculty member to achieve excellence in all (or at least two of the three) roles. As noted earlier, however, this expectation is unreasonable at best and grossly unfair at worst. This expectation is analogous to expecting that every class admitted to the institution will be made up of students who were valedictorians, captains of their (basketball, swimming, soccer, etc.) team, and achieved prominence in their community as model charitable citizens. Although we might be able to make up a couple of classes like that, we couldn't hold that expectation for every class admitted.

Obviously, a static faculty role model cannot adequately represent the reality of the diversity of responsibilities and values of the faculty in a faculty evaluation system. In order to develop a fair faculty evaluation system a better approach is to define a dynamic faculty role model that establishes parameter values for each role. That is, determine the minimum and maximum weights that could be assigned to a role within the institution's faculty evaluation system to adequately represent the full scope of configurations of professional responsibilities and assignments. Thus, in developing a comprehensive faculty evaluation system that furthers the institutional goal of achieving excellence in teaching, scholarship, etc., the evaluation system must be designed to permit a *differentiated staffing model* for faculty: It must enable faculty to play to their strengths and be recognized and rewarded appropri-

ately. A differentiated staffing model permits faculty who are excellent teachers to engage primarily in teaching, permits faculty who are excellent in scholarly and creative activities to engage primarily in pursuing various expressions of scholarship or creation, and so on. A faculty evaluation system based on a dynamic faculty role model enables faculty to play to their strengths and be appropriately recognized. In reality, then, a differentiated staffing model can facilitate an institution's goal of achieving excellence in its major missions of teaching, scholarship, and service by focusing the talents of faculty.

Figure 2.2 shows a dynamic faculty role model developed by one institution using the process described here. Note that values or weights for the teaching role range from a minimum of 50% to a maximum of 85%. This is be interpreted to mean that teaching performance can count *no less* than 50% and *no more* than 85% of the final evaluation of a faculty member's overall performance. This does *not* necessarily mean that a faculty member may have a 50% to 85% teaching load or that they spend 50% to 85% of their time teaching. Rather, these numbers are an expression of how much impact or weight performance in the role of teaching can have on the faculty member's overall evaluation. Although there should be some correspondence between the configuration of professional duties a faculty member may have and the value selected for each role in the final evaluation, it is generally *not* recommended that such values be directly associated with the number of hours spent by the faculty member engaged in any one role or activity within a role. To define the faculty evaluation system in that way would tend to reduce faculty to hourly employees rather than professionals. As professionals faculty should be recognized on the basis of the importance or value of the professional service they provide, not on the basis of how long it took them to provide that service. Thus, in the example of a dynamic faculty role model shown in Figure 2.2, an individual faculty member may or may not have a full-time teaching load, but the value associated with teaching performance in this evaluation system could range from 50% to 85%.

Figure 2.2 Example of a Dynamic Faculty Role Model

Minimum Weight (%)	Faculty Role	Maximum Weight (%)
50%	Teaching	85%
0%	Scholarly/Creative Activities	35%
10%	Service to the College	25%
5%	Service to the General Community	10%

The dynamic faculty role model shown in Figure 2.2 clearly indicates that a faculty member's total evaluation will be based not only on teaching, but on performance in other roles as well. What is communicated to the faculty is that simply doing well in their teaching assignment is not enough. Obviously, between 15% and 50% of the evaluation will be based on something else. In the example shown in Figure 2.2, that "something else" includes scholarly/creative activities, faculty service, and community service. Here, scholarly/creative activities can count as little as 0% and as much as 35%. The 0% minimum weight communicates that the activities that define scholarly/creative activities are not required. The 35% maximum weight communicates that such scholarly/creative activities cannot constitute the entire, or even the majority, of the activities on which a faculty member will be evaluated. The minimum and maximum weights for service to the college (10%–25%) and service to the general community (5%–15%) communicate the fact that performance in these two roles are expected of everyone to some degree. The smaller values also indicate that neither of these roles can constitute the primary or majority activity for a faculty member insofar as the evaluation system is concerned.

In this step in building a comprehensive faculty evaluation system, each department should do the initial work of developing a dynamic faculty role model that reflects the activities and values of the faculty and administration of that department. It is possible for different departments to develop somewhat different preliminary faculty role models. Later, it will be the task of the Committee to analyze and reconcile the various faculty role models from different departments in completing the design of the institution's overall faculty role model.

Similar to Step 1, before initiating Step 2 the Committee must determine whether any administrative mandates exist that may proscribe the process. For example, an institution's board may have issued a policy or administrative mandate specifying that at least 50% of a faculty member's evaluation will be based on teaching. Or, the institution's president may have established the principle that all faculty must engage in some form of service to the community—which would mandate not only the inclusion of the role of "service to the general community" but also some minimum value other than 0%. Such administrative mandates must be made clear to all concerned prior to starting Step 2.

Several forms have been developed to facilitate the process of carrying out Step 2. These forms, FORMs 2A, 2B, and 2C, are shown in Figures 2.6, 2.7, and 2.8 respectively, at the end of this chapter. Using copies of FORM 2B each department should list the roles identified on FORM 1B completed in Step 1. Each department must determine

its own dynamic faculty role model that specifies the minimum and maximum weights for each as agreed to by the faculty and administration of the department. FORM 2A is provided as a faculty worksheet that may be distributed to faculty in preparation for meeting together to determine a final, consensus-based dynamic faculty role model for the department that will be expressed on FORM 2B. Faculty may be asked to complete FORM 2A individually, on their own time. However, *the department as a whole must complete* FORM 2B, which can be done in a faculty meeting called for this specific purpose.

■ DETERMINING COLLEGE OR INSTITUTIONAL PARAMETER VALUES

In practice, determining the actual parameter values for the institution's faculty role model is a political process that involves consensus building between faculty and administration. The minimum and maximum weights should reflect the values and the priorities of the administration as well as the general sentiment of the faculty. This is best accomplished by integrating the various departmental faculty role model values (as expressed in each department's FORM 2B) and those that may have been specified by the administration into a singular faculty role model for the institution. The Committee may accomplish this task by using FORM 2C or some variation of it.

For example, assume that an institution had only two departments (designated as D1 and D2 in Figure 2.3). Each department would go through the process of determining the minimum and maximum weights for its faculty role model. The results taken from their respective FORM 2Bs would be displayed in FORM 2C as shown in Figure 2.3.

In preparing the parameter values of a faculty role model for the institution, care must be given to ensure that the combination of any maximum value and the remaining minimum values does not exceed 100%. Ideally, any combination of maximum and remaining minimum values should fall somewhere in the range of 65%–100%. A larger range is permissible but not desirable since it would tend to indicate that there still exists considerable differences of opinion among the faculty on which weights should be given to various faculty performances in the faculty evaluation system. Care must be taken, however, to make sure that the sum total of all minimum values does not equal 100% since that would essentially produce a static faculty role model with all its inherent problems.

The preliminary institutional faculty role model would be comprised of the lowest and highest values for each role as shown in parenthesis in Figure 2.3. The resulting institutional faculty role model, shown in Figure 2.4,

Figure 2.3 Recording of all departmental faculty role models for one institution on FORM 2C with the smallest minimum and the largest maximum for each role put in parenthesis

FORM 2C: Institutional Faculty Role Model—Committee Worksheet						
Departmental Minimum Weights			Role	Departmental Maximum Weights		
D1	D2	D3		D1	D2	D3
(50%)	55%		Teaching	(85%)	75%	
(0%)	10%		Scholarly/Creative Activities	25%	(35%)	
15%	(10%)		Faculty Service	(25%)	15%	
(5%)	(5%)		Community Service	(25%)	15%	

has been mathematically *balanced:* It is possible for an individual faculty member to select the maximum value for any one role and still be assured that they can meet the minimum requirements for the remaining roles. For example, a faculty member might select 35% as the weight to be applied to the evaluation of his or her performance in scholarly/creative activities, but still be able to meet the requirements of at least 50% minimum for teaching, 10% for faculty service, and 5% for community service (i.e., 35% + 50% + 10% + 5% = 100%).

The institutional faculty role model resulting from the individual departmental faculty role models represents the composite institutional value system and allows for diversity in values among departments. Although the institutional faculty role model may list the minimum value allowable for teaching as 50% and the maximum 85%, various departments could have different values as long as they fell within those limits. Department D2 as shown in Figure 2.3 would be one such department since it would have a minimum weight for teaching of 55% and a maximum weight of 75%.

■ DEALING WITH "OUTLIERS"

Occasionally one department or another may develop a faculty role model that is so different from the rest that it cannot reasonably be folded into the institutional faculty role model. This is sometimes true of departments involved in agricultural extension, or some other discipline where the faculty activities required to achieve the department's missions and goals are of a significantly different nature from faculty activities in disciplines such as English, psychology, mathematics, or music. In such cases it is appropriate to determine separate faculty role models that are incorporated into the comprehensive faculty evaluation system in addition to the institutional faculty role model. This strat-

egy does not in any way compromise, or unnecessarily complicate, the final evaluation system. Rather, it simply means that faculty within that department will be evaluated in accordance to the definitions and values established by their departmental faculty role model. In essence, for such outlier departments the departmental faculty role model becomes the institutional faculty role model. The institution, then, may legitimately have a faculty role model that has more than one variation. This may be necessary in order to accommodate the full spectrum of academic units needed to meet the missions and goals of the institution. As will be seen later, the determination of the evaluation procedure for faculty in such outlier departments will fit smoothly and seamlessly into the overall faculty evaluation system.

Figure 2.4 Mathematically Balanced Institutional Faculty Role Model

Minimum Weight	Role	Maximum Weight
50%	Teaching	85%
0%	Scholarly/Creative Activities	35%
10%	Faculty Service	25%
5%	Community Service	25%

Balance Calculations: Each maximum value plus the remaining minimum values must be less than, or equal to 100%.

Teaching:	85% + (0% + 10% + 5%)	= 100%
Scholarly Activities:	35% + (50% + 10% + 5%)	= 100%
Faculty Service:	25% + (0% + 50% + 5%)	= 80%
Community Service:	25% + (10% + 0% + 50%)	= 85%

Figure 2.5   Action Checklist for Completing Step 2

Action Checklist for Completing Step 2*

Expected Outcomes: Each department will complete and submit to the Committee a copy of FORM 2B that represents its faculty's consensus on the minimum and maximum weights to be assigned to the various roles in the faculty role model. The Committee, using FORM 2C, will reconcile the various departmental faculty role models into an institutional faculty role model. Note: It may be possible that certain "outlier" departments may exist which require their own separate faculty role model.

____ Prepare packets for each department that contain at least one copy of FORM 2A for each faculty member in the department.

____ Distribute the FORM 2A packets to the department chairs and ask them to distribute them to their faculty with instructions to complete the form in preparation for a faculty meeting to determine the final departmental faculty role model.

____ Each department conducts a faculty meeting in which faculty reach consensus on what minimum and maximum values they believe should be assigned to the roles they specified in their department's FORM 1B.

____ Each department completes FORM 2B and submits it to the Committee.

____ Assemble the separate departmental faculty role model parameter values into a single worksheet (FORM 2C).

____ Determine the preliminary institutional faculty role model by using the absolute maximum and minimum values from the worksheet. Prepare additional outlier faculty role models if necessary.

____ Present the preliminary institutional faculty role model derived from the departmental input to the administration for review and approval in accordance with your institution's policies and procedures. Ideally, the institution's administrators, sitting as a separate department should complete a FORM 2B prior to such a presentation to have a clear frame of reference of the procedure and thus be able to provide the Committee with focused input in developing the final institutional faculty role model.

____ Resolve any discrepancies between the administratively determined parameter values and those of the preliminary institutional faculty role model parameter values. Experience has shown that generally there is very little discrepancy between these two sets of values. If a large discrepancy does exist there may be a significant conflict between the values of the administration and those of the faculty. If such a conflict does exist, it is not advisable to proceed with the project until the conflicts are resolved.

____ Once any discrepancies have been resolved the Committee should publish a report to the faculty which delineates the adopted faculty role model for the institution (including outliers if needed). This report should include not only the minimum and maximum values but also the role definitions that will be determined in Step 3.

---

* See action checklist for Step 3 for an alternate procedure for completing this step in conjunction with the completion of Steps 1 and 3.

Arreola, R. A. (2007). *Developing a comprehensive faculty evaluation system* (3rd ed.). Bolton, MA: Anker.

Step 2: Determining Faculty Role Model Parameter Values 13

Figure 2.6 Form for use in gathering input from individual faculty concerning the values they believe should be given, as a minimum and maximum, to the roles identified in Step 1

FORM 2A: Setting Faculty Role Model Parameter Values (Individual Worksheet)		
Minimum Value or Weight	Role	Maximum Value or Weight

Directions: List the roles that were identified in Step 1 and recorded on FORM 1B for your department. Indicate the *minimum* and *maximum* percentage values or weights you believe should be placed on each role. For example, if "teaching" is one of the roles that was identified to be evaluated, and you feel that, at minimum, faculty performance in teaching should count as at least 65% of their overall evaluation, you would place 65% in the minimum value column for teaching. On the other hand, if you feel that faculty performance in teaching should count no more than 85% of their overall evaluation, you would place the number 85% in the maximum value column for teaching. *Note: The sum total of all minimum values you record may be less than, but must not exceed, 100%. However, the sum total of the maximum value column may exceed 100%.*

Arreola, R. A. (2007). *Developing a comprehensive faculty evaluation system* (3rd ed.). Bolton, MA: Anker.

Figure 2.7 Form for use by individual departments in reporting the minimum and maximum values the faculty has agreed should be placed on the various roles in the faculty role model

FORM 2B: Dynamic Faculty Role Model For: _____

Minimum Value or Weight	Role	Maximum Value or Weight

Directions:

A) Enter the name of the academic unit (department, division, etc.) at the top of the form.

B) List the roles that have been identified on the department's FORM 1B completed as part of Step 1.

C) Reach consensus among the faculty on the departmental minimum and maximum weight for each role. That is, determine how much a faculty member's performance in that role should count in the overall faculty evaluation system. (Individual faculty may have filled out FORM 2A in preparation for the departmental discussion of what minimum and maximum weights should be set for each role.)

D) In completing this form make sure the values entered *balance*. That is, every maximum value, when added to the *remaining* minimum values, should total no less than 70% but no greater than 100%. If the total exceeds 100%, you must reduce the value of one or more of the weights. Reduce either the maximum weight of the role being considered or one or more of the minimum weights in the remaining roles. (A simple computer spreadsheet may be developed to facilitate this process.)

E) Repeat step D above using the maximum weight of each role in turn and the minimum weights of ALL the remaining roles. If more than six roles have been identified, first examine them to determine if one or more roles is really a subset of another and should thus be combined. If it is determined that more than 6 different roles have been identified then simply insert additional rows into the table above.

Arreola, R. A. (2007). *Developing a comprehensive faculty evaluation system* (3rd ed.). Bolton, MA: Anker.

Step 2: Determining Faculty Role Model Parameter Values

Figure 2.8   Form for use by the Committee in developing the institutional faculty role model

FORM 2C: Institutional Faculty Role Model (Committee Worksheet)

Departmental Minimum Values					Role	Departmental Maximum Values				
D1	D2	D3	D4	D5		D1	D2	D3	D4	D5

Directions:

A) List the roles that have been identified in each department's FORM 2B. Note that not all departments may have the exact same roles. Wherever possible list like roles on the same row. For example, one department may list the role of "teaching" and another list the role of "instruction." If both roles refer to the same type of activities they may both be listed under the more generic name of "teaching." One department may list the role of "faculty development" while another may list the role of "professional growth." Again, if both roles refer to essentially the same type of activities they may both be listed under the more generic name of "professional growth and development."

B) Examine the range of *minimum* and *maximum values* for each role. The general 'rule of thumb' here is to pick the lowest value as the preliminary institutional minimum value for that role, and pick the highest value as the preliminary institutional maximum value for that role.

C) In some instances outlier departments exist that have either significantly different maximum and minimum values for a given role compared to the remaining departments, and/or may list one or two roles that are significantly different from the remaining departments. In this instance it may be necessary to complete an *additional* faculty role mode for each outlier department. That is, within the design of the institution's comprehensive faculty evaluation system, there may need to be more than one faculty role model in order to accommodate departments, divisions, or even colleges whose missions and activities differ significantly from the remaining academic units.

D) Complete the institution's faculty role model by repeating steps A through C above until the minimum and maximum values for all roles have been determined.

E) Finally, balance the resulting faculty role model. Since some values may have to be adjusted, when reporting out the final product to the faculty it is important to communicate clearly why this needed to be done and that their initial values were not being rejected.

Arreola, R. A. (2007). *Developing a comprehensive faculty evaluation system* (3rd ed.). Bolton, MA: Anker.

Step 3: Defining Roles in the Faculty Role Model

The definition of the specific roles in which faculty engage is the last step in the process of building the faculty role model upon which the evaluation system will be based. As noted earlier, it is assumed that a specially appointed Committee will coordinate the detail work associated with this project. Step 3 involves reaching a consensus on how each of the roles identified and briefly defined in the previous steps are to be completely defined. For example, the role of teaching will readily be agreed upon. However, faculty from different disciplines or with different styles may mean different things when they use the word "teaching." Teaching a basic psychology course in a large lecture hall is different from teaching a lab course in biology is different from teaching a vocational course in air conditioner manufacturing on the floor of a factory. Teaching a graduate course is different from teaching an undergraduate course. Some faculty define meeting and counseling with students as part of teaching. Librarians consider the orientation seminars they give to students and new faculty as teaching. Thus, to say we are going to evaluate teaching doesn't necessarily mean the same thing to everyone—even though we may all agree that it is important to evaluate it.

The key to the development of a successful faculty evaluation system is to engage faculty and administrators in discussions of the conceptual underpinnings of the definition of any role in the faculty role mode. It is important that both groups come to an agreement about how each role should be defined for the system.

The importance of carefully defining the roles in your faculty role model cannot be overstated. Accordingly, this chapter presents detailed discussions concerning the devel-

opment of definitions of several common faculty roles. These definitions include the detailed development of the definition of the teaching role as well as suggested definitions of scholarly and creative activities, service, and other roles. Although the definitions provided have been found to be useful in the design of many faculty evaluation systems, it is important to consider these definitions as simply *examples* rather than the "correct" definitions. Thus, although you may not agree with the definition of teaching or any of the other roles developed in what follows, it should be noted that the intent here is to show an example of the *process* involved and to provide a jumping off point for your own campus discussions. In any case, a consistent definition for each role in your faculty role model must be developed in completing Step 3. It is important that any final definitions adopted by your institution be developed in consultation with the faculty. However, for the purposes of consistency and clarity throughout the remainder of this book, the definition of teaching and the other roles derived here will be used in all examples.

▣ DEFINING THE TEACHING ROLE: PERSPECTIVES ON THE DEFINITION OF TEACHING

In the broadest sense, we can define teaching as involving an interaction between a teacher and a student such that learning occurs on the part of the student. Of course, the crux of the matter in defining teaching is to specify what kind of interaction occurs between teacher and student. Over the years, three different perspectives or philosophical positions have evolved on what does, or should, occur when a teacher interacts with a student to produce learning. These perspectives are founded on different assumptions that significantly affect how we approach the evaluation of teaching.

Teaching as Providing the Opportunity to Learn

Under this perspective teaching is conceptualized as *an interaction between a teacher and a student conducted in such a way that the student is provided with the* opportunity *to learn.* In this definition the assumption is that a student has essentially the entire responsibility for learning and that the primary responsibility of the teacher is to provide the student with the appropriate opportunity to learn.

If we accept this definition in which it is the teacher's responsibility to simply give the students the opportunity to learn (a very popular definition among college faculty), then the defining characteristic of a good teacher would simply be content expertise. Under this definition, the teacher's primary responsibility would be to maintain his or her content expertise, usually through research, and to share this expertise with students. The act of teaching would consist of sharing knowledge, insights, hypotheses, and professional experiences through lectures, seminars, presentations, individual consultations, and mentoring. The primary role of the teacher would be that of scholar, knowledge generator, knowledge resource, role model, and, ideally, mentor.

Obviously, with this definition of teaching, student ratings or so-called "student evaluations" would be at best useless and at worst insulting. Students, by definition, would not have the teacher's content expertise and would thus not be qualified to make any sort of evaluative statements or conclusions concerning the teacher's competence. The faculty criticism of student ratings which says, "If students were competent to evaluate me, *they* would be up here teaching the course!" would be entirely correct and justified under this assumed definition of teaching. If this definition is assumed, then peer evaluation or department head evaluation becomes the only acceptable type of evaluation. It would be assumed that these individuals would be content experts and thus qualified to adequately assess the instructor's expertise.

Teaching as Enabling Learning

The second perspective conceptualizes teaching as *an interaction between a teacher and a student conducted to* promote *and* facilitate *student learning.* This perspective of teaching still assumes that a student has the primary responsibility for learning. However, implied in this perspective is the assumption that a teacher has some responsibility for student learning, because now the teacher has the task of facilitating or somehow enabling that learning.

If we choose this definition of teaching in which the teacher facilitates students' learning, then teaching becomes more complex. Under this definition, students still have the primary responsibility for learning, but the teacher has the responsibility for promoting or facilitating that learning. As with the first definition of teaching, the teacher must still be the source of knowledge and must possess content expertise, but now must also have the skills required to create and maintain an environment that is conducive to learning.

Implicit in this definition is the idea that the teacher must have the kind of social or human interactive skills that can engender interest in students and motivate them to learn. Teaching, under this definition, implies not only content expertise, but affective or personality traits not always under the direct conscious control of the teacher. People assuming this definition often say, "Good teachers are born and not made" or "Teaching is an art" or "You either have it or you don't." Such comments or beliefs reflect a heavy emphasis on the affective or personality component of this definition of teaching.

Under this definition peer or department head evaluations would still be considered most valid but student ratings could be viewed as having some use, because students can report how interested or motivated the teacher made them feel. Faculty subscribing to the first definition of teaching (i.e., providing the *opportunity* to learn) who encounter other faculty who subscribe to this second definition often charge that student ratings are "just a popularity contest."

Teaching as Causing Learning

Finally, the third perspective conceptualizes teaching as *an interaction between a teacher and a student conducted in such a way as to* cause *the student to learn.* This is the most severe definition of teaching insofar as teacher responsibility is concerned. This definition clearly implies that the teacher has the primary, if not the sole, responsibility for student learning.

If we assume a definition of teaching wherein the teacher has the primary or sole responsibility for student learning, we are led to a somewhat different set of defining characteristics of a good teacher. This, of course, affects the ways in which we would set about evaluating teaching. Under this definition, the simplistic sine qua non of good teaching is student learning: A good teacher is one who produces the most learning in students.

In this case, if one wished to evaluate how good a teacher was, one would simply test the students. Those teachers whose students performed the highest on some prescribed test would be, ipso facto, the best teachers. The appeal of this definition, especially to the lay public and state legislators in particular, is so strong that we need to address it in more detail.

Because, as noted earlier, the entire faculty evaluation movement has grown out of the larger issue of accountability in education, it is apparent that for the foreseeable future teachers at all levels will be assumed to be responsible for student learning to one degree or another. This is not necessarily a bad thing.

▪ DEFINING TEACHING FOR FACULTY EVALUATION AND DEVELOPMENT SYSTEMS

Virtually every educator's conception of what constitutes good teaching involves one, or some combination, of these three conceptualizations of teaching. If we choose any one of these as the "right" one, we can easily demonstrate how these incomplete assumptions have led us astray in our efforts to develop a generally acceptable means for defining teaching for the purpose of evaluation. However, if we take our three partially right, partially wrong, definitions of teaching and try to integrate them into a coherent whole, we get a more useful definition that enables us to do a more effective job of evaluating teaching.

If we are to evaluate faculty performances in carrying out these aspects of teaching it is necessary to consider not only the precise performances to be carried out, but also the specific skills required to do so. For example, although it is obvious that faculty must know the subject matter being taught we find that *content expertise, although necessary, is insufficient for good teaching.* Faculty must be able to design instructional experiences so that there is some assurance that learning will occur when students engage the experience. They must also be able to present that subject matter so that it piques student interest and encourages them to learn, and they must by able to provide meaningful feedback on student learning. Of course, teachers must also successfully deal with the myriad of bureaucratic tasks involved in managing a course, including: ordering laboratory supplies and maintaining inventories, making arrangements for guest lecturers, reserving library materials, arranging and coordinating field trips, turning in drop/add slips and final grades on time, and posting and maintaining office hours.

Thus the total teaching act involves being able to interact with students to 1) provide them an opportunity to learn; 2) create conditions that support and facilitate learn-

ing; and, 3) utilize techniques and methods that, although not causing learning, at least create a high probability that learning will occur. Also, it is obvious that the teacher must have expertise in the content being taught.

From this examination at least five broad skill dimensions required for teaching emerge:

- Content expertise
- Instructional design skills
- Instructional delivery skills
- Instructional assessment skills
- Course management skills

Before specific performance-oriented definitions of each of these dimensions of teaching can be developed, we must first develop an overarching general definition of the term *teaching* and then develop more specific definitions of *learning* and *instruction.*

Teaching

Teaching, in a global, general sense, may be defined as the process of engaging in specifically designed interactions with the student that facilitate, promote, and result in student learning.

Learning

Learning may be defined as a specific, measurable, persistent change in the performance of the student resulting from an experience designed by the teacher. Such a definition, of course, has technical limitations. A teacher who hits a student soccer player on the knee with a bat so that the student can no longer run as fast or kick as far, fits this definition of learning. Obviously, this is not the kind of experience that is being referred to in this definition of learning. Any text in educational psychology can provide us with a number of more psychologically correct definitions of learning. However, here we wish to develop a definition that will facilitate the ultimate objective of defining teaching in such a way that makes it more amenable to effective evaluation. So, for our purposes we will assume that the experience designed by the teacher is intended to promote the achievement of the specified goals and objectives of a course or other approved instructional unit.

Instruction

Instruction may be defined as delivering specifically designed experiences that, when engaged in by the type of individual for whom it was intended, results in predictable learning outcomes. With this definition, we take into account the issue of the teacher being responsible for causing learning to occur. This definition also encompasses two other critical issues. First, the learner must *engage* in the experience. Thus the responsibility of the learner to become a willing and active participant in the teaching/learning experience is acknowledged. Second, the experience must be engaged in by *the type of person for whom it was intended*. This portion of the definition acknowledges the necessity for the learner to come to the instructional experience with the prerequisite knowledge, skills, and ability to successfully engage in the experience. This issue is a double-edged sword: The process of selecting (admitting) individuals to engage in the instructional experience must ensure that everyone selected possesses the necessary prerequisites. Thus it is incumbent upon the instructor to carefully determine those prerequisites, to specify them in advance for selection purposes, and to design the instructional experience so that the prerequisites form a complete foundation for the additional knowledge and skills to be learned by the student. Finally, notice that by this definition, instruction has not occurred unless learning has occurred. With the terms teaching, instruction, and learning so defined, we can go on to develop our definitions of the skills required of faculty in carrying out the performances involved in the five broad dimensions of teaching.

Content Expertise

Content expertise is the body of skills, competencies, and knowledge in the specific subject area to be taught in which the faculty member has received advanced education, training, and/or experience. From the point of view of evaluating this component, we can readily agree that, with the exception of advanced doctoral candidates or postdoctoral fellows, students are generally not competent to assess the degree to which a teacher is knowledgeable in the content being taught. In fact, rarely does a well-designed student rating form ask students to evaluate the content expertise of the teacher. However, students *are* competent to report the degree to which the faculty member *appears* to be knowledgeable in the subject matter being taught. This issue, however, is associated with the instructional delivery skills dimension.

Instructional Design Skills

Instructional design skills are those technical skills in designing and sequencing experiences which, when engaged by a qualified learner, result in a high probability that speci-

fied learning outcomes will be achieved by the student. The relationship between this definition and the definitions of learning and instruction is direct and intentional. If instruction is defined essentially as an activity that induces learning, and if learning is defined as a specified change in student performance that must persist and be measurable, then the teacher must possess the skills to execute the necessary tasks involved. Such skills as conducting a task analysis, preparing learning objectives, developing syllabi, and handouts (and other such instructional support materials), properly using media and other forms of instructional technology, and organizing lectures and presentations for maximal instructional impact are included in this dimension.

Several sources of information are available to aid in evaluating instructional design skills. Although students would not generally be considered competent to evaluate the correctness of the instructional design of the course, they could report their observations, perceptions, and reactions to certain aspects of the design of the course. For example, if students report their opinion that the course examinations did not appear to be related to the course objectives, this reaction could serve as a flag for the instructor, department head, and/or peer review committee that there may be some problem with the instructional design of the course. Likewise, if the students report that the course appeared to be too difficult, this could serve as a flag that perhaps the material was inappropriate for the level of the course or that important connecting information between topics was missing. These ratings may also indicate that a curriculum problem exists such that students are not being adequately prepared prior to taking the course being evaluated; the students may lack the prerequisite skills and knowledge the instructor assumed they would have when the course was designed. In any case as a general principle department heads and/or other instructional leaders and peers in the department would most likely be the best evaluators of this dimension. These and other qualified people could conduct a more detailed and expert analysis of the syllabus, handouts, content, and general instructional design of the course, and make appropriate interpretations of the flags raised by the students' responses on the rating forms.

Instructional Delivery Skills

Instructional delivery skills are human interactive skills and characteristics that promote or facilitate learning, including the ability to motivate students, generate enthusiasm, and communicate effectively using various forms of information transmittal technology. The instructional delivery skills dimension can be further classified in terms of *oral presentation skills, written communication skills,* and *skills in using various forms of information technology.* Thus, having the appropriate (and somewhat different) oral presentation skills required for effective teaching in a variety of environments (e.g., large lecture, standard classroom, small seminar or practicum, tutoring, or distance education) are included here. Written communication skills are called into play in the production of syllabi, handouts, written feedback to students, the production of graphs, charts, and maps, and the development of study notes and case studies. Skills in using information technology include being able to produce materials for and effectively utilize such mechanisms as overhead projectors, slide projectors, videocassette recorders, video projectors, and computers in the delivery of instruction.

The instructional delivery dimension also includes the skills to be able to create an overall learning environment appropriate to the content being taught. These instructional delivery characteristics have been shown to be associated to varying degrees with student learning (Abrami, Cohen, & d'Appollonia, 1988; Cohen 1981; Feldman, 1996). Interestingly, it is from the instructional delivery dimension that a great deal of the confusion and misconceptions concerning the validity and utility of student ratings originates.

We can readily agree that some teachers are better classroom performers than others. Someone who is organized, possesses a clear and pleasant speaking style, has the ability to set a class at ease when appropriate, who can motivate and capture the interest of students, and who demonstrates an enthusiasm toward the subject matter and student learning would be a highly prized teacher—if that person were also competent in the subject matter being taught and if the students taking the course actually learned the subject material. Certainly, such a person would be preferable to one who, though equally competent in the subject matter and whose students learned equally as much, was perceived by students as uncaring, unenthusiastic, or even hostile, and left the students feeling as if they had had an unpleasant experience in the course. It is interesting to note that if we define teaching as consisting of only instructional delivery skills, it becomes clear why we might see a lot of "good" teaching going on but very little learning occurring. Having good instructional delivery skills but poor content expertise is analogous to gunning the engine in your car but not putting it in gear. It sure sounds like you're racing along, but in reality you're not getting anywhere. Examining the relationship between the various components of teaching can provide insights into the design of your faculty evaluation system and your faculty development or professional enrichment program. For example, Figure 3.1 relates the issues of real and apparent content expertise relative to instructional delivery skills.

Ideally, instructors should be competent in the subject being taught and appear competent to students. This type of teacher is identified as Type A, shown in Figure 3.1 (this is not to be confused with the popular *type A* personality construct, but is simply the first cell in the matrix and is thus labeled "A"). Some research has indicated that, given two instructors who are equally competent in their content area, students tend to learn more from the one who *appears* most competent (Sullivan & Skanes, 1974; Leventhal, Perry & Abrami, 1977; Ware & Williams, 1975; Williams & Ware, 1976). This stands to reason because, on the whole, students are likely to pay more attention to those whom they believe know what they are talking about than they would to someone whom they think does not.

Thus, from an evaluative point of view, faculty members who are competent in their content area but do not appear so to their students (Type B) could not be considered to be performing at the same level in their overall role as teachers. Type B teachers, however, are ideal candidates for professional enrichment experiences such as those that focus on public speaking or giving organized oral presentations. Already expert in their content field, all Type B teachers might need is some assistance in becoming more effective in their presentational or instructional delivery skills to move into the Type A category and thus realize their full potential as excellent teachers.

Of course, appearing to be knowledgeable is not the same thing as actually being knowledgeable. This brings us to the Type C teachers—faculty members who may not

Figure 3.1   Categories of Types of Teachers Based on the Interaction of the Content Expertise Dimension and the Instructional Delivery Skills Dimension

	Good *Content Expertise*	**Poor** *Content Expertise*
Good *Instructional Delivery Skills*	Type A	Type C *(Dr. Fox effect)*
Poor *Instructional Delivery Skills*	Type B	Type D

possess the desired level of content expertise but are skilled in putting on a good show. This phenomenon is generally referred to as the *Dr. Fox effect* (Perry, Abrami, & Leventhal, 1979; Meir & Feldhusen, 1979; Abrami, Leventhal, & Perry, 1982; Marsh & Ware, 1982).

The Dr. Fox effect was first confirmed in an experiment conducted in 1973 by Donald H. Naftulin from the University of Southern California School of Medicine, John E. Ware from the Southern Illinois University School of Medicine, and Frank A. Donnelly from the University of Southern California. In the experiment a professional actor, introduced as Dr. Myron L. Fox, a psychiatrist, delivered a lecture on "Mathematical Game Theory as Applied to Physical Education" to three separate audiences composed of educators, school administrators, psychiatrists, psychologists, and social workers. Each one-hour lecture was followed by a 30-minute question and answer session. After each session rating forms were administered asking the participants to rate Dr. Fox's lecture. Approximately 80% of the participants rated Dr Fox as "an outstanding psychiatrist," and agreed that "he used enough examples to clarify the material," that "the material was well-organized," and that the lecture "stimulated their thinking." Of course, Dr. Myron Fox was not a real psychiatrist and did not have a doctorate in the subject but simply delivered a lecture scripted by the experimenters. The important point here, however, is that Dr. Fox's presentation (instructional delivery) skills were so good that he was able to convince knowledgeable observers (at least for a short period of time) of his nonexistent content expertise.

Of course, in real life we are unlikely to find a true Dr. Fox on the faculty—that is, someone who has no content expertise at all in the subject they are teaching. However, the occasional Type C faculty member (one who is a good presenter but who may not be completely current in their field) may benefit from traditional faculty development efforts such as attending seminars or workshops in their content field or sabbaticals to study with another expert in the field.

Finally we see in Figure 3.1 that, logically, we can have a category of instructors who are not competent in their content area and do not appear competent to their students (i.e., possess poor content expertise *and* poor instructional delivery skills). This type of person is labeled in Figure 3.1 as a Type D faculty member. An effective faculty evaluation system can provide insights and mechanisms for ensuring that such individuals do not get hired in the first place. Candidates may be asked to conduct a class in their area as a guest lecturer and then be subject to the same student rating experience as a faculty member. Candidates may be asked to submit a syllabus for a course

they would teach if hired, which could then undergo the same scrutiny as in the annual evaluation of regular faculty's syllabi. Many institutions hire faculty on the basis of their research record and thus can be reasonably assured that they will not end up with a Type D faculty member. However, selecting candidates for the faculty solely on the basis of their content expertise, as expressed in their research record, may result in the appearance of many Type B instructors, since no relationship has been found between research productivity and teaching effectiveness (Harry & Goldner, 1972; Feldman, 1987; Barnett, 1992; Hattie & Marsh, 1996; Marsh & Hattie, 2002). In this regard, it has always seemed ironic that institutions that apparently place such high value on research, and thus hire their faculty to teach primarily on the basis of their research record, ignore the research—which has consistently shown that the relationship between research performance and teaching performance is essentially *zero*.

To the extent, then, that research productivity is an indicator of content expertise, we can relate this back to the earlier statement that content expertise is a necessary, but insufficient quality for effective teaching. Clearly, teaching effectiveness will depend in part on the interplay between content expertise and several other dimensions, including instructional delivery skills. In that regard, Figure 3.1 provides an interesting insight into the relation between Type B faculty and Type C faculty. If both types exist on the same campus, one effective faculty development or professional enrichment strategy might be to engage the Type C faculty members in assisting Type B faculty in their presentation skills. Of course, in the rare event that a Type B and Type C faculty member are teaching in the same discipline, the benefits of these two types helping each other are obvious.

Insofar as the evaluation of content expertise is concerned, students should be able to provide information on the degree to which a faculty member *appears* competent in a given subject area (an *instructional delivery* issue). However, it should be kept in mind that this information may not necessarily reflect the true competence of an instructor as a content expert. Obviously, the true content expertise of an instructor, if it is to be evaluated at all, must be assessed in some other way, usually by peers. But to the degree that it is important to know how knowledgeable the instructor *appears* to the students, rating forms, appropriately constructed, can provide useful and reliable information.

Student rating forms used in faculty evaluation systems almost always include items that ask students to provide information concerning the instructional delivery skills and characteristics of the instructor, although the forms may not label such items that way. From this fairly common practice has grown the often-heard charge that student ratings are "just a popularity contest." This charge generally comes from those faculty who tend to assume that content expertise is the sole defining characteristic of good teaching. However, taken in its proper perspective in an overall faculty evaluation system, the "popularity" of an instructor (as an indicator of the their instructional delivery skills) is important information to have if we are to obtain a comprehensive picture and thus produce a fairer evaluation of the instructor's total teaching performance.

There appears to be an underlying assumption that if an instructor is a good performer, he or she must not really be a good teacher (i.e., possess a high level of content expertise). Fortunately, or unfortunately, depending on your perspective, such assumptions are generally not true. Teachers who are popular because they are good performers in the classroom are not automatically poor in their content expertise, although we must watch out for the occasional Type C faculty member (Dr. Fox).

For the instructional delivery skills dimension, we can generally consider students competent to report their reactions to the performance characteristics of a faculty member relative to classroom presentations. Asking students to rate those human interactive skills and traits which, in and of themselves, do not produce learning, but rather create an appropriate situation or affective environment which promotes and facilitates it, is a valid endeavor. It should be noted that charges by faculty that student ratings can be raised by making classroom presentations more entertaining do have a basis in fact. To the extent that a faculty member becomes a better performer, those elements of student rating forms that reflect instructional delivery skills will be affected, as they should be. The danger in this arises when student rating forms are overloaded with items that measure *only* instructional delivery skills or when the tacit assumption is made by those reviewing the ratings that good instructional delivery skills are the predominate defining characteristic of good teaching. Of course, more sophisticated approaches besides student ratings can be taken in attempting to evaluate this dimension. Videotaping classroom presentations for later analysis by professionals, peers, and the instructor has been found to be highly effective. Classroom visitation by peers, on the other hand, has not necessarily proven itself to be the most *efficient* means of evaluating this dimension of teaching and is generally not recommended (Aleamoni, 1982; Centra, 1975, 1979, 1993; Cohen & McKeachie, 1980). Although many current researchers advise caution in using peer observations of classroom performance, especially for personnel decisions, a 1932 study by William R. Wilson, reprinted in 1999, eloquently expresses the underlying concern:

It would unquestionably be a splendid thing if mature and experienced persons could be induced to visit classes and appraise and criticize them. The judgment of an outsider, however, is at best a second-hand impression of the effectiveness of a course. Presumably the mature visitor would appraise the course by better standards than students possess. They would not, however, reveal the effect of the course upon the students who take it. If the students report that the course is interesting and the visitor reports that it is dull, the only conclusion that can be drawn is that the course is interesting to the students and dull to the mature visitor. If either set of appraisals is taken as a criterion, the other set is invalid. A distinguished scholar, dissatisfied with the ratings that he received from a large beginning class, complained that he was casting pearls before swine. The mature visitor doubtless would have agreed. But does the wise swineherd continue to lavish pearls upon his charges after he has found that the diet cannot be assimilated? (Wilson, 1932/1999, p. 568)

Unfortunately, with the exception of those faculty whose area of content expertise encompasses educational psychology, instructional design, or teaching methodology, most college faculty have had little or no formal training in the technical areas of instructional design, delivery, and assessment. All too often faculty simply employ the same teaching strategies they experienced as students. It is ironic that most college faculty have never received even minimal formal exposure to the skills involved in these three key dimensions of teaching.

Double-Blind Peer Evaluation of Teaching

Instructional Assessment Skills

Instructional assessment skills are those skills in developing tools, procedures, and strategies for assessing student learning and providing meaningful feedback to students. This definition acknowledges the fact that one performance required of virtually every teacher is to determine whether, and to what degree, students have learned what is being taught. Every teacher, at one point or another, must construct some sort of examination or test to determine if students are learning. At the very least this is required in order to give a grade to the student completing the course. Ideally, assessments of student learning should be carried out during the progress of the course to provide the learner with meaningful feedback to help them guide their studying and overall learning activities.

As with the instructional design dimension, entire doctoral degrees are offered in the field that encompasses psychological assessment (*psychometrics)*. The field of psychometrics involves not only knowledge and skill in statistics but also such skills as conducting task analyses of the material to be learned, developing test questions from learning objectives, and utilizing item analyses to enhance the reliability of the test and control the difficulty and discriminating power of each item. Psychometrics also involves understanding the design and use of alternate grading systems and grading practices. There is a substantial body of knowledge that may be brought to bear in properly assessing student-learning outcomes. However, since most faculty have little or no formal education or training in psychometrics, this is a component of teaching in which faculty may find themselves receiving less than satisfactory evaluations. Accordingly, the issues involved in instructional assessment often form an ideal first topic for faculty development or professional enrichment programs.

Course Management Skills

Course management skills are those skills in configuring, maintaining, and managing the resources and facilities required to provide an appropriate teaching/learning environment. The tasks involved in course management include, but are not limited to, such things as ordering and configuring laboratory equipment; arranging for and coordinating guest lecturers; placing readings on library reserve; ensuring that appropriate computer software is loaded in computers used by students; arranging field trips; monitoring and updating the course web site. Also included are the timely execution of such tasks as grading examinations, completing drop/add and incomplete grade forms, and generally handling all the paper work that may be required by the institution in conducting a course.

By defining the total teaching act in terms of these five broad components or dimensions—content expertise, instructional design, instructional delivery, instructional assessment, and course management—it becomes clear that the evaluation of teaching cannot be accomplished by using simply one student rating form or another; nor can it be done solely on the basis of the judgment of one administrator or peer committee based on a few classroom visits. No one person or group can have a sufficiently detailed and complete view of the entire process involved in the role of teaching. A more accurate and valid assessment of teaching performance would, of necessity, involve gathering information on the faculty member's performance in all five dimensions. This might include 1) student perceptions and reactions to various aspects of the instructor's delivery, the course design, and the instructional assessment procedures; 2) information from peers, and perhaps informed experts, on the instructor's instructional design and instructional assessment skills; 3) information from peers and department heads on the instructor's content expertise (primarily expressed in terms of the level, currency, and appropriateness of the content represented in the course design and its supporting materials); and 4) information from the department head, or perhaps even the department office administrator, on the instructor's course management performance. Additionally, we would want information from students concerning the instructor's apparent content expertise as well as their reactions to several aspects of the course operation from which we could make inferences about the instructor's instructional design skills and the level and utility of the content (value of course to the student). Thus, the key to more effective evaluation of teaching is to carefully take all the parts of this mosaic and put them together in such a fashion that it accurately reflects the faculty member's overall teaching competence. This process is described in detail in Chapter 9.

Teaching Excellence

At this point it is useful to address the popular notion of *teaching excellence*. The word "excellence," like the word "diversity," has become so overused (and often inappropriately used) in higher education that it has lost its meaning. Once used to designate the "best" or "superior," the word "excellence" has come to mean a sort of a minimal expectation in virtually every faculty evaluation system. There are many problems with the use of this word in faculty evaluation—the main one being that excellence is a term of relative position. That is, in order to be excellent a person must be *better than* someone or some group of individuals. Excellence is a norm-referenced term, not a criterion-referenced one. Yet, in most faculty evaluation systems the expectation persists that all faculty are to achieve excellence. This can be considered the "Lake Woebegone" model of faculty evaluation. As a profession, higher education is stuck in the silly verbal knot of expecting everyone to be what, by definition, only one or a few can be. As a consequence, the pursuit of excellence in higher education (usually translated into efforts to obtain ever-increasing numbers of research dollars) has resulted in many faculty receiving neither the time, resources, nor incentives, to develop the skills necessary to become competent teachers. The societal lament over poor teaching in higher education, and the resulting demands for accountability, reflect this situation. Given this discussion we may conclude then, that the pursuit of excellence at the expense of competence leads to mediocrity.

The vast, underlying problem in the evaluation of teaching has been the fact that the professoriate has not come forward with a universally accepted definition of what constitutes an excellent teacher. Although there is considerable research on which teacher characteristics and performances positively influence learning (cited throughout this work), no universally accepted definition or list of qualities has entered the higher education lexicon. If there existed some universally accepted and recognized list of

characteristics, some specific description of the qualities and skills, that define an excellent teacher, then the evaluation of teaching would be relatively easy. As noted earlier, many faculty and academic administrators consider the main component of teaching excellence to be content expertise. Others hold that teaching excellence is some sort of ephemeral, immeasurable characteristic that results in some long-term (and perhaps never-to-be-seen by the instructor) effect on student lives. We may never solve this particular problem to the satisfaction of all. However, based on our earlier discussion of teaching and its defining components, as well as a career-long assimilation of research literature and professional experience, I suggest Table 3.1 as a jumping off point for discussions concerning the development of a list of qualities and characteristics of an excellent teacher. I offer no specific defining research study or list of references to support this list other than those appearing at the end of the chapters that discuss the issues included in Table 3.1.

■ DEFINING OTHER ROLES

The following are brief definitions of other roles commonly found in faculty role models underpinning a comprehensive faculty evaluation system. Although these

Table 3.1   Some Qualities and Characteristics of an Excellent Teacher

Content Expertise	Obviously faculty must be knowledgeable in their content field in order to teach it. However, content expertise, although necessary is an *insufficient* quality for teaching excellence.
Affective Traits/Skills	• Enjoys teaching as much or more than they enjoy working in their field • Models the best characteristics of an accomplished *practitioner* in the field they are teaching • Models the best characteristics of a *lifelong learner* • Is demanding but fair • Is ethical and honest • Is comfortable admitting ignorance
Performance Skills	• Speaks clearly • Is organized when making a presentation • Uses personal examples when teaching • Uses humor effectively • Creates an appropriate psychological environment for learning
Cognitive Skills	• *Instructional design*—develops and uses learning objectives in designing effective learning experiences • *Instructional delivery*—skill in presenting information in a variety delivery modes • *Instructional assessment*—skill in the design and use of a variety of tools and procedures to assess student learning

Arreola, R. A. (2007). *Developing a comprehensive faculty evaluation system* (3rd ed.). Bolton, MA: Anker.

definitions are recommended and have been constructed to facilitate the evaluation process, they are offered here primarily as a resource to provoke thought and discussion relative to developing your own definitions.

Scholarly and Creative Activities

Annual reviews of college faculty performance have traditionally focused on three major faculty roles: teaching, research, and service. A great deal of literature exists relative to the evaluation of teaching, some of which has been discussed earlier. Also, the evaluation of service is, in large measure, a function of how a department or college chooses to define it. However, the evaluation of the research role (as the primary, if not exclusive, expression of scholarship) has always posed a complex problem within the context of an overall faculty evaluation system.

The conventional approach has been to base the evaluation of research on the number of publications a faculty member has amassed. Usually articles in refereed journals "count" more than those in non-refereed journals, with books, monographs, and other such publication outlets valued to differing degrees. This approach often produces considerable concern among faculty in those disciplines in which such publications are either more difficult to attain, or not necessarily deemed to be the best indicator of scholarly achievement (such as can sometimes be found in the arts). For this reason the role of research in the traditional faculty role model of teaching, research, and service is expanded here to a more inclusive definition. *Scholarly and creative activities* may be defined as those activities associated with the faculty member's recognized area of content expertise including maintaining proficiency, discovering, developing, or creating new knowledge; disseminating information and knowledge; and translating information and knowledge into products or services of value to society.

From an evaluative perspective the components of the role of scholarly and creative activities are not identical to the components of scholarship as defined by Boyer (1990; i.e., discovery, integration, application, and teaching). In the Boyer model teaching is seen as an expression of scholarship in that it serves to increase the scholar's knowledge level—not the student's. Boyer's perspective in this regard is clearly expressed in his citation of Aristotle that "Teaching is the highest form of understanding" (p. 151). However, from the perspective of a comprehensive faculty evaluation system, teaching is considered a separate, identifiable activity with the student at its center. That is, teaching is seen as an activity that involves not only scholarship (in the sense of knowledge and expertise in one's content

field) but also the additional professional skills and expertise of instructional design, delivery, and assessment.

In this context, as noted in the introduction of this book, the members of the professoriate are seen as belonging to a meta-profession. The meta-profession concept assumes faculty possess the knowledge and skills associated with their base profession (an element of the traditional concept of scholarship), but adds equally high levels of skill, knowledge, and performance in the areas of instructional design, instructional delivery, and instructional assessment, not to mention management, group process, and a number of other skills (Arreola, R., Aleamoni, L., & Theall, M., 2001, 2003).

By keeping the roles of teaching and service separate from the broader role of scholarly and creative activities, we can define its components in a way that is more amenable to evaluation. Briefly, scholarly and creative activities can be classified into the four categories of proficiency, discovery/creation, dissemination, and translation. Keeping in mind that the primary intent of this classification is to facilitate the evaluation of faculty performance within the context of a conventional annual review process, these categories may be defined as follows.

The scholarship of proficiency. Proficiency speaks to the issue of maintaining currency within one's chosen discipline (base profession). That is, a faculty member must continue to keep abreast of the latest research findings or developments in his or her field with concomitant enhancements of professional practice or clinical skills as appropriate. Such practice or clinical skills, of course, vary according to the academic field of the faculty member. For a chemist it might mean learning a new lab technique resulting from research in the field. For a sculptor it might mean learning how to use new tools to shape some newly developed plastic or artificial granite. For a musical composer it might mean learning how to use new computer programs that synthesize music in ways never before possible.

In addition, the pursuit of advanced degrees, certification (if applicable), postdoctoral study, internships, fellowships, or professional workshops may be seen as appropriate evaluative indicators of this area of scholarly and creative activities. In short, proficiency, from an evaluative perspective, speaks to the activities and accomplishments of a faculty member in maintaining a continuing effort of personal professional growth commensurate with the growth of knowledge in their base profession (content field).

The scholarship of discovery/creation. That portion of scholarly and creative activities referred to here as discovery/creation speaks to two distinct expressions. The first, most familiar, expression is conducting any form of research that is appropriate to a faculty member's discipline.

However, it also speaks to creative (artistic) endeavors that produce new styles or modes of expression, usually in the arts. The activities associated with discovery, or creativity, may be messy and appear initially inconclusive. Some faculty may engage in research or creative endeavors that are time consuming and require great expertise and intellectual effort, but have no immediate product. What is important to note here is that although these activities may eventually result in a definitive product or finding (i.e., published article, new form of music, etc.), the activities in and of themselves demonstrate knowledge of the field, high levels of professional skill, and innovation in strategy and thinking. Therefore the evaluation of discovery/creation must involve peer review of process, as much as product.

In contrast to the conventional research category in which anonymously peer-reviewed publications of research findings are the primary (if not exclusive) evaluative indicators, discovery/creation requires a more local, collegial, qualitative assessment of the ongoing research and discovery activities of the faculty member. Thus, in addition to the conventional indicators of research productivity such as number of publications or total amount of grant money brought in for the year, this broader perspective on scholarly and creative activities also permits and encourages the inclusion of many other indicators of scholarly activity that may still be in process or that have not yet produced a result or a final observable product.

The scholarship of dissemination. Dissemination speaks to the issue of transmitting and sharing information about one's field of academic expertise (base profession). For the purposes of evaluating this expression of scholarly and creative activities, we can easily see the relevance and value of the publication of peer-reviewed articles. However, we can also expand it to include a broader and more useful (from an evaluative perspective) set of professional activities. Such activities must simply meet the criterion of serving to disseminate information concerning one's academic field not only within the professional community but throughout the general society as well. Thus, a more complete list of activities that may be considered appropriate within the evaluative category of dissemination might include:

• Publishing articles (refereed and nonrefereed)

• Publishing books, monographs, pamphlets

• Paper presentations at national professional meetings or conferences

• Making keynote or invited addresses

• Writing articles for the popular press

• Producing educational television and radio series (e.g., Carl Sagan's *Cosmos* television series)

• Artistic exhibitions, performances, displays

• New artistic interpretations of previous works

• Conducting professional workshops or seminars

This list is by no means exhaustive but is intended to merely suggest, from an evaluative perspective, a broader range of legitimate forms of the scholarly and creative activity of dissemination. Each academic discipline would need to determine for itself the full range of possible means of dissemination appropriate to the discipline. Note, however, that dissemination is not defined as being identical to, or congruent with, teaching—although some of the skills involved in dissemination may be used in instructional delivery.

Scholarship of translation. This category speaks to the issue of translating research findings into new products, services, or artistic expressions of benefit to either the professional or the larger general society. Academic health science institutions have long recognized this form of scholarly and creative activity. In fact, the term *translational research* has emerged from the health sciences arena where it is defined as the scientific work required to develop a clinical or commercial application from a basic science discovery. For example, as when a faculty-researcher is able to develop a technique for mass-producing a newly developed drug to make it available for large-scale patient care. Some health science centers apply considerable resources to centers for translational research—which take research findings in the basic biomedical sciences and turn them into treatment protocols, medications, or medical procedures that contribute to the public health.

To varying degrees, however, the scholarship of translation may be applied across all academic fields. In physics, for example, the discovery of the laser was a significant achievement within the field and resulted in many peer-reviewed articles and publications. However, the development of laser-based applications such as DVD players, CD burners in computers, laser leveling devices used in construction, not to mention the use of lasers in vision correction surgery, plastic surgery, sculpting, and holography, are all expressions of the scholarly activity of translation. However, the scholarly and creative activity of translation may not have equal application in all academic fields. Translating research in basic physics may be easier than translating research in linguistics or philosophy into usable, commercial products or services. It is acknowledged that some translational activities may be carried out in industrial or commercial settings rather than within the strictly academic environment. However, to the degree that a faculty member is engaged in the process, it is a legitimate expression of scholarly and creative activities from an evaluative perspective and should be included in a comprehensive faculty evaluation system.

The division of the role of scholarly and creative activities into the four categories of proficiency, discovery/creation, dissemination, and translation can serve to clarify not only the evidence required for evaluating faculty performance within this role, but can also serve to guide faculty professional growth and development.

The Scholarship of Teaching and Learning

One of the issues associated with the evaluation of scholarly and creative activities that frequently arises is that of evaluating the scholarship of teaching and learning (SOTL). Having previously defined scholarly and creative activities in terms that are more amenable to measurement and evaluation (proficiency, discovery/creation, dissemination, and translation), and using the meta-profession model shown in Table A (in the introduction), it becomes possible to more specifically identify the performances and their attendant skill sets that define the scholarship of teaching and learning. Although the meta-professional conceptualization of the professoriate moves teaching out of the realm of the conventional concept of scholarship and into a separate, clearly definable professional role, considerable interest remains in how to evaluate the scholarship of teaching and learning as defined by Boyer (1990). Table 3.2 (based on the work of Mike Theall) shows an expanded conceptualization of the role of scholarly and creative activities that enables us to see the scholarship of teaching and learning as simply a special case of the larger meta-professional model. As can be seen in Table 3.2, the key to linking the meta-professional model to the scholarship of teaching and learning is to expand the definition of scholarship to include those activities involved in the faculty member's base profession and the faculty member's meta-profession (Theall & Arreola, 2001). That is, rather than using Boyer's (1990) conceptualization of teaching as an extension of the scholarship associated with one's base profession, the meta-profession model enables us to define scholarship in terms of activities and performances associated with a faculty member's meta-professional practice. A variety of skill sets are called into play to varying degrees in carrying out those activities and performances that define traditional base-profession-oriented scholarship and the meta-profession performances that define the scholarship of teaching and learning (see Table 3.2). With this concep-

tualization it now becomes possible to measure those performances as well as design and provide appropriate resources to assist faculty in gaining and/or enhancing the required skills.

The Service Role

In order to facilitate the measurement and evaluation of the service role, it has been found useful to identify three different categories of service: 1) service to the institution, 2) service to the professional community, and 3) service to the general community.

Service to the institution may be defined as carrying out assigned non-teaching responsibilities or duties, not necessarily related to one's recognized area of expertise or even academic in nature, that contribute to the functional operation of the institution.

Thus service to the institution may involve such activities as:

- Serving on committees (curriculum, promotion and tenure, admission, etc.)

- Supervising student clubs and organizations

- Managing projects

- Advising, mentoring

- Recruiting, fundraising

- Participating in community outreach activities

Service to the profession may be defined as voluntarily carrying out responsibilities or duties, not necessarily related to one's recognized area of expertise, which contribute to the functional operation of a professional organization within one's content field.

Service to the profession may include such activities as:

- Serving as a journal or newsletter editor

- Serving as a paper reviewer for a journal, newsletter, or national conference

- Serving as a conference organizer

- Serving as an officer of a professional organization (president, secretary, treasurer, etc.)

- Serving as an organizational representative

Service to the general community may be defined as the application of a faculty member's recognized area of expertise in the community without pay. Service to the general community, or community service as it is often

Table 3.2   Skill Sets Defining the Scholarship of Teaching and Learning (SoTL)

SKILL SETS	SCHOLARLY & CREATIVE ACTIVITIES				Special Case: *Scholarship of Teaching & Learning*			
	Base Profession				**Meta-Profession**			
	Proficiency	Discovery/Creation	Dissemination	Translation	Proficiency	Discovery/Creation	Dissemination	Translation
Base Profession Skill Sets								
Content Expertise			●●●			●●●	●●●	
Practice/Clinical Skills			●●◉			●●◉	●●◉	
Research Skills			●◉◉			●◉◉	●◉◉	
Instructional Design			●●●			●●●	●●●	
Instructional Delivery			●●●			●●●	●●●	
Instructional Assessment			●◉◉			●◉◉	●●●	
Instructional Research			●●●			●●●	●●●	
Psychometrics/Statistics			●◉◉			●◉◉	●◉◉	
Epistemology			●◉◉			●◉◉	●●◉	
Learning Theory			●●◉			●◉◉	●◉◉	
Human Development			●◉◉			●◉◉	●◉◉	
Information Technology			●◉◉			●◉◉	●●●	
Technical/Scientific Writing			●◉◉			●◉◉	●◉◉	
Graphic Design			●◉◉			●◉◉	●◉◉	
Public Speaking			●◉◉			●◉◉	●◉◉	
Communication Styles			●●●			●●●	●●●	
Conflict Management			●◉◉			●◉◉	●◉◉	
Group Process/Team Building			●◉◉			●◉◉	●◉◉	
Resource Management			●●◉			●◉◉	●◉◉	
Personnel Management			●◉◉			●◉◉	●◉◉	
Budget Analysis/Management			◉◉◉			◉◉◉	◉◉◉	
Policy Analysis/Development			◉◉◉			◉◉◉	◉◉◉	

Additional

META-PROFESSION Skill Sets Required by Various Faculty Roles

Legend

Almost Always	●●●
Frequently	●●◉
Occasionally	●◉◉
Almost Never	◉◉◉

Source: Based on Theall (n.d.).

Arreola, R. A. (2007). *Developing a comprehensive faculty evaluation system* (3rd ed.). Bolton, MA: Anker.

called, can turn out to be one of the most contentious in the design of a comprehensive faculty evaluation system. Although the issue of providing service to the general community may be conceived differently by different institutions depending upon their value system and mission, the definition provided above is recommended. In this definition two primary issues are addressed. First, the service provided must be within one's area of expertise formally recognized by the institution. If decisions concerning promotion, tenure, continuance, and pay are going to be determined in part upon performance in this role, one must be careful not to require performances that, although they may constitute expressions of good citizenship, have no direct relationship to the faculty member's academic responsibilities. Second, the issue of providing the service without pay is included simply to differentiate it from consulting activities, which may be an appropriate expression of either dissemination or translation in the scholarly and creative activities role depending upon the precise form or type of consulting service provided.

A closer look at some examples can serve to help us clarify the defining characteristics of service to the community in a well-designed faculty evaluation system. For example, suppose a faculty member in the music department directs the adult choir in a local community arts theater (without pay). That faculty member may be considered as performing a service to the community insofar as the faculty evaluation system is concerned. If, however, that same faculty member serves as an accountant for the theater, this would not be considered community service for the purposes of faculty evaluation, since the service would not be in the area of the faculty member's recognized area of expertise. The reason for this is that good or poor performance on the part of the faculty member as an accountant would not necessarily reflect on the quality of the music program at the institution. On the other hand, good or poor performance in directing the adult choir could. If the choir performs poorly, an inference could be made about the quality of the music program at the institution, since the person conducting the choir is a music faculty member. No similar inference could be made to the quality of the accounting department if the music faculty member did a poor job of keeping the books for the theater. However, if the faculty member was found to have embezzled a large amount of money from the theater, and was convicted for doing so, this "performance" would more correctly be addressed in the charter of the institution and/or the faculty handbook, not in the faculty evaluation system. In order to be relevant to the faculty evaluation system, the definition of community service

must be restricted to those activities that could reasonably reflect, positively or negatively, on the academic program in which the faculty member teaches. Exceptions to this approach may be found, however, in faith-based institutions in which all faculty accept that the terms of their employment require specific service to the community reflective of the institution's moral, religious, or ethical values and mission.

In many faculty evaluation systems there is often a temptation to include such activities as serving on the United Way board, or serving as a girl or boy scout leader, or participating in organizations that feed the homeless, as being acceptable as evidence of community service. However, as soon as such an activity becomes an acceptable expression of community service in a formal faculty evaluation system we cross over to the realm of good citizenship. Although we would certainly want all faculty to be good citizens, it is unwise to include such activities as part of your faculty evaluation system. Doing so tends to open the doors to grievances and potential lawsuits. This may occur when faculty members perceive themselves as being denied promotion or tenure simply because they chose to stay home on the weekends rather than coach a city soccer team, volunteer to clean a city park, or raise money for the poor by baking goods for a church bake sale.

In defining the role of service to the general community it is useful to further subdivide it into *voluntary service* and *institutionally assigned service*. The best way to demonstrate the difference between these two subcategories is to provide an example. Suppose a nursing faculty member has voluntarily undertaken to visit a homeless shelter once a week and minister to the health needs of the individuals there. This activity, being an application of the faculty member's recognized area of expertise without pay, may legitimately be counted as service to the community in the annual evaluation. However, suppose that mid-year the dean initiates a college-wide outreach program that includes a health fair at a local shopping mall, the operation of a bloodmobile, and various other activities intended to serve the community. The dean issues various faculty assignments to carry out all these activities. The faculty member who has been visiting the homeless shelter is assigned to visit that very same homeless shelter once a week and continue ministering to the health needs of those living there. In this situation, the same activity that previously could be counted as service to the community in a faculty evaluation system, must now, more appropriately, be counted as service to the institution since it is the institution that is providing the service to the community and the faculty member is simply the instrument by which the service is being provided.

Thus, insofar as its application in a faculty evaluation system, assigned service to the community is identical to, and becomes, service to the institution for the faculty member being evaluated.

Service to the profession is defined as voluntarily carrying out responsibilities or duties, not necessarily related to your recognized area of expertise, which contribute to the functional operation of a professional organization within your content field. Providing a service to one's (base) profession may sometimes be found as part of the service role. Generally the activities defining this type of service are identical to some of the activities in the scholarly and creative activities role. In fact, service to the profession is often better placed as one of the menu items that define the scholarly and creative activities role and, as noted earlier, may include:

- Serving as a paper reviewer or journal/newsletter editor

- Organizing conferences or national meetings

- Serving as an officer of the organization

- Serving as an organizational representative

Consulting is defined as the application of a faculty member's recognized area of expertise in the community for pay. Consulting, on the other hand, is to be differentiated from moonlighting, in which a faculty member may have another job (full- or part-time) outside the faculty. Depending upon the nature of the consulting service performed, this activity may fit in either the dissemination or the translation performances in the scholarly and creative activities role. The important principle here is that the faculty member's performance be in their institutionally recognized area of expertise so that a reasonable inference may be drawn relative to the quality of the academic program in which they teach. A faculty member whose skills and expertise in their content field are so valued that other institutions or organizations are willing to pay for their consulting services, is assumed to reflect well on their institution and thus enhance its prestige.

Advising

Advising is a generic term that may take on many meanings within a college or university. However, if advising is to be considered a role that may be evaluated, it is best to subdivide this role into two different expressions—*academic advising* and advising as *counseling*.

- *Academic advising* is defined as consulting with students on an individual basis for the purpose of providing guidance and advice concerning their academic endeavors.

- *Counseling* is defined as consulting with students on an individual basis for the purpose of providing guidance and advice concerning their personal, emotional, and psychological concerns.

Collegiality

Collegiality has emerged as an issue of growing concern in the evaluation of faculty. No consistent body of literature yet exists on how to evaluate collegiality, and the practice of including it as a separate performance category in a faculty role model is discouraged by the American Association of University Professors (AAUP; 1999):

> Relatively little is to be gained by establishing collegiality as a separate criterion of assessment.... the separate category of "collegiality" should not be added to the traditional three areas of faculty performance. Institutions of higher education should instead focus on developing clear definitions of scholarship, teaching, and service, in which the virtues of collegiality are reflected. (¶s 6–7)

By including this brief consideration of collegiality it should not be construed that the author is advocating its use as a role in a faculty role model. Rather, the author supports the AAUP position. However, since the issue of collegiality comes up so often when considering the design of comprehensive faculty evaluation systems, it is appropriate to at least address the issue within the context of developing definitions of the roles in a faculty role model.

In most cases the issue of the collegiality of an individual tends to focus on the negative. Such statements as "he doesn't fit in" or "she doesn't get along with anyone" may often be heard. However, in considering the issue of collegiality from an evaluative perspective it is clear that simply not liking someone, or saying they don't fit in is woefully insufficient in any sort of faculty evaluation system. Rather, the issue of the collegiality of an individual, at least insofar as a faculty evaluation system is concerned, must focus on the effect the individual has on the performance and productivity of colleagues. This is separate from the performance and productivity of the faculty member in question. The following definition encapsulates this concept: *The collegiality of an individual is a measure of the effect his or her interactions have on his or her colleagues' professional productivity and performance.*

Two examples may serve to clarify the principle underlying collegiality as a faculty evaluation issue. First, suppose that there was a faculty member whom you did not like. Perhaps you objected to his or her lifestyle or sense of ethics or professionalism, or simply found him or her to be the kind of person with whom you would prefer not to associate. Further suppose that every time the two of you were on the same committee or were assigned to work on a project together, the intellectual interaction between you was stimulating and resulted in high quality performance on your part. In this case, although you may not like the individual, your professional interactions served to enhance your professional performance. In this case, the collegiality of the individual might be considered positive even though you did not like him or her.

On the other hand, suppose there was another colleague whom you liked, or at least to whom you had no particular personal objection. Further suppose that every interaction with this individual, either personal or professional, inevitably ended up with his or her complaining about the lack of sufficient resources for teaching, or the poor quality of the support staff, or the inherent incompetence and cruelty of the administration. After such interactions you invariably found yourself angry and frustrated with the situations the individual talked about and wondering if maybe you shouldn't try to find a job at another institution. Suppose that after such interactions it was difficult to regain your enthusiasm to finish grading those exams, or write that report for the curriculum committee, or work on the manuscript for your book. In any case suppose it took you several minutes, hours, or even days to regain your normal enthusiasm for your professional responsibilities. Such a person, regardless of his or her individual professional productivity, might be said to have a negative collegiality effect.

If collegiality is to be considered as a role in a faculty evaluation system, care must be taken not to couch the discussion in terms of whether the person fits in to the existing group, or has a disagreeable personality, lifestyle, personal habits, or values. Rather, collegiality must be considered in terms of its effect on the professional productivity of an individual's colleagues. In any case, the valid and reliable measurement of collegiality would be extremely difficult and would most likely have to be based on principles articulated primarily in the field of social psychology. However, it must be emphasized that insufficient research exists concerning any effective and efficient means to validly and reliably measure a faculty member's collegiality. In fact, no universally agreed-upon definition of collegiality has yet emerged in the literature. Thus, it is strongly recommended that collegiality *not* be

included in the faculty role model of an institution's faculty evaluation system. Instead, focus should be placed on developing clear definitions of teaching, scholarly and creative activities, and service in which the virtues and characteristics of collegiality are reflected.

■ COMPLETING STEP 3: DETERMINING ROLE DEFINITIONS FOR YOUR FACULTY ROLE MODEL

With the previous discussion and recommendations concerning the definitions of common faculty roles, the purpose of Step 3, then, is to reach some agreement about defining the various roles that have been adopted as the formal faculty role model of your institution. However, in order to give your faculty evaluation system a measure of objectivity, or at least to control the effects of the unavoidable subjectivity, it is important to define each of the roles in terms of observable or documentable achievements, products, or performances. This is obviously easier said than done. For this reason the definitions in this chapter have been provided as a way to begin defining several traditional roles to make them more amenable to measurement and thus evaluation. It is not reasonable to expect faculty to readily come up with concise definitions of the roles adopted in the faculty role model if they do not have the benefit of some prior thought on the matter. The discussion presented on the development of the definition of the teaching role demonstrates the kind of work the Committee may wish to undertake in considering each role. Therefore, it is recommended that the Committee, as one of its first efforts, develop preliminary definitions of the roles in the proposed faculty role model. In this way, when the questionnaire soliciting faculty values (Step 2) and their role definitions (Step 3) is distributed, it will contain some definitions to which the faculty can refer in expressing their own views.

Figure 3.2 provides an example of FORM 3A that is recommended for use in carrying out that part of Step 3 in which the faculty within a department 1) define each role; 2) identify possible subdivisions (components) of each role; and 3) indicate (list) the specific activities (from Step 1) that constitute the performances involved in each role. Figure 3.3 provides an example of FORM 3B with which departments may summarize the definitions of each role and the definitions of each identified component of each role. The definition of teaching, as well as the components of instructional design, instructional delivery, and instructional assessment defined earlier, are provided as examples to guide the process. Also, the Committee coordinating the process may wish to share the definitions of the roles of scholarly and creative activities and service developed earlier as examples. However, these definitions should not be presented to the faculty as the correct definitions, but as suggestions to facilitate their discussion. It is important that the faculty feel that they are free to develop definitions that meet their own assumptions, priorities, and values.

When FORMS 3A and 3B have been completed and collected it will be the work of the Committee to use them to develop consistent, institutional definitions of the identified roles. In doing so it is important for the Committee to keep in mind the differing views that may be represented on your campus relative to each role. Remember that the ultimate objective is to arrive at a definition that will be generally acceptable to everyone subject to the evaluation system. This means that you may have several subdefinitions. For example, you may have to define teaching differently for vocational education courses than you might for the traditional academic curriculum. You may have to define scholarly and creative activities differently for faculty in the arts than you would for faculty in the sciences. There is no hard and fast rule, and no single definition will necessarily work for all institutions—although the more generic definitions developed earlier may serve to orient and guide the development of your institution's definitions. The important issue here is the process of developing these definitions by consensus so that the evaluation system will be seen as functionally valid by the faculty. That is, it will be seen as measuring something that the faculty and administration agree ought to be measured. As with previous chapters an action checklist for completing this step is provided (see Figure 3.4); this checklist also presents an accelerated process for carrying out Steps 1, 2, and 3.

Figure 3.2 FORM 3A for use in gathering departmental definitions of the role components and their specific defining activities for the faculty role model developed by each department in Step 2

FORM 3A: Role Component Names With Defining Activities
(Use as many sheets as needed to define each component for each role)

Department or Discipline Group Name:_____

Role:_____

In the spaces below indicate the name(s) of the component(s) the group has identified for the role named above. Provide a short definition/description of the component in the space provided below the component name. Finally, below each component name list the activities and/or professional performances that further define and specify the component. Each component list should be a subset of the larger role list provided by the group on FORM 1B.

Role Name	**Role Name**
*Brief Definition:*_____	*Brief Definition:*_____
_____	_____
_____	_____
_____	_____

Activities Defining This Role

1._____	1._____
2._____	2._____
3._____	3._____
4._____	4._____
5._____	5._____
6._____	6._____
7._____	7._____
8._____	8._____
9._____	9._____
10._____	10._____
11._____	11._____
12._____	12._____
13._____	13._____
14._____	14._____
15._____	15._____

Arreola, R. A. (2007). *Developing a comprehensive faculty evaluation system* (3rd ed.). Bolton, MA: Anker.

Developing a Comprehensive Faculty Evaluation System

Figure 3.3 FORM 3B on which departments may summarize the definitions of each role and the definitions of each identified component of each role

FORM 3B: ROLE AND ROLE COMPONENT SUMMARY		
(Use as many sheets as needed to summarize all defined roles and their components)		

Department or Discipline Group Name:_____

List each role and write its general definition as identified in FORM 1B. List the components of each role and include a brief description of the component as indicated on FORM 3A. Each group must prepare a copy of FORM 3B that summarizes the group's consensus on the names of the roles, their definitions, the names of their components, and brief component definitions.

Example:

Role: TEACHING	Components	Component Definitions (Brief)
Role Definition: *Engaging in specifically designed interactions with students that facilitate, promote, and result in specific student learning.*	Instructional Design	*Syllabus, grading standards, learning objectives*
	Instructional Delivery	*Presentation skills, clarity of speech, use of media*
	Instructional Assessment	*Valid & reliable exams, timely feedback*
	Content	*Currency, accuracy, appropriate level*
	Resource Management	*Availability of learning support materials, proper physical environment*
Role:	**Components**	**Component Definitions (Brief)**
Role Definition:		
Role:	**Components**	**Component Definitions (Brief)**
Role Definition:		
Role:	**Components**	**Component Definitions (Brief)**
Role Definition:		

Arreola, R. A. (2007). *Developing a comprehensive faculty evaluation system* (3rd ed.). Bolton, MA: Anker.

Figure 3.4   Action Checklist for Completing Step 3

Action Checklist for Completing Step 3

Expected Outcomes: Each department will complete and submit to the Committee a copy of FORM 3A that represents its faculty's consensus on the subdivisions (if any) identified for each role and the specific activities associated with each subdivision. These activities should come from the information developed in Step 1. Each department will also complete FORM 3B, which summarizes the definitions of the roles developed and brief definitions of the components or subdivisions of those roles.

____ Prepare packets for each department that contain at least one copy of FORM 3A for each faculty member in the department.

____ Distribute the FORM 3A packets to the department chairs and ask them to distribute them to their faculty with instructions to complete the form in preparation for a faculty meeting to determine the final departmental faculty role model with its role and role component definitions and specific activities.

____ Each department conducts a faculty meeting in which faculty reach consensus on how to define each role and any role components identified within each role. The department then completes one FORM 3A for the entire department that includes the specific activities, which for that department constitute the specific performances that define each role and each role component. Each component list should be a subset of the larger role list provided by the group on FORM 1B.

____ Each department completes FORM 3B by listing each role and writing its general definition as identified in FORM 1B. The components of each role are to be listed and should include a brief description of the component as indicated on FORM 3A. Each group must prepare a copy of Form 3B that summarizes the group's consensus on the names of the roles, their definitions, the names of their components, and brief component definitions. The department submits departmental FORMS 3A and 3B to the Committee.

____ The Committee reviews all FORMS 3A and 3B submitted by each department and begins the process of synthesizing and integrating them into an institutional faculty role model definition set on FORM 2C. That is, consistent definitions for each role should be developed for the institution as a whole. In those circumstances in which Step 2 indicated that multiple faculty role models may be needed, specific definitions for the roles in those role models must be developed from the forms submitted by the departments to form their own separate faculty role model.

Alternate (Accelerated) Process for Carrying out Steps 1, 2, & 3

A unique approach to carrying out the first three steps that accelerates the process considerably has been successfully used by a number of institutions developing a comprehensive faculty evaluation system. However, this approach involves a major commitment of time and resources and may not be feasible for every institution. The approach involves holding a daylong meeting of all faculty to conduct the activities involved in carrying out Steps 1, 2, and 3. However, this meeting must be preceded by careful training and preparation by the Committee members to serve as facilitators during the day with one Committee member serving as the main facilitator/presenter. The following is a typical agenda for such a session in which the author served as the facilitator/presenter.

Arreola, R. A. (2007). *Developing a comprehensive faculty evaluation system* (3rd ed.). Bolton, MA: Anker.

AGENDA FOR ACCELERATED APPROACH FOR CARRYING OUT STEPS 1, 2, & 3	
8:00 AM 8:30 AM	Check in and pick up workshop materials. Faculty may be seated by disciplines or program areas as they choose.
8:30 AM 10:00 AM	**Overview of 8-Step Process.** Presentation of an overview of the entire 8-step process for developing a comprehensive faculty evaluation system. The objective of this session is to provide the participants with a clear perspective on the work they will be doing in completing the first three steps of the process.
10:00 AM 10:15 AM	**BREAK**
10:15 AM 12:00 PM	**Step 1: Determining the Faculty Role Model.** The objective of this session is for the faculty within a division or discipline to produce a single list of activities that define specific roles such as teaching (or instruction), service (to the institution, discipline, community, etc.), and any other roles. The session will begin with each participant filling out FORM 1A individually. Then FORM 1B will be used to prepare the list of agreed-upon activities that define each role. By the end of this session each division or discipline-specific group must have completed a FORM 1B that represents the consensus of the group on what activities will define each role to be evaluated.
12:00 PM 12:45 PM	**LUNCH BREAK.** Participants may continue their work if they wish.
12:45 PM 2:00 PM	**Step 2: Determining the Faculty Role Model Parameter Values.** Based on the work completed in Step 1 in which the several roles were identified and their subordinate activities defined, the participants will determine the minimum and maximum values to be assigned to each role and record them on FORM 2A. Note that in completing FORM 2B for the department, the sum of each maximum value with the remaining minimum value should equal 100. Each division or discipline group must produce a single FORM 2B that represents its agreed-upon parameter values.
2:00 PM 3:00 PM	**Step 3: Defining the Roles in the Faculty Role Model.** Using FORM 3A the participants will determine/define the components of each role and record their results. Then a subset of activities and/or performances from FORM 1B will be used to further define each component. The group will produce a single FORM 3B for each role that represents the group's consensus.
3:00 PM 3:15 PM	**BREAK.** *All group work reports (paper summary sheets) must be turned in by this time in preparation of the closing Summary, Synthesis, & Planning session.*
3:15 PM 4:30 PM	**Summary, Synthesis, & Planning for Next Steps.** A brief presentation of each group's work. Each group will identify a member to present a short (2–3 minute) presentation of the group's work. After all groups have made their presentation, the workshop presenter/facilitator will present a preliminary summary and synthesis of all the work. The individual group work and the preliminary synthesis will be used to guide the final development of the Comprehensive Faculty Evaluation System.

Comment: A key element in the successful execution of this approach is to provide each breakout (department or discipline) group with a laptop computer on which electronic versions of the various forms have been preloaded. In this way, the work that is done by each group is easily captured and makes the final session much more effective since each group's work can be easily displayed and shared by using a video projector connected to a laptop computer. Depending upon the institution's size, this type of one- or two-day workshop has been found to be very effective in accelerating the process of completing Steps 1, 2, and 3. Experience with such workshops in which 300+ faculty gather in the same room have been found to be very successful in building consensus and developing well-configured faculty role models.

Arreola, R. A. (2007). *Developing a comprehensive faculty evaluation system* (3rd ed.). Bolton, MA: Anker.

■ References

Abrami, P. C., Cohen, P. A., & d'Appollonia, S. (1988). Implementation problems in meta-analysis. *Review of Educational Research, 58*(2), 151–179.

Abrami, P. C., Leventhal, L., & Perry, R. P. (1982). Educational seduction. *Review of Educational Research, 52*(3), 446–464.

Aleamoni, L. M. (1982). Components of the instructional setting. *Instructional Evaluation, 7,* 11–16.

American Association of University Professors. (1999). *On collegiality as a criterion for faculty evaluation.* Washington, DC: Author.

Arreola, R. A., Aleamoni, L. M., & Theall, M. (2001, February). *College teaching as meta-profession: Reconceptualizing the scholarship of teaching and learning.* Paper presented at the annual American Association for Higher Education conference on Faculty Roles and Rewards, Tampa, FL.

Arreola, R. A., Aleamoni, L. M., & Theall, M. (2003, April). *Beyond Scholarship: Recognizing the multiple roles of the professoriate.* Paper presented at the annual meeting of the American Educational Research Association, Chicago, IL.

Barnett, R. (1992). Linking teaching and learning: A critical inquiry. *Journal of Higher Education, 63*(6), 619–636.

Boyer, E. L. (1990). *Scholarship reconsidered: Priorities of the professoriate.* Princeton, NJ: The Carnegie Foundation for the Advancement of Teaching.

Centra, J. A. (1975). Colleagues as raters of classroom instruction. *Journal of Higher Education, 46*(3), 327–337.

Centra, J. A. (1979). *Determining faculty effectiveness.* San Francisco, CA: Jossey-Bass.

Centra, J. A. (1993). *Reflective Faculty Evaluation: Enhancing Teaching and Determining Faculty Effectiveness.* San Francisco, CA: Jossey-Bass.

Cohen, P. A., & McKeachie, W. J. (1980). The role of colleagues in the evaluation of college teaching. *Improving College and University Teaching, 28*(4), 147–154.

Cohen, P.A. (1981). Student ratings of instruction and student achievement: A meta-analysis of multi-section validity studies. *Review of Educational Research, 51*(3), 281–309.

Feldman, K. A. (1987). Research productivity and scholarly accomplishment of college teachers as related to their instructional effectiveness: A review and exploration. *Research in Higher Education, 26*(3), 227–298.

Feldman, K. A. (1996). Identifying exemplary teaching: Using data from course and teacher evaluations. In M. Svinicki & R. Menges, (Eds.). *New directions for teaching and learning: No. 65. Honoring exemplary teaching* (pp. 41–50). San Francisco, CA: Jossey-Bass.

Harry, J., & Goldner, N. S. (1972). The null relationship between teaching and research. *Sociology of Education, 45*(1), 47–60

Hattie, J., & Marsh, H. W. (1996). The relationship between research and teaching—A meta-analysis. *Review of Educational Research, 66*(4), 507–542.

Leventhal, L., Perry, R. P., & Abrami, P. C. (1977). Effects of lecturer quality and student perception of lecturer's experience on teacher ratings and student achievement. *Journal of Educational Psychology, 69*(4), 360–374.

Marsh, H. W., & Hattie, J. (2002). The relationship between research productivity and teaching effectiveness. *The Journal of Higher Education, 73*(5), 603–641.

Marsh, H. W., & Ware, J. E., Jr. (1982). Effects of expressiveness, content coverage, and incentive on multidimensional student rating scales: New interpretations of the Dr. Fox effect, *Journal of Educational Psychology, 74*(1), 126–134.

Meier, R. S., & Feldhusen, J. F. (1979). Another look at Dr. Fox: Effect of stated purpose for evaluation, lecturer expressiveness, and density of lecture content on student ratings, *Journal of Educational Psychology, 71*(3), 339–345.

Naftulin, D. H., Ware, J. E., Jr., & Donnelly, F. A. (1973). The Doctor Fox lecture: A paradigm of educational seduction. *Journal of Medical Education, 48*(7), 630–635.

Perry, R. P., Abrami, P. C., & Leventhal, L. (1979). Educational seduction: The effect of instructor expressiveness and lecture content on student ratings and achievement. *Journal of Educational Psychology, 71*(1), 107–116.

Sullivan, A. M., & Skanes, G. R. (1974). Validity of student evaluations of teaching and the characteristics of successful instructors. *Journal of Educational Psychology, 66*(4), 584–590.

Theall, M. (n.d.). *Skill sets.* Retrieved July 21, 2006, from: http://www.cedanet.com/meta/SOTLmatrix.htm

Theall, M., & Arreola, R. A. (2001, April). *Beyond the scholarship of teaching: Searching for a unifying metaphor for the college teaching profession.* Paper presented at the annual meeting of the American Educational Research Association, Seattle, WA.

Ware, J. E., Jr., & Williams, R. G. (1975). The Dr. Fox effect: A study of lecturer effectiveness and ratings of instruction. *Journal of Medical Education, 50*(2), 149–156.

Williams, R. G., & Ware, J. E. (1976). Validity of student ratings of instruction under different incentive conditions: A further study of the Dr. Fox effect. *Journal of Educational Psychology, 68*(1), 48–56.

Wilson, W. R. (1999, September/October). Students rating teachers. *Journal of Higher Education, 70*(5), 562–571. (Original work published 1932)

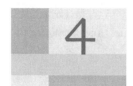

Step 4: Determining Role Component Weights

At this point, you will have developed definitions for the various roles in your faculty role model (Step 3). You will also have determined the relative impact or parameter values that the different roles can take in the overall evaluation of a faculty member (Step 2). Depending upon the definitions developed for each role in Step 3, you may have also identified specific subsets of performances or *components* of various roles. For such roles it now becomes important to consider how much weight or relative importance the various components of each role should have in the overall evaluation of that specific role. That is, we must express the proportion or weight that will be given to the performance of each component in the evaluation of the total role.

In carrying out the procedure for establishing the weights for the components of each role we must consider three different cases:

- *Case 1.* Performance in every component is required with weights of each component fixed.

- *Case 2.* Performance in some components is required and performance in others is optional (with weights for the components either fixed or variable).

- *Case 3.* The role is comprised of a menu of optional components (with either fixed or variable weights) from which the faculty member must select as defining the role.

◼ CASE 1: COMPONENT WEIGHTS FIXED

In our example in Step 3, we defined teaching as involving five components: content expertise, instructional delivery, instructional design, instructional assessment, and course

management. In Step 4 the issue is to determine how much relative importance each of these five defining components should have in the evaluation of the teaching role as a whole.

To aid in the process of determining the role component weights we begin using a tool that will play an important part in the final design of our system—the Source Impact Matrix. This tool enables us to control the effect of the subjective data gathered as part of the overall evaluative process. The full Source Impact Matrix will be completed in Step 6; however, at this point it is used to begin indicating the values you wish to associate with the various components of each role. Figure 4.1 shows a worksheet variation of a Source Impact Matrix that includes examples of selected component weights for the teaching role in which performance in each component is required (since it fully defines the role), and the values or weights associated with each component have been determined and are fixed.

Note that in Figure 4.1 content expertise has not been listed although it was earlier defined as one of the five components of teaching. The reason for this is that the content expertise of the instructor is not going to be evaluated separately here but as part of the fabric the entire teaching role as expressed in the design, delivery, and assessment components. The currency, level, and appropriateness of the content presented in the course will be reflected in the design of the instruction (instructional design), the strategies used to deliver the instruction (instructional delivery), and the design and development of the tests and other assessment devices and strategies (instructional assessment).

As we begin using the matrix shown in Figure 4.1, notice that the sources of information have not yet been determined (signified by the question marks) and are left blank at this time. Also, the Source Weight and Impact Weight cells have been left blank and will be completed in Step 6. In this example the instructional design component is weighted as 40%, the instructional delivery component as 40%, the instructional assessment component as 25%, and the course management component as 5%. These weights reflect the relative importance that the various defining components of the teaching role hold for the faculty in our hypothetical institution. Thus, whatever rating is provided for the instructional design component for a given faculty member, that rating will count for only 40% of the total evaluation of the teaching role. Likewise, the rating of the instructional delivery component will count for 30%, and so on. The weights used in this example are entirely subjective. The weights you determine and the components you define for your institution may vary considerably from these examples.

Although the Committee may choose to solicit information from the faculty concerning the weights for each component, it is recommended that the Committee first determine a preliminary estimate of the component weights. The weights selected should be based on careful deliberation and examination of the role and component definitions and their underlying activities, which have been previously provided by the faculty in Steps 1, 2, and 3. Completed matrices for each role, such as the one shown in Figure 4.1, may be distributed to the faculty for their comment and confirmation. Or, if the Committee wishes to solicit direct individual or departmental input into the determination of the role component weights, it may do so by simply using matrices for each role in which the components have been listed on the left side and the value column on the right side left blank such as those shown in Figure 4.2.

■ Case 2: Required and Optional Components With Fixed or Variable Weights

In this case the faculty role has been defined to specify that performance in certain components is required and performance in others is optional. Figure 4.3 shows the role of scholarly and creative activities with this configuration.

Note in the Case 2 example shown in Figure 4.3 that the role of scholarly and creative activities has been determined (in Step 3) to have four possible components: proficiency, discovery/creativity, dissemination, and translation. In this example the faculty have determined that proficiency must be maintained (is required) and that at least 50% of the evaluation of the scholarly and creative activities role will be based on that component. Notice, also, that the remaining components are optional, with

Figure 4.1   Example of a Case 1 worksheet version of the Source Impact Matrix in which the components of Teaching and their fixed weights are shown

Source Impact Matrix Worksheet for Teaching							
Role Components	Sources						*Component Weight*
	??		??		??		
	Source Weight	*Impact Weight*	Source Weight	*Impact Weight*	Source Weight	*Impact Weight*	
Instructional Design							40%
Instructional Delivery							30%
Instructional Assessment							25%
Course Management							5%
TOTAL Source Impact Weights							*100%*

Arreola, R. A. (2007). *Developing a comprehensive faculty evaluation system* (3rd ed.). Bolton, MA: Anker.

Figure 4.2   Example of a simplified format that may be used in Step 4 to gather role component weight values from individual faculty or intact departments

Teaching Role	
Role Components	*Desired Component Weights*
Instructional Design	
Instructional Delivery	
Instructional Assessment	
Course Management	
Please record the percentage weight you feel each of the components listed should carry in the overall evaluation of teaching. The values you enter should total 100%	**100%**

Figure 4.3   Example of a Case 2 worksheet version of the Source Impact Matrix that shows the components of scholarly and creative activities and their fixed or variable weights

values ranges of 0–50%. With this configuration of weights it is possible for a faculty member to assemble any combination of components, and component weights, to form an appropriate expression of their particular mix of activities in performing the role of scholarly and creative activities.

■ CASE 3: MIX OF REQUIRED AND OPTIONAL COMPONENTS WITH FIXED OR VARIABLE WEIGHTS

As you develop your various role definitions, it is possible that some roles may not have a fixed set of separate defining components. In the event a role is defined in such a way that it stands as a complete singular statement, it is not necessary to develop separate role component weights. In some instances, however, you may need to develop "menus" of activities, any combination of which may define a role. In this case a useful strategy is to assign percentage weights to each item on the list and give the faculty member the option of selecting any set of performance items as long as the total of the weights of the individual items equals 100%. Also, there may be some items on the list that are absolutely required and some that are optional. Again, an effective strategy is to assign component weights to each of the required items as well as the optional items. The faculty member would have the option of selecting any set of performance items, including the required items, as long as the total weight of all items equals 100%. For example, suppose we have a role in our fac-

Source Impact Matrix Worksheet for: Scholarly and Creative Activities							
Role Components	Sources						Component Weight or Weight Range
	??		??		??		
	Source Weight	*Impact Weight*	*Source Weight*	*Impact Weight*	*Source Weight*	*Impact Weight*	
Proficiency							50–100%
Discovery/Creativity							0–50%
Dissemination							0–50%
Translation							0–50%
TOTAL Source Impact Weights							*100%*

Arreola, R. A. (2007). *Developing a comprehensive faculty evaluation system* (3rd ed.). Bolton, MA: Anker.

ulty role model we have identified as *administration and management* that has certain required and optional activities. In completing Step 4 for a role such as administration and management specific values would have been assigned to each activity and, depending upon the specific administrative or management responsibilities a faculty member may have, sufficient activities must be selected to total 100% of the assignment. Figure 4.4 shows an example of one possible value configuration for the required and optional activities that may have been identified as defining the administrative and management role. Thus, anyone engaged in the administration and management role as defined in Figure 4.4 would have to determine the appropriate configuration of required and optional items that matched his or her specific assignment and whose values totaled 100%.

Another variation of Case 3 may occur when certain activities are absolutely required, while other activities in a menu are optional but are each assigned a weight. In this situation the absolutely required items may have no weight associated with them. That is, they are activities that must be completed before consideration may be given to the quality of performance in the remaining activities. Thus, in such a situation, failure to perform one of the absolutely required activities will automatically result in the lowest possible rating for the role regardless of the faculty member's performance in the remaining optional activities. Figure 4.5 shows an example of such a situation.

In the variation of Case 3 shown in Figure 4.5 the faculty member must attend graduation and the annual faculty convocation meeting and must serve on at least one committee. The faculty member must also participate in some combination of the optional activities to the extent that the total value of all such activities equals 100%. In this situation the optional activities are provided with a range of values with the lowest value being 0%. The minimum value of 0% indicates that the activity is truly op-

tional since performance in that activity can count for as little as nothing. Giving each activity a range permits variable weights to be assigned depending upon the specific expression of that activity. It should also be noted that the strategy of using ranges of values for the optional items might also be applied to the example shown in Figure 4.4.

GATHERING THE ROLE COMPONENT WEIGHT INFORMATION

It is necessary at this point in our procedure to begin ascertaining the relative importance or weights your institution holds for the different components for each role it has defined. Figure 4.6 shows a master Source Impact Matrix worksheet form (FORM 4) for making working copies. Begin one matrix for each role by first listing the role components down the left side. The weights for each component should be listed down the right side. Note that the weights may be either fixed (Case 1) or may take on a range (Case 2). Note that if the role components have fixed weights, they must equal 100%. If each component has a value range (or if there are a combination of components, some with fixed weights and some with value ranges), it must be possible to select various combinations of components and weights such that the weights total 100%. If components with value ranges have a minimum weight of 0%, indicate that performance in that component is truly optional (i.e., does not have to be performed).

In the event a role is defined with a menu of required and/or optional activities (Case 3) simply use a variation of the forms shown in Figures 4.4 or 4.5 to gather and record the data. When you have completed one matrix for each role for which you have developed defining components, place it aside. These matrices will be completed in Step 6. Do not enter anything into the other cells in each matrix at this time. Figure 4.7 provides an action checklist for completing Step 7.

Figure 4.4   Example of a role with a list of required activities and a menu of optional activities with fixed values associated with each menu item (Case 3)

Administration and Management Role	
Required Activities/Responsibilities	*Optional Activities/Responsibilities*
(35%) Prepare annual budget (10%) Prepare annual board report (25%) Coordinate accreditation	(10%) Supervise staff (15%) Coordinate fundraising campaign (20%) Coordinate graduate events (5%) Serve on grievance review board (5%) Federal regulation compliance (5%) Maintain equipment inventory (5%) Serve as building manager

Arreola, R. A. (2007). *Developing a comprehensive faculty evaluation system* (3rd ed.). Bolton, MA: Anker.

Figure 4.5   Example of a variation of Case 3 in which a role is defined by a list of absolute required activities (with no weight) and a menu of optional activities with an associated value or range of values for each

Service to the Institution Role	
Required Activities/Responsibilities	*Optional Activities/Responsibilities*
Attend graduation **Attend annual convocation** **Serve on at least one committee** [Failure to perform any one of these activities automatically drops the rating of the service to the institution role to the lowest rating of "1." Exemptions may be granted for illness or other documented circumstance that prevented participation in these activities.]	**Serve on Departmental Committees** 20% Curriculum 20% Promotion and tenure 20% Admission 0–10% Other departmental committees **Serve on Institutional Committees** 30% Accreditation compliance committee 30% Institutional promotion and tenure committee **Other Service** 0–15% Supervise student clubs/organizations 0–15% Managing projects 0–35% Advising students 0–15% Recruiting 0–25% Fundraising 0–15% Community outreach program 0–15% Mentoring new faculty 0–15% Conducting campus faculty workshops

Developing a Comprehensive Faculty Evaluation System

Figure 4.6 Sample of a Source Impact Matrix worksheet form (FORM 4) for roles in which the values assigned to each component may take on either a fixed value or a range of values (Case 1 & Case 2 situations) *(Make as many copies of this form as needed).*

FORM 4: Source Impact Matrix Worksheet for:

Role Components	Source — Y/N	Wt.	Source — Y/N	Wt.	Source — Y/N	Wt.	Source — Y/N	Wt.	TOTAL of all Source Weights	Role Component Weight or Weight Range
									= 100%	
									= 100%	
									= 100%	
									= 100%	
Total Source Impact Weights										= 100%

Directions: This form is to be used by the Committee to begin recording the various decisions as to:

1) The values to be given to each component of each role
2) The sources of information for each component of each role
3) The values to be associated with each source
4) The *impact* the information from each source will be allowed to have on the overall evaluation of the role

At this point the Committee should record only the weights that have been determined for each role component in the "Role Component Weight" column on the right. Note that if the role components have fixed weights they must total 100%. If the components have a value range it must be possible to select values within those ranges whose total equals 100%. A minimum value of 0% within a range indicates that performance in that component is not required.

Arreola, R. A. (2007). *Developing a comprehensive faculty evaluation system* (3rd ed.). Bolton, MA: Anker.

Figure 4.7   Action Checklist for Completing Step 4

Action Checklist for Completing Step 4

Expected Outcomes: The outcome of Step 4 is the specification of the values to be given to the individual components of each role as determined and defined in Steps 1, 2, and 3. Step 4 begins the process of completing the Source Impact Matrices that will provide the final value system to be used in the operational faculty evaluation system.

OPTION 1

____ The Committee assembles and reviews all the data provided primarily on FORMS 3A and 3B and establishes preliminary weights or values for each component of each role. The Committee then records these weights on an appropriate Source Impact Matrix worksheet (FORM 4). There should be one worksheet matrix for each role.

____ The Committee distributes its preliminary source impact matrices to the departments for comment and discussion. If a department wishes to recommend an adjustment to the values it should do so on forms provided by the Committee similar to those shown in Figure 4.2.

____ The Committee reconciles the input from the various departments into a single Source Impact Matrix worksheet (FORM 4) for each role for the institution.

OPTION 2

____ The Committee prepares blank Source Impact Matrix worksheets (FORM 4) for each of the roles identified in earlier Steps. The blank matrices list only the role components but not the role component weights. All other cells in matrix are grayed-out at this time as shown in Figure 4.6.

____ The Committee distributes blank versions of FORM 4 (with only the names of the role components listed for each role) to the departments.

____ Each department conducts a faculty meeting to come to an agreement on the values that they feel should be associated with each component of each role. The department then completes a FORM 4 for each role entering the component weights agreed upon by the faculty and submits it to the Committee.

____ The Committee reviews all the FORM 4s submitted by each department and reconciles the input from the various departments into an institutional faculty role model that includes the weights for each component for each role. In those instances where there is a need to develop a unique faculty role model for an outlier department, the component values determined by that department should be the ones used as long as they total 100%. However, as noted in Figures 4.4 and 4.5 some roles may not have components but menu lists of items that may have different values that may be combined in different ways to produce a 100% assignment.

Arreola, R. A. (2007). *Developing a comprehensive faculty evaluation system* (3rd ed.). Bolton, MA: Anker.

Step 5: Determining Appropriate Sources of Information

In Steps 1–4, we focused on determining and defining the roles that should be evaluated, how much weight or value should be placed on the performance of each role in the overall evaluation, and how much weight the individual components of each role contribute in the evaluation of that role. The next step is to decide who should provide the information on which the evaluations will be based. Too frequently students are automatically selected as the sole or primary source of the information used in a faculty evaluation system. Students are certainly appropriate sources of information for certain kinds of activities, but they are by no means always the best source of information for all the activities in which faculty engage and on which they may be evaluated. The most important principle in identifying and selecting sources of information is to make certain that the source identified has first-hand knowledge of the performance being evaluated. Too often peers or administrators are included in the evaluation of a faculty member's classroom performance when they have never, or rarely, seen that performance. However, peers and various administrators often believe they have a good idea of the quality of such performance. The question is where did they get the information on which their belief or opinion is based? The answer is almost always "from students." If you are ultimately going to depend upon students for information, go directly to the source—don't rely on second-hand information. Using second-hand information may give the random, or non-systematically obtained, input of a few students an inordinate effect on a faculty member's evaluation.

Here we will use another worksheet variation of the Source Impact Matrix developed in Step 4, for each of our roles. That is, we need to begin determining who are

the most appropriate sources of information concerning each of those activities by means of an analysis of the specific component activities that define each role. This is an activity that should be undertaken by the Committee only. Figure 5.1 shows simplified example of a completed Source Impact Matrix worksheet appropriate for the teaching role as defined earlier (see Figure 4.1).

As can be seen in Figure 5.1, teaching has previously been defined in terms of four separate components: instructional design, instructional delivery, instructional assessment, and course management. Depending on the definition developed for your institution for the teaching role, you may have three, four, five, or more defining components for teaching. These components are listed down the left side of the matrix. A number of possible sources of information are listed across the top of the matrix. In our example, we have listed only students, peers, and the department head; however, other sources such as self, alumni, parents, and external consultants are also possible.

The Source Impact Matrix worksheet for Step 5 provides a tool for making important decisions concerning the design of the faculty evaluation system. In completing the matrix, "yes" or "no" decisions are made about whether a particular source of information should be tapped for the role component in question. For example, in Figure 5.1 teaching is defined, in part, as consisting of effective instructional delivery which includes those human interaction and communication events that the students experience every time they are in class. In examining the situation represented by the cell at the intersection of students as a source and instructional delivery as the teaching component, students would appear to be a good source of information since they have first-hand experience with the performance in question, so a "yes" is entered in that cell. However, note that a "no" has been entered in the cells representing the intersection of peers and department head as sources for the instructional delivery component. If, however, the decision were made to gather this information from peers and/or the department head then classroom visitation issues must be discussed. In this case unless the department is willing to undertake a peer visitation program or the department head is willing and able to regularly sit in on a faculty member's class, neither of those sources would really have first-hand information concerning the instructional delivery of the instructor and should not be included. However, in our example, teaching has been defined, in part, as also consisting of instructional design. As noted earlier, instructional design includes technical skills in designing the course, developing instructional events or experiences, and sequencing presentations. For these kinds of skills, peers may be an excellent source of information; thus, a "yes" has been entered in the appropriate cell. Students, too, could provide certain kinds of information about these skills as they are exhibited in the course.

Proceeding in this way through each role's defining components, it is possible to make rational decisions and determinations as to what sources of information would be appropriate and acceptable to the faculty. Again, the important principle to follow in identifying sources is always to select the source which has the best opportunity to observe first-hand the performance to be evaluated.

The "yes" and "no" decisions represented in Figure 5.1 are merely examples and are not intended to represent the right decision in each case. The example merely serves to demonstrate the process of using the simplified worksheet version of the Source Impact Matrix tool in planning the design of a faculty evaluation system. The teaching components you develop and the sources you identify may be different from those shown in the example in Figure 5.1.

The process of identifying the sources for each of the roles in the institution's faculty role model is best accomplished by the Committee working independently as a deliberative body. Appropriate input from the faculty may be solicited in the form of consultants to the Committee. It is *not* recommended that faculty be consulted on a broad scale as has been the case in earlier steps, since this can become cumbersome and may delay the process considerably. Rather, the Committee, through a series of discussions and meetings with faculty groups, can determine what source or sources would be most appropriate for each of the roles' defining activities.

The simplified version of the Source Impact Matrix shown in Figure 5.1 illustrates the intermediate process to be carried out in Step 5. However, in fully completing this step another worksheet variation of the Source Impact Matrix developed in Step 4 should be used. Figure 5.3 contains a master of the worksheet variation of the Source Impact Matrix (designated as FORM 5) for use in completing Step 5. This master may be used to make copies for the Committee's work. The directions for completing this matrix are included at the bottom of the form.

Figure 5.1 Simplified Source Impact Matrix worksheet for identifying the sources of information for each component of the Teaching Role

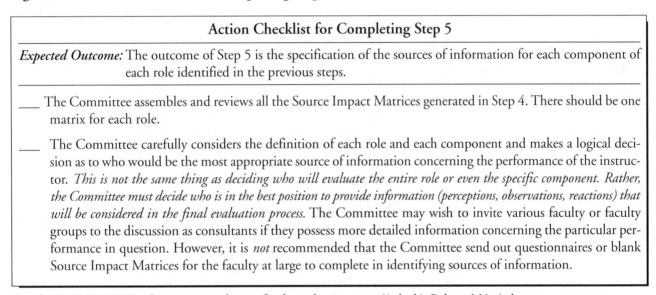

Source Impact Matrix for: TEACHING				
Simplified Worksheet for Step 5				
Role Components	Sources			
	Students	Peers	Dept. Chair	_____
Instructional Design	YES	YES	NO	
Instructional Delivery	YES	NO	NO	
Instructional Assessment	YES	YES	YES	
Course Management	NO	NO	YES	

Figure 5.2 Action Checklist for Completing Step 5

Action Checklist for Completing Step 5
Expected Outcome: The outcome of Step 5 is the specification of the sources of information for each component of each role identified in the previous steps.
___ The Committee assembles and reviews all the Source Impact Matrices generated in Step 4. There should be one matrix for each role.
___ The Committee carefully considers the definition of each role and each component and makes a logical decision as to who would be the most appropriate source of information concerning the performance of the instructor. *This is not the same thing as deciding who will evaluate the entire role or even the specific component. Rather, the Committee must decide who is in the best position to provide information (perceptions, observations, reactions) that will be considered in the final evaluation process.* The Committee may wish to invite various faculty or faculty groups to the discussion as consultants if they possess more detailed information concerning the particular performance in question. However, it is *not* recommended that the Committee send out questionnaires or blank Source Impact Matrices for the faculty at large to complete in identifying sources of information.

Arreola, R. A. (2007). *Developing a comprehensive faculty evaluation system* (3rd ed.). Bolton, MA: Anker.

Figure 5.3   Source Impact Matrix Worksheet for Completing Step 5
(Make as many copies as needed.)

FORM 5: Source Impact Matrix Worksheet for:

Role Components	Source		Source		Source		Source		TOTAL of all Source Weights	Role Component Weights
	Y/N	Wt.	Y/N	Wt.	Y/N	Wt.	Y/N	Wt.		
									= 100%	
									= 100%	
									= 100%	
									= 100%	
Total Source Impact Weights										= 100%

Directions: This form is to be used by the Committee to begin recording the decisions as to the appropriate *sources* of information for each component of each role. One FORM 5 must be completed for each role in the faculty role model. In completing this form:

1) Enter the name of one of the roles in the Faculty Role Model (as determined in Step 1) at the top of the form.
2) Enter the names of the role components for that role (as determined in Step 3) on the left side of the matrix.
3) Enter the value or weight for each component of each role (as determined in Step 4).
4) Enter the names of possible sources of information concerning the components listed (students, peers, department head, alumni, external peers, etc.).
5) Consider each source in relation to each role component. Determine whether the source can reasonably provide first-hand information concerning the faculty member's performance in that role component. If so, place a "Y" or "YES" in the cell. If not place an "N" or "NO" in the cell.

Arreola, R. A. (2007). *Developing a comprehensive faculty evaluation system* (3rd ed.). Bolton, MA: Anker.

Step 6: Determining the Source Impact Weights

In any well-designed faculty evaluation system, the evaluative judgments concerning faculty performances in the various expressions or components of the roles should be based on information derived from multiple sources. The issue of the appropriateness of those sources is addressed in Step 5. Having determined where this information is to come from, now the issue of the credibility of those sources needs to be addressed. Thus, specify the *weight* or *impact* the information from each source will have in the overall evaluation. In completing Step 6 two separate tasks must be accomplished: 1) determining the individual source weights based on the values of the faculty, and then 2) computing the final source impact weights for the system. The objective of Step 6 is to specify how much impact information from each source will ultimately have on the overall evaluation of an individual in the comprehensive faculty evaluation system.

Remember that the essence of a workable faculty evaluation system is that the value structure implicit in the system be clearly evident and agreed upon by the majority of the faculty being evaluated. If this is not the case, the system, no matter how technically correct its structure, has little chance of long-term success. Thus, in determining the impact weights for the various sources that are to provide information concerning faculty performances in each of the components of each role, it is best to follow the same general procedure of gathering data from the faculty as described in earlier steps.

■ DETERMINING THE SOURCE WEIGHTS

It is a normal human characteristic to consider information from some sources as more important or valuable than information from other sources. It is this issue that is addressed in Step 6. In previous steps we determined the values we wished to associate with the roles in the faculty role model as well as the values we wished to assign to the components of those roles. In this step we will establish the values we wish to associate with the identified sources of information for each component of each role. That is, we must now build into our value system a reflection of the fact that people assign different value to information depending upon its source.

For example, suppose you are driving in to work and see a new billboard advertising a new restaurant that says: "Grand Opening! The Steak Emporium! Serving the Best Steaks in Town!" Now, suppose later in the day you go to lunch with a friend who tells you "We went to that new Steak Emporium restaurant last night. For my money they've got the best steaks in town." In this situation you have received the same information (the Steak Emporium serves the best steaks in town) from two sources—a billboard by the side of the road and a friend whom you trust. So here the simple question is, which source of that particular information do you trust more? Which source of information will be more likely to move you to act? Most likely you will believe your friend more than just words printed on a billboard. You might even be moved to go to the restaurant yourself (if you like steaks).

It is clear that simply specifying what information should be gathered is not sufficient in designing our faculty evaluation system. We must also consider where the information comes from, since we may value that information differently depending upon the source. In many faculty evaluation systems, the most common sources of information are students, peers, and administrators at various levels. This is true whether data from these sources are systematically gathered or randomly acquired. Depending on the situation and the performance being evaluated, the credibility of the information coming from these sources varies. For example, students may be a credible source of information concerning classroom performance but not as credible for information concerning the faculty member's research activities. Likewise, peers may be a credible information source concerning the professional standing and publication record of an individual but not as credible for information concerning his or her classroom teaching style. The credibility of any information source in a faculty evaluation system depends as much on the opportunity that source has to be a first-hand observer of the performance in question as it does on our willingness to accept and believe what that source has to say. Thus, our next step in developing a comprehensive faculty evaluation system is to arrive at some consensus on the credibility of the various sources of information that have been previously identified. More specifically, we must determine how much weight we wish information from any given source to have on the overall evaluation of a given role. In short, we must determine and define the impact we wish the information from these sources to have in the overall evaluation of faculty. The tool used for this is another worksheet variation of the Source Impact Matrix developed in Step 4 (Figure 4.1). An example of this worksheet variation is shown in Figure 6.1 that reflects the original "yes" and "no" decisions made in completing the Source Impact Matrix worksheet in Step 5 (Figure 5.1). Also shown are the values to be assigned to the information indicated by percentage weights in each cell.

Because students and peers have been determined to be appropriate sources of information for the instructional design component, the task is now to divide the 100% total weight across these two sources. This decision is a subjective one which is based, in large measure, on how these elements of teaching are defined and weighted (Steps 3 and 4) and how much credibility these two sources have with the faculty relative to the activities defining instructional design. If we can assume that instructional design speaks more to the technicalities of course design (i.e., designing appropriate experiences, specifying learning outcome objectives, ensuring the currency of content, etc.), then it might be considered appropriate to place the bulk of the weight (75%) on the input from faculty peers and 25% of the weight on input from students. In a similar fashion appropriate weights must be determined for each cell in the matrix. However, as noted earlier, this is a subjective decision. The decision you make for your system, as well as the role components you define, may be quite different.

In deciding what values are to be associated with each source for each component it is recommended that the Committee make worksheet versions of each matrix developed in Step 5. These worksheets may then be distributed to the departments to once more gather value information from the faculty. These worksheets should include the previously determined role components and identified sources but leave a blank space for faculty to enter a value or weight figure. Figure 6.2 shows an example of such a worksheet for use in gathering faculty input

Figure 6.1   Example of a Source Impact Matrix worksheet for Step 6 showing Source Weights for teaching role components

	Source Impact Matrix Worksheet for Step 6						
	Source Weight Specification Form						
Role Components	Sources						Total of Role Component Weights
	Students		**Peers**		**Dept. Chair**		
	Source?	*Weight*	*Source?*	*Weight*	*Source?*	*Weight*	
Instructional Design	YES	25%	YES	75%	NO	0%	= 100%
Instructional Delivery	YES	100%	NO	0%	NO	0%	= 100%
Instructional Assessment	YES	20%	YES	50%	YES	30%	= 100%
Course Management	NO	0%	NO	0%	YES	100%	= 100%

Arreola, R. A. (2007). *Developing a comprehensive faculty evaluation system* (3rd ed.). Bolton, MA: Anker.

concerning the weights to be placed on the previously identified sources of information for each component of the teaching role.

Note that the example shown in Figure 6.2 already has the value (0%) entered into cells where a "NO" was previously entered in Step 5 since no information is being gathered from that source for that component of the teaching role. Also note that a value of (100%) has also already been entered in those cells in which the information concerning that component is to be gathered from only that source. These cells have been "grayed out" to designate previously made decisions and the resulting (default) weights determined by those decisions. Also, note that since the values across any one role component must equal 100%, the last column on the right has 100% already entered to remind anyone entering individual source weights that those weights must total 100%. Figure 6.4 shows FORM 6A, a master Source Impact Matrix worksheet for completing the first part of Step 6 from which copies may be made. In actual practice, of course, the Committee would need to prepare such forms with the previously determined information already entered. These prefilled forms could then be used by faculty and/or departments to arrive at a consensus on the specific values or weights for each defining component of each role. A mock-up of a prefilled FORM 6A that could be used in gathering this information is shown in Figure 6.3.

■ DETERMINING THE SOURCE IMPACT

To this point we have reflected the credibility of various sources of information by gathering from the faculty the individual source weights for each role. Also, previously in Step 4, we reflected the relative importance of each of the defining components for every role by determining the role component weights. The purpose of these exercises was to lead us to the point of determining (and thus permitting us to specify and control) the total impact information from each source would have on the overall evaluation of a faculty member. Now we must determine our final source impact weights by using the full Source Impact Matrix that is designated as FORM 6B. A master copy of FORM 6B is provided in Figure 6.8 at the end of this chapter.

Figure 6.5 shows an example of a completed FORM 6B using the information first provided in Figure 4.1 in which a value of 40% was assigned to the instructional design component of teaching. Further, in Figure 6.1, it was determined that 75% of the information concerning instructional design skills would be provided by peers, so "75%" has been entered in the source weight box of the upper left-hand corner of the peer instructional design cell of the FORM 6B (Figure 6.5). Now, by multiplying the role component weight of 40% by source weight of 75%, we arrive at a source impact

Figure 6.2   Example of a worksheet version of the Source Impact Matrix for use in gathering information from departments on their recommended values for each source

Source Impact Matrix Worksheet for Step 6							
Source Weight Specification Form							
Role Components	Sources						Total of Source Weights
	Students		Peers		Dept. Chair		
	Source?	Weight	Source?	Weight	Source?	Weight	
Instructional Design	YES		YES		NO	0%	= 100%
Instructional Delivery	YES	100%	NO	0%	NO	0%	= 100%
Instructional Assessment	YES		YES		YES		= 100%
Course Management	NO	0%	NO	0%	YES	100%	= 100%

Arreola, R. A. (2007). *Developing a comprehensive faculty evaluation system* (3rd ed.). Bolton, MA: Anker.

Figure 6.3 Mock-up of prefilled FORM 6A to be prepared by the Committee for use by departments in providing their input as to the values to be assigned to each source for each component

Role Components	Students Source		Peers Source		Dept. Chair Source		___ Source		TOTAL of all Source Weights	Component Weights
	Y/N	Wt.	Y/N	Wt.	Y/N	Wt.	Y/N	Wt.		
Instructional Design	YES		YES		NO	0%			= 100%	40%
Instructional Delivery	YES		NO	0%	NO	0%			= 100%	30%
Instructional Assessment	YES		YES		YES				= 100%	25%
Course Management	NO	0%	NO	0%	YES	100%			= 100%	5%
										= 100%

FORM 6A: Source Impact Matrix Worksheet for: TEACHING

Directions: This form is to be used by your department in providing the Committee with the values you wish to place on each of the identified sources for each role component. Recall that earlier your department provided the information on which each role and its components were defined. The decisions on who should provide the information have been made based on an analysis of the type of information to be provided and who or what source would be in the position to have first-hand information concerning the instructor's performance in each area. In completing this form please:
1) Examine the sources for each role component for which the word "yes" has been entered indicating that this will be a source of information for the role component.
2) In the blank cell to the right of each "yes" indicate how much you think the information from that source should count.
3) The value you place should be a percentage value between 1% and 100%.

Note: The source weights entered for each role component (row) must equal 100%

Arreola, R. A. (2007). *Developing a comprehensive faculty evaluation system* (3rd ed.). Bolton, MA: Anker.

weight of 30% for peers. The number "30%" is then recorded in the impact weight cell for peers. In a similar fashion the source impact weights are computed and entered in the appropriate cells. By adding all the source impact weights in each column, we can compute the total impact weight for the information coming from each source. It is clear from the values shown in the full Source Impact Matrix (Figure 6.5) that peer input will account for 45% of the overall evaluation of teaching, student input will account for 45%, and department head input will account for 10%.

It is critical at this point in the process to discuss the appropriateness of the final source impact weights as computed for each role. In this case the result of all of the definitions, decisions, and weights determined in the previous steps has led us to the point where the evaluation of teaching will be based 45% on student input, 45% on peer input, and 10% on department head input. If it were felt, for example, that the department head should have a greater impact on the evaluation of teaching, this would be the point to make the necessary adjustments.

Suppose it was determined at this point that a more appropriate mix of the impact weights of the three sources would be students 35%, peers 40%, and department head

25%. These weights are shown in Figure 6.6 in the "proposed revised weights" row at the bottom of the matrix.

If we wished to adjust the total Source Impact Weights to reflect the preferred values, it would be necessary, then, to revisit the decisions that led to the original weights of 45% for students, 45% for peers, and 10% for department head. If it were determined that the department head's impact should be 25% rather than the original 10%, a decision would need to be made to either involve the department head in providing information on additional components of teaching, or to give more weight to those components for which the department head already provides information. Likewise, since the impact weight of the students and peers would be reduced to 35% and 40% respectively, decisions would need to be made to correspondingly reduce either the value of the components for which they provide information or the number of components for which they serve as information sources. If the total Source Impact Weights do not correspond to the expressed values of the institution, adjustments can now be made to bring the total final weights into agreement with the faculty's collective value structure. Note that the sums of the component weights and source impact weights must each total 100%. Figure 6.7 provdides an action checklist for completing Step 6.

Figure 6.4 **FORM 6A: Source Impact Matrix worksheet master for gathering individual source values from the faculty.**
(Make as many copies as necessary).

FORM 6A: Source Impact Matrix Worksheet for:

Role Components	Source		Source		Source		Source		TOTAL of all Source Weights	Component Weights
	Y/N	Wt.	Y/N	Wt.	Y/N	Wt.	Y/N	Wt.		
									= 100%	
									= 100%	
									= 100%	
									= 100%	
									= 100%	

Directions: This form is to be used by your department in providing the Committee with the values you wish to place on each of the identified sources for each role component. Recall that earlier your department provided the information on which each role and its components were defined. The decisions on who should provide the information have been made based on an analysis of the type of information to be provided and who or what source would be in the position to have first-hand information concerning the instructor's performance in each area. In completing this form please:

1) Examine the sources for each role component for which the word "yes" has been entered indicating that this will be a source of information for the role component.

2) In the blank cell to the right of each "yes" indicate how much you think the information from that source should count. The value you enter should be a percentage value between 1% and 100%.

Note: The source weights entered for each role component (row) must equal 100%.

Arreola, R. A. (2007). *Developing a comprehensive faculty evaluation system* (3rd ed.). Bolton, MA: Anker.

Figure 6.5 Full Source Impact Matrix for the Teaching Role with computed source impact weights

FORM 6B: FULL Source Impact Matrix for: TEACHING							
Role Components	Sources						Component Weight
	Students		Peers		Dept. Chair		
	Source Weight	Impact Weight	Source Weight	Impact Weight	Source Weight	Impact Weight	
Instructional Design	25%	10%	75%	30%	0%	0%	40%
Instructional Delivery	100%	30%	0%	0%	0%	0%	30%
Instructional Assessment	20%	5%	60%	15%	20%	5%	25%
Course Management	0%	0%	0%	0%	100%	5%	5%
TOTAL Source Impact Weights		45%		45%		10%	100%

Figure 6.6 Full Source Impact Matrix for the teaching role with proposed revised weights for the various sources

FORM 6B: FULL Source Impact Matrix for: TEACHING							
Role Components	Sources						Component Weight
	Students		Peers		Dept. Chair		
	Source Weight	Impact Weight	Source Weight	Impact Weight	Source Weight	Impact Weight	
Instructional Design	25%	10%	75%	30%	0%	0%	40%
Instructional Delivery	100%	30%	0%	0%	0%	0%	30%
Instructional Assessment	20%	5%	60%	15%	20%	5%	25%
Course Management	0%	0%	0%	0%	100%	5%	5%
Total Source Impact Weights		45%		45%		10%	100%
Proposed Revised Weights		35%		40%		25%	

Arreola, R. A. (2007). *Developing a comprehensive faculty evaluation system* (3rd ed.). Bolton, MA: Anker.

Figure 6.7 Action Checklist for Completing Step 6

Action Checklist for Completing Step 6

Expected Outcome: The outcome of Step 6 is the final specification of the impact (weight) that is to be given to the input from the various sources providing information concerning the faculty member's performance in the various components of the several roles in the Faculty Role Model.

___ The Committee assembles prefilled copies of FORM 6A for each of the roles identified in previous steps. The FORM 6A for each role should include the role components and indications of which sources have been previously selected to provide the information. The Committee should enter "0%" in the appropriate source weight cell if a source has not been identified to provide information for a particular component. For those sources that are serving as the *only* source of information for a component, the Committee should enter "100%" in the appropriate cell.

___ The Committee distributes its prepared copies of FORM 6A for each role to the department chairs.

___ As in previous steps each department conducts a faculty meeting to determine the source values it wishes to submit to the Committee. Each department completes a FORM 6A for each role and submits it to the Committee.

___ *Compiling the Data.* The task before the committee at this point is to aggregate and combine all the data to most appropriately reflect the expressed values of each department. This is best done by making a rough distribution of the data for each cell and determining whether to use the mean, median, or modal value for the final source value. This determination is made, in part, by considering the range of the distribution. If the range is extremely wide or if the distribution is bimodal, these are signs that considerable disagreement exists among the faculty and must be resolved. However, if the greatest bulk of the faculty responses appear to cluster together, the mean or average may be used.

___ *Assembling the full Source Impact Matrix for each role.* Once the Committee has reconciled the input from the various departments into a singular source impact value for each component of each role you are ready to compute the final full source impact matrices (FORM 6B) for your system. (A master copy of FORM 6B is provided in Figure 6.8.)

   1) For each role for which you have previously completed a Weighted Source by Role Component Matrix, copy the source weights from that matrix into the small boxes in the upper left-hand corner of the corresponding cells in FORM 6B.

   2) At this point the FORM 6B Source Impact Matrix for each role should contain component weights down the right side and source weights in the small boxes in the upper left corner of each cell. Multiply the values in the small boxes in the upper left corner of each cell by the component weight for the row of that cell. Write the resulting product (source impact weight) in the larger portion of each cell.

   3) Compute each of the column totals of the source impact weights and record them at the bottom of the matrix. These column totals are the total source impact weights for the given role. Note that the sum of the component weights and the sum of the source impact weights must each equal 100%.

Arreola, R. A. (2007). *Developing a comprehensive faculty evaluation system* (3rd ed.). Bolton, MA: Anker.

Figure 6.8 FORM 6B: Full Source Impact Matrix master to be used by the Committee when inputting the final source impact weights for each role (*Make as many copies as needed.*)

FORM 6B: Full Source Impact Matrix for:

Role Components	Source		Source		Source		Source		Component Weights
	Source Weight	Impact Weight	Source Weight	Impact Weight	Source Weight	Impact Weight	Source Weight	Impact Weight	
								= 100%	
								= 100%	
								= 100%	
								= 100%	
Total Source Impact Weights									= 100%

Directions: This form is to be used by the Committee in determining the final source impact weights for each role. In completing this form please:

1) Enter the name of the role at the top of the form and list the role components down the column on the left side.

2) Enter the role component weights as previously determined down the column on the right side.

3) Enter the final source weight for each component as determined from the synthesis of the departmental data provided on FORM 6A.

4) Compute the individual source impact weights for each component by multiplying the individual source weight by its corresponding role component weight and enter it in the impact weight column for each source.

5) Sum all the impact weights for each source and enter them in the total source impact weights row.

Note that the total of all the source weights for a component must equal 100%, the sum of all component weights must equal 100%, and the sum of the total source impact weights must equal 100%.

Arreola, R. A. (2007). *Developing a comprehensive faculty evaluation system* (3rd ed.). Bolton, MA: Anker.

Developing a Comprehensive Faculty Evaluation System

7

Step 7: Determining How Information Should Be Gathered

Once the sources of the information for the evaluation system and their impact weights have been determined, we begin moving into the less political and more technical area of measurement. It is best at this point to enlist the aid of those people on your faculty whose area of expertise is tests and measurement. They will certainly be required in the next step, and it is generally a good idea to have this expertise represented on the Committee in the first place if possible.

In this step, we set about determining how the information we have specified in our role definitions is to be gathered from the sources we have identified and agreed are appropriate. This is a relatively simple process. However, it does require a careful review of the roles and the development of an operational plan for the final faculty

evaluation system. In completing this step, we will make use of a new matrix worksheet, the Data-Gathering Tool Specification Matrix designated as FORM 7. Figure 7.1 shows an example of a completed Data-Gathering Tool Specification Matrix (FORM 7) for the teaching role.

This matrix follows the example that has been used in previous chapters. Note that the cells that contained zeros (0%) in the previous Source Impact Matrix (Figure 6.5) that was completed in Step 6 are blanked out on this matrix. Since we will not be gathering data from those sources for these elements, we will not need to specify the tools or means for doing so. In the cells that are not vacant, however, we are faced with the task of determining how we will gather information from students, peers, and the department head. For example, if we wish to gather information

Figure 7.1   Example of a Completed Data-Gathering Tool Specification Matrix for the Teaching Role

FORM 7: Data-Gathering Tool Specification Matrix for: TEACHING						
Role Components	Sources					
	Students		Peers		Dept. Chair	
	Source?	*How?*	*Source?*	*How?*	*Source?*	*How?*
Instructional Design	YES	*Rating Form*	YES	*Peer Analysis of Syllabus and Course Materials*	NO	
Instructional Delivery	YES	*Rating Form*	NO		NO	
Instructional Assessment	YES	*Rating Form*	YES	*Peer Analysis of Exams*	YES	*Review of Grading Practice*
Course Management	NO		NO		YES	*Checklist*

Arreola, R. A. (2007). *Developing a comprehensive faculty evaluation system* (3rd ed.). Bolton, MA: Anker.

from students concerning a faculty member's instructional delivery, there are several possible alternatives:

- Interview each student.

- Interview a random sample of students from each class.

- Administer a questionnaire or rating form to a random sample of students from each class.

- Administer a rating form to each student.

Unless the classes are unusually small and an appropriate team of individuals can be identified to serve as nonthreatening interviewers, interviewing students is generally not done. However, if that approach *were* desired, then an appropriate interview protocol would have to be developed. For example, in a music curriculum there may exist a number of courses that are individual tutorials. That is, each class has only one student in it. In such a case we might consider a structured exit interview as a means for gathering data.

A more common situation is shown in Figure 7.1 where a rating form has been identified as the way in which student information is to be gathered. This does not mean that a system that uses rating forms and some type of follow-up interview could not also be implemented. Only by discussing what is desired, what is acceptable, and what is feasible and affordable can an appropriate decision be made about the best way the information for each role is to be gathered.

Referring to the example in Figure 7.1, note that peers have been identified as appropriate sources of infor-mation for the instructional design and the content expertise components of the teaching role. For instructional design, a group of knowledgeable peers will review the course materials—the course syllabus, handouts, assignments, sequence, and general design. This assessment may require a specific checklist and a set of standards by which the peers are to rate the course materials. (See the case studies in Chapter 16 for examples of some of these kinds of materials.) Likewise, the peer source will provide information concerning the content expertise of the faculty member as reflected in the course materials. This may involve a careful analysis and review of the course in terms of the currency, appropriateness, and level of the content presented in the materials and exercises, as well as the sequencing of the content itself in the design of the course. Note that gathering the information required for a given role or role component may require a form, a set of forms, a specified procedure or protocol, or some combination of forms and procedures.

Figure 7.2 contains a blank data-gathering tool specification matrix worksheet (FORM 7) master for making working copies. Using all the information resulting from Steps 1–6, make a preliminary judgment on what means will be used to gather the information from each source. The activities listed in each department's FORM 1B should be especially helpful in determining which information-gathering strategy or procedure should be used for each component of each role. Develop a brief explanation and rational for the data-gathering approach you identify for each cell.

Figure 7.2   Data-Gathering Tool Specification Matrix Worksheet Master

FORM 7: Data-Gathering Tool Matrix for:

Role Components	Sources							
	Sources		Sources		Sources		Sources	
	Y/N	Tool or Data-Gathering Strategy	Y/N	Tool or Data-Gathering Strategy	Y/N	Tool or Data-Gathering Strategy	Y/N	Tool or Data-gathering Strategy

Directions: This form is to be used by the Committee to begin recording the decisions as to the appropriate tool or data-gathering strategy, protocol, or rubric to be used in gathering information from each source for each component of each role. One FORM 7 must be completed for each role in the faculty role model. In completing this form:

1) At the top of the form enter the name of the role to be considered (from the Faculty Role Model list as determined in Step 1).
2) Enter the names of the role components for that role (as determined in Step 3) on the left side of the matrix.
3) Enter the possible sources selected for the role placing a "Y" (yes) or "N" (no) in the "Y/N" column for each component for each source (as determined in Step 5). Blank out the "Tool or Data-Gathering Strategy" cell to the right of any cell for which you have entered a "N."
4) Consider each source in relation to each role component. Determine what would be the best tool or data-gathering strategy to use in obtaining the information required. It may be necessary for the Committee to consult with campus measurement and assessment experts in making these determinations.

Arreola, R. A. (2007). *Developing a comprehensive faculty evaluation system* (3rd ed.). Bolton, MA: Anker.

Figure 7.3   Action Checklist for Completing Step 7

Action Checklist for Completing Step 7

Expected Outcome: The outcome of Step 7 is the specification of the kinds of tools or data-gathering strategies (questionnaires, rating forms, interviews, etc.) to be used in obtaining information from the various sources concerning faculty performance in the components of the roles in the Faculty Role Model.

_____ The Committee fills out FORM 7 for each role in the faculty role model recording the earlier decisions made in Step 5 about where the information for each component will come from (FORM 5 for each role). Make certain to "blank out" the cells where no information will be gathered (as shown in Figure 7.1).

_____ The Committee makes a preliminary judgment on the types of forms or data-gathering strategies to be used for each source for each component for each role by listing them in the tool or data-gathering strategy cell for each component.

_____ The Committee may wish to hold hearings or consult with individual departments concerning their recommendations as to the most appropriate data-gathering strategy or type of tool. Information provided on each department's completed FORM 1B may be of considerable value at this point.

_____ The Committee completes a final FORM 7 for each role with the final form type or data-gathering strategy specified in the appropriate cells and moves to Step 8.

_____ It is helpful if the Committee issues a report to the faculty that includes the specification of the tools to be developed and used, as well as a brief explanation of how the determination was made as to which data-gathering strategy to use. It is helpful in such a report to cite the information provided by the faculty in Step 1 of the process in their departments' FORM 1B.

Arreola, R. A. (2007). *Developing a comprehensive faculty evaluation system* (3rd ed.). Bolton, MA: Anker.

8

Step 8: Completing the System: Selecting or Designing Forms, Protocols, and Rating Scale

We now arrive at the last step in developing a comprehensive faculty evaluation system—designing the questionnaires and other forms. Constructing valid and reliable rating forms, questionnaires, or other tools needed to implement the data-gathering strategies specified in Step 7 is a complex technical task requiring expertise in psychometrics. It must be remembered that what is being developed are tools to measure, in a valid and reliable way, complex psychological phenomena (e.g., opinions, reactions, observations, rankings, etc.). Even selecting published forms or other commercially available tools requires fairly sophisticated psychometric skills in order to adequately assess their appropriateness and utility for the faculty evaluation system you have designed.

This chapter is not intended to be a short course in psychometrics but simply a guide to the major issues that must be addressed in constructing and/or selecting the appropriate tools to use in gathering the information required by your faculty evaluation system. As noted in Step 7, it is recommended that the Committee utilize campus experts in psychometrics. If none are available on your campus, the Committee may wish to consult with such experts at other colleges or universities in your area.

It should be apparent at this point that designing forms without first having clearly identified what is to be measured (Steps 1–4), and deciding from whom the information will be gathered (Step 5), could lead to the development of inappropriate and perhaps invalid forms or other data-gathering strategies. Unfortunately, the first step that many institutions take when designing a faculty evaluation system is to design, or at least revise, a specific form—usually the student rating form. *This is a serious error that can stymie the*

entire process. Committees charged with such tasks can argue interminably over specific questions to be included on the form. Even if they do develop a technically correct form, the faculty almost always universally criticize the resultant product. The reason for this is simple: Any questionnaire, rating form, or other instrument, even if it meets professional psychometric standards, is predicated on certain assumptions, definitions, and values. If a committee designs and develops a form with which it is satisfied, it will have been based on the assumptions, definitions, and values of the members of the committee. However, the general faculty may not share these assumptions, definitions, and values. Thus, any form produced by the committee is almost inevitably criticized, if not rejected outright, by the faculty. Even if the faculty shares the committee's assumptions, definitions, and values, there is a strong feeling of disenfranchisement since they were not systematically consulted. The steps described in this book are designed to ensure that when the time comes to develop and/or select the tools to be used, the faculty feeling of disenfranchisement will have been drastically reduced, since they will, in fact, have been systematically consulted in the design of the entire system.

After systematic consultation with the faculty, you will have 1) clearly defined what it is you wish to measure, 2) determined from whom you wish to get the information, and 3) specified how you are going to gather the information. Now the design and/or selection of the forms and procedures becomes a relatively straightforward technical matter. There is no specific recipe for accomplishing the development of your forms and procedures. Rather, what is provided here is simply a word of caution and some resources.

The word of caution is, "Don't reinvent the wheel." Many rating forms have already been developed and are used in faculty evaluation systems around the country. In addition, there are a number of commercially available forms and systems available. Chapter 15 contains a description and technical review of several of the better-known commercially available student rating forms. In addition Chapter 15 provides guidelines for constructing a customized student rating form and includes a catalog of more than 500 sample items. Chapter 16 contains several case studies from institutions that developed their faculty evaluation systems using the approach in this book. Within these case studies are several examples of different forms and other documents developed and used by these institutions that may serve as useful guides in the design and/or selection of tools for your system.

Again, it is strongly recommended that experts in psychometrics be commissioned to design and develop a final set of forms. The Committee coordinating this project should not take on the task of developing and/or selecting the forms by itself—unless, of course, there are members of the Committee who possess expertise in psychometrics. The Committee, by going through the various steps in this book, will have determined all the specifications for *what* is to be measured and *who* is to be tapped for the information. These specifications, along with the data provided by faculty in FORMS 2A and 2B, provide sufficient directions for the technical team to follow in developing the questionnaires, rating forms, and protocols. Experience has shown that if the full Committee takes on this task, previous agreements can unravel once the item-by-item determination of the forms and questionnaires gets under way. Faculty unfamiliar with the principles of psychological measurement are likely to overlook the fact that well-designed questionnaires may include questions that, when taken in isolation, may appear inappropriate, but when taken in aggregate provide valid and reliable measures of the characteristic or role component in question. Anyone who has taken such instruments as the Minnesota Multiphasic Personality Inventory or the Myers-Briggs Type Indicator can appreciate the fact that questions, which individually may not seem to be related or even relevant can, in aggregate, provide accurate, valid, and reliable measures of various psychological characteristics.

COMMON NUMERICAL RATING SCALE

It is necessary to clarify one assumption before we move to actually constructing the forms, questionnaires, and protocols. We must assume that all information gathered from each source will be reported on a common scale.

That is, regardless of whether we use a questionnaire, a rating form, an interview schedule, or some other technique in gathering information from the various selected sources, that data needs to be reported on the same scale. For example, we may agree to assume that all information will use a 4-point scale where 1 is the lowest rating and 4 is the highest. That is, student ratings of instructional delivery would be reported on a scale from 1 to 4. Likewise, peer ratings of instructional design would be reported on a scale from 1 to 4, and so on. Thus, the Committee would need to specify the numerical scale to be used by all the tools before the various questionnaires, forms, and protocols were developed. The numerical scales used on most commercial forms, and in most comprehensive faculty evaluation systems, are the 4-point and 5-point scales. Neither scale is the best or right one. Rather, the scale you select should be appropriate to, and easily used in, the forms designed and/or selected for your system. Although it is possible to use scales with more points such as 7-point or 10-point scales, these larger scales are *not* recommended for the tools in your faculty evaluation system. Experience has shown that these scales give a false impression of providing a larger spread among the scores obtained by faculty. Frequently, however, the scores just tend to bunch up at the high end of the scale. Thus, for 7-point scales we often see the bulk of the scores at the 5, 6, and 7 end, and for 10-point scales the scores tend to fall at the 7, 8, 9, and 10 end. The better approach is to use a 4- or 5-point scale and make certain that the forms are constructed in accordance with professional psychometric procedures. Such well-designed forms can provide accurate information that can clearly discriminate between levels of performance without introducing the false accuracy of a 7- or 10-point scale.

FACULTY EVALUATION TOOLS AND PROCEDURES

Different forms in our system will ask different questions and will thus require different response options. Some forms may require the individual completing the form to either agree or disagree with certain statements. Some forms may require the individual to rate some performance as either satisfactory or unsatisfactory. Therefore, care must be exercised in choosing the correct response scale for each form. The response scale selected must fit the type of questions being asked and contain the same number of response categories as the *numerical* scale selected by the Committee. Figure 8.1 shows several examples of different response scales, all using a 4- or 5-point format, which would be appropriate for different types of questions.

Figure 8.1   Sample rating form response formats using either a 4- or 5-point common numerical scale

Agree–Disagree Scale				Good–Poor Scale				Satisfactory Scale			
(SA)	=	Strongly Agree	= 4	(VG)	=	Very Good	= 4	(HS)	=	Highly Satisfactory	= 4
(A)	=	Agree	= 3	(G)	=	Good	= 3	(S)	=	Satisfactory	= 3
(D)	=	Disagree	= 2	(P)	=	Poor	= 2	(U)	=	Unsatisfactory	= 2
(SD)	=	Strongly Disagree	= 1	(VP)	=	Very Poor	= 1	(HU)	=	Highly Unsatisfactory	= 1
(SA)	=	Strongly Agree	= 5	(VG)	=	Very Good	= 5	(HS)	=	Highly Satisfactory	= 5
(A)	=	Agree	= 4	(G)	=	Good	= 4	(S)	=	Satisfactory	= 4
(NA/D)	=	Neither Agree nor Disagree	= 3	(NG/P)	=	Neither Good nor Poor	= 3	(NS/U)	=	Neither Satisfactory nor Unsatisfactory	= 3
(D)	=	Disagree	= 2	(P)	=	Poor	= 2	(U)	=	Unsatisfactory	= 2
(SD)	=	Strongly Disagree	= 1	(VP)	=	Very Poor	= 1	(HU)	=	Highly Unsatisfactory	= 1

Arreola, R. A. (2007). *Developing a comprehensive faculty evaluation system* (3rd ed.). Bolton, MA: Anker.

Table 8.1 is a summary of a number of tools and procedures that have been used in evaluating faculty performance in teaching. It briefly overviews the strengths, weaknesses, and characteristics of each tool or procedure.

This listing is by no means exhaustive but, rather, simply summarizes a number of more commonly used tools and procedures for gathering data on teaching performance in faculty evaluation systems.

Table 8.1   Summary of tools and procedures used in evaluating faculty performance in teaching

Data-Gathering Approach	Student Ratings
Description of this approach	Students rate an instructor's performance through a structured or unstructured questionnaire or interview.
Purposes for which this approach is most appropriate	Help instructors improve. Identify faculty for merit recognition. Make personnel decisions.
Strengths of this approach	Can produce extremely reliable and valid information concerning faculty classroom performance, because students observe the teacher every day. Instructors are often motivated to change as a result of student feedback. Results show high correlation with other peer and supervisor ratings if a professionally designed student rating form is used. Assessments are reliable and not affected by grades if well-designed form is used.
Weaknesses	Unless a professionally developed student rating form is used, factors other than teacher performance (e.g., class size, time of day) may inappropriately contribute to student ratings. Students may tend to be generous in their ratings.
Conditions for effective use	Need student anonymity. Need teacher willingness to accept student feedback. Instruments must be carefully developed by appropriate reliability and validity studies.
Nature of evidence produced	Student perceptions of what they have learned, how they have changed. Student opinions of how various teaching acts affected them. Student reactions to instructor actions. Student perceptions of what they like and dislike about an instructor.

Data-Gathering Approach	Tests of Student Performance
Description of this approach	Measures of what students have learned or how they have changed over a period of time in working with the instructor.
Purposes for which this approach is most appropriate	Improve student learning. Identify teachers for merit recognition.
Strengths of this approach	Student attainment of objectives is a legitimate source of data on faculty performances. Measures impact of instructor on students over a period of time.
Weaknesses	Difficulty of designing appropriate tests. Gains on standardized tests often an inadequate measure of performance. Other factors may considerably affect performance (e.g., student intelligence, family background, previous schooling).
Conditions for effective use	Must have systematic and comprehensive data collection plan. Need personnel skilled in collecting performance data.
Nature of evidence produced	Student work samples. Test results (standardized and others). Attitude measures.

Data-Gathering Approach	Simulated Teaching
Description of this approach	Brief unit taught to a special selected group of students on content normally *not* taught by the instructor with pre- and post-test measures of student gains in the content.
Purposes for which this approach is most appropriate	Improve student learning. Make personnel decisions.
Strengths of this approach	Evaluates instructor skills in terms of student learning. Provides short-term feedback. Increases control over non-teacher variables assumed to influence student.
Weaknesses	Does not allow for assessing student growth over time. Expensive to conduct. Not a normal classroom situation.
Conditions for effective use	Need personnel trained in design of controlled situation evaluations and in student performance testing. Requires extra teacher preparation time.
Nature of evidence produced	Evidence on student learning under controlled conditions.

Arreola, R. A. (2007). *Developing a comprehensive faculty evaluation system* (3rd ed.). Bolton, MA: Anker.

Data-Gathering Approach	Self-Evaluation
Description of this approach	Instructor uses various means to gather information to assess performance relative to own needs, goals, and objectives.
Purposes for which this approach is most appropriate	Help instructors improve. Determine best assignments.
Strengths of this approach	May be used as part of a program of continuous assessment. Faculty are more likely to act on data that they collect themselves. The data collected are more clearly related to a faculty member's own goals and needs.
Weaknesses	Results not consistent with other raters. May be unwilling to collect and/or consider data relative to own performance. Tend to rate themselves higher than students do.
Conditions for effective use	Instructor must have self-confidence and security. Need skills in identifying goals and collecting appropriate data. Must not be weighted highly in the determination of personnel decisions (promotion, tenure, merit pay, etc.)
Nature of evidence produced	Information on progress toward one's own goals.
Data-Gathering Approach	**Department Head Observation**
Description of this approach	Administrators evaluate an instructor's performance through classroom observation, review of student learning data, feedback from students.
Purposes for which this approach is most appropriate	Guide professional growth and development *only.* The information produced should *not* be used for personnel decisions unless the supervisor is a part of a team of observers who use a standardized observation tool on which they have been trained, and have made sufficiently frequent observations to produce measures with high inter-rater reliabilities.
Strengths of this approach	Supervisor is familiar with college and community goals, priorities, and values and may often have additional information about faculty performance. Can compare instructors within the college, school, division, or department. Requires minimal resources for observation, feedback, and follow up.
Weaknesses	Bias due to previous data, personal relationships, reason for observation, own values, and favored teaching methods. Situation being observed is, by definition, not normal because the observer is present.
Conditions for effective use	Supervisor/peer must have adequate time and observational and review skills. Observation must focus on characteristics of teaching that research has established relates to desired student outcomes.
Nature of evidence produced	Comments on relations between instructor acts and student behaviors. Information on how instructors compare on certain factors. Comparisons with other methods supervisors may consider to be good. Directions on changes to be made.

Arreola, R. A. (2007). *Developing a comprehensive faculty evaluation system* (3rd ed.). Bolton, MA: Anker.

Data-Gathering Approach	Peer Ratings and Observations
Description of this approach	Other faculty rate an instructor's performance through classroom observation, and the review of the course design, the appropriateness and effectiveness of instructional support materials, and the appropriateness of instructional assessment strategies and tools.
Purposes for which this approach is most appropriate	Guide professional growth and development. Information produced should *not* be used for personnel decisions unless peer is a part of a team of observers who use a standardized observation tool and who have been trained and have made sufficiently frequent observations to produce inter-rater reliability of the data. (See Chapter 11 for a more detailed discussion of the characteristics of peer evaluation.)
Strengths of this approach	Familiar with college (department/division) goals, priorities, values, and problems facing the faculty. Encourages professional behavior (e.g., motivation to help upgrade own profession). Can be chosen from instructor's subject area and thus may be able to give content-specific suggestions and recommendations.
Weaknesses	Bias due to previous data, personal relationships, or peer pressure to influence evaluation. Relationships among peers may suffer. Possible bias due to evaluator's preference for his or her own teaching method.
Conditions for effective use	Requires high degree of professional ethics and objectivity. Requires training in observational and analysis skills. Need time for multiple reviews.
Nature of evidence produced	Comments on relations between instructor acts and student behaviors. Comparisons with other methods peers may consider to be good. Suggestions for instructors on methods, etc., to use.

Data-Gathering Approach	Visiting Team of Experts
Description of this approach	People external to the system recognized as qualified in faculty (teacher) evaluation procedures observe faculty performance and/or review student learning data.
Purposes for which this approach is most appropriate	Guide professional growth and development. Aid in making personnel decisions. If data are to be used for personnel decisions, the team of experts must have been trained and have made sufficiently frequent observations to produce inter-rater reliability of the data.
Strengths of this approach	Can select evaluators with special skills. External to politics, problems, and biases of the institution. Provides reliable data through pooling of independent ratings.
Weaknesses	Bias of evaluators due to own values, preferences, etc. Evaluators not accountable to the academic unit (college, school, division, department, etc.).
Conditions for effective use	Experts must be properly selected, oriented, and trained. Need time for multiple observations and reviews. Must use a standardized observer rating form on which team has been trained.
Nature of evidence produced	Comments on relations between instructor acts and student behaviors. Comparisons with other methods the experts may consider to be better or more effective. Suggestions for teachers on methods, etc., to use.

Arreola, R. A. (2007). *Developing a comprehensive faculty evaluation system* (3rd ed.). Bolton, MA: Anker.

Once the questionnaires, protocols, checklists, and other forms have been designed, the system is ready to be implemented. This assumes, however, that the appropriate support systems have been developed and put in place as noted in the introduction of this book.

The following timetable (Table 8.2) has been found to be typical in the successful development of a comprehensive faculty evaluation system.

Table 8.2   Timetable for Developing and Implementing a Comprehensive Faculty Evaluation System

	Typical Timetable for Development and Implementation of a Comprehensive Faculty Evaluation System
Month 1	Appoint the Committee responsible for coordinating the development of the comprehensive faculty evaluation system. Familiarize the Committee with system development procedures. Hold general faculty meeting, sponsored by the Committee, during which the steps in the procedure to be carried out are presented and explained.
Months 2–6	The Committee distributes the FORMS specified in the various steps to departments and proceeds with the development of the faculty role model, definitions of roles and role components, specification of the weights for the roles and role components, identification of sources of information, and determination of weights for each source. *Note: This part of the process can be accelerated considerably by conducting Steps 1, 2, and 3 in a single, all-day faculty workshop as described in the action checklist in Step 3.*
Month 7	The Committee reports to the general faculty the total value structure and role definitions as determined by faculty input.
Months 7–12	System forms and protocols are designed, selected, and developed. Policy decisions concerning confidentiality and the use of the information in promotion, tenure, and merit pay decisions are finalized.
Months 12–24	Pilot the system. Debug system and make adjustments. One common strategy is to use volunteers among the faculty for the pilot run. At the end of the trial the Committee and the volunteers may present the results of using the system to the general faculty. This is a time of stress, however, because decisions concerning promotion, tenure, and merit pay will still have to be based on the old system that is to be modified or phased out.
Month 25	Full implementation of the completed system.

Arreola, R. A. (2007). *Developing a comprehensive faculty evaluation system* (3rd ed.). Bolton, MA: Anker.

Figure 8.2   Action Checklist for Completing Step 8

Action Checklist for Completing Step 8

Expected Outcome: The outcome of Step 8 is the development of the tools or data-gathering strategies (questionnaires, rating forms, interviews, etc.) to be used in obtaining information from the various sources concerning the faculty performance in the components of the roles in the Faculty Role Model.

____ The Committee should consult with test and measurement experts when beginning the process of developing the tools and procedures required. It is *not* recommended that the Committee simply start developing forms by assembling questions or items submitted by faculty or committee members. It must be kept in mind that a form designed to gather opinions, reactions, observations, etc., must accurately and reliably measure sophisticated psychological phenomena. The Committee may wish to consult the resources listed below in completing this step:

Brace, I. (2004). *Questionnaire design: How to plan, structure, and write survey material for effective market research.* Sterling, VA: Kogan Page.

Bradburn, N. M., Sudman, S., & Associates (1979). *Improving interview method and questionnaire design.* San Francisco, CA: Jossey-Bass.

Converse, J. M., & Presser, S. (1986). *Survey questions: Handcrafting the standardized questionnaire.* Beverly Hills, CA: Sage.

Payne, S. L. (1951). *The Art of Asking Questions.* Princeton, NJ: Princeton University Press.

Sudman, S., & Bradburn, N.M. (1983). *Asking questions: A practical guide to questionnaire design.* San Francisco, CA: Jossey-Bass.

Arreola, R. A. (2007). *Developing a comprehensive faculty evaluation system* (3rd ed.). Bolton, MA: Anker.

Generating an Overall Composite Rating

In developing your comprehensive faculty evaluation system as specified in Steps 1–8, you have made the following determinations:

1) Which faculty roles should be evaluated

2) To what degree the evaluation of any one role may impact the total evaluation of an individual

3) What the defining activities or components for each role are

4) How much weight each component contributes to the overall role definition

5) Where information about each role is to be gathered

6) How much the information from each source will impact or influence the total evaluative outcome

7) What methods and forms should be used to gather the information specified from the various sources

8) Developed and/or selected appropriate valid and reliable forms, protocols, or other data-gathering tools and strategies for obtaining the required information from the specified sources

At this point you are ready to begin using the system. The task now is to combine all the data resulting from the system into a usable form. Previously it was determined that all information gathered from each source would be reported on a common scale. In our examples we have used a common 1 to 4 scale where 4 is the highest rating and 1 is the lowest. That is, regardless of whether a questionnaire, an interview schedule, or some other technique has been used in gathering evaluative information from the various sources identified, that data will be reported on the same 1 to 4 scale. Thus, student ratings, peer ratings, department head ratings, et cetera will all be reported on a scale of 1 to 4. This is not to suggest that 5-point or other point scales may not be used in a comprehensive system, merely that whatever scale is used must be consistent throughout the system.

COMPUTING THE COMPOSITE ROLE RATING

Having determined and specified the weights to be assigned to various activities and sources in the overall faculty evaluation system, it is now possible to compute an overall rating for each role that reflects the collective values of the faculty. This rating will be referred to as the composite role rating (CRR) because it will be derived from information from a variety of sources. Each source will provide information concerning various components of each role. The information from each source concerning each component of each role will be weighted in ways that reflect the consensus value structure of the institution. That is, the overall rating will be determined using the principle of controlled subjectivity discussed in the introduction. The following is an example of how the composite role rating for teaching would be computed.

In Figure 6.5 we determined that the information students provided concerning the faculty member's instructional delivery would impact the overall rating of the teaching role by 30%. Likewise, student information concerning the instructional design component would count 10%, and peer information would count 30%. We also determined that student input on instructional assessment would count 5%, peer input would count 15%, and department head input would count 5%. Finally, it was determined that department head input concerning course management would count 5% of the overall rating on teaching.

Figure 9.1 shows these weights along with the rating each source has given each role component. Note that all ratings, shown in brackets, use the common scale of 1 to 4. Here the students rated the instructor 4 on instructional delivery. Because it was determined in Figure 6.5 that whatever data the students provided concerning the instructional delivery component would count as 30% of the overall evaluation of the teaching role, we simply multiply the rating of 4 by 30% to arrive at a weighted rating of 1.2. In a similar fashion, the ratings provided by the various sources on the different components of the teaching role are multiplied by their impact weights. Finally, all weighted ratings are added together to form a CRR of 3.45. For ease of computation, the ratings in Figure 9.1 are shown as whole numbers. In actual practice, the ratings may be averages and may thus include decimal values.

Note that the CRR of 3.45 was not determined or assigned by any one student, peer, or administrator. Rather, this value represents a composite of the information concerning activities the faculty agreed should be evaluated, collected from sources that were agreed to be appropriate,

and weighted to reflect the credibility of the sources and the relative importance of each component of the entire role. Although the CRR does not represent an objective measure, the subjectivity involved in computing it has been carefully controlled and prescribed by the values assigned to the sources and role components. Thus, any two faculty members with the exact same component ratings would obtain the exact same composite role rating. This demonstrates the essence of controlled subjectivity in that we are able to obtain consistency of evaluative conclusions based on the same data. A similar procedure would be followed in determining the composite role ratings for the other roles (e.g., scholarly and creative activities, service to the institution, etc.)

■ INDIVIDUALIZING THE EVALUATIONS: THE OVERALL COMPOSITE RATING (OCR)

One of the first steps in developing our comprehensive faculty evaluation system was to establish a faculty role model with minimum and maximum parameter values, reflecting the values and priorities of the faculty and administration of the institution. These minimum and maximum values were expressions of the variability that may appropriately occur in faculty assignments. Using the matrices and values developed to this point, it is now possible to begin individualizing the evaluations of different faculty.

Figure 9.1   Computation of the Composite Role Rating for Teaching

Role Components	Sources						Weighted Rating
	Students		Peers		Dept. Chair		
	Source Impact Weight	Source Rating	Source Impact Weight	Source Rating	Source Impact Weight	Source Rating	
Instructional Design	[10% x	3] +	[30%	x 3] +	0%		= 1.20
Instructional Delivery	[30% x	4] +	0%		0%		= 1.20
Instructional Assessment	[5% x	3] +	[15%	x 4] +	(5%	x 4)	= .95
Course Management	0%		0%		(5%	x 2)	= .10
Composite Role Rating							*3.45*

Arreola, R. A. (2007). *Developing a comprehensive faculty evaluation system* (3rd ed.). Bolton, MA: Anker.

Assume that Professor Drake has received the composite role ratings shown in Figure 9.2. The individual composite role ratings for all the roles shown for Professor Drake were computed in the same way as the CRR for teaching was computed in Figure 9.1. That is, each composite role rating is the result of gathering specific information from specified sources, weighted in ways that reflect the value system of the faculty and the institution. Of course, it is possible to stop at this point and use the various CRRs separately. However, using them in isolation does not permit us to reflect the specific nature of Professor Drake's assignment and thus produce a fairer evaluation picture.

Assume that Professor Drake is on the faculty at an institution that has the faculty role model as shown in Figure 9.3. This model specifies a minimum of 50% weight on teaching and a maximum of 85%; a minimum of 0% and a maximum of 35% for scholarly and creative activities; a minimum of 10% and a maximum of 25% for service to the institution; and a minimum of 5% and a maximum of 15% for service to the community. Further, assume that Professor Drake's specific combination of professional duties and responsibilities has been assigned the weights shown in Figure 9.4.

In Figure 9.4 the 50% weighting for teaching for Professor Drake does not necessarily imply a 50% teaching load. Rather, it simply reflects the fact that, given the particular roles the faculty member is engaged in, it has been agreed that whatever rating Professor Drake receives for the teaching role will count 50% of the comprehensive overall rating.

To combine Professor Drake's several separate CRR ratings into an overall composite rating, we simply multiply each composite role rating by the assignment weights shown in Figure 9.4 and compute the total. These computations are shown in Figure 9.5.

Note that Professor Drake's OCR of 3.34 was not determined by any single individual or group. Rather, the OCR may be considered a true evaluation since it was assembled by gathering information from multiple (agreed-upon) sources, weighted in ways that reflect the agreed-upon credibility of those sources, and further weighted by the assignment emphasis for this faculty member. That is, given the particular assignment Professor Drake had this year, the various appropriate sources provided a mosaic of information that is expressed in the OCR. This approach permits us to more fairly compare the ratings of two faculty who may have considerably different assignments. For example, look at the OCR computation for a different faculty member, Professor Lamb, as shown in Figure 9.6.

The assigned role weights for Professor Lamb differ considerably from those of Professor Drake. Note that Pro-

Figure 9.3   Hypothetical Faculty Role Model for Professor Drake's Institution

Minimum Weight	Faculty Role	Maximum Weight
50%	Teaching	85%
0%	Scholarly and Creative Activities	35%
10%	Service to the Institution	25%
5%	Service to the Community	15%

Figure 9.2   Composite Role Ratings for Professor Drake

Role Ratings for Professor Drake	
Roles	Composite Role Ratings
Teaching	3.45
Scholarly and Creative Activities	3.20
Service to the Institution	3.60
Service to the Community	2.60

Figure 9.4   Assigned Role Weights for Professor Drake

Role Assignment Weights for Professor Drake	
Role	Assigned Weight
Teaching	50%
Scholarly and Creative Activities	35%
Service to the Institution	10%
Service to the Community	5%

Arreola, R. A. (2007). *Developing a comprehensive faculty evaluation system* (3rd ed.). Bolton, MA: Anker.

fessor Lamb did not engage in any scholarly and creative activities, as indicated by the absence of that role. This was permissible since the faculty role model for this faculty member (shown in Figure 9.3) allows a minimum value of 0% to that role. However, Professor Lamb's greater emphasis in teaching is reflected in the maximum weight (85%) given the teaching role. Thus, if we consider the OCR to be an index of success within their different configurations of professional responsibilities and duties, it can readily be seen that Professor Drake and Professor Lamb, with OCR's of 3.34 and 3.35, respectively, were rated as essentially equally successful in accomplishing their specific assignments. Again, it should be noted that no one individual assigned these rating values to professors Drake and Lamb. Rather, their overall composite ratings are the result of information gathered from a number of appropriate sources, weighted so that they reflect the value structure of the institution as well as the individual faculty member.

▪ RESPONDING TO CONCERNS IN USING A SINGLE NUMERICAL INDEX (OCR)

The development of the OCR as a single numerical index representing a summary of a faculty member's professional performance provides the academic decision-maker with the kind of numerical index that student rating averages are often used as, but never really are. That is, a singular value has been computed which represents a valid and reliable measure of a complex set of behaviors and performances and which takes into account the interaction between the values of the institution and the person being evaluated. Although the assignment of a singular numerical index to represent complex human performance may be criticized, it is a practice used throughout society and in education especially. Colleges and universities routinely make critical decisions and award scholarships, certificates and degrees on the basis of summary singular numerical

Figure 9.5   Computation of Professor Drake's Overall Composite Rating

OCR Computation for Professor Drake					
Role	Assigned Weight		Composite Role Rating (CRR)		Weighted Composite Rating
Teaching	50%	x	3.45	=	1.73
Scholarly & Creative Activities	35%	x	3.20	=	1.12
Service to the Institution	10%	x	3.60	=	0.36
Service to the Community	5%	x	2.60	=	0.13
Overall Composite Rating (OCR)					*3.34*

Figure 9.6   Computation of Professor Lamb's OCR

OCR Computation for Professor Lamb					
Role	Assigned Weight		Composite Role Rating (CRR)		Weighted Composite Rating
Teaching	85%	x	3.53	=	3.00
Service to the Institution	10%	x	2.00	=	0.20
Service to the Community	5%	x	2.90	=	0.15
Overall Composite Rating (OCR)					*3.35*

Arreola, R. A. (2007). *Developing a comprehensive faculty evaluation system* (3rd ed.). Bolton, MA: Anker.

indices of complex human behavior (i.e., student GPAs). As a profession, we are not unfamiliar or unskilled in this practice.

Criticisms may also be made that using a singular numerical index such as the OCR can fool us into making significant decisions on the basis of insignificant differences, such as in the examples of Professors Drake and Lamb whose ratings differed by only 0.01. This is an important issue that must be considered.

The criticism that small numerical differences in faculty evaluation results cannot be used to make significant decisions would be well founded if the OCR were a singular measure. It is important to recognize that an OCR value represents an aggregate of measurements. More specifically, it is computed as the weighted sum of a variety of measures derived from tools and procedures specifically designed and/or selected to produce valid and reliable data gathered as objectively as possible. The OCR, then, is a numerical expression of the sum of the measurement data weighted by subjective values. However, these subjective values have been predetermined in the design of the system and are specifically reflective of the institution's value system. These values are embedded in the definition of each role and the specification of the role weights, role component weights, identified sources, source weights, and individual assignment weights.

Of course appropriate care must be taken to ensure that the forms, protocols, or other measurement strategies provide accurate, valid, and reliable measures of faculty performance. Careful attention to, and application of, professional psychometric principles in the design and/or selection of such tools and strategies will ensure this. In considering this issue it is important to ask what alternative may be used in making significant decisions on the basis of what some may consider insignificant differences in the numerical ratings of individuals.

One alternative often mentioned is to round the OCR values from the nearest hundredth to the nearest tenth. However, this provides no real solution since the same objection can still be made in the difference between tenths of a point as it was between hundredths of a point.

A second alternative often suggested is to take other factors into account besides the OCR in making decisions. The flaw in this suggestion, however, is that if the faculty evaluation system were developed as specified in Steps 1 through 8, all relevant performances and evidence would have already been taken into account. Thus, to consider any other factor at the time of making a significant

decision would be, by definition, to inject irrelevant data into the evaluation system.

A third alternative that is sometimes suggested is that faculty be placed within groups representing a range of rating values and that everyone within the group is treated the same in terms of any personnel decisions. Although this approach can find some use in the distribution of merit pay (see Chapter 10), the flaw in this suggestion is that someone may still miss being put into a particular grouping by a hundredth or tenth of a point and we are left with the same problem.

The only practical response to this situation is to make sure that the all definitions, criteria, and standards within the faculty evaluation system have been clearly specified and that they relate to observable or documentable products, performances, or achievements. Further, ensure that all forms used in the system have been constructed using accepted professional psychometric techniques and that all forms are as valid, reliable, objective, and accurate as possible. However, regardless of the accuracy of the measures they are not going to be perfect. No matter where the cutoff for a decision point is set, there is always the possibility that someone will just miss it. Since mathematical and psychometric accuracy can take us just so far, we must be prepared to take a policy stance and stick to it. Nothing is worse than an inconsistent evaluation process.

Finally, make certain that those performances considered important (significant) and those which are considered less important (not significant) are given the appropriate values or weights in the faculty evaluation system. If this is done then the final aggregate of measures, even though they may differ by only a tenth or hundredth of a point, will reflect issues and performances that the faculty considers to be important. It is preferable to make significant decisions on the basis of small differences along relevant and appropriate dimensions than to make significant decisions on the basis of larger differences in irrelevant and inappropriate dimensions. See the section in Chapter 11 on the alternate peer review model (Figure 11.5) for a more detailed discussion on policy strategies for dealing with this and other problems.

With the computation of an individualized OCR, which can be correctly characterized as an index of perceived success, we now possess an aggregate measure that may appropriately be used in decisions concerning promotion, tenure, continuation, and merit pay. The OCR also provides important information for post-tenure review considerations.

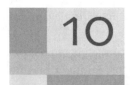

10

Using the OCR in Promotion, Tenure, Merit Pay, and Post-Tenure Review Decisions

Computing an overall composite rating (OCR) in the manner described to this point greatly simplifies the use of faculty evaluation information in making several personnel decisions including:

- Promotion

- Continuation of contract

- Tenure

- Post-tenure review

- Merit pay raises

Decisions regarding the determination and distribution of merit raises are fundamentally different from those concerning other personnel decisions. It is important to recognize this difference in the establishment of the policies that will guide these decisions.

Promotion, tenure (or continuation), and post-tenure review decisions are based essentially on a prediction concerning the faculty member's *future* performance. When we promote someone from the rank of assistant professor to that of associate professor, the underlying prediction is that the faculty member will continue to perform at a level that is appropriate to an associate professor. If we decide to tenure or award a continuing contract to someone, we are making a prediction that they will continue to perform in a manner that will be of value to the institution. If a post-tenure evaluation determines that a tenured professor is performing below minimally acceptable standards despite opportunities to improve, the prediction is that the faculty member will persist in that poor performance and thus the institution may initiate termination procedures.

Merit pay decisions, on the other hand, are based on the recognition of meritorious performance during the evaluation period. The intent is to reward that meritorious performance and encourage continued meritorious performance. Thus, promotion, tenure, continuation, and post-tenure review decisions require data on which to base a prediction of future performance, and merit pay decisions require data on which to base a reward for *past* performance.

The best data we can use on which to base a prediction concerning a person's future performance is their *pattern of performance over time.* Personnel decisions should be based on information that clearly demonstrates the pattern of performance of a faculty member over a specified length of time, preferably several years. The particular student ratings for one class, the peer critiques of a single article, or similar such specific data are rarely appropriate for making decisions of this sort. Thus, for a faculty evaluation system to be truly effective for personnel decisions, it must gather an aggregate of relevant performance data and demonstrate a pattern of performance over some specified length of time. Generally, positive personnel decisions are based on a body of evidence that says, in essence, "no matter what the professional responsibilities assigned, this faculty member achieves a certain level of success time after time." The system you will have developed up to this point using the steps specified in this book can provide the academic decision-maker with valid, reliable, relevant information concerning the pattern of performance and level of success of a faculty member over time.

■ PROMOTION DECISIONS

Making the decision whether to promote a faculty member is significantly simplified using the OCR. It is assumed, of course, that the institution has policies concerning the length of time faculty members must be in a given rank or level before they are eligible for promotion to the next rank or level. The following is an example of a simplified version of such a policy that specifies the use of the OCR in promotion decisions:

Promotion Policy Statement

Promotions from one rank to the next are based on the achievement of a specified minimum overall composite rating (OCR) for a specified number of years. Ratings are based on a 4-point scale where 4 is the highest rating and 1 is the lowest.

To be promoted from assistant professor to associate professor, the applicant must have served as an assistant professor, or the equivalent, for at least four consecutive years and must have achieved a minimum OCR of 2.75 for the three consecutive years prior to consideration for promotion.

Note this policy statement indicates that the applicant must have served a specified minimum number of years as an assistant professor and must have achieved a specified minimum overall composite rating for a set number of years prior to the application for promotion. The minimum number of years in rank in this example is arbitrary, as is the value of 2.75. Different institutions may have varying requirements concerning length of time in rank. However, the point is that such a policy statement makes it clear that the applicant must achieve and sustain a certain level of success for the three years prior to applying for promotion from assistant to associate professor. An effective way to display the information required in making personnel decisions is to maintain a graph of the yearly OCR values of the a faculty member. The following graph (Figure 10.1) shows a faculty member's pattern of performance over several consecutive years. The graph is prepared by plotting the OCR value resulting from the annual faculty evaluation process for each year the instructor has been on the faculty.

In Figure 10.1 we can see that, although the faculty member got off to a slow start, over the years the pattern of performance shows continuous growth. Not only does

Figure 10.1 Graph of a Faculty Member's OCR Values From 2001–2007

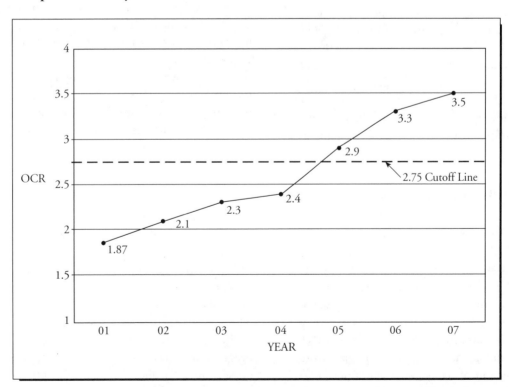

Arreola, R. A. (2007). *Developing a comprehensive faculty evaluation system* (3rd ed.). Bolton, MA: Anker.

the faculty member meet the technical requirements for promotion from assistant to associate professor (OCR greater than 2.75 for the last three consecutive years), but the overall pattern of performance gives us confidence in predicting that the faculty member will continue to perform at a high level.

Note that it is the pattern of performance over time that is important. Also, by specifying a minimum overall composite rating (in this case 2.75), one can ensure that, regardless of the assignment given, this faculty member is able to consistently achieve a level of success that is comparable to faculty already at the associate professor level. One suggested approach to determining the cutoff value for the overall composite rating for promotion from assistant to associate professor is to determine the *average* overall composite rating for associate professors and set the minimum entry level at one-half of one standard deviation below that average. Similar policy statements with different times in rank and different (higher) cutoff values could be developed for promotion from associate to full professor.

■ TENURE DECISIONS

Even more than decisions concerning promotion, the decision whether to tenure or grant a continuing contract needs to be based on the complete performance history. Again, the concern is what prediction concerning future performance can be made from the faculty evaluation data. As noted in the preceding example, promotion decisions may be based on an individual's achieving and sustaining a specified level of performance in the three years prior to application for promotion. Tenure decisions, however, should be based on the individual's pattern of performance over the *entire* span of time the faculty member has been employed at the institution. The following is a simplified example of the type of policy statement that applies the OCR to tenure decisions:

Policy for Awarding Tenure

The awarding of tenure is determined, in part, on achieving a minimum average overall composite rating (OCR) of 2.5 for the entire length of time the faculty member has been employed by the college. Tenure may not be granted to anyone who has had more than two consecutive years of declining OCR values below 2.5 even if they meet the 2.5 average OCR value criterion. No faculty member may be awarded tenure before the completion of five years of continuous employment with the institution. However, credit may be given for previous employment as specified in the initial appointment letter. It is noted that the number of applicants for tenure in any given year may exceed the number of available tenure positions as determined by the Board of Regents. Thus achieving the required OCR in the fifth year of employment does not automatically ensure the granting of tenure in the subsequent academic year.

This policy statement specifies a level of success as indicated by the average overall composite rating for the entire length of time the faculty member has worked at the institution. Again, it is the pattern of performance over time that is being used to make the decision. This policy implies that, regardless of the mix of professional responsibilities or the normal ups and downs that affect most careers, on the average the faculty member is able to perform at such a level that the college is willing to make a long-term commitment for continued employment. The policy also specifies that a prolonged decline in performance (more than two years) below the cutoff value of 2.5 disqualifies the applicant for tenure regardless of their average OCR value over the length of their employment. By using the complete OCR pattern, one or two bad years do not automatically disqualify the person from applying for and being awarded tenure, although prolonged decline does. The following examples provide three general possibilities.

Figure 10.2 shows the pattern of performance over time for a faculty member being considered for the granting of tenure (or continuing contract). Note that the pattern of performance, as indicated by the OCR values in the graph, shows a consistent growth in performance level from year to year. This graph takes on special significance when we realize that the OCR values are expressions of the success the faculty member achieved in a given year's assignment of professional duties. Thus, even if a faculty member's mix of professional duties changes from year to year, the OCR graph gives us a powerful tool in making decisions. In this first example not only does the faculty member qualify technically (i.e., the average OCR value across the length of time of employment is 2.5 or greater), the pattern of performance over time strongly suggests a high probability of continued high levels of performance.

The growth in performance documented in Figure 10.2 might be the function of simple maturation on the part of a new doctoral graduate in his or her first academic position, the result of a concerted faculty development program offered by the institution, or both.

Figure 10.3 shows a somewhat different pattern of performance over time. As with the previous example, the faculty member technically qualifies for tenure since the average OCR value is greater than 2.5. However, this pattern demonstrates another benefit of maintaining OCR graphs. The obvious dip that occurs in the middle of the graph in this example is indicative of a sudden change in the performance level. The cause for such a change in performance could be due to many factors, including a death in the family, a divorce, a stroke, an accident, or a departmental change in the required texts of several courses. Or, it could have been the result of a new experimental teaching technique that required some adjustment but ultimately resulted in even better performance after the adjustment was completed. Noting sudden declines in performance at the time they occur provides a powerful tool for identifying faculty who may require support and thus provides a link to possible faculty development efforts. The OCR graphs also provide a useful tool as part of departmental, college, or institutional program evaluations in providing evidence of faculty performance without the necessity of identifying individuals. OCR graphs may also be used to monitor the effect of administrative changes in policy or the restructuring of resources.

Figure 10.4 shows an OCR graph of a faculty member whose performance started out well upon hiring but has progressively deteriorated over time. This might be called the flash-in-the-pan faculty performance pattern. Here, the faculty member achieves an average OCR value greater than 2.5 for the entire length of employment. However, the pattern of performance indicates several years of continuous decline below the 2.5 level. This pattern strongly supports a prediction that the faculty member's performance may continue to deteriorate in the future. Accordingly, the policy requirement that no one may be tenured if they have a decline below the 2.5 cutoff value for more than two years disqualifies this person from being granted tenure.

Again, the OCR graph provides decision-makers with a means of taking appropriate action on declining performance at the time it occurs. In the case of the faculty member whose graph is shown in Figure 10.4, some sort of professional development intervention would be well advised at the time of the third consecutive year of decline before it falls below the established cutoff of value of 2.5.

In reality, the pattern of performance shown in Figure 10.4 should never be allowed to occur. Such patterns on the part of one or more faculty within an academic unit may serve as indicators of possible poor performance on the part of the academic administrator responsible for monitoring faculty performance and assisting in their continued growth and development.

Figure 10.2 Pattern of Performance Indicating Continuous Growth

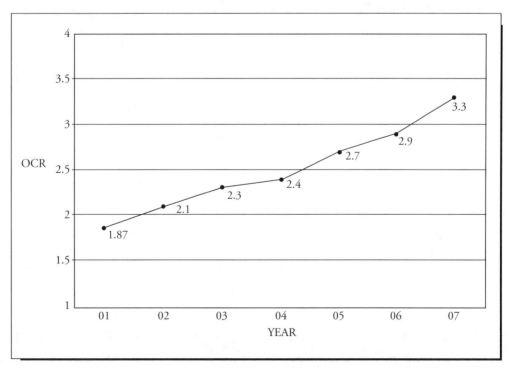

Arreola, R. A. (2007). *Developing a comprehensive faculty evaluation system* (3rd ed.). Bolton, MA: Anker.

In response to intense societal demands for accountability, there is a growing movement in the direction of a tenure-free academic environment among colleges and universities. The increased use of adjunct and nontenure-track faculty is partial evidence of this movement. The other is the adoption and implementation of a post-tenure review process.

Although virtually every post-tenure review policy speaks to the intent to promote continuous professional growth and development and thus facilitate and promote

Figure 10.3 Pattern of Performance Indicating a Sudden Change

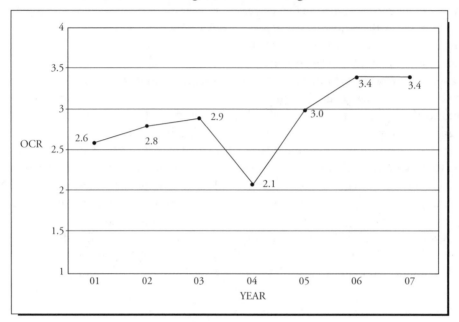

Figure 10.4 Declining Pattern of Performance

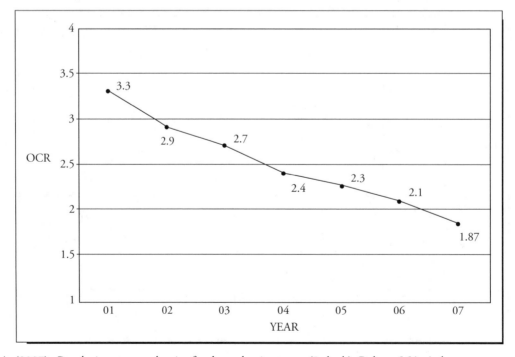

Arreola, R. A. (2007). *Developing a comprehensive faculty evaluation system* (3rd ed.). Bolton, MA: Anker.

excellence, the heart of each policy statement is to provide a mechanism for the termination of tenured faculty. Thus there is little doubt that the primary purpose of the post-tenure review process is to provide a mechanism for systematically gathering data on which to base the termination of tenured faculty whose performance no longer meets accepted professional standards.

Although proponents of post-tenure review speak to its value in promoting professional development, opponents see it as a threat to the entire concept of academic freedom (American Association of University Professors, 1998). In truth, post-tenure review is the academic community's response to society's demand to get rid of the deadwood among the faculty (i.e., those tenured faculty who have ceased to perform at an acceptable professional level but remain employed simply by virtue of being tenured).

The relationship among tenure, post-tenure review, and faculty evaluation in general is best understood in terms of the shifting of responsibilities. Before granting tenure it is the responsibility of the faculty member to provide evidence to the institution in support of continued employment. That is, prior to tenure, a faculty member may be terminated without great effort. His or her faculty appointment simply does not have to be renewed the following year. Of course institutions have different policies on how and when and under what conditions a nontenured faculty member may be terminated. Fundamentally, however, it is the responsibility of the faculty member to provide evidence in support of the continuation of their faculty appointment.

After the granting of tenure the responsibility shifts. Whereas before tenure it is the responsibility of the faculty member to show why he or she should continue to be employed, after tenure it becomes the institution's responsibility to provide evidence for why the faculty member should not continue to be employed. This constitutes a subtle but significant shift in responsibility with great ramifications. There have always been policies in place to terminate tenured faculty, which have generally revolved around egregiously offensive and/or illegal behavior on the part of the faculty member. The post-tenure review process, however, adds the element of nonsatisfactory professional performance to this mix.

This shift in responsibility is based on a new assumption. Prior to post-tenure review the underlying assumption has been that tenured faculty would continue to perform at a satisfactory professional level and that no further evaluation was necessary. However, the underlying assumption of post-tenure review policies is that the professional performance of tenured faculty may fall to unacceptable levels and remain there.

The previous assumption speaks to an earlier, golden age when college professors where held in high regard by society—often on par with physicians and clergy. The latter assumption speaks to the practical reality of today's information-age society. Under post-tenure review it becomes the responsibility of the tenured faculty member to periodically provide evidence that his or her professional performance has not fallen to an unacceptable level.

Interestingly, this subtle but significant shift in responsibility does little to change the landscape in terms of faculty evaluation. Prior to tenure faculty evaluation data is generally gathered systematically every year. It is in the faculty member's best interest to participate in the faculty evaluation system and systematically gather evidence in support of his or her continued employment. In addition, as discussed elsewhere in this book, gathering evidence that conveys an accurate picture of the faculty member's pattern of professional performance over time can provide substantial support for promotion and tenure applications.

Traditionally, tenured faculty have not had to be overly concerned with faculty evaluation. Historically, colleges and universities have tended to make participation in the faculty evaluation process optional for tenured faculty. Some universities have even adopted polices which specify that tenured faculty are never to be evaluated again. Most post-tenure review policies, however, specify that a preliminary evaluation, or check of a tenured faculty member's performance take place once every five or seven years. If the check is negative, then the full-blown, post-tenure review process is initiated. These post-tenure review processes often take a form similar, if not identical to, the evaluation procedure used for awarding tenure in the first place. Heavy peer evaluation is often a component, with special emphasis placed on research. Student ratings may also be seen as a component in providing evidence of the quality of teaching performance. If substandard performance or performance that would be inconsistent with the granting of tenure in the first place is detected, then a process of focused improvement efforts are initiated. If performance does not improve, then termination procedures are initiated. (Banks, 1997)

Although continuous participation by tenured faculty in the faculty evaluation may be recommended, generally most post-tenure review policies do not mandate it. However, since a significant responsibility has been shifted back to the faculty member (i.e., to provide evidence that his or her professional performance has *not* fallen to unacceptable levels), it continues to be in their best self-interest to participate continuously in a systematic faculty evaluation process. In the absence of the data provided by continuous participation in the faculty evaluation process, the tenured faculty member may find himself or herself in a position of having to assemble evidence for a post-tenure review committee in a fashion similar to when he or she first applied for tenure.

Suppose, for example, that the post-tenure review process requires an evaluation once every six years (see Figure 10.5). Further suppose that a tenured faculty member's performance has been at acceptably high levels for five of those years but on the sixth year he or she experiences problems. Perhaps a death in the family, a divorce, or an accident affects his or her professional performance. The post-tenure review finds an unacceptable level of professional performance in that sixth year and triggers the entire focused development activities and round of subsequent evaluations pursuant to the possibility of termination. The faculty member is now in the position of trying to reconstruct his or her positive performance for the previous five years. If, however, the tenured faculty member had participated continuously in the faculty evaluation process he or she would have considerable evidence as to his or her actual pattern of performance over time as shown in Figure 10.5. Thus, the poor performance in the sixth year may more accurately be seen as an aberration rather than an indication that the faculty member's performance has sunk to an un-

acceptably low level. If, however, the pattern of performance over time for the tenured faculty member shows a significant and consistent decline in professional performance similar to that in Figure 10.4, then appropriate termination procedures may be initiated on this firm evidence. More importantly, continuous participation by tenured faculty in the faculty evaluation process provides an early indication as to when they may need to engage in focused professional enrichment activities before their performance sinks to an unacceptable level.

From a comprehensive faculty evaluation system perspective, it is recommended that all faculty, tenured and nontenured, full- and part-time, regular and adjunct, participate in the annual evaluation process. The data for nontenured or nontenure-track faculty may be used for promotion, tenure, and merit pay decisions as specified earlier. The data for tenured faculty should be maintained by the faculty members to monitor their own performance and provide an early warning system for a potential serious decline in performance. This data may be made available for presentation at five-, six-, or seven-year intervals to provide evidence that their level of professional performance has not declined to an unacceptable level. In addition continuous participation in the faculty evaluation process would provide normative data on the performance level of

Figure 10.5 Assumption of Poor Performance of Tenured Faculty Member

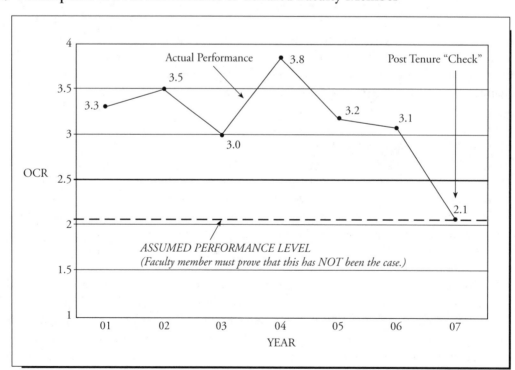

Arreola, R. A. (2007). *Developing a comprehensive faculty evaluation system* (3rd ed.). Bolton, MA: Anker.

Developing a Comprehensive Faculty Evaluation System

tenured faculty for use in program evaluations, legislative or board inquiries, and/or accreditation reviews.

In summary, the use of OCR graphing techniques and appropriate promotion, tenure (continuation), and post-tenure review decision policies, moves us further in the direction of consistency in the faculty evaluation process. Using this approach, no single person makes the tenure decision. Here the decision-making rationale of the administration has been codified in terms of policy statements and it is clear what conditions must be met before tenure may be granted. The same holds true for the promotion decisions described previously. Post-tenure review becomes a matter of periodically checking the records indicating the tenured faculty member's pattern of performance over time as part of the enhanced evaluation procedure often prescribed by post-tenure review policies. It must be emphasized that these procedures do not restrict, or in any way limit, the decision-making authority of the administration. Rather, the authority of the administration is codified in the policy statements and decision-making rules built into the procedure for using the faculty evaluation data, instead of being left to the subjective interpretation of the individual administrator or review committee.

▪ USING THE OCR IN MERIT PAY DECISIONS

In addition to its applicability in making promotion, tenure, or continuation decisions, the overall composite rating provides a powerful tool for use in distributing money to faculty on the basis of meritorious performance. In the discussion that follows we must first clearly delineate between raises that are given as a function of a promotion and merit raises. Although faculty must obviously perform at a sufficiently high level to qualify for promotion from one rank to another and thus qualify for an increase in salary, distributing special moneys to faculty as a direct result of their meritorious performance on an annual basis is quite different. Thus, the focus in this section is on what are generally referred to as merit raises—given in recognition of meritorious performance the previous year.

Before considering the use of the OCR in making merit raise decisions, it must be acknowledged that merit pay, as a concept to be applied in higher education, is highly criticized by the general academic community. Conversely, it is highly valued by state legislators, boards of trustees or regents, and the general public. Of course, the general concept of recognizing and rewarding meritorious performance is a good one. However, the problem arises when the distribution of moneys on the basis of meritorious performance is done incorrectly—which it often is.

The underlying intention of relating money to meritorious performance is essentially to serve two functions: to recognize and reward past meritorious performance and to encourage future meritorious performance. In actual practice merit pay plans rarely successfully meet either of these two objectives because critical errors are often made in setting up the merit pay distribution systems in the first place.

Critical Errors in Implementing Merit Pay Systems

Error 1. The first most common error is to specify that *all* raises will be based on merit (a popular position often taken by state legislatures and governing boards). This approach serves to immediately antagonize faculty since cost-of-living adjustments are generally swept away by such systems. This means that if faculty perform satisfactorily, but do not warrant a special merit increase, their earning power is progressively eroded. Thus, satisfactory performance in such systems is seen by faculty as resulting in a functional *decrease* in salary. This approach can also lead to charges of discrimination if equity adjustments in salary are swept under the same rug.

Error 2. Another common error is when administrative or board policy specifies that only a certain percentage of the faculty may be deemed meritorious in any given year. When this policy is put in place with the system described above in which *all* raises are to be based on merit, faculty tend to see the merit pay program as essentially just another way to continually decrease the pay of the majority of faculty.

Error 3. A third common error that causes faculty to see the entire merit pay distribution system as unfair, even if the first two errors cited above are not made, is to compute merit pay as a percentage of existing salary and then add it to the permanent base pay of the individual. This approach is seen as promoting a situation that is fundamentally unfair in which the rich get richer. That is, a 5% merit raise for someone earning a salary of $70,000 results in a larger increase than someone who gets a 5% merit raise but is earning $50,000. Thus, although the two faculty members may have been evaluated as being equally meritorious (qualifying each of them for a 5% raise) one individual gets a smaller raise in terms of absolute dollars. Also, if market forces result in a new, younger faculty member coming in with a higher salary than an older, senior faculty member, then the inequity cited above can cause even greater distress and distrust in the merit pay system. In addition, adding the merit increase to the base pay (thus permanently raising the salary by that amount) firmly solidifies the impression of unfairness in the system, since the individual getting the raise will enjoy a career-long compounding reward for a one-time performance.

Principles in Implementing a True Merit Pay Program

As noted earlier, the intention of a true merit pay program is to recognize and reward past meritorious performance and to encourage future meritorious performance. It is possible to construct a merit pay program that works in this way. However, certain principles must be followed, including:

- Merit pay, however it is computed, should be distributed only after cost of living, market, and equity adjustments have been addressed.

- Merit pay amounts should be calculated as portions of the existing pool of merit money, not as a proportion of the faculty member's current salary. In this way every faculty member who achieves the same level of merit will receive the same dollar amount.

- Merit pay should be distributed as an annual *bonus* payment. An institution rarely has a large enough merit pay fund to provide sufficiently high amounts of money that would make the recipients feel truly rewarded solely on the basis of money. Therefore, in the absence of significant amounts of money available for merit raises, we must concern ourselves with more effective strategies for the distribution of the money that is available in order to meet these desired purposes. For example, a pay raise of $1,200 spread over 12 months, when adjusted by taxes and other deductions, may amount to an increase of $70 in take-home pay each month. Not much to celebrate about. But a check for $850 (taxes and other deductions prepaid), given as part of an awards dinner along with a plaque or certificate and a round of applause from peers, has a greater chance of achieving the objective of giving the faculty member a sense of appreciation and reward for meritorious performance. While a check for $10,000 by itself might also achieve the effect of giving the faculty member a sense of appreciation and reward, it is unlikely that the institution will have a sufficiently large merit pay pool to enable it to routinely provide merit pay bonuses of that size. Thus, to achieve the psychological effect of having the faculty feel rewarded for meritorious performance and encouraged to continue performing at a meritorious level, merit pay moneys should be distributed as a one-time bonus at the end of the year.

Such merit pay bonuses should not be added permanently to the faculty member's base pay. Depending upon the culture and traditions of the institution, the desired psychological effect is best achieved if the bonus payments, accompanied by a certificate of merit, are made as part of an end-of-year event recognizing and honoring faculty excellence. In this way, for those years in which a faculty member performs at a meritorious level, there will be a clearly evident reward and public recognition.

Computing Merit Pay

In the examples that follow, it is assumed that the amount of money available in the merit pay pool has been determined in the customary fashion for a given institution. State-supported institutions may have their merit pay pool determined by state legislators, while private institutions may have their merit pay pool determined by their board of governors. In any case, it is assumed that a pool of funds is available for distribution on the basis of demonstrated merit. Also, the term *merit pay* will be used instead of the term *merit raise*. This is in keeping with the principle stated earlier that, ideally, merit pay moneys should be distributed as a bonus rather than a permanent addition to the base pay of an individual. However, it is recognized that state or other regulations that bind the institution may not allow for a bonus but only for permanent increases in base pay. Thus, although the examples that follow refer to a merit bonus rather than a merit raise, the amounts computed could just as easily be added as a permanent raise to the base pay of an individual.

In computing the merit bonus for a faculty member based on evidence provided by the faculty evaluation system, it is important to make the merit bonus amount a direct function of the faculty member's overall composite rating. The first step in this process is to compute what can be called the merit unit amount (MUA). The MUA will then serve as the basis for the final determination of the merit bonus amount for an individual. Computation of the MUA assumes that:

1) The academic unit within which all meritorious faculty will receive a merit bonus has been determined. The academic unit may be a department, division, college, or an entire university.

2) A pool of merit money has been made available by whatever process is customary at the institution.

3) A specified OCR value has been set which defines the eligibility of faculty for merit pay.

4) A specific decision regarding the model of merit pay money distribution has been established. Merit pay distribution models include the following:

- *Large distribution range.* A large range in merit bonus amounts is distributed to faculty and the bonus is in proportion to their OCR values. Faculty who attain the highest meritorious levels are to be rewarded to a significantly greater degree than those who barely make it into the meritorious category.

- *Moderate distribution range.* A moderate range in merit bonus amounts is distributed to faculty and pay is in proportion to their OCR values with only a moderate difference between faculty who attain the highest meritorious level and those who barely make it into the meritorious category.

- *Intact group distribution.* Everyone within the same meritorious range receives the same merit bonus amount. Levels of meritorious performance are established based on different OCR ranges, and everyone within the same level receives the same merit bonus. Under this approach faculty are placed in groups defined by a preset range of OCR values and all faculty within the same group receive the same merit bonus amount.

The following examples demonstrate the use of the OCR in computing the merit bonus amounts to be distributed to eligible faculty under the different distribution models. In each case, it is also assumed that the faculty evaluation system has used the same common 4-point rating scale that has been used in the examples throughout this book.

Large Distribution Range

Under this approach, the merit unit amount would be computed as follows:

$$MUA = \frac{\text{Total funds available in merit pay pool*}}{\text{Grand total of the excess of OCRs of eligible faculty}}$$

* The academic unit may be a department, division, or entire college.

For example, assume that a policy has been established which states that only faculty members who achieve an OCR greater than 3.00 on our 4-point scale are eligible for a merit bonus. In accordance with our earlier discussion, the merit bonus is to be given in addition to any cost of living or across-the-board raises. Further assume for our example that our academic unit is a department with 10 faculty members, and $10,000 has been made available for its merit pool. The faculty in this department with their various assignments have achieved the OCRs shown in Table 10.1 for the year just completed.

We have previously encountered Professors Drake and Lamb and their OCR values as computed in Figures 9.5 and 9.6, respectively. As shown in Table 10.1 Professors Fox, Greer, and Smith do not qualify for merit bonuses this year, because their OCRs are less than 3.00. The first step under this option is to compute how much the seven remaining eligible faculty members exceeded the minimum OCR cutoff for merit raise eligibility. This is computed by simply subtracting the OCR cutoff value of 3.0 from each faculty member's individual OCR:

Table 10.1   OCRs of Faculty in a Department With a Large Distribution Range

Name	OCR	Name	OCR
Professor Cole	4.00	Professor Lamb	3.35
Professor Drake	3.34	Professor Phillips	3.96
Professor Fox	2.45	Professor Smith	2.99
Professor Greer	2.89	Professor Thomas	3.77
Professor Jones	3.01	Professor Woods	3.63

Table 10.2   Calculating the OCR Values in Excess of the Minimum

Name	OCR		Cutoff		OCR Excess
Professor Cole	4.00	-	3.00	=	1.00
Professor Drake	3.34	-	3.00	=	.34
Professor Jones	3.01	-	3.00	=	.01
Professor Lamb	3.35	-	3.00	=	.35
Professor Phillips	3.96	-	3.00	=	.96
Professor Thomas	3.77	-	3.00	=	.77
Professor Woods	3.63	-	3.00	=	.63
Total of OCRs in excess of			*3.00*	=	*4.06*

Arreola, R. A. (2007). *Developing a comprehensive faculty evaluation system* (3rd ed.). Bolton, MA: Anker.

The merit unit amount for this department is then computed as:

$$MUA = \frac{\$10,000}{4.06} = \$2,463.00$$

The merit bonus for each faculty member is then computed by multiplying the OCR excess by the MUA as in Table 10.3.

Note the large difference between the merit bonus of Professor Jones, who barely makes it into the meritorious category, and Professor Cole who is at the top of the meritorious category.

Moderate Distribution Range

This approach takes the position that those who barely make it into the meritorious range are still meritorious and should receive more than a token merit bonus. With this approach, the merit unit amount is computed as follows:

$$MUA = \frac{\text{Total funds available in merit pay pool*}}{\text{Grand total of OCRs of eligible faculty}}$$

* The academic unit may be a department, division, or entire college.

For example, in this situation again assume that only faculty who achieve an OCR greater than 3.00 on a 4-point scale are eligible for a merit bonus. Further assume that the academic unit is a department that has been given $10,000 for its merit pay pool.

Once again the faculty in this department, with their various different assignments, have achieved the OCRs shown in Table 10.4 for the year just completed.

As before, Professors Fox, Greer, and Smith do not qualify for merit bonuses this year because their OCRs are equal to or less than 3.00. Under this option, we simply add all the OCRs for the eligible faculty (Table 10.5) and divide that total into the merit pay pool to compute our MUA.

Table 10.3   Computing the Merit Bonus for Each Faculty Member

Name	OCR Excess	x	MUA	=	Merit Bonus
Professor Cole	1.00	x	$2,463.00	=	$2,463.00
Professor Drake	.34	x	$2,463.00	=	$ 837.42
Professor Jones	.01	x	$2,463.00	=	$ 24.63
Professor Lamb	.35	x	$2,463.00	=	$ 862.05
Professor Phillips	.96	x	$2,463.00	=	$2,364.48
Professor Thomas	.77	x	$2,463.00	=	$1,896.51
Professor Woods	.63	x	$2,463.00	=	$1,551.69

Table 10.4   OCRs of Faculty in the Department

Name	OCR	Name	OCR
Professor Cole	4.00	Professor Lamb	3.35
Professor Drake	3.34	Professor Phillips	3.96
Professor Fox	2.45	Professor Smith	2.99
Professor Greer	2.89	Professor Thomas	3.77
Professor Jones	3.01	Professor Woods	3.63

Table 10.5   Faculty Eligible for Merit Bonuses

Name	OCR
Professor Cole	4.00
Professor Drake	3.34
Professor Jones	3.01
Professor Lamb	3.35
Professor Phillips	3.96
Professor Thomas	3.77
Professor Woods	3.63
TOTAL OCR	25.06

Arreola, R. A. (2007). *Developing a comprehensive faculty evaluation system* (3rd ed.). Bolton, MA: Anker.

$$\text{MUA} = \frac{\$10,000}{25.06} = \$399.04$$

Computing the individual merit bonus amount then becomes a simple matter of multiplying each faculty member's OCR by the MUA for the department. The resulting merit bonus amounts, which are now computed as a direct function of the faculty member's OCR, are shown in Table 10.6.

Under this option, there is less variability among bonuses. Professor Jones receives a merit bonus of $1,201.11 for an OCR of 3.01, whereas in the large distribution range option the computed merit raise was only $24.63. Which approach you choose to use depends upon the particular value system of your institution.

Intact Group Distribution

Another approach is to place the eligible faculty into intact groups based on specific OCR ranges and give the same merit bonus amount to everyone within the group. Although this approach sounds simple, it is mathematically a little more complex than the previous distribution models. The following are the steps for computing the merit raise amount for blocks or groups of meritorious faculty:

1) Before implementing the merit bonus system, establish policies that specify:

   - The number of meritorious levels or groups you wish to have in your system

   - The OCR value ranges for each meritorious level

2) Define the group with the lowest OCR value range as the baseline group. Establish, by policy, how much more (on a percentage basis) the faculty in Group 2 will receive over those in Group 1 (the baseline group); decide how much more (on a percentage basis) faculty in Group 3 will receive over those in the baseline group, and so on.

3) Use the following general formula to compute the MUA:

$$\text{MUA} = \frac{\text{Total money available in merit pay pool}}{[G_1 + G_2(1 + P_1) + \ldots + G_i(1 + P_{i-1}) + G_N(1 + P_{i-N})]}$$

N = the total number of groups
i = 1, 2, 3, ..., N
G_i = the number of faculty in a given group
P_{i-N} = the percentage increase over the first group a given group is to receive (this value must be expressed in its decimal equivalent)
P_0 = 0.0 (by definition)

4) Compute the merit bonuses for the faculty in each group. The general formula for computing the merit bonus amount (MBA) for a given group is:

MBA for Group i = $\text{MUA}(1.00 + P_{i-1})$

Where i = 1 to N and P_0 is defined as being equal to zero (0.0).

For example, assume again that we have $10,000 in our merit pay pool. Further assume that we have established the following OCR ranges for the different levels of meritorious performance:

- Group 1: Faculty with OCR values ranging from 3.01–3.50

- Group 2: Faculty with OCR values ranging from 3.51–3.80

Table 10.6 Computing the Merit Bonus for Each Faculty Member

Name	OCR Excess	x	MUA	=	Merit Bonus
Professor Cole	4.00	x	$399.04	=	$1,596.16
Professor Drake	3.34	x	$399.04	=	$1,332.79
Professor Jones	3.01	x	$399.04	=	$1,201.11
Professor Lamb	3.35	x	$399.04	=	$1,336.78
Professor Phillips	3.96	x	$399.04	=	$1,580.20
Professor Thomas	3.77	x	$399.04	=	$1,504.38
Professor Woods	3.63	x	$399.04	=	$1,448.52

Arreola, R. A. (2007). *Developing a comprehensive faculty evaluation system* (3rd ed.). Bolton, MA: Anker.

- Group 3: Faculty with OCR values ranging from 3.81–4.00

As before, we will use the same faculty with the same OCR values as in previous examples. First we sort meritorious faculty into groups based on the cutoffs established and count the number of people in each group. Label the lowest group (the baseline group) as Group 1, the next higher group as Group 2, and so on up to the highest group.

As we can see in Table 10.7 Group 1 (the baseline group) contains three faculty, Group 2 contains two, and Group 3 contains two. Further assume that we have established, by policy, that faculty in Group 2 will receive 20% more than those in the baseline group (Group 1), and faculty in Group 3 will receive 30% more than those in the baseline group (Group 1).

Thus, in terms of our formula for the MUA

N = 3 (Number of Groups)
G_1 = 3 (Number of faculty in Group 1)
G_2 = 2 (Number of faculty in Group 2)
G_3 = 2 (Number of faculty in Group 3)
P_0 = 0.0 (By definition)
P_1 = 0.20 (Faculty in Group 2 will get 20% more)
P_2 = 0.30 (Faculty in Group 3 will get 30% more)

Then, computing

$$MUA = \frac{\text{Total money available in merit pay pool}}{[G_1 + G_2(1 + P_1) + \ldots. + G_i(1 + P_{i-1}) + G_N(1 + P_{i-N})]}$$

$$MUA = \frac{\$10,000}{[3 + 2(1.20) + 2(1.30)]}$$

$$MUA = \$1,250$$

Group 1: MBA = \$1,250 x (1 + 0.00) = \$1,250.00
Group 2: MBA = \$1,250 x (1 + 0.20) = \$1,500.00
Group 3: MBA = \$1,250 x (1 + 0.30) = \$1,625.00

Thus, the faculty would receive the merit bonus payments shown in Table 10.8.

Performance-Based Pay Raises

It is useful at this point to briefly mention performance-based pay raise systems as contrasted to merit pay systems. Merit pay is here defined as moneys distributed solely on the basis of, and in proportion to, evidence of meritorious performance. In contrast, in a performance-based pay system a raise in the base pay is granted upon the demonstration that the faculty member has achieved a certain level of performance and is thus eligible to receive the pay scale associated with that level. In certain respects the standard pay raises given for promotion in rank are a form of performance-based pay raises. In performance pay models the levels of performance are usually defined in terms of specific accomplishments or the demonstration of certain skills and competencies

Institutions may determine any number of performance levels, although they generally tend to range from three to nine levels, with a different pay increment associated with the achievement of each level. To be faithful to the principle behind performance-based pay, faculty should be able to move up *or down* the levels in accordance to their performance with appropriate adjustments in pay. In other words placement in a level is not permanent but, rather, contingent upon the continued demonstration of the required level of performance.

Table 10.7 Sorting Faculty Into Groups for Merit Pay

Group	Name	OCR
Group 1	Professor Jones	3.01
	Professor Drake	3.34
	Professor Lamb	3.35
Group 2	Professor Woods	3.63
	Professor Thomas	3.77
Group 3	Professor Phillips	3.96
	Professor Cole	4.00

Table 10.8 Merit Bonuses Based on Intact Group Distribution

Group	Name	OCR	Merit Bonus
Group 1	Professor Jones	3.01	$ 1,250
	Professor Drake	3.34	$ 1,250
	Professor Lamb	3.35	$ 1,250
Group 2	Professor Woods	3.63	$ 1,500
	Professor Thomas	3.770	$ 1,500
Group 3	Professor Phillips	3.96	$ 1,625
	Professor Cole	4.00	$ 1,625
	Total		*$10,000*

Arreola, R. A. (2007). *Developing a comprehensive faculty evaluation system* (3rd ed.). Bolton, MA: Anker.

Developing a Comprehensive Faculty Evaluation System

By policy, different levels of performance could be established on the basis of the average OCR range for a specific length of time. For example, several performance-based pay levels are defined here in terms of the average OCR achieved by the faculty member and the length of time employed:

- Level 1 = Average OCR 2.0–4.0 (during first three years of employment)

- Level 2 = Average OCR range of 2.5–2.9 (after at least three years of employment)

- Level 3 = Average OCR range of 3.0–3.5 (after at least four years of employment)

- Level 4 = Average OCR range of 3.6–4.0 (after at least five years of employment)

Thus, faculty in their first three years of employment may only be placed in Level 1, assuming they are performing well enough to achieve an average OCR of 2.0 or greater on a 4-point scale. Faculty may achieve Level 2 after they have been employed three or more years, Level 3 after four or more years, and Level 4 after five or more years, assuming their average OCR falls within the specified range.

The base pay level should be established as a specific dollar amount. For example,

- Level 1 = $45,000 per year

- Level 2 = $50,000 per year

- Level 3 = $57,500 per year

- Level 4 = $65,000 per year

Thus, someone moving from Level 2 to Level 3 would receive an increase of $7,500. Conversely, someone moving from Level 4 back to Level 3 would return to Level 3 base pay. Of course, the OCR average ranges and the length of employment requirements used in this example are arbitrary and are only meant to demonstrate the application.

SUMMARY

Note that in each of the examples given in this chapter, no single administrator or decision-maker determined, in isolation, whether to promote, tenure, or grant merit pay to any given individual. Each decision was arrived at by the application of policies based on the performance of the individual as reflected by the OCR. To be sure, the use of the OCR in making personnel decisions does not eliminate the ability of an administrator or administration to exercise its authority in setting standards. Decisions such as setting cutoff values or determining the merit pay pool amounts to be given to any particular department may still need to be made by the administration; however, these decisions would need to be implemented as a matter of established policy. What the OCR and its application does constrain is capriciousness—that is, the inconsistent application of agreed-upon criteria, standards, and procedures in making personnel decisions. In this way, the faculty may have greater confidence in the fairness of the personnel decision-making mechanism. Although the use of the OCR in making personnel decisions does not eliminate faculty complaints and grievances, it does tend to protect the administration from unwarranted charges of prejudice, bias, and unfairness in making personnel decisions.

REFERENCES

American Association of University Professors. (1998). *Post-tenure review: An AAUP response.* Washington, DC: Author.

Banks, R. F., (1997). *Post-tenure review: A summary of other comparable university policies.* East Lansing, MI: Michigan State University.

Operating the Faculty Evaluation System: Peer Input and Review Issues

In keeping with the definitions of measurement and evaluation specified in the introduction to this book, this chapter deals with peers as a source of information that will become part of the *measurement* data entered into the computation of the overall composite rating (OCR). Thus, the term *peer evaluation* will not be used, since the assumption is being made that peers will not be called upon to make any kind of evaluative judgment concerning the overall performance of an individual. We wish to avoid and recommend against systems in which peers evaluate one another in some global sense. Although such systems may appeal to a sense of elitism and prestige, they have generally been shown not to produce consistent or reliable evaluative results (Centra, 1975). At least one study found that peer ratings of teaching effectiveness were related to office location (Centra, 1979), suggesting that peer evaluation may result in little more than an indication of popularity.

Experience has shown that faculty evaluation systems that rely on peers to provide the overall evaluations of colleagues tend to generate hostility and negativity out of proportion to the value of any obtained results. The concern for this possible effect is so strong that in some unionized institutions the contract specifically prohibits peer evaluation. Rather, this chapter examines the issues of who can serve as peers and what kind of information they can most appropriately provide. This peer information, like student ratings, becomes part of the data entered into an appropriate matrix (such as that shown in Figure 9.1) in computing the OCR for a specific role.

WHO IS A PEER?

The first issue we must address is defining what constitutes a peer—at least insofar as the design of our comprehensive faculty evaluation system is concerned. As sources of information appropriate to our evaluation system, peers fall into three basic categories:

- Internal content peer
- External content peer
- Internal non-content peer

In this context, an *internal content peer* is a faculty member within the same institution (and perhaps the same department) who possesses the same content expertise as the individual being evaluated. On the other hand, an *external content peer* is an individual external to the institution, who possesses the same content expertise as the individual being evaluated. An *internal non-content peer* is a faculty member within the same institution (although not necessarily in the same department) who does not possess the same expertise as the individual being measured. In setting up the peer component of our comprehensive faculty evaluation system we must consider these types of peers in relation to the kind of information required.

WHAT INFORMATION CAN PEERS PROVIDE?

In defining the roles in our faculty role model as specified in Steps 1, 2, and 3, the specific activities or performances that define each role were identified and defined. In establishing the peer component of your faculty evaluation system, those performances should now be examined to determine which are content dependent and which are non-content dependent.

Content-Dependent Performance

For example, suppose we have identified peers as an appropriate source of information for the instructional design component of teaching as shown in Figure 5.1. Further, suppose that peers are to provide information concerning such things as the currency of the content of a course, the appropriateness of the level of the content presented for the level of the course, and the appropriateness of the sequencing of the content to best achieve the learning objectives for the course. Then, clearly, those peers providing the information would need to have the same content expertise as the faculty member being evaluated. Thus, for that piece of the faculty evaluation system content peers would be required. If peers exist within the same institution (or department) that possess the same content expertise as the faculty being evaluated, then we would use internal content peers. However, suppose that no one at the institution possesses the same content expertise as the faculty member being evaluated. In this case, appropriate individuals outside the institution would have to be consulted. The faculty member being evaluated may identify several qualified external content peers, and the materials to be examined would be sent to one or more of them for review. In such instances, however, it is critical that an external content peer agree to use, and be provided with, the standards and criteria established in the design of your comprehensive faculty evaluation system. What must be avoided at all costs is the situation where an external content peer uses either their personal values or the values of their institution to rate or otherwise review the materials. It is critical that the values determined by the faculty in the design of the comprehensive faculty evaluation system be respected and applied even if an external content peer must be consulted.

Content-Independent Performance

Other aspects of faculty performance that may play a significant role in the evaluation of a faculty member, such as service to the institution, may not depend in any way on content expertise. For example, the faculty member being evaluated may have served on a fundraising committee for the institution with a number of colleagues throughout the institution, none of whom share each other's content expertise. However, input from those non-content peers could provide the kind of peer information required concerning performance on that committee. Thus, as before, the various faculty performances identified in Steps 1, 2, and 3, should be examined to determine which non-content peers might be the most appropriate sources of information.

In any case, whether a content peer (internal or external) or a non-content peer is the most appropriate source of information for a given faculty performance, the best source principle must still be applied. That is, we must identify those peers who are in the best position to have first-hand knowledge of the performance in question. Of course, if the services of an external content peer are required, either the evidence must be sent to them or they must be invited to the campus to obtain first hand the evidence they need to provide the information required by the evaluation system.

■ GATHERING PEER INPUT

In Step 7 the specific data-gathering procedures for each source for each role would have been determined. Thus, for those components of the several roles in the faculty role model in which peers were identified as meeting the best source principle (i.e., in a position to have first-hand knowledge of the performance in question), specific tools and data-gathering procedures would have been specified. In Step 8, those specific tools and data-gathering procedures would have been developed and/or selected. Again it must be stressed that the design of such tools and data-gathering procedures must adhere to professional psychometric standards. In addition to references concerning the psychometric technicalities of questionnaire and rating design, see Chism (1999) for examples of structured peer-review procedures as well as suggested tools or instruments.

If the value structure of the institution has been determined and carefully integrated into the construction of the faculty evaluation system as specified in earlier chapters, peer input and review can assume a much more consistent and valuable role. A graphic representation of the relationship among student, peer, and administrative input is shown in Figure 11.1.

As can be seen in Figure 11.1 peers are shown as one source of information, not as an overarching peer evaluation committee. Rather, the actual evaluation is carried out by the institutional/college/departmental value filter that is comprised of all the matrices developed in the system that specify the sources and weights to be applied to each piece of information. That is, as noted in earlier chapters, all sources of information in the faculty evaluation system—students, peers, self, department head, dean, and others—have been identified and the appropriate information has been gathered from each. Information has been weighted in accordance with the consensus value structure of the institution and combined with all other information to form the overall composite rating or the overall evaluation. This process of gathering, weighting, and combining information can be thought of as the application of the value filters for the department, college, and institution. The outcome of such a process may then be interpreted through the previously determined set of policies governing promotion, tenure, and so on. These policies form the decision-making rule system for the institution. Notice that with this approach the power and authority of the administration is neither diminished nor diluted. Rather, the decision-making rule system followed by the administration is simply codified in advance so everyone knows what it is. As noted earlier, this approach does limit the administration's authority to set criteria and performance standards; however, it does constrain the administration from being capricious. The administration may still determine procedures, criteria, and standards by which faculty performance will be judged. However, because the decision-making rule system is codified and built into the evaluation system, this approach constrains the administration to apply these procedures, criteria, and standards consistently to all faculty. In this model, a very specific peer committee structure is recommended—*the triad peer review committee.*

Figure 11.1 Graphic Representation of the OCR Model (Comprehensive Faculty Evaluation System) Resulting From Steps 1–8

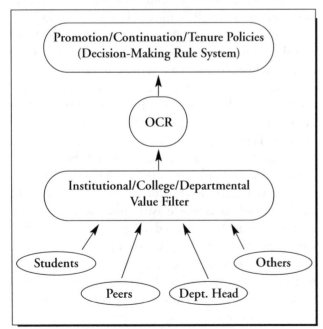

Arreola, R. A. (2007). *Developing a comprehensive faculty evaluation system* (3rd ed.). Bolton, MA: Anker.

A good mechanism to use in gathering peer input data is a three-member, or triad, peer committee structure (Figure 11.2). The task of the triad peer committee is not to conduct an overall evaluation of the faculty member. Rather, its task is to gather appropriate peer information that either the members can provide, or that is provided by someone else at the request of the triad peer committee. In the triad peer committee model, a three-person committee is appointed for every faculty member. The department head selects one member of the committee, one member is selected from a group of peers recommended by the faculty member being evaluated (usually an internal content peer), and one member is appointed from the faculty at large, perhaps by the dean. In this way, no one faculty member will have to sit on more than three peer review committees, and each committee will concern itself with only one faculty member.

Under this triad approach, the third member appointed from the faculty at large should be an internal non-content peer. The primary function of the third member is to ensure that proper deliberative process, prescribed by the faculty evaluation system, is followed. It is assumed that the other two members will adequately represent the perspective of professionals from the content field. Also, because the faculty member being evaluated will have one person on the committee that he or she nominated, it is unlikely that any negative biases on the part of the other two members will unduly affect the outcome of the committee's deliberations. Likewise, the assumed neutrality of the at-large member will offset any unwarranted positive biases by the two content peers.

Because the triad peer review committee concerns itself with only one faculty member, it is much easier to assign it more detailed and evaluatively relevant tasks. Such tasks may include in-depth review and rating in accordance with prescribed criteria and standards of such things as course design, course materials, examinations, professional development activities, and service activities. In the event that a content peer is needed to provide certain information, but no internal content peer exists or is available, it would be the task of the triad peer committee to:

- Identify and locate an appropriate external content peer

- Communicate the institution's criteria and standards for rating or otherwise considering evidence concerning a specific performance

- Provide appropriate evidence of faculty performance to the external content peer

- Record the results in the appropriate matrix as part of the computation of the OCR

Figure 11.2 Triad Peer Input Coordinating Committee Model

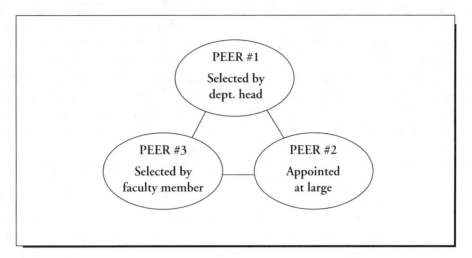

Thus, the operational principles to be followed here are: 1) each triad committee considers the performance of only one individual, and 2) the triad committee is responsible for gathering and assembling appropriate information based on the best source principle.

■ ADAPTING TRADITIONAL PEER REVIEW AND EVALUATION SYSTEMS

In considering the issue of peer input in a comprehensive faculty evaluation system it must be acknowledged that institutions may have traditions or even specific mandates that require some sort of peer review or peer evaluation. Thus, it is important to examine the possible structures that are required and determine how best to revise them so as to realize the benefits of the processes described in this book.

Generally, peer review components of traditional faculty evaluation systems involve a committee, sometimes made up of the tenured faculty, all the senior faculty, or some similar combination. The function of such a peer committee is to review all the evidence (e.g., student rating forms, letters of recommendation, other peer or colleague comments, and published articles) and make a decision or recommendation to the administration. When there are a number of faculty submitting their materials for review at the same time, the task can be daunting. In addition, such committees can often bring subjective impressions, friendships, and hostilities into the decision-making process. Such an approach also has the unfortunate side effect of giving second-hand information or hearsay evidence much greater impact than should be the case. Committee members may bring to the

deliberations positive or negative opinions concerning the faculty member's teaching performance based on random or limited student comments. This approach may be considered as the *traditional hierarchical peer review model* (Figure 11.3).

Note that there is repeated processing of the same material in the traditional hierarchical peer review model. That is, the peer committees, the department head, and the dean all have the opportunity to examine all of the information available in the faculty member's file. This information may include student ratings; peer or colleague reports concerning research, teaching, or college service; self-reports; as well as the reports of others such as alumni or employers of graduating students. With the traditional hierarchical peer review model, opportunities exist at each level for the entry of new or anecdotal information that may or may not be relevant to the decision being made. Such information may have the effect of biasing the recommendations made at each level. In these situations, it is possible for a faculty member to be recommended positively at each level for promotion, tenure, or some other personnel action, yet be turned down at the highest level. The converse is also possible, although less frequent. This result occurs in the traditional hierarchical peer review model, because different value systems may be applied in evaluating the data provided. What a peer review committee or administrator at one level may define as good and valuable performance, a peer review committee or an administrator at another level may define as being of little or no value.

An approach developed to deal with the problems inherent in the traditional hierarchical peer review model (Figure 11.3) is the portfolio approach. The portfolio approach is a modification of the traditional hierarchical peer review model that interposes what may be called a contextual filter between the input from the various sources and the various peer review and evaluation groups considering the input (see Figure 11.4). In the portfolio approach the intent is to provide a leveling context for the interpretation of the student, peer, and other data. The faculty member being evaluated prepares a portfolio in which such issues as the individual's goals and objectives are described, philosophy of education, professional growth activities, and other explanatory information is provided. It is intended that such a document will promote the consistent interpretation of the data as it moves up the chain of reviewers. Notice also that the faculty member is given the opportunity to provide either additional information that only they have or to provide a separate self-evaluation to the first level peer review committee. Unless it is part of some concerted, psycholog-

ically based, self-improvement program, self-evaluations seldom have much value in a formal faculty evaluation system other than to assuage some political need. Generally all that a self-evaluation component of a faculty evaluation system does is add a constant to the evaluative data. Not many people will give themselves a bad self-evaluation (although those that do probably deserve it).

Neither the traditional hierarchical peer review model nor the traditional hierarchical peer review model with contextual filter solves the problems of the repeated processing of identical information, the numerous opportunities for the entry of irrelevant or biasing information, or the possibility of different value systems being applied to the information at various levels. The system designed in accordance with Steps 1–8, (e.g., the OCR model shown in Figure 11.1) does successfully address these problems and results in a fairer and more consistent faculty evaluation system.

Figure 11.3 The Traditional Hierarchical Peer Review Model

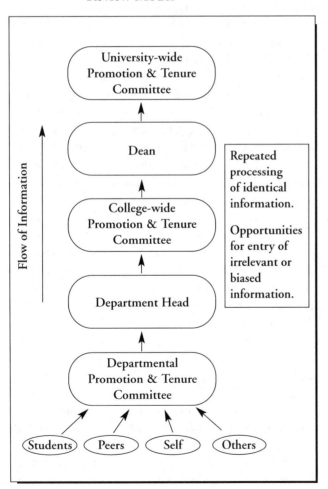

Figure 11.4 Traditional Hierarchical Peer Review Model With Portfolio Filter

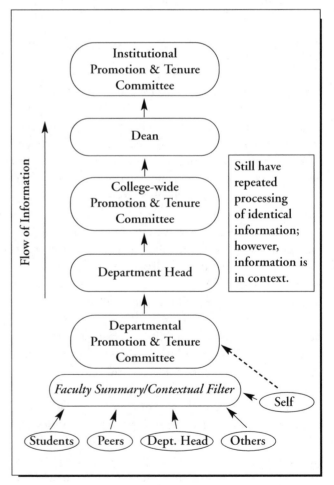

Arreola, R. A. (2007). *Developing a comprehensive faculty evaluation system* (3rd ed.). Bolton, MA: Anker.

Developing a Comprehensive Faculty Evaluation System

As noted earlier, the development of a successful faculty evaluation system requires that we pay careful attention to political and psychometric issues; therefore, it should be recognized that for political reasons it might be necessary to have a peer review oversight committee somewhere in the faculty evaluation system. Figure 11.5 shows a variation of the OCR model shown in Figure 11.1, which accommodates this requirement.

In this variation, it is recommended that the peer review oversight committee limit its work to simply ensuring that the prescribed process has been followed in gathering and assembling the information from the various sources and that the appropriate value filter has been correctly applied to the data. If the peer review oversight committee concerns itself with reevaluating all the data provided by the various sources, we are once again faced with the possibility of the entry of irrelevant or biasing information into the decision-making process. This possibility is somewhat less than in the traditional hierarchical peer review model (Figure 11.3). If a strong need is felt to have a peer review oversight committee, two questions must be asked:

- What information is the committee going to consider that has not been considered earlier by someone closer to the source of information?

- What criteria for judging the information is the peer review oversight committee going to apply that have not been applied to the data earlier?

If some new criteria, values, or information need to be considered by the peer review oversight committee, then those criteria, values, and information requirements should be built into the system at an earlier level.

The primary need for a peer review oversight committee generally grows out of the situation where the values and criteria for evaluating faculty performance at the department or college level differs markedly from that at the institutional or university-wide level. If the process for developing a comprehensive faculty evaluation system described in earlier chapters has been followed, such differences should have already been resolved and the need for a peer review oversight committee obviated.

PEER OBSERVATION OF CLASSROOM PERFORMANCE

The first and most vigorous statement here concerning peer observation of classroom performance is *DON'T DO IT if the data is to be used for anything other than personal feedback to the instructor for his or her use in teaching improvement efforts.* However, for a variety of political reasons peer observation of classroom teaching performance is becoming a more frequent part of the faculty evaluation landscape. From a measurement perspective, valid and reliable peer observation data is costly to obtain. Researchers in the field of faculty evaluation generally do not recommend that peer observation data be used in summative faculty evaluation (Aleamoni, 1982; Centra, 1979; Cohen & McKeachie, 1980). Further, Centra (1993) claims that it would be a mistake to design peer evaluation procedures to rely heavily on classroom observations. Although peer observation of classroom performance may provide useful data for self-improvement purposes, such data should play little or no part in a summative faculty evaluation on which personnel decisions (promotion, tenure, etc.) may be based.

However, since peer observation as part of the faculty evaluation system is sometimes mandated by regulation, contractual agreement, or board policy, it is important to at least consider the basics. If classroom observations of teaching performance are to be undertaken, we must consider them to be simply another measure of a performance component of teaching and must thus be concerned with the reliability and validity of the data being produced.

Figure 11.5 Alternate OCR Model With Mandated Peer Review Oversight Committee

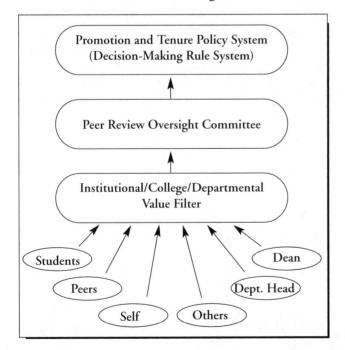

Arreola, R. A. (2007). *Developing a comprehensive faculty evaluation system* (3rd ed.). Bolton, MA: Anker.

One of the issues of the measurement of complex behavior is that of *sampling:* How can we be sure that the slice of teaching that has been observed is truly representative? Another issue revolves around the old scientific principle that one cannot measure a phenomenon without affecting the phenomenon itself. Thus we must be concerned with what effect the observation has on the performance being observed.

The following suggestions address these issues and other practical matters related to observing classroom performance for the purpose of gathering data that may impact personnel decisions.

Develop or Adopt a Valid, Reliable Observational Checklist

Any two people observing a performance may not see the same thing if their attention is not focused on the specific performance elements of interest. Therefore, it is necessary to design and construct an observational checklist based on agreed-upon performances to be observed. The checklist should undergo standard reliability and validity studies to ensure that the resulting data is valid and reliable. One of the more popular processes for coding teacher behaviors is the Flanders Interaction Analysis System. Another is the Cognitive Interaction Analysis System, which is described by Chism (1999) with appropriate forms.

Assemble Peer Observer Team

In order to obtain inter-rater reliability and thus ensure the overall reliability of the data from classroom observations, it is necessary to have at least three, or preferably four, members on a peer review team. The team may not necessarily be composed of content peers if the behaviors to be observed are content independent.

Train Peer Observer Team

To further ensure the reliability of the peer observation data the observers must be trained in the use of the observational checklist. Training the observers increases the probability that their observations will be valid and consistent and thus result in acceptable inter-rater reliability. The inter-rater reliability of the team must be confirmed prior to the team's actual observations.

Schedule Multiple Visits

As noted earlier, we must make certain that a sufficient sampling of the behavior or performances in questions. To do this it is important to schedule at least 8 to 10 visits to the class by the peer observation team. It is recommended that the entire team not attend class at the same time.

Prepare the Students

Since having a team of peer observers in the classroom is likely to significantly alter the learning environment, it is important to prepare and desensitize the students to the presence of the observation team. The class should be prepared for the visitations by having the instructor explain the purpose of the team's visits. Each member of the team should be introduced to the class and students should be allowed to ask questions of the team members. It is important that team members visit the class two or three times each before undertaking the actual observations so that the students become accustomed to having them in the room. In this way, once the real observations begin to take place, the performance being observed and the students' reactions to it will have a greater probability of being representative of the instructor's teaching performance.

Prepare the Instructor

Millis (1992) recommends a pre-visit conference between the observers and the instructor. During a pre-visit conference, the two parties should review the instrument the observers will use to familiarize the instructor with the issues of importance. The instructor should communicate to the observers any teaching strategies or issues he or she considers important. In addition, an agreement should be reached with the observers on what role student input will play in the observation.

It is generally not recommended that members of the observation team ask any questions or otherwise participate in the classroom activities, even if the instructor invites such them to do so. Any activity by the visitors other than observing further serves to affect the learning environment, thus increasing the likelihood that the performance being observed is not truly representative of normal classroom activity.

Schedule a Post-Observation Conference

Once all the observation visits have been completed it is recommended that a conference be held with the instructor to review the overall conclusions of the team. It is recommended that the feedback be honest, accurate, focused, concrete, positively phrased, and action-oriented to facilitate individual faculty self-improvement (Millis, 1992; Chism, 1999).

■ CONCLUSION

Peer input can and should play a significant role in a comprehensive faculty evaluation system. The steps for building such a faculty evaluation system, as described in this book, provide many opportunities for specifying peer input. In certain roles, such as scholarly and creative activities, peers may be the single most important source of information. Care should be taken, however, not to insert peers as a source of information into those areas where others may be better sources of that information. Chief among these are the gathering of data from peers concerning classroom performance. It is strongly recommended that peer observation of classroom performance not be part of a summative faculty evaluation system. The cost in time and effort of gathering valid and reliable peer observation data that may legitimately be used to support personnel decisions (e.g., promotion, tenure, etc.) is generally prohibitive. However, if peer observation of classroom performance is required for policy or political reasons, the data gathered from such observations should be provided, in confidence, to the faculty member for their personal use in self-improvement. Finally, if the peer observation data is required to be used as part of the personnel decision-making process, such data should be given as little weight as possible.

■ REFERENCES

Aleamoni, L. M. (1982). Components of the instructional setting. *Instructional Evaluation, 7,* 11–16.

Centra, J. A. (1975). Colleagues as raters of classroom instruction. *Journal of Higher Education, 46*(3), 327–337.

Centra, J. A. (1979). *Determining faculty effectiveness.* San Francisco, CA: Jossey-Bass.

Centra, J. A. (1993). *Reflective Faculty Evaluation: Enhancing Teaching and Determining Faculty Effectiveness.* San Francisco, CA: Jossey-Bass.

Chism, N. V. N. (1999). *Peer review of teaching: A sourcebook.* Bolton, MA: Anker.

Cohen, P. A., & McKeachie, W. J. (1980). The role of colleagues in the evaluation of college teaching. *Improving College and University Teaching, 28*(4), 147–154.

Millis, B. J. (1992). Conducting effective peer classroom observations. In D. H. Wulff & J. D. Nyquist (Eds.), *To improve the academy: Vol. 11. Resources for faculty, instructional, and organizational development* (pp. 189–206). Stillwater, OK: New Forums Press.

Student Ratings:
What More Than 80 Years
of Research Tell Us

Student ratings are one of the most common features of faculty evaluation systems. More than 85% of all faculty evaluation systems make regular and routine use of student ratings (Seldin, 1993). Despite the continued recommendations in the literature that faculty evaluation systems use multiple sources of data, many working faculty evaluation systems continue to use student ratings of instructor and instructions as their only component. It is not surprising, therefore, that student ratings have tended to become synonymous with faculty evaluation. And, because the evaluation of faculty performance, especially for the purpose of making personnel decisions, is not always the most popular and well-received administrative activity, faculty and administrators continue to ask questions concerning the factors that may, or may not, influence student ratings of instructors and instruction.

The literature concerning student ratings is immense. Far more than 2,000 articles have been written on this one aspect of faculty evaluation alone (Cashin, 1999). Although the great body of research on student ratings has taken place in the last 30 years, studies on student ratings go back more than 80 years (Guthrie, 1954, cites a study on student ratings dating all the way back to 1924). Even today the design, development, use, and interpretation of student ratings continues to be one of the most heavily researched topics in the general area of faculty evaluation. The results of all this research have led to the fairly firm conclusion, at least among the educational research community, that properly constructed, appropriately administered, and correctly interpreted student ratings can be valid and reliable measures indicating the quality of teaching (Aleamoni, 1999).

With all the evidence for the validity and reliability of student ratings in the literature, the basic belief in higher education that student ratings are not valid persists. Before providing an overview and summary of what the large body of research on student ratings says to us, it is useful to examine why this belief persists.

■ WHAT IS VALIDITY?

Decades of research have demonstrated that tools used in faculty evaluation systems, especially student rating forms, can be designed to be valid and reliable. So why does the belief that student ratings are not valid still reverberate throughout higher education despite so much research? My experience with hundreds of colleges and universities facing the task of revising or building their faculty evaluation systems has led me to conclude that there are three main reasons:

1) Many of the tools used in faculty evaluation systems are homemade and are thus of dubious validity and reliability.

2) Most academic administrators are not conversant with the finer points of psychometrics.

3) Higher education has yet to establish a universally accepted definition of the characteristics and skills necessary for teaching excellence.

These three conditions lead to a cascading set of circumstances that profoundly affect the general professoriate's perception, and willingness to accept, the possibility that student rating data is, or can be, valid. A brief examination of these conditions reveals the underlying problem.

Homemade Faculty Evaluation Tools

Faculty evaluation tools have, by and large, been dominated by the use of some form of student rating form. Student rating forms have been, and continue today, to be the primary common element of all faculty evaluation systems. In many cases student ratings constitute the only systematically gathered data used in a faculty evaluation system. Unfortunately, the great bulk of student rating forms in use across higher education in America today are homemade. That is, they have been constructed by committees comprised of various combinations of faculty, academic administrators, and students. Owing to the lack of psychometric expertise or rigor in constructing these forms, they are of dubious (and often undetermined) validity and reliability. This common situation has resulted in a rich and voluminous storehouse of anecdotes and stories leading to a number of myths, including the ever-popular myths that student ratings are just a popularity contest and that faculty can buy good ratings by giving easy grades. Unfortunately, these and many other such myths likely have a basis in fact since they may possibly be true for poorly constructed forms. The anecdotes that have produced these and other myths about faculty evaluation tools are so common, so voluminous, and so widespread throughout the culture of higher education that they have taken on an aura of common knowledge. Thus, in the minds of the professoriate and academic administrators, this common knowledge is so pervasive that it far overshadows the truth concerning student ratings and other faculty evaluation tools that are buried in the pages of psychometric journals.

What Is Psychometrics?

It is unfortunate but true that the majority of academic administrators are unfamiliar with the finer points of psychometrics. Deans and vice presidents for academic affairs are usually the ones faced with the task of gathering some form of evaluative information concerning their faculty's performance for the purpose of making promotion, tenure, continuation, or similar personnel decisions. Of the many hundreds of academic administrators with whom I have had the occasion to interact on the issue of faculty evaluation, I could number on one hand the ones that have been sufficiently conversant with psychometrics to understand the subtle differences between, say, content validity and construct validity. These individuals (biolo-gists, musicians, historians, physicists, physicians, etc.) not only are generally unfamiliar with the finer points of psychometrics but rarely, if ever, read articles in such publications as *Journal of Educational Psychology* (American Psychological Association) or *Review of Educational Research* (American Educational Research Association).

From the perspective of many academic administrators responsible for making significant decisions concerning the design, structure, and format of faculty evaluation systems (especially those administrators that come from the so-called "hard sciences"), the entire field of research that speaks to the issues of psychological measurement is, at best, a little-known area and, at worst, considered a phony or illegitimate area of study on par with research on ghosts and leprechauns. Thus, when the issue of the validity of student ratings is raised, the definition or conception of validity used is much more likely to be that of colloquial usage rather than technical precision. It is useful to look at a dictionary definition of *valid* and the technical, psychometric definition of *validity:*

Main Entry: **val·id** [Dictionary definition]

1 : having legal efficacy or force; *especially* : executed with the proper legal authority and formalities <a *valid* contract>

2 a : well-grounded or justifiable : being at once relevant and meaningful <a *valid* theory> **b** : logically correct <a *valid* argument> <*valid* inference>

3 : appropriate to the end in view : **EFFECTIVE** <every craft has its own *valid* methods>

VALID implies being supported by objective truth or generally accepted authority <a *valid* reason for being absent> <a *valid* marriage> (Miriam-Webster OnLine, 2005–2006)

Validity. [Psychometric technical definition] The effectiveness of the test in representing, describing, or predicting the attribute that the user is interested in. *Content validity* refers to the faithfulness with which the test represents or reproduces an area of knowledge. *Construct validity* refers to the accuracy with which the test describes an individual in terms of some psychological trait or construct. *Criterion-related validity,* or *predictive validity,* refers to the accuracy with which the test scores make it possible to predict some criterion variable of educational, job, or life performance. (Thorndike & Hagen, 1969, pp. 163–177).

Looking at the differences between these definitions, and realizing that the majority of faculty and academic administrators use the dictionary definition rather than the psychometric one, it is easy to see why the belief that student ratings are not valid persists. There is no body of anecdotes and stories comparable to the myths supporting the proposition that faculty evaluation data (especially student ratings) are "well-grounded or justifiable, being at once relevant and meaningful, logically correct, or supported by objective truth or generally accepted authority."

■ WHAT DOES THE RESEARCH TELL US?

Having acknowledged the cultural aspects of the higher education community that lead to the constant doubting of the utility of student ratings, we can now explore some of the more common questions about student ratings and examine what the research tells us.

In interpreting the research findings relative to the most common questions concerning student ratings, it is important to note that the conclusions drawn are based on the assumed use of professionally developed, valid, and reliable student rating forms. What the literature demonstrates to be a reliable finding concerning how student ratings work may, in fact, not be true for student rating forms that have been homemade by student, faculty, or administrative groups. Such forms have generally not undergone the rigorous psychometric and statistical procedures required to construct a valid and reliable rating. Most of the answers provided to the following common questions concerning student ratings are derived from several reviews of the literature, especially Lawrence M. Aleamoni's (1999) excellent review of the literature on student rating research. The questions addressed are:

- Aren't student ratings just a popularity contest?

- Aren't student rating forms just plain unreliable and invalid?

- Aren't students too immature, inexperienced, and capricious to make any consistent judgments about the instructor and instruction?

- Isn't it true that I can buy good student ratings just by giving easy grades?

- Isn't it generally easier to get good ratings in higher level courses?

- Isn't it true that students who are required to take a course tend to rate the course more harshly than those taking it as an elective?

- Isn't there a gender bias in student ratings? Don't female faculty tend to get lower ratings than male faculty?

- Isn't it more difficult for math and science faculty to get good ratings?

- Isn't it true that the only faculty who are really qualified to teach or evaluate their peers' teaching are those who are actively involved in conducting research in their field?

- Don't students have to be away from the course, and possibly the college, for several years before they are able to make accurate judgments about the instructor and instruction?

- Isn't it true that the size of the class affects student ratings?

- Does the time of the day the course is taught affect student ratings?

- Do majors in a course rate it differently than nonmajors?

- Does the rank of the instructor (instructor, assistant professor, associate professor, or professor) affect student ratings?

- Why bother with 20 or 30 questions on a student rating form? Can't we just use single general items as accurate measures of instructional effectiveness?

- What good are student ratings in efforts to improve instruction?

Aren't student ratings just a popularity contest? The answer to this first most vexing of questions is "no"—if you are using a student rating form that has been constructed using professional psychometric procedures and has demonstrated reliability and validity. Well-designed student rating forms (i.e., those designed according to professional psychometric standards) carefully measure many different aspects of faculty performance. While these may include the approachability or friendliness of a faculty member, which might be interpreted as a popularity issue, well-designed forms also measure many other factors that are unrelated to the popularity issue. Thus, the complete student rating is *not* simply a measure of popularity, but a measure of various instructional design and delivery skills and characteristics. Many studies show that, given a well-designed form, students can be reliable judges of instructional effectiveness.

There is one qualification, however: Student rating forms that have *not* been constructed according to professional psychometric standards may be unreliable and thus able to be influenced by such factors as popularity, temperature of the classroom, instructor gender, or anything else. Unfortunately, many institutions do use student rating forms that have not been constructed and validated using professional psychometric standards. Without rigorous reliability and validity data on such forms, it is impossible to tell for certain what influences the final student rating. (See: Aleamoni, 1999; Aleamoni & Spencer, 1973; Aleamoni, 1976; Arreola, 1983; Feldman, 1989; Tang, 1997; Beatty & Zahn, 1990; Benz & Blatt, 1995, Costin, Greenough, & Menges, 1971; Dukes & Victoria, 1989; Frey, 1978; Grush & Costin, 1975; Johannessen & Associates, 1997; Krehbiel & Associates, 1997; Macdonald, 1987; Marlin, 1987; Marsh & Bailey, 1993; Perry, Abrami, & Leventhal, 1979; Rodabaugh & Kravitz, 1994; Shepherd & Trank, 1989; Tollefson, Chen, & Kleinsasser, 1989; Ware & Williams, 1977; Waters, Kemp, & Pucci, 1988.)

Aren't student rating forms just plain unreliable and invalid? The answer to this question is, surprisingly, "yes and no." Most student rating forms in use today suffer from unreliability and invalidity problems. As noted in the earlier discussion concerning the issue of validity, the great preponderance of student rating forms used by colleges and universities have been developed by committees comprised of students, faculty, and/or administrative groups who have not followed the rigorous psychometric and statistical procedures required to produce a valid and reliable student rating form. Well-developed instruments have been shown to be reliable and valid. Costin et al. (1971) and Marsh (1984) reported reliabilities for such forms to be about 0.90. Aleamoni (1978a) reported reliabilities ranging from 0.81 to 0.94 for items and from 0.88 to 0.98 for subscales of the Course/Instructor Evaluation Questionnaire (CIEQ; see www.cieq.com). It should be noted, however, that wherever student rating forms are not carefully constructed with the aid of professionals, as in the case of most student- and faculty-generated forms (Everly & Aleamoni, 1972), the reliabilities may be so low that they completely negate the evaluation effect and its results.

Validity, in the psychometric sense, is much more difficult to assess than reliability. Most student rating forms have been validated by the judgment of experts that the items and subscales measure important aspects of instruction (Costin et. al., 1971). These subjectively determined dimensions of instructional setting and process have also been validated using statistical tools, such as factor analysis (Aleamoni & Hexner, 1980; Burdsal & Bardo, 1986; Marsh, 1984). Further evidence of validity comes from studies in which student ratings are correlated with other indicators of teacher competence, such as peer (colleague) ratings, expert judges' ratings, graduating seniors' and alumni ratings, and student learning. The 14 studies cited by Aleamoni and Hexner (1980) in which student ratings were compared to colleague ratings, expert judges' ratings, graduating seniors' and alumni ratings, and student learning measures all indicated the existence of moderate to high positive correlations, which can be considered as providing additional evidence of validity. The one or two studies that have found a negative relationship between student achievement and instructor rating have been found to be methodologically flawed by several researchers (Centra, 1973b; Frey, 1973; Gessner, 1973; Menges, 1973).

Aren't students too immature, inexperienced, and capricious to make any consistent judgments about the instructor and instruction? The answer to this question is "no." Evidence dating back to 1924, according to Guthrie (1954), indicates that this commonly held belief is not true. The stability of student ratings from one year to the next results in substantial correlations in the range of 0.87 to 0.89. More recent literature on the subject cited by Costin, Greenough, and Menges (1971) and studies by Gillmore (1973) and Hogan (1973) indicated that the correlation between student ratings of the same instructors and courses ranged from 0.70 to 0.87.

Isn't it true that I can buy good student ratings just by giving easy grades? There has been more research conducted on this one question than almost any other in the field of student ratings and faculty evaluation. Nearly 500 studies have been conducted in trying to answer this question. The reason for the numerous studies is not that the question is so difficult to answer—it's that faculty generally don't like the answer the literature provides. The answer is that there is *no* consistent correlation between the grades a faculty member gives and the ratings he or she receives from a well-designed student rating form. No clear positive correlation between grades and student ratings has emerged in the literature. The bulk of the correlations appearing in the literature have been quite weak ranging from -.18 to + .18 (i.e., average r = 0.0).

Considerable controversy has centered around the relationship between student ratings and actual or expected course grades. The general feeling is that students tend to rate courses and instructors more highly when they expect to, or actually receive, good grades. Correlational studies have reported widely inconsistent grade-rating relationships. Twenty-two studies have reported zero relationships (Aleamoni & Hexner 1980), and 28 studies have reported significant positive relationships (Aleamoni & Hexner, 1980). In most instances however, these relationships were relatively weak, as indicated by the fact that the median correlation was approximately 0.14, with the mean and standard deviation being 0.18 and 0.16, respectively. The clear outcome from the studies on this issue is that, at best, the relationship between grades and ratings is extremely weak, with the average correlation across all studies being 0.0. Clearly, the idea that student ratings are highly correlated with grades is not supported by the literature (Frey, 1973; Gessner, 1973; Sullivan & Skanes, 1974). Again, however, it must be noted that we can't be sure what will influence the ratings of individual homemade student rating forms that have not been designed in accordance with professional psychometric standards.

Isn't it generally easier to get good ratings in higher level courses? The answer to this question is "yes." Actually, freshmen tend to rate a course more harshly than sophomores, sophomores more harshly than juniors, juniors more harshly than seniors, and seniors more harshly than graduate students. The majority of studies on this issue tend to support this belief. Aleamoni and Hexner (1980) cited 18 investigators who reported that graduate students and/or upper division students tended to rate instructors more favorably than did lower division students. They also cited eight investigators who reported no significant relationship between student status (freshman, sophomore, etc.) and ratings assigned to instructors.

Isn't it true that students who are required to take a course tend to rate the course more harshly than those taking it as an elective? Interestingly, the answer to this question is "yes." The bulk of the literature tends to support this conclusion. Several investigators have found that students who are required to take a course tend to rate it lower than students who elect to take it (Cohen & Humphreys, 1960; Gillmore & Brandenburg, 1974; Pohlmann, 1975). This finding is also supported by Gage (1961) and Lovell and Haner (1955) who found that instructors of elective courses were rated significantly higher than instructors of courses considered required by the students. In contrast, Heilman and Armentrout (1936) and Hildebrand, Wilson, and Dienst (1971) reported no differences between students' ratings of required courses and elective courses.

Isn't there a gender bias in student ratings? Don't female faculty tend to get lower ratings than male faculty? The literature on this question is not as plentiful as it is on other issues in student rating research, but the research that has been done appears to be fairly consistent in answering the question as "no." Earlier research provided conflicting results relating the gender of the student to student evaluations of instruction. Aleamoni and Thomas (1980), Doyle and Whitely (1974), Goodhartz (1948), and Isaacson, McKeachie, Milholland, Lin, Hofeller, Baerwaldt, et al. (1964) reported no differences between faculty ratings made by male and female students. In addition, Costin et

al. (1971) cited seven studies that reported no differences in overall ratings of instructors made by male and female students or in the ratings received by male and female instructors. Conversely, Bendig (1952) found female students to be more critical of male instructors than their male counterparts. Aleamoni and Hexner (1980) cited five studies which reported female students rated instructors higher on some subscales of instructor evaluation forms than did male students. (See Basow & Howe, 1987; Basow & Silberg, 1987; Feldman, 1992, 1993; Ferber & Huber, 1975; Goodwin & Stevens, 1993; Kaschak, 1978.) Walker (1969) found that female students rated female instructors significantly higher than they rated male instructors. This finding was confirmed by Centra and Gaubatz (2000), but they concluded that even though the differences in ratings given by male and female students were statistically significant, they should not make much difference in personnel decisions. Thus, although it appears that female students may tend to rate female instructors higher than they rate male instructors, overall the literature does not indicate a consistent difference in the student ratings received by male and female instructors.

Isn't it more difficult for math and science faculty to get good ratings? Surprisingly the answer to this question is "yes." This does not necessarily mean that all math and science faculty are poor teachers. Rather, the normative data gathered on thousands of courses show that courses in the fields of math and science tend to get lower ratings than those in the humanities. No definitive reason for this tendency has yet been determined, but we do know that different disciplines produce different rating norms. That is, student ratings can be affected by the discipline being taught. It is important, therefore, in interpreting student rating results that we do so by using the appropriate norm group.

Isn't it true that the only faculty who are really qualified to teach or evaluate their peers' teaching are those who are actively involved in conducting research in their field? The answer to this question is "no." At one time it was believed that good instruction and good research were so closely allied that it was unnecessary to evaluate them independently (Borgatta, 1970; Deming, 1972). Some studies have found weak positive correlations between research productivity and teaching effectiveness (Maslow & Zimmerman, 1956; McDaniel & Feldhusen, 1970; McGrath, 1962; Riley, Ryan, & Lipschitz, 1950; Stallings & Singhal, 1968). On the other hand, Aleamoni and Yimer (1973), Guthrie (1949, 1954), Hayes (1971), Linsky and Straus (1975), and Voeks (1962) found no significant relationship between instructors' research productivity and students' ratings of their teaching effectiveness. One study

(Aleamoni & Yimer, 1973) also reported no significant relationship between instructors' research productivity and colleagues' ratings of their teaching effectiveness. More recently Hattie and Marsh (1996) and Marsh and Hattie (2002) have shown rather conclusively that the relationship between research productivity and teaching effectiveness is effectively zero. It is ironic that those individuals who apparently value research highly but persist in believing that only those involved in research can be effective teachers apparently do not read the literature on this issue.

Don't students have to be away from the course, and possibly the college, for several years before they are able to make accurate judgments about the instructor and instruction? The answer to this question is a qualified "no." This very popular belief is continuously bolstered by anecdotes passed from teacher to teacher. However, conducting research on this issue has proven to pose certain problems. For example, it is very difficult to obtain a comparative and representative sample in longitudinal follow-up studies. The sampling problem is further compounded by the fact that almost all student attitudinal data relating to a course or instructor are gathered anonymously, thus no true pre- and post-test research designs are possible. Most studies in this area, therefore, have relied on surveys of alumni and/or graduating seniors. Early studies by Drucker and Remmers (1951) showed that alumni who have been out of school 5 to 10 years rated instructors much the same as students currently enrolled. More recent evidence by Aleamoni and Yimer (1974), Marsh (1977), Marsh and Overall (1979), and McKeachie, Lin, and Mendelson (1978) further substantiated the earlier findings. Thus, the literature up to this point leads to the conclusion that this popularly held belief is not generally true.

Isn't it true that the size of the class affects student ratings? The answer to this question appears to be "no." Taken in its entirety, the literature has not indicated consistent relationship between class size and student ratings. Aleamoni and Hexner (1980) cited eight studies that indicate that class size has an effect on student ratings, and seven others that found no relationship between class size and ratings. Some investigations have also reported curvilinear relationships between class size and student ratings (Gage, 1961; Kohlan, 1973; Lovell & Haner, 1955; Marsh, Overall, & Kesler, 1979; Pohlmann, 1975; Wood, Linsky, & Straus, 1974). There does appear to be a substantial body of literature that student ratings are positively correlated with student learning, as measured by student performance on standardized final exams (Cohen, 1981, 1986; d'Apollonia & Abrami, 1988; McCallum, 1984). Also, there is evidence that students tend to rate most highly those courses in which they learn the most (Centra, 1977) with students who perceive the instructor to be well prepared and highly organized achieving the highest gains in learning (Pascarella, 2001). To the degree that faculty teaching courses of smaller size appear to the student to be better organized and prepared, or to the degree that students learn more in smaller classes, there may be some relationship between class size and student ratings. However, taken in its entirety, the literature does not support the position that a consistent relationship between class size (alone) and student ratings of any sort exists.

It is interesting to note, however, that most large, required courses tend to be offered early in the curriculum of a college. Thus, most of the large, required courses may be offered in the freshman and sophomore years, just the time when students tend to rate their teachers most harshly. It would be easy to conclude from personal experience with such courses that the problem lies with the size of the course when, in fact, the research indicates it is the level (freshman, sophomore, etc.) and the fact that the course is required that are the factors which contribute to generally lower student ratings.

Does the time of the day the course is taught affect student ratings? The answer to this question is "we don't think so." There hasn't been much research on this question, but the limited amount of research in this area (Feldman, 1978; Guthrie, 1954; Yongkittikul, Gillmore, & Brandenburg, 1974) indicates that the time of day the course is offered does not influence student ratings.

Do majors in a course rate it differently than nonmajors? The answer to this question is "no." Although there is only a limited amount of research in this area (Aleamoni & Thomas, 1980; Cohen & Humphreys, 1960; Null & Nicholson, 1972; Rayder, 1968), all studies indicate that there are no significant differences and no significant relationships between student ratings and whether students were majors or nonmajors.

Does the rank of the instructor (instructor, assistant professor, associate professor, or professor) affect student ratings? The answer to this question is "not really." The literature on this issue, in general, does not support the idea that faculty of higher professorial rank get higher student ratings, because no consistent relationship between faculty rank and student ratings has been found. Although some investigators reported that instructors of higher rank receive higher student ratings (Clark & Keller, 1954; Downie, 1952, Gage 1961; Guthrie, 1954; Walker, 1969), others reported no significant relationship between instructor rank and student ratings (Aleamoni & Graham, 1974; Aleamoni & Thomas, 1980; Aleamoni & Yimer, 1973; Linsky & Straus, 1975; Singhal, 1968).

Conflicting results have also been found when comparing teaching experience to student ratings. Rayder (1968) reported a negative relationship, whereas Heilman and Armentrout (1936) found no significant relationship.

Why bother with 20 or 30 questions on a student rating form? Can't we just use single general items as accurate measures of instructional effectiveness? The use of single general items on student rating forms has been popular for some time. These items can be very reliable but do not provide information that is as useful as that produced by the multiple-item student rating form. The limited amount of research in this area (Aleamoni & Thomas, 1980; Burdsal & Bardo, 1986) indicates that there is a low relationship between single general items and specific items and that the single general items had a much higher relationship to descriptive variables (gender, status, required-elective, etc.) than did the specific items. These findings suggest that the use of single general items should be avoided, especially for tenure, promotion, or salary considerations. In any case, single general items provide little useful diagnostic information for use in faculty development efforts compared to multiple items that measure specific components of teaching performance.

What good are student ratings in efforts to improve instruction? The answer to this question is "under the right conditions, student ratings can be very helpful in assisting faculty to improve their instruction." Studies by Braunstein, Klein, and Pachla (1973), Centra (1973a), and Miller (1971) were inconclusive with respect to the effect of feedback at midterm to instructors whose instruction was again evaluated at the end of the term. However, Marsh, Fleiner, and Thomas (1975), Overall and Marsh (1979), and Sherman (1978) reported more favorable ratings from and improved learning by students by the end of the term. In order to determine if a combination of a printed report of the results and personal consultations would be superior to providing only a printed report of results, Aleamoni (1978b), McKeachie (1979), and Stevens and Aleamoni (1985) found that instructors significantly improved their ratings when personal consultations were provided. The key finding that emerges here is that student ratings can be used to improve instruction if used as part of a personal consultation between the faculty member and a faculty development resource person.

■ SUMMARY

Given the use of a well-designed, valid, and reliable student rating form, the literature indicates that:

- Faculty cannot buy good ratings by giving easy grades.

- Teaching a small class does not automatically guarantee high student ratings, nor does teaching a large class automatically guarantee low ratings.

- Lower level students (freshman, sophomore) do tend to rate more harshly than upper level students (seniors, graduate students).

- Students in required courses tend to rate their instructors more harshly than students in elective courses.

- Math and science courses tend to be rated more harshly than courses in the humanities.

- There is no overall gender bias in student ratings (i.e., one gender of faculty does not consistently get higher, or lower, ratings than the other).

- The time of day a class is taught does not affect the student ratings of the instructor (i.e., students do not automatically rate faculty lower in classes taught early in the morning or right after lunch).

- Student ratings can be quite helpful in instructional improvement efforts when used as part of a faculty development program that includes personal consultations.

Obviously the proper interpretation of student ratings must take a variety of issues into account. The important conclusion to be drawn here is the necessity to systematically incorporate research findings into the interpretation of student ratings in a comprehensive faculty evaluation system. See Chapter 14, especially the section on the Course Instructor Evaluation Questionnaire (CIEQ), for ways professionally developed, commercially available student rating form services address these issues.

Developing a Comprehensive Faculty Evaluation System

■ REFERENCES

Aleamoni, L. M. (1976). Typical faculty concerns about student evaluation of instruction. *National Association of Colleges and Teachers of Agriculture Journal, 20*(1), 16–21.

Aleamoni, L. M. (1978a). Development and factorial validation of the Arizona Course/Instructor Evaluation Questionnaire. *Educational and Psychological Measurement, 38*(6), 1063–1067.

Aleamoni, L. M. (1978b). The usefulness of student evaluations in improving college teaching. *Instructional Science, 7*(1), 95–105.

Aleamoni, L. M. (1999). Student rating myths versus research facts from 1924 to 1998. *Journal of Personnel Evaluation in Education, 13*(2), 153–166.

Aleamoni, L. M., & Graham, M. H. (1974). The relationship between CEQ ratings and instructor's rank, class size, and course level. *Journal of Educational Measurement, 11*(3), 189–202.

Aleamoni, L. M., & Hexner, P. Z. (1980). A review of the research on student evaluation and a report on the effect of different sets of instructions on student course and instructor evaluation. *Instructional Science, 9*(1), 67–84.

Aleamoni, L. M., & Spencer, R. E. (1973). The Illinois Course Evaluation Questionnaire: A description of its development and a report of some of its results. *Educational and Psychological Measurement, 33*, 669–684.

Aleamoni, L. M., & Thomas, G. S. (1980). Differential relationships of student, instructor, and course characteristics to general and specific items on a course questionnaire. *Teaching of Psychology, 7*(4), 233–235.

Aleamoni, L. M., & Yimer, M. (1973). An investigation of the relationship between colleague rating, student rating, research productivity, and academic rank in rating instructional effectiveness. *Journal of Educational Psychology, 64*(3), 274–277.

Aleamoni, L. M., & Yimer, M. (1974). *Graduating Senior Ratings Relationship to Colleague Rating, Student Rating, Research Productivity and Academic Rank in Rating Instructional Effectiveness* (Research Report No. 352). Urbana, IL: University of Illinois, Office of Instructional Resources, Measurement and Research Division.

Arreola, R. A. (1983). Students can distinguish between personality and content/organization in rating teachers. *Phi Delta Kappan, 65*(3), 222–223.

Basow, S. A., & Howe, K. G. (1987). Evaluations of college professors: Effects of professors' sex-type, and sex, and students' sex. *Psychological Reports, 60*, 671–678.

Basow, S. A., & Silberg, N. T. (1987). Student evaluations of college professors: Are female and male professors rated differently? *Journal of Educational Psychology, 79*(3), 308–314.

Beatty, M. J., & Zahn, C. J. (1990). Are student rating of communication instructors due to "easy" grading practices? An analysis of teacher credibility and student-reported performance levels. *Communication Education, 39*(4), 275–282.

Bendig, A. W. (1952). A preliminary study of the effect of academic level, sex, and course variables on student rating of psychology instructors. *Journal of Psychology, 34*, 2–126.

Benz, Z., & Blatt, S. J. (1995). Factors underlying effective college teaching: What students tell us. *Mid-Western Educational Researcher, 8*(1), 48–54.

Borgatta, E. F. (1970). Student ratings of faculty. *American Association of University Professors Bulletin, 56*, 6–7.

Braunstein, D. N., Klein, G. A., & Pachla, M. (1973). Feedback, expectancy, and shifts in student ratings of college faculty. *Journal of Applied Psychology, 58*(2), 254–258.

Burdsal. C. A., & Bardo, J. W. (1986). Measuring students' perceptions of teaching: Dimensions of evaluation. *Educational and Psychological Measurement, 56*, 63–79.

Cashin, W. E. (1999). Student ratings of teaching: Uses and misuses. In. P. Seldin & Associates, *Changing practices in evaluating teaching* (pp. 25–44). Bolton, MA: Anker.

Centra, J. A. (1977). Student ratings of instruction and their relationship to student learning. *American Educational Research Journal, 14*(1), 17–24.

Centra, J. A. (1973a). Effectiveness of student feedback in modifying college instruction. *Journal of Educational Psychology, 65*(3), 395–401.

Centra, J. A. (1973b). The student as godfather? The impact of student ratings on academia. In A. L. Sockloff (Ed.), *Proceedings of the First Invitational Conference on Faculty Effectiveness as Evaluated by Students*. Philadelphia, PA: Temple University Measurement and Research Center.

Centra, J. A., & Gaubatz, N. B. (2000). Is there gender bias in student evaluations of teaching? *The Journal of Higher Education, 70*(1), 17–23.

Clark, K. E., & Keller, R. J. (1954). Student ratings of college teaching. In R. A. Eckert & R. J. Keller (Eds.), *A university looks at its program: The report of the University of Minnesota Bureau of Institutional Research, 1942–1952*. Minneapolis, MN: University of Minnesota Press.

Cohen, P.A. (1981). Student ratings of instruction and student achievement: A meta-analysis of multi-section validity studies. *Review of Educational Research, 51*(3), 281–309.

Cohen, P. A. (1986, April). *An updated and expanded meta-analysis of multisection validity studies*. Paper presented at the annual meeting of the American Educational Research Association, San Francisco, CA.

Cohen, J., & Humphreys, L.G. (1960). *Memorandum to faculty*. Unpublished manuscript, University of Illinois Department of Psychology.

Costin, F., Greenough, W. T., & Menges, R. J. (1971). Student ratings of college teaching: Reliability, validity, and usefulness. *Review of Educational Research, 41*(5), 511–535.

d'Apollonia, S., & Abrami, P.C. (1988, April). The literature on student ratings of instruction: Yet another meta-analysis. Paper presented at the annual meeting of the American Educational Research Association, New Orleans, LA.

Deming, W. E. (1972). Memorandum on teaching. *The American Statistician, 26*(1), 47.

Downie, N. W. (1952). Student evaluation of faculty. *Journal of Higher Education, 23*, 495–496, 503.

Doyle, K. O., & Whitely, S. E. (1974). Student ratings as criteria for effective teaching. *American Educational Research Journal, 11*(3), 259–274.

Drucker, A. J., & Remmers, H. H. (1951). Do alumni and students differ in their attitudes toward instructors? *Journal of Educational Psychology, 42*(3), 129–143.

Dukes, R. L., & Victoria, G. (1989). The effects of gender, status, and effective teaching on the evaluation of college instruction. *Teaching Sociology, 17*(4), 447–457.

Everly, J. C., & Aleamoni, L. M. (1972). The rise and fall of the advisor ... students attempt to evaluate their instructors. *Journal of the National Association of Colleges and Teachers of Agriculture, 16*(2), 43–45.

Feldman, K. A. (1978). Course characteristics and college students' ratings of their teachers: What we know and what we don't. *Research in Higher Education, 9,* 199–242.

Feldman, K. A. (1989). The association between student ratings of specific instructional dimensions and student achievement: Refining and extending the synthesis of data from multisection validity studies. *Research in Higher Education, 30*(6), 583–645.

Feldman, K. A. (1992). College students' views of male and female college teachers: Part I—Evidence from the social laboratory and experiments. *Research in Higher Education, 33*(3), 317–375.

Feldman, K. A. (1993). College students' views of male and female college teachers: Part II—Evidence from students' evaluations of their classroom teachers. *Research in Higher Education, 34*(2), 151–211.

Ferber, M. A., & Huber, J. A. (1975). Sex of student and instructor: A study of student bias. American Journal of Sociology, 80, 949–963.

Frey, P. W. (1973). Student ratings of teaching: Validity of several rating factors. *Science, 182,* 83–85.

Frey, P. W. (1978). A two-dimensional analysis of student ratings of instruction. *Research in Higher Education, 9*(1), 69–91.

Gage, N. L. (1961). The appraisal of college teaching: An analysis of ends and means. *Journal of Higher Education, 32,* 17–22.

Gessner, P. K. (1973). Evaluation of instruction. *Science, 180,* 566–569.

Gillmore, G. M. (1973). *Estimates of reliability coefficients for items and subscales of the Illinois Course Evaluation Questionnaire* (Research Report No. 341). Urbana, IL: University of Illinois Office of Instructional Resources, Measurement, and Research Division.

Gillmore, G. M., & Brandenburg, D. C. (1974). *Would the proportion of students taking a class as a requirement affect the student rating of the course?* (Research Report No. 347). Urbana, IL: University of Illinois Office of Instructional Resources, Measurement, and Research Division.

Goodhartz, A. S. (1948). Student attitudes and opinions relating to teaching at Brooklyn College. *School and Society, 68*, 345–349.

Goodwin, L. D., & Stevens, E. A. (1993). The influence of gender on university faculty members' perceptions of "good" teaching. *Journal of Higher Education, 64*(2), 166–185.

Grush, J. E., & Costin, F. (1975). The student as consumer of the teaching process. *American Educational Research Journal, 12,* 55–66.

Guthrie, E. R. (1949). The evaluation of teaching. *Educational Record, 30,* 109–115.

Guthrie, E. R. (1954). *The evaluation of teaching: A progress report.* Seattle, WA: University of Washington.

Hattie, J., & Marsh, H. W. (1996). The relationship between research and teaching—A meta-analysis. *Review of Educational Research, 66*(4), 507–542.

Hayes, J. R. (1971). Research, teaching, and faculty fate. *Science, 172,* 227–230.

Heilman, J. D., & Armentrout, W. D. (1936). The rating of college teachers on ten traits by their students. *Journal of Educational Psychology, 27,* 197–216.

Hildebrand, M., Wilson, R. C., & Dienst, E. R. (1971). *Evaluating university teaching.* Berkeley, CA: University of California Center for Research and Development in Higher Education.

Hogan, T. P. (1973). Similarity of student ratings across instructors, courses, and time. *Research in Higher Education, 1*(2), 149–154.

Isaacson, R. L., McKeachie, W. J., Milholland, J. E., Lin, Y. G., Hofeller, M., Baerwaldt, J. W., & Zinn, K. L. (1964). Dimensions of student evaluations of teaching. *Journal of Educational Psychology, 55,* 344–351.

Johannessen, T. A., & Associates. (1997). What is important to students? Exploring dimensions in their evaluations of teachers. *Scandinavian Journal of Educational Research, 41*(2), 165–177.

Kaschak, E. (1978). Sex bias in student evaluations of college professors. *Psychology of Women Quarterly, 2*(3), 235–243.

Kohlan, R. G. (1973). A comparison of faculty evaluations early and late in the course. *Journal of Higher Education, 44,* 587–597.

Krehbiel, T. C., & Associates. (1997). Using student disconfirmation as a measure of classroom effectiveness, Journal of Educational Psychology, 82(2), 224–229.

Linsky, A. S., & Straus, M. A. (1975). Student evaluations, research productivity, and eminence of college faculty. *Journal of Higher Education, 46*(1), 89–102.

Lovell, G. D., & Haner, C. F. (1955). Forced-choice applied to college faculty rating. *Educational and Psychological Measurement, 15,* 291–304.

Macdonald, A. (1987). Student views on excellent courses. *Agricultural Education Magazine, 60*(3), 19–22.

Marlin, J. W., Jr. (1987). Student perception of end-of-course evaluations. *Journal of Higher Education, 58*(6), 704–716.

Marsh, H. W. (1977). The validity of students' evaluations: Classroom evaluations of instructors independently nominated as best and worst teachers by graduating seniors. *American Educational Research Journal, 14*(4), 441–447.

Marsh, H. W. (1984). Students' evaluations of university teaching: Dimensionality, reliability, validity, potential biases, and utility. *Journal of Educational Psychology, 76*(5), 707–754.

Marsh, H. W., & Bailey, M. (1993). Multidimensionality of students' evaluations of teaching effectiveness: A profile analysis. *Journal of Higher Education, 64*(1), 1–18.

Marsh, H. W., Fleiner, H., & Thomas, C. S. (1975). Validity and usefulness of student evaluations of instructional quality. *Journal of Educational Psychology, 67*(6), 883–889.

Marsh, H. W., & Overall, J. U. (1979). Long-term stability of students' evaluations: A note on Feldman's consistency and variability among college students in rating their teachers and courses. *Research in Higher Education, 10*(2), 139–147.

Marsh, H. W., Overall, J. U., & Kesler, S. P. (1979). Class size, students' evaluations, and instructional effectiveness. *American Educational Research Journal, 16*(1), 57–69.

Marsh, H. W., & Hattie, J. (2002). The relationship between research productivity and teaching effectiveness. *The Journal of Higher Education, 73*(5), 603–641.

Maslow, A. H., & Zimmerman, W. (1956). College teaching ability, scholarly activity, and personality. *Journal of Educational Psychology, 47,* 185–189.

McCallum, L. W. (1984). A meta-analysis of course evaluation data and its use in tenure decisions. *Research in Higher Education, 21*(2), 150–158

McDaniel, E. D., & Feldhusen, J. F. (1970). Relationships between faculty ratings and indexes of service and scholarship. *Proceedings of the 78th Annual Convention of the American Psychological Association, 5,* 619–620.

McGrath, E. J. (1962). Characteristics of outstanding college teachers. *Journal of Higher Education, 33,* 148–152.

McKeachie, W. J. (1979). Student ratings of faculty: A reprise. *Academe, 65*(6), 384–397.

McKeachie, W. J., Lin, Y. G., & Mendelson, C. N. (1978). A small study assessing teacher effectiveness: Does learning last? *Contemporary Educational Psychology, 3*(4), 352–357.

Menges, R. J. (1973). The new reporters: Students rate instruction. In C. R. Pace (Ed.), *New directions in higher education: No. 4. Evaluating learning and teaching* (pp. 59–75). San Francisco, CA: Jossey-Bass.

Merriam-Webster OnLine. (2005–2006). *Valid.* Retrieved June 28, 2006, from http://www.m-w.com/dictionary/valid

Miller, M. T. (1971). Instructor attitudes toward, and their use of, student ratings of teachers. *Journal of Educational Psychology, 62*(3), 235–239.

Null, E. J., & Nicholson, E. W. (1972). Personal variables of students and their perception of university instructors. *College Student Journal, 6,* 6–9.

Overall, J. U., & Marsh, H. W. (1979). Midterm feedback from students. Its relationship to instructional improvement and students' cognitive and affective outcomes. *Journal of Educational Psychology, 71,* 856–865.

Pascarella, E. T. (2001). Cognitive growth in college: Surprising and reassuring findings from The National Study of Student Learning. *Change, 33*(6), 21–27.

Perry, R. P., Abrami, P. C., & Leventhal, L. (1979). Educational seduction: The effect of instructor expressiveness and lecture content on student ratings and achievement. *Journal of Educational Psychology, 71*(1), 107–116.

Pohlmann, J. T. (1975). A multivariate analysis of selected class characteristics and student ratings of instruction. *Multivariate Behavioral Research, 10*(1), 81–91.

Rayder, N. F. (1968). College student ratings of instructors. *Journal of Experimental Education, 37,* 76–81.

Riley, J. W., Ryan, B. F., & Lipschitz, M. (1950). *The student looks at his teacher.* New Brunswick, NJ: Rutgers University Press.

Rodabaugh, R. C., & Kravitz, D. A. (1994). Effects of procedural fairness on student judgments of professors. *Journal on Excellence in College Teaching, 5*(2).

Seldin, P. (1993). How colleges evaluate professors: 1983 vs. 1993. *AAHE Bulletin, 46*(2), 6–8, 12.

Shepherd, G. J. & Trank, D. M. (1989). Individual difference in consistency of evaluation: Student perceptions of teacher effectiveness. *Journal of Research and Development in Education, 22*(3), 45–52.

Sherman, T. M. (1978). The effects of student formative evaluation of instruction on teacher behavior. *Journal of Educational Technology Systems, 6,* 209–217.

Singhal, S. (1968). *Illinois course evaluation questionnaire items by rank of instructor, sex of the instructor, and sex of the student* (Research Report No. 282). Urbana, IL: University of Illinois Office of Instructional Resources, Measurement, and Research Division.

Stallings, W. M., & Singhal, S. (1968). *Some observations on the relationships between productivity and student evaluations of courses and teaching* (Research Report No. 274). Urbana, IL: University of Illinois Office of Instructional Resources, Measurement, and Research Division.

Stevens, J. J., & Aleamoni, L. M. (1985). The use of evaluative feedback for instructional improvement: A longitudinal perspective. *Instructional Science, 13*, 285–304.

Sullivan, A. M., & Skanes, G. R. (1974). Validity of student evaluations of teaching and the characteristics of successful instructors. *Journal of Educational Psychology, 66*(4), 584–590.

Thorndike, R.L. & Hagen, E. (1969). *Measurement and evaluation in psychology and education* (3rd ed.). New York, NY: John Wiley & Sons.

Tollefson, N., Chen, J. S., & Kleinsasser, A. (1989). The relationship of students' attitudes about effective teaching to students' ratings of effective teaching. Educational and Psychological Measurement, 49(3), 529–536.

Voeks, V. W. (1962). Publications and teaching effectiveness. *Journal of Higher Education, 33*, 212–218.

Walker, B. D. (1969). An investigation of selected variables relative to the manner in which a population of junior college students evaluate their teachers. *Dissertation Abstracts, 29*(9–B), 3474.

Ware, J. E., Jr., & Williams, R. G. (1977). Discriminant analysis of student ratings as a means of identifying lecturers who differ in enthusiasm or information giving. *Educational and Psychological Measurement, 37*(3), 627–639.

Waters, M., Kemp, E., & Pucci, A. (1988). High and low faculty evaluations: Descriptions by students. *Teaching of Psychology, 15*, 203–204.

Wood, K., Linsky, A. S., & Straus, M. A. (1974). Class size and student evaluation of faculty. *Journal of Higher Education, 45*(7), 524–534.

Yongkittikul, C., Gillmore, G. M., & Brandenburg, D. C. (1974). *Does the time of course meeting affect course ratings by students?* (Research Report No. 346). Urbana, IL: University of Illinois Office of Instructional Resources, Measurement, and Research Division.

Portions of this chapter appeared in the following article. Used by permission.

Aleamoni, L. M. (1999). Student rating myths versus research facts from 1924 to 1998. *Journal of Personnel Evaluation in Education, 13*(2), 153–166.

13

Operating the Faculty Evaluation System: Issues in Designing and Using Student Rating Forms

▨ LEGAL ISSUES

Easily the largest and most visible component of a faculty evaluation system is the student rating form and its computerized output. Over the years, for good or ill, student ratings have come to be the single most heavily weighted component of faculty evaluation systems. In response, many institutions have developed their own student rating forms, generally designed either by faculty, students, administrators, or a committee made up of some combination of these. Experience has shown that in the majority of cases these student rating forms have not been constructed in accordance with professional psychometric principles and standards. Thus, the forms may be of inadequate, or at least indeterminate, reliability and/or validity. The use of these forms may pose a legal liability for the institution.

In the general area of faculty evaluation the courts have tended to accept faculty-determined criteria and standards of professional performance, focusing instead on the consistent application of contractual conditions or procedures (Kaplin, 1978). Centra (1993) points out that, from a legal perspective, institutions must take care to comply with faculty evaluation procedures specified in the contract or faculty handbook. In addition, an institution may not use criteria or processes that create a discriminatory assessment based on ethnic background, race, or gender (Braskamp & Ory, 1994). Thus, the issues of *what* to measure and *how* to measure it have tended to be left to faculty to determine. Primarily, institutions must have procedures in place that do not violate basic civil rights and, in the event of an audit, must be able to provide evidence that their procedures have been applied correctly and consistently. The legal ramifications surrounding the design and use of student rating forms in a faculty evaluation system must be considered within the context of these principles.

Carr & Padgett (1992) reviewed the legal liability in all 50 states concerning the design and use of student rating forms. They concluded that the primary legal issue revolves around statistical validity and reliability of such forms. Legal liability is posed when unreliable and invalid student rating forms are used in support of personnel decisions. The legal liability of the institution includes discrimination, defamation, and violations of individual privacy and academic freedom.

> State laws provide an additional environmental element creating possible legal liability. Of particular concern are the open records laws. Unless exceptions are made, these laws provide that employment records such as salary and performance evaluations of public employees are public information. Some colleges and universities publish the results of student ratings of faculty. Some do not. Under open records laws, ratings would have to be made public for a single faculty member or for all faculty members if an individual or group requested this information. In this litigious society liability for publishing student evaluations of faculty members based on forms of dubious statistical validity seems rather apparent. (Carr & Padget, 1992, p. 69)

An examination of the states' open records laws indicates that all states have laws allowing public access to government records; however, various states provide certain exceptions or limitations relative to access to faculty personnel records.

All Personnel Records Public—No Exceptions

The following states provide for no exception to state statutes pertaining to the release of public employee records, including faculty personnel records:

- Alaska
- Arizona
- Arkansas
- Georgia
- Massachusetts
- Maine
- Minnesota
- Missouri
- Montana
- North Carolina
- North Dakota
- Ohio
- Tennessee
- Texas
- Utah
- Virginia
- Wisconsin

All Personnel Records Public—General Exceptions

The following states grant only general exceptions pertaining to the release of faculty personnel records. These exceptions pertain to withholding information that would invade a person's privacy but do not specify what this information may be.

- Washington, DC
- Kentucky
- Louisiana
- Nevada
- Pennsylvania
- Washington
- West Virginia

Specific Exception for Faculty

The following states specifically exclude faculty personnel records, including student ratings, from release to the public:

- Florida
- New Mexico
- Oregon
- South Carolina

Personnel Records Not Public

The following states specifically prohibit the release of personnel records including faculty evaluation results:

- Alabama
- California
- Colorado
- Connecticut
- Delaware
- Hawaii
- Iowa
- Idaho
- Illinois
- Indiana
- Kansas
- Maryland
- Michigan
- Mississippi

- Nebraska
- New Hampshire
- New Jersey
- New York
- Oklahoma
- Rhode Island
- South Dakota
- Vermont
- Wyoming

Institutions in states that have no or only general exceptions to public records laws may find themselves at greater risk for possible legal action revolving around the publication of faculty records that include data from unreliable and invalid student rating forms. In those states where public disclosure of faculty records is less likely owing to specific exceptions, the risk of legal liability still exists if faculty personnel decisions are challenged in court.

In terms of the design or adoption of student rating forms, the key issue is to establish their reliability and validity prior to their use in a faculty evaluation system. The adoption of commercially available student rating forms such as those reviewed in Chapter 15 ensures that the forms are reliable and valid, since they have undergone rigorous psychometric procedures in their development. It is generally recommended that an institution consider the adoption of a commercially available student rating form before embarking on the task of building one from scratch. However, if the institution chooses to design and use its own student rating form, the administration must be willing to commit to the yearlong rigorous psychometric process involved producing a reliable and valid instrument. To fail to do so places the institution at unnecessary legal risk.

> Civil rights legislation has provided a legal environment in which employment tests and performance evaluations must in most cases be statistically reliable and valid. That is, there must be statistical documentation that they are reliable measures, are job related and predict job performance. Otherwise, the employer's legal defense is likely to be inadequate in cases of discrimination. (Carr & Padgett, 1992, p. 68)

■ DESIGNING A VALID AND RELIABLE STUDENT RATING FORM

As frequently noted in previous chapters the design and development of a valid, reliable form intended to measure the teaching performance of an instructor and/or the perceived effectiveness of a course, is a technical task requiring professional expertise in statistics and psychological measurement. It is a common fallacy among educators that all that is required to develop a questionnaire is to sit down and write a set of questions. It should be noted that what is being constructed is an instrument designed to measure psychological phenomena (i.e., perceptions, opinions, reactions, etc.). As such its development must be held to the same high professional standards of accuracy, reliability, and validity as any other scientific measurement tool or instrument. In fact, since non-physical (psychological) phenomena are being measured, the task of designing the measurement tool is that much more complex and difficult to accomplish. To assume that all one has to do to construct a psychometric instrument is to write a set of questions is analogous to assuming that all one has to do to construct an automobile is to get a motor and attach some wheels to it. Both tasks are easier said than done. And both tasks require not only precision and skill but also an understanding of the underlying principles and science involved.

As noted earlier, many student rating forms in use are homemade—constructed by faculty, students, administrators, and/or committees who lacked questionnaire design and scaling expertise. Such instruments typically are not subjected to reliability and validity studies and, therefore, may be easily influenced by extraneous variables in the classroom such as time of day, class size, and the instructor's personality.

In order for student ratings to be considered an integral part of a comprehensive instructional evaluation system, they must be reliable and valid. As a practical matter, certain issues must be considered when designing and/or selecting a student rating form.

Student Ratings Versus Student Evaluations of Teaching

One of the core issues that must be addressed in considering the process of designing a valid and reliable instrument to be completed by students as part of the assessment of faculty teaching performance is the differentiation between student ratings and student evaluations. As noted in the introduction, the term *evaluation* is defined as: The process of interpreting a measurement (or aggregate of measurements) by means of a specific value construct to determine the degree to which the measurement(s) represent a desirable condition. Considering this definition of evaluation, and examining the role of student input into the evaluation of teaching performance, we can take one of two directions: 1) Construct a form that asks students to make judgments on the desirability of certain instructor performances or characteristics (i.e., evaluate teaching and the teacher), or, 2) construct a form that measures the impact of the instructor's performance on the students and from which a judgment on the desirability of the per-

formance (evaluation) will be made later by the systematic application of a specific, predetermined value construct.

Taking the first approach results in constructing student *evaluation* forms. On these forms students are asked such questions as "How would you rate this instructor compared to all the other teachers you have had?" or, "Overall, how would you rate this teacher?" These questions ask the student to classify the faculty member in such ways as "among the top 10%," "exceptional," "unsatisfactory," or "among the worst." The problem with this approach is that the judgment about whether the faculty member's performance represents a desirable or undesirable condition is being made on the basis of the student's individual value construct. Each student's individual value construct may not only be unknown to either the faculty member or the administrator reading the results, but may differ from student to student. It is for this reason that student evaluation forms (that is, forms designed only to gather student evaluative judgments concerning faculty performance) may be considered inherently flawed. The reason for this is that no matter how technically correct the items may be in terms of their psychometric characteristics, there is no assurance that the value construct being applied by the student to interpret their observations and experiences (and thus make evaluative judgments) either matches that of the faculty or is even consistent from student to student. This flaw in many of the forms used in higher education generates the common conception that student evaluations are merely a popularity contest.

In contrast to student evaluation forms, student *rating* forms take the approach of measuring student perceptions and reactions rather than asking for an evaluation of some aspect of teaching. These forms measure those psychological phenomena that the student is best qualified to provide—their own reactions. Well-designed student rating forms include such items as "The objectives of the course were clear," "The audiovisuals used in class helped me to learn the material," and "The instructor's speaking style made it difficult for me to understand what he/she was saying." Students are then provided a "Strongly Agree–Strongly Disagree" or similar scale with which to respond to each item. In this way, measures of the students' perceptions and reactions to certain aspects of the instructor's performance are gathered. The evaluation of the instructor's performance is then made by someone else using an agreed-upon value construct to interpret the students' reactions as being indicative of either a desirable or undesirable teaching performance. As noted earlier, the use of a previously agreed-upon value construct in the evaluation process is the essence of *controlled subjectivity*. And, it is controlled subjectivity that makes possible a fair and consistent faculty evaluation system.

Unfortunately, the terms *student rating* and *student evaluation* have come to be used interchangeably in higher education, and even in the professional literature. Not all so-called student evaluation forms truly call for the student to make an evaluative judgment, but are, in fact, student rating forms (although they may contain one or two items calling for an evaluative conclusion). On the other hand, not all student rating forms are designed to simply measure student perceptions and reactions, but include many items that call for students to come to an evaluative conclusion. It is likely that it is this mixture of terms and approaches (i.e., measurement of student perceptions and reactions versus requests for students to draw evaluative conclusions) that has led to much of the confusion and continuing concern over the use of student input in the evaluation of faculty performance.

In any case, as has been described in greater detail elsewhere, the evaluation of teaching performance must be based on multiple sources of data, not just student rating data which, of necessity, can only provide part of the picture of the complex (meta-) professional performance we call teaching.

Validity and Reliability of the Student Rating Form

The validity of student ratings is an issue of continuing discussion and disagreement, perhaps due in part to the confusion between the concepts of student ratings and student evaluations (the underlying reasons for this continuing confusion are explored in Chapter 12). Basically, the source of this disagreement is the fact that a universally accepted definition or description of the characteristics of an excellent teacher does not exist. While the student rating literature provides an indication of the aspects of faculty classroom performance that impact learning, there is still no precise formula for being a good teacher to which everyone subscribes.

Although from a professional psychometric perspective the validity of a given student rating form may be calculated, determination of validity is predicated on some underpinning construct or assumptions of what should be measured. Should a student rating form measure only those things that affect immediate learning outcomes? Should a student rating form measure some longer-term impact on students' perspectives, motivations, or values? Should a student rating form measure the degree to which a faculty member's style of dress or speech offends students? Faculty will answer these and many similar questions differently depending on what they consider to be

relevant and important (of value). Thus, from a practical perspective, the real problem in determining the validity of any student rating form is to determine a priori what aspects of teaching performance should be measured. There is no fixed answer to this problem. Although there is strong evidence that teacher preparation and organization positively affects student learning (Pascarella, 2001), different faculty value systems may dictate that different aspects of faculty performance (beyond those that affect immediate learning outcomes) be measured. For example, in certain faith-based institutions a faculty member's teaching performance may be required to include an expression of faith in the style of delivery and the context in which the content is presented.

In addition to the issue of the validity of student rating forms, there is the issue of reliability. From a practical perspective, a student rating form is reliable if it accurately and consistently measures students' perceptions and reactions to previously agreed-upon faculty teaching performances and characteristics. If the form does not measure those aspects of teaching performance that the faculty feel are relevant and important, it doesn't matter how accurate and consistent its measurements are. In fact, experience has shown that faculty prefer a form that they perceive as valid even if the evidence shows that the form is not reliable. Many institutions fall into the trap of using a student rating form that appears to be measuring the "right things," without being concerned whether the form is in fact producing consistent and accurate measures of those right things.

From a strict, professional psychometric perspective, an instrument must be reliable before it can be determined whether it is valid. That is, the instrument must be measuring something with accuracy and consistency before it can be confirmed that it is measuring what we want to measure. Unfortunately, however, in common practice institutions accept a student rating form as being valid in the sense that it asks questions that the faculty and/or the administration think should be asked, without checking to make sure that the form is reliable first. Such institutions may be at risk (see discussion on legal issues).

Designing a Student Rating Form

The following is a brief discussion and overview of the procedures required in building a valid and reliable student rating form. This section is not intended to serve as a technical reference on the issue of psychometrics. Rather, what follows is a summary, with examples, of the various phases an institution must go through to design and develop its own valid and reliable student rating form. It is assumed in this discussion that the institution will consult with appropriate professionals in psychometrics when carrying out the following procedures.

Phase I: Determine the issues to be measured by the form. While the student rating literature indicates that the broad dimensions of teacher preparation and organization, clarity of communication, and rapport with students are among those that tend to impact student learning, it is important at this point to gain consensus among the faculty and administration on the major issues they feel should be considered. For example, if there is a concern that sexism or racism not be expressed or demonstrated in any way by the teacher, then this should be made clear. It is critical that the individuals involved in this discussion do not fall into the trap of beginning the process by simply sitting down and writing the items for the form. This discussion should steer away from specific questions and focus on the underlying issues and values on which the questions may be based.

The following strategy has been employed successfully in carrying out this step:

• Ask the faculty to develop a list of one-, two-, or three-word descriptors of an *excellent* teacher and another list of one-, two-, or three-word descriptors of a *poor* teacher.

• Ask the students to develop the same two lists.

• Examine the faculty-generated and student-generated lists of terms used to describe excellent and poor teachers and find those descriptors used by the faculty and students to describe each type of teacher.

• Use the list of common descriptors (those used by both faculty and students) for excellent and poor teachers to develop items for the student rating form.

Phase II: Write or select the items. Once the issues or characteristics to be measured are determined, the process of either writing new items or selecting them from existing catalogs (such as the one in Chapter 14) may proceed. As much as possible, the items should use the common list of descriptors determined in Phase I.

• Each item should be written to measure only one perception, reaction, etc.

• For each issue to be measured be certain to write and/or select at least six to eight items.

Phase III: Develop/select appropriate response scales. A key element in building a valid and reliable student rating form is the scale that is used to elicit student responses. It is critical that the response scale used for each item meets certain logical and technical requirements, including:

1) The response scale must be *appropriate.* Response choices must logically follow from the item/question. For example, the item "Was the instructor organized?" logically calls for a "yes" or "no" response. To ask such a question and then give the student a response scale such as Excellent–Poor or Strongly Agree–Strongly Disagree will result in unreliable data.

2) The response scale must be *parallel.* That is, the scale must not mix two or more types of responses. The following is an example of a *nonparallel* scale:

• Very Good

• Above Average

• Satisfactory

• Unsatisfactory

Very Good fits with a Very Good–Very Poor scale; Above Average fits with a scale that provides indications of performance above, at, or below Average; and Satisfactory and Unsatisfactory belong to a separate satisfaction scale. A nonparallel scale compromises the reliability of the student ratings.

3) The response scale must be *balanced:* There must be an equal number of positive and negative choices. An *unbalanced* scale is one that has either more positive or more negative choices. Obviously if you have more opportunities to make a positive response than a negative one, the responses will tend to be skewed in that direction. The converse applies if there are more negative responses than positive. Also, it is generally recommended that odd-numbered scales in which the middle response is "Neutral" or "Don't Know" *not* be used unless the middle position has a specific meaning relative to the item. Otherwise some students will use the middle response simply to avoid answering the item. The following are examples of a balanced, parallel scale and a scale that is unbalanced and nonparallel:

Balanced Parallel Scale	Unbalanced and Nonparallel Scale
(+) Strongly Agree	(+) Excellent
(+) Agree	(+) Outstanding
(+) Disagree	(+) Satisfactory
(+) Strongly Disagree	(+) Unsatisfactory

4) Every point on the scale must be defined. Do *not* use a scale where only the end points are defined such as "Low 1 2 3 4 5 High." With such a scale you can never be sure what the student is thinking when they

pick a "2," for example. Such scales tend to compromise the reliability, and perhaps even the validity, of the response data.

5) Make certain to use abbreviations to denote points on the response scale, *not* numbers or the letters A, B, C, D, E. For example, if your response scale is Strongly Agree–Strongly Disagree, use the abbreviations SA for Strongly Agree, A for Agree, D for Disagree, and SD for Strongly Disagree. Do not use 4 for Strongly Agree, 3 for Agree, and so forth. Also, do not use A for Strongly Agree, B for Agree, C for Disagree, and D for Strongly Disagree. Again, when either numbers or letters are used instead of the abbreviations for the responses, you can never be certain what the students are thinking when they respond. The letters A, B, C, and D can easily be interpreted as grades rather than varying degrees of agreement. The numbers 4, 3, 2, and 1 can mean different things to different people, including being interpreted as ranking system. Therefore it is critical that the response choices on the student rating form either use the full words describing the choice points or an appropriate abbreviation of those words.

Phase IV: Conduct field trials to gather the data needed for subsequent validity and reliability determination. At this point you may be testing 50, 60, or even 100 items. Separate subsets of these items should be placed on different forms and administered to all kinds of classes. Once you have at least 200 responses for each item (that is, each item will have appeared on one form or another so that at least 200 students have had the opportunity to respond to it) you are ready to move to the next step.

Phase V: Conduct a factor analytic study. It is critical to determine the reliability and validity of the form and the degree to which the items reliably measure each issue or characteristic of interest. Nationally standardized forms, such as those reviewed in Chapter 15, should be used as the vehicle for developing your own form: Insert the items developed for your form in the optional items section of the commercial form and then conduct factor analytic studies on the responses to the commercial rating form items and the items written for your form. In this way it is possible to compare the results of the analysis of your items with the analyses of the items on the commercial form. Although the factor analytic study must be conducted by individuals proficient in statistics and psychometrics, the outcome of such an analysis should produce at least four items for each issue of interest. In order to adequately measure a specific perception of or reaction to an

issue of interest, at least four items measuring that perception or reaction must be used. From a technical perspective the factor loadings of these items on the dimension being measured should be .400 or higher.

Phase VI: Develop subscales based on the result of the factor analysis. The form should produce separate scores for each of the dimensions or characteristics being measured by the form. Such subscales provide more detailed diagnostic information for instructor use in improving or enhancing their performance and fairer comparisons across time and across different courses.

Phase VII: Refine the form based on the results of the factor analytic study to ensure reliability of each subscale and the form as a whole. Ideally, the reliability values should be .60 or higher.

Phase VIII: Establish norms. Since no specific, agreed-upon set of criteria for what constitutes an excellent teacher exists, we must use a norm-referenced model of evaluation. That is, we cannot simply say that someone is an excellent or poor teacher based on a specific rating value derived from the student rating form. It is important to develop a way to interpret the ratings relative to an appropriate cohort group. This part of the process is the most time consuming, since data on the form must be gathered for at least three years before any kind of appropriate normative interpretation may be made. Data from all classes should be accumulated without replacement into a normative database that can then be used to properly interpret the student ratings of an individual faculty member. Thus, it will become possible to interpret the student ratings for an individual in terms of where the faculty member stands relative to others in the norm group. The commercially available forms reviewed in Chapter 15 all make use of norms—developed over decades of use across a broad spectrum of courses and course types—to provide appropriate interpretations of an individual's ratings.

Phase IX: Organize the items. The final step in developing your student rating form is to decide how the items are to be grouped and labeled in the final design of the form: Determine how the items should be organized for easy reading and answering and how and where the responses should be recorded. If there is a logical or chronological flow to the items, then their organization on the form should reflect that. If there are only a few negative items, then one or two should appear very early in the instrument to avoid positive response set mistakes (i.e., before students get in the habit of thinking the response to the extreme right is always the most positive). It is advisable to have a few negatively stated items in the instrument, but only if they can be stated negatively in a logical manner.

At this point it should be clear that constructing a valid and reliable student rating form is a time-consuming, technical process that requires various studies and analyses. As stated before, it is recommended that experts in psychometrics and statistics be consulted in undertaking such a project. A good example of a study that demonstrates the technicalities involved in constructing a valid and reliable student rating form is "Differential Relationship of Student, Instructor, and Course Characteristics to General and Specific Items on a Course Evaluation Questionnaire" (Aleamoni & Thomas, 1980).

Phase X: Implement the Student Rating System. Once the student rating form has been completely developed and has been shown to be valid and reliable, it can be placed into operation within the comprehensive faculty evaluation system. The overall usefulness of the student rating form can be maximized, however, if it is constructed so that it has not only the standard, validated, and reliable items, but also room for additional optional items that may be unique to either a department or an individual faculty member. Forms constructed in such a manner allow the instructor to select supplementary (or more diagnostic) items from a catalog. Each commercial student rating form reviewed in Chapter 15 is designed in this manner. For example, the Course/Instructor Evaluation Questionnaire (CIEQ) provides the standard 21 items (from which the five subscale scores are derived and for which normative data are provided), and two optional 21-item response sections. The optional item response sections allow instructors to select up to 42 additional items from the 373-item CIEQ optional item catalog.

A more sophisticated approach to maximizing the utility of student rating forms is to develop multiple standard forms. This requires the institution to possess a great deal of in-house expertise in psychological measurement and statistics and be willing to undertake the major research and development projects involved. Under this approach optional items and optional item sections are generally not available to the individual instructor. Instead the instructor is given a choice among forms that more closely match specific teaching/learning environments. For example, the University of Washington Instructional Assessment System provides six valid and reliable forms to their faculty, one for small lecture/discussion courses, one for large lecture courses, one for seminar courses, one for problem-solving courses, one for skills-oriented or practicum courses, and one for quiz sections (Abrami & Murphy, 1980).

■ ADMINISTERING STUDENT RATING SYSTEMS

After an appropriate instrument has been developed or selected, administrative procedures need to be established. If possible the responsibility for managing and directing a campus-wide program of distributing, administering, and collecting student ratings should be given to a unit such as a teaching and learning center, a professional development center, a testing and evaluation center, or an office of institutional research. The responsibility for operating the system should be given to the student government or distributed to either individual college deans or department chairs. As a last option, the responsibility for operating the system may be assumed by the chief academic officer of the institution, since the danger of having the program perceived as a "watchdog" program of the administration is increased by doing so. Ideally, the unit that operates the student rating system should be seen, legitimately, as one dedicated to providing services to the faculty.

In keeping with the concept of designing and operating the faculty evaluation system to serve formative and summative purposes, several guidelines related to student rating systems may be stated. First, it must be recognized that the value of any student rating system relies on the confidence the students have that their input will cause them no harm, and have some effect on the instructor (Arreola, 1987). In actual practice, operating a student rating system requires a careful balancing of the needs and concerns of the students, faculty, and administration. These needs and concerns are sometimes antithetical to one another. This can often place the person in charge of the office or agency running the student rating system in a very difficult and tricky situation.

On the one hand, faculty may be fearful and distrustful of the administration. Faculty go through a predictable set of stages in resisting or attempting to escape from a faculty evaluation system. On the other hand, students may be fearful of retribution by the faculty if they give negative ratings, and they might not believe the faculty or the administration will pay attention to what they say anyway. Finally, the administration may desperately want any kind of quantitative or hard data on which to base difficult personnel decisions. Long experience with these circumstances leads to the following practical guidelines pertaining to running a student rating system:

1) If at all possible, do not locate a student rating coordination or processing agency in the office of a dean, vice president, or other major administrator. Such placement only reinforces the idea that the student

rating system and the faculty evaluation office are simply watchdog agencies of the administration.

2) Try to locate the student rating form processing office in a test-scoring center, computer center, media center, or, ideally, in a faculty professional enrichment center.

3) Arrange the processing schedule so that the completed analyses of the student rating forms are not available until after final grades have been reported.

4) Conduct a program to maintain the credibility of the students in the student rating system. Include regular contacts with student government, appoint student representative(s) to the Committee charged with developing the comprehensive faculty evaluation system. Submit articles to the student newspaper describing the importance and use of student ratings at least once each term. A constant communication campaign with the students must be maintained which informs them that the faculty member will not see the student rating results until after grades have been reported and that the student ratings are taken seriously by the faculty and the administration (Arreola, 1983). Without such a campaign, the student rating system will experience serious problems, including refusal of the students to complete forms, completing forms by simply marking the same response for all items, and covering the forms with various types of graffiti.

5) Make it clear that the student rating form processing office is a service to the faculty and not the administration or the student government. Do not automatically send results of the ratings to the administration or the student newspaper, even though written permission has been given by the instructor. Such actions will forever taint the credibility of the processing office. Require anyone wanting information concerning the student ratings of a faculty member to get them from that faculty member.

6) Make certain that the issue of the distribution of copies of the individual faculty student rating reports is a matter between the administration and the faculty or between the students and the faculty. Provide the faculty member with multiple copies of the student rating report form containing the analyses or other results; do not keep copies in the processing office. Make it physically difficult to recover or reconstitute a given faculty member's student rating report. The best approach is to maintain only raw data computer files. Then, if a request is received by the processing office to provide copies of a particular faculty member's evaluation results, it can truthfully be said that the processing office has no copies but that the faculty member has several.

The issue of the confidentiality and distribution of individual faculty member's student rating reports should be a matter between the faculty member and the administration and not between the processing office and the administration. The processing office must not be perceived as an arm of a "big brother" administration.

The method of administering and gathering student responses can determine the quality of the resulting data. It is advisable to administer the instrument in a formalized manner in the classroom by providing a standard set of instructions and enough time to complete all the items. If the instrument is administered in an informal manner, without a standard set of instructions and a designated time to fill it out, the students tend not to take it seriously and possibly do not bother to turn it in. Furthermore, if the students are permitted to take the instruments home to fill them out and return them at the next class meeting, very few instruments will be returned.

The following practical procedures have been successfully used in managing large student rating systems. These procedures assume that the faculty member will not be the primary person administering the rating forms in class to the students.

1) Set up a log system for maintaining control of student rating form distribution and collection. This log should contain the name of the faculty member, the number of the course, and the enrollment. Such information is generally available from the registrar's office.

2) Prepare student rating packets with at least five more sheets than the official number enrolled in the course. Log in the actual number of sheets sent to the instructor.

3) In addition to the student rating forms, the packet should contain a standardized script to be read when administering the forms and a proctor identification form (PIF). Upon receipt of the packet, the faculty member should remove the PIF and indicate the name of the student in the class who has been selected to administer the rating forms. The faculty member must sign the PIF and return it separately to the processing office. The processing office should log in the date of the receipt of the form and the name of the student proctor.

4) After removing the PIF, the faculty member should give the student rating form package to the chosen student proctor. The student proctor removes and distributes the student rating forms and removes and reads a special form identified as the proctor administration form. It contains the standardized script for administering the student rating form. In addition to the standard information concerning the use of a #2 pencil to record student responses, the script should note that

- The faculty member is not in the room.

- The results of the rating will not be returned to the instructor until after final grades have been turned in.

- The students' responses will be an important part of the information considered in improving the course or making promotion, tenure, retention, and merit pay decisions.

5) The proctor must sign the proctor administration form, certifying that the student rating forms were administered in accordance to the instructions, that the script was read as part of the administration, and that the faculty member was not in the room.

6) Finally, cross-checking items should be included on the student rating forms that ask such questions as, "Was the instructor in the room when this form was administered?" "Did the proctor read the administration directions out loud to the class?" and, "Do you have confidence that your responses will make a difference?"

7) After the forms are completed and returned to the proctor, they should all be placed in the envelope, along with the signed proctor administration form, and dropped in the campus mail to the processing office.

8) Upon receipt of the packet, the date of receipt should be logged in; the name on the proctor administration form should be checked against the name reported by the instructor on the proctor identification form. A count is made of the incoming completed student rating forms to make sure that the number does not exceed the official enrollment figure for the class. This latter step is designed to discourage stuffing of completed student rating packets by either students or, in certain instances, the faculty themselves.

9) Before machine processing, the student rating forms must be visually scanned for stray marks. Often the students doodle in the margins or simply cross out an incorrect response rather than erase it. These types of marks must be erased before the sheets can be processed. Experience has shown that the student rating processing office would be well advised to buy electric erasers rather than using the eraser end of a pencil. The time and staff size required to carry out this necessary step is often much larger than would first be anticipated. This is especially true if the system is new and the students are not yet familiar with the rating forms.

10) Finally, log the date when the completed computer analysis and student rating forms were returned to the faculty member.

◼ OPTIONS FOR ADMINISTERING RATING FORMS IN CLASS

The steps described in the previous section assume that a student proctor, selected from the class itself, administers the rating form. Other options, more or less desirable, are possible.

Self-Administered

In systems where instructors administer their own student rating forms, they should also read the standard set of instructions after the forms have been distributed and then remain in the front of the room until all forms have been completed. The instructor may then select a student from the class to gather the completed forms and deposit them in the campus mail. As before, the statement read should specify that the instructor will not see the results until after the term grades have been turned into the admissions and records office. The exception to this procedure is when the instructor has informed the students that their responses will be used in a formative way to improve the current course.

Student Government Administered

Another option is to have representatives of the student government association administer the student rating forms if the faculty and department or college administrators are willing or request them to do it. The students administering the instruments should also read a similar standard set of instructions and request that the instructor leave during the administration. The student organization could use the campus newspaper to announce when the instruments are going to be used and how they will be administered as a final cross-checking procedure.

Staff Administered

If an administrator decides to designate a staff member to administer the student rating form, then the same procedures should be followed as suggested above. This option should be avoided, however, unless there is no other way to ensure a common administration of the instruments. As noted earlier, faculty and students tend to feel threatened if they know that an administrator is controlling and directing the administration or processing of the instruments.

When the student rating form is administered, the students should have all necessary materials. Students should generally fill out the forms in their regular classroom near the beginning of a particular class session. Above all, the students must be left with the impression that their frank and honest comments are desired and not that this is their chance to get back at the instructor. If the students get the impression that the instructor is not really interested in their responses, they will not respond seriously. If the students feel the instructor is going to see their responses before final grades are in, they will respond more positively and write very few comments. This is especially true if the students are asked to identify themselves on the student rating form. If the form is administered immediately before, during, or after the final examination (or any other meaningful examination, homework, or term paper deadline), the students tend to respond in an inconsistent manner. If students are allowed to discuss the course and instructor while filling out the forms, then biases may enter into their ratings.

■ THE STUDENT RATING REPORT

One of the most important aspects of any program is the method of reporting the results. If the results are not reported in an appropriate, accurate, and timely manner, the usefulness of the student rating form and the system as a whole will be seriously compromised. When tabulating and summarizing item responses, the following procedures should be considered:

- The item responses should be given numerical values in order to calculate descriptive statistics, and the descriptive statistics should be reported. However, the response positions on the form should be labeled only with abbreviations and *not* the numerical values used in later computations.

- The results should be reported by item and subscale, if appropriate.

- The results should be summarized by class section, department, college, and so on.

Directionality of Numerical Scale

When items are presented with defined response scales, such as Strongly Agree, Agree, Disagree, and Strongly Disagree, they should be weighted to reflect direction and ideal response when the results are tabulated and summarized. For example, if this response scale were weighted 4, 3, 2, and 1, respectively, it would indicate that the item was positively stated with the ideal response being Strongly Agree. With such a weighting, it is possible to calculate a mean and standard deviation for each item for a given class of students. The mean value indicates their average rating and the standard deviation indicates how similar or dissimilar their responses were. With such a weighting scheme and the resulting means and standard deviations, the results can then be reported for items and subscales. The results can also be summarized and reported by class section, course, selected courses, courses within a department, courses within a college, and courses within the university. Such complete reporting schemes permit meaningful comparisons when necessary.

Distributing Rating Results—Voluntary Systems

An important aspect of any system of reporting student rating results is who will or should actually see the results. If the administration of the instruments is completely voluntary, then only the faculty members themselves should receive the results. As noted earlier, the processing office is ill advised to enter into an arrangement that places it between the faculty and the administration.

Distributing Rating Results—Mandatory Systems

If the administration of the student rating form is mandatory, as is the case in many systems, then every effort should be made by the processing office to remove itself from the responsibility of distributing rating results directly. However, if the processing office has no choice and the system must be designed to provide faculty with the option of releasing copies of their results to other interested parties, great effort must be taken to ensure that the instructor feels no pressure to release the results. In such a circumstance, a procedure must be implemented that requires a formal written release by the instructor. The processing office would be well advised to consult with the college or university attorney in developing the wording of such a release. Every effort must be made to make faculty members aware of who is to receive copies of their results and how frequently. Under no circumstances, however, should students' written comments be reported to administrators or student organizations, because those comments tend to be susceptible to widely discrepant subjective interpretations by the reader.

Publishing Rating Results

If the faculty or administration has entered into an agreement with the campus student organization to publish the results of the student ratings, every effort should be made to ensure fair and accurate reporting of the results. Such results may be reported in a book divided by discipline or content area or published on a web site. Student-published books are usually promoted as course and instructor guides for prospective student enrollees as well as vehicles to encourage instructional improvement. Unfortunately, due to the zealousness of some student editors and the vendettas of others, such publications have tended to simply generate antagonistic relationships between the rated faculty and student editors.

Recently the Internet has become an outlet for student rating results. Student organizations may publish student ratings on a web site and, in a few instances, invite comments to be made via email. These anonymous email comments are then posted to the site. This approach to distributing faculty rating data poses new challenges, not the least of which is the issue of confidentiality. In a setting where it is illegal for faculty to publicly post student grades with identifying names and social security numbers, it is likely that the emerging practice of posting faculty ratings on the Internet will generate legal challenges in the future. In any case, care must be taken to respect the legal requirements of your state relative to the release of faculty personnel records as discussed at the beginning of this chapter.

■ FORMAT OF THE STUDENT RATING FORM COMPUTERIZED ANALYSIS OUTPUT

It has been assumed that virtually every operational student rating form system produces some form of computerized analysis output. This output may range from a simple frequency count for each response to each item up to a very sophisticated printout showing normative data of various sorts. Experience has shown that most faculty react to a sophisticated printout that contains page after page of indices, norms, graphs, and tables with something less than total enthusiasm. Although professional standards demand that the analysis of student rating data be accurate and statistically sound, it must be remembered that most faculty are not well versed in the intricacies of item analysis, measurement theory, or statistical analysis. Moreover, most faculty have no real desire to become well versed in these areas. Thus, for the computerized analysis of stu-

dent rating results to have the desired effect of providing useful information that may be acted upon by the faculty member for self-improvement, an effort must be made to make these computerized analyses user friendly. One way to do this is to provide a verbal summary sheet that translates the statistical information into general statements.

For example, if the student rating form has four response choices per item, it is clear that a standard deviation exceeding 1.00 would indicate wide disparity of responses to the item. In such a case, the mean value of the item would have little value other than to represent the numerical average of the responses. The computer program can be written to produce a statement such as the following:

> On item 6, the standard deviation was 1.3. This can be interpreted to mean that there was CONSIDERABLE DISAGREEMENT among the students on this item and thus the average response value should NOT be interpreted as representing a consensus rating by the class.

Or, the program could present a statement such as

> On item 18, the average response was 3.1 and the standard deviation was 0.4. This can be interpreted to mean that the students rated you as being MODERATELY HIGH on this item and there was a HIGH degree of consensus among the students in this rating.

Ideally, such statements should be printed as either the first or the last page in a computer analysis so they are easily found. Obviously, the program must be written to make the proper interpretations of various combinations of data relative to the appropriate norms. The point is that even though the processing office may produce reports which are statistically sophisticated and correct, one must never lose sight of the fact that for the analyses to be useful they must be understood and used by the faculty. As a practical guideline providing computerized, written interpretations of the statistical information listed in the printout is highly effective in helping to promote the effectiveness of the student rating information.

■ INTERPRETING AND USING STUDENT RATING RESULTS

Although we may want our analyses to be user friendly, they must still present data of sufficient clarity and detail to permit sophisticated interpretations. How accurately and meaningfully the results of student ratings are interpreted and used depends on the type of information provided to the participating faculty member and other interested parties. The research on student ratings has revealed a definite positive response bias, which needs to be addressed when interpreting and using the results. That is, if students are asked to respond to positively stated items using a 4-point scale of Agree Strongly, Agree, Disagree, and Disagree Strongly, the responses tend to be distributed as shown in Figure 13.1.

To someone unfamiliar with statistics, the midpoint of the 4-point scale (2.5) could easily be interpreted as average, and any rating higher than 2.5 could be interpreted as a positive rating. But, as Figure 13.1 shows, the easy interpretation that any rating of 2.5 or higher is good can be seen as being substantially in error. In fact, because the distribution of student ratings is skewed, the average or mean rating tends to fall closer to 3.0 than 2.5.

One effective way to report student-rating data is to present decile information based on the appropriate norm base. In this way, the bias of the student rating distribution can be taken into account. Figure 13.2 shows one way to represent student rating data in deciles.

The use of comparative (normative) data, such as the deciles shown in Figure 13.2, when reporting results can serve to counteract the positive response bias and result in a more accurate and meaningful interpretation of the ratings. For example, comparative data gathered on freshmen-level courses in the anthropology department allow the instructors to determine how they and their courses are perceived in relation to the rest of the courses in the department. When such comparative data are not available,

the instructor will be interpreting and using results in a void with very little substantiation for the resulting conclusions and actions taken.

Qualitative judgments can also be provided to the instructor by identifying course mean intervals in the comparative data, which can be defined as representing levels of excellence or needed improvement. For example, the comparative data for the freshmen courses in the anthropology department consisting of course means on student rating questionnaires could be divided into 10 equal portions. Each portion could be defined as representing a 10% interval of rated courses with a defined minimum and maximum course mean. These 10 intervals could then be defined as follows:

- *VP = Very Poor.* Any course mean falling in the lowest 10%, 20%, or 30% interval is defined as being of unacceptably low quality insofar as the elements being measured by the student rating form are concerned.

- *P = Poor (Improvement Required).* Any course mean falling in the 40% or 50% interval is defined as being of low quality (insofar as the elements being measured by the student rating form are concerned) and indicates that improvement is required.

- *G = Good.* Any course mean falling in the 60% or 70% interval is defined as being of solid professional quality (insofar as the elements being measured by the student rating form are concerned) and, although improvement is always desirable, no improvement is required.

Figure 13.1 Skewed Student Rating Response Curve

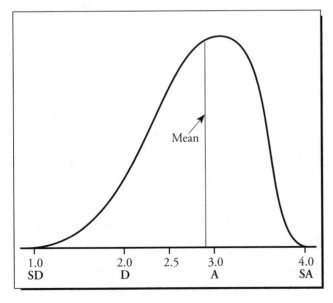

Figure 13.2 Decile Interpretation of Student Ratings

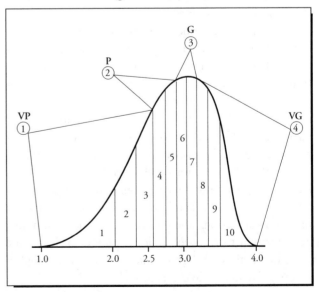

- *VG = Very Good.* Any course mean falling in the upper 80%, 90%, or 100% interval is defined as being of high quality (insofar as the elements being measured by the student rating form are concerned) surpassing standard professional performance.

This information could be provided to each participating instructor in a computerized format along with the appropriate interpretive materials. Or, as noted earlier, these values could be built into the computer program to produce appropriate written interpretive statements.

Further, the numerical values of 1, 2, 3, and 4 have been assigned to the labels VP, P, G, and VG, respectively. Thus, a raw student rating average of 3.2 may translate into either a decile of 8, a category rating of Very Good, or provide an appropriately norm-referenced summary qualitatively determined value of 4 since VG = 4. In computing the composite role rating (CRR) for teaching, the norm-referenced summary value of 4 in this example would be entered into the matrix in Figure 9.1 if this data were indicative of faculty performance in instructional delivery for instance. If student rating data from more than one course were being used in the matrix in Figure 9.1, then the norm-referenced value of 4 in this example would be averaged with the comparable data from the other courses.

Once established on a representative number of courses, the normative database should not change appreciably from year to year. Additional courses can be added to the normative database without significantly changing the distribution and comparative judgments. For some of the sources of invalidity identified as nontrivial by research studies, such as class level and required–elective status, comparative data stratified by course level and required–elective status will provide meaningful interpretations of the results. Aleamoni and Stevens (1986) include particular examples.

Once faculty members are provided with comparative data and interpretive materials, they are then ready to interpret their results. The comparative interpretations result from the normative data provided, and the subjective interpretations result from reflections on what took place in the classroom that could be related to the comparative interpretations. Using this procedure, in addition to a careful reading of the students' written comments (if available), each instructor should be able to generate diagnostic interpretations of instructional strengths and weaknesses in the course. If an instructor has results on two or more similar sections, then the ratings of one section may be compared to those of another section to determine what instructional behaviors may have led to the higher comparative ratings in one section.

If the faculty are not able to generate any diagnostic interpretations, they may need to talk with the department head, dean, or instructional development specialist about the results. This assumes, of course, that these individuals know how to interpret the results. Finding that this approach still does not adequately identify the source of instructional difficulty, the instructor may want to consider other procedures (e.g., the use of additional diagnostic optional items, classroom visitation, videotaping, etc.) in future evaluations.

After identifying their instructional strengths and weaknesses, instructors can use the information to plan an improvement strategy. In some instances, the strategy may simply require minor modifications in the course or teaching method. In other instances, the strategy may require a substantial commitment of time and resources on the part of the faculty member and the department. It has been through a process such as this that instructors have been able to use student ratings to identify instructional problems and then rectify them. Obviously, the success or failure of such a venture rests solely with the instructors and their willingness to gather and use the data provided.

If faculty members decide to submit copies of their student rating results to their department head or dean for rank, pay, and tenure considerations, then all of the appropriate interpretive materials should also be provided. Ideally, the student rating results should be interpreted by someone with expertise in the field of measurement and instructional development. Deans and department heads should be made aware of the necessity of using the comparative data to interpret the results rather than relying on the more subjective and highly unreliable written and oral comments of students. Interpretations of student rating results may also be carried out by peer review triads using several other assessments of instructional effectiveness such as self-evaluation, quality of student learning, and peer ratings of content (Aleamoni, 1987).

Student course/instructor rating data should never be used alone in evaluating instructional effectiveness for rank, pay, and tenure decisions, because such data are not completely diagnostic of all elements in the instructional domain. How such student rating data should be used in a comprehensive system of instructional evaluation and how much weight they should carry is something that should be determined at the department level.

■ FACULTY EVALUATION AND PROFESSIONAL ENRICHMENT

Experience has shown, time and again, that a faculty evaluation system implemented without reference or connection to a professional enrichment program will generate greater amounts of anxiety and resistance among the faculty than if it is part of a larger faculty development or instructional improvement effort. Likewise, experience has also shown that faculty professional enrichment programs, operated in isolation or without reference to a faculty evaluation program, tend to attract mainly those faculty who need their services the least.

Ideally, a faculty evaluation system should be an integral part of a larger faculty evaluation/professional enrichment program. To achieve maximal benefit from these two programs, each element of the faculty evaluation system should have a corresponding and concomitant element in the professional enrichment program. Thus, if the faculty evaluation system is going to evaluate how well faculty teach courses or how frequently they publish scientific articles, there should be professional enrichment seminars, advanced workshops, and instructional materials available to assist them in learning how to teach better or how to write manuscripts that are more likely to be accepted for publication. In short, the faculty evaluation system should provide diagnostic information on the strengths and weaknesses a faculty member possesses and then follow up with programs or materials to aid the faculty member in enhancing strengths or overcoming weaknesses.

Again, as a practical matter, the computerized report derived from student ratings should include written comments that not only highlight the major areas of concern but also provide information on where to seek assistance. For example, a computer printout could include a statement such as:

> On the TESTING AND GRADING section of the student rating form, the majority of the students (87%) indicated that your tests did not seem to relate well to the course objectives. The Office of Assessment and Professional Enrichment offers a seminar for faculty on Test Construction that may be of some interest. Call 555-1234 for information about the next seminar.

Thus, to be truly effective, a faculty evaluation program must be linked to, and work in concert with, a structured and supported professional enrichment program. Only in this way will both programs stand a reasonable chance of achieving the common goals of improving instruction and enhancing faculty performance.

ONLINE STUDENT RATINGS

The administration and use of conventional paper-and-pencil student rating forms clearly involves cost and intrusion in class time. The advent of Internet technology, however, has made possible the use of online student rating forms which may be completed outside of class and which cost less to administer. Despite the continuing problem of low response rates to online student ratings, and even though the research concerning the utility, reliability, and validity, of online student ratings is just beginning to emerge, there appears to be a rush to adopt this technology. In fact, the popularity of online student rating systems has begun to grow to such an extent that more than 60 universities report their use (Clark, 2003). Online student rating systems are seen as having a number of advantages over paper-and-pencil systems including ease of administration, more complete data collection, longer, more thoughtful student responses, reduced processing time and costs, more accurate data collection and reporting, and more detailed, user-friendly reports (Hmielski & Champagne, 2000; Johnson, 2003). Theall (2000) has questioned these preliminary findings. The fact is that using technology to streamline data handling does nothing to address a fundamental lack of sufficient research concerning online teaching and learning, the quality of the underlying faculty evaluation systems making use of online student rating data, and the quality and appropriateness of the reporting and interpretation of such data (Franklin & Theall, 1989). In the larger context of considering the development of a comprehensive faculty evaluation system, it must be concluded that insufficient literature and experience exists within the higher education community to make definitive recommendations concerning online student ratings at this point. It is recommended, however, that institutions interested in this technology explore the literature that currently exists. See Sorensen and Johnson (2003) for an excellent starting point for entering this literature.

REFERENCES

Abrami, P. C., & Murphy, V. (1980). *A catalogue of systems for student evaluation of instruction.* Montreal, Canada: McGill University Centre for Teaching and Learning.

Aleamoni, L. M. (1987). Evaluating instructional effectiveness can be a rewarding experience. *Journal of Plant Disease, 71*(4), 377–379.

Aleamoni, L. M., & Stevens, J. J. (1986). *Arizona course/instructor evaluation questionnaire (CIEQ): Results interpretation manual.* Tucson, AZ: Office of Instructional Research and Development, University of Arizona.

Aleamoni, L. M., & Thomas, G. S. (1980). Differential relationships of student, instructor, and course characteristics to general and specific items on a course questionnaire. *Teaching of Psychology, 7*(4), 233–235.

Arreola, R. A. (1983). Establishing successful faculty evaluation and development programs. In A. Smith (Ed.), *Evaluating faculty and staff, new directions for community colleges: No.41* (pp. 83–90) San Francisco, CA: Jossey-Bass.

Arreola, R. A. (1987). The role of student government in faculty evaluation. In L. M. Aleamoni (Ed.), *New Directions for Teaching and Learning, No. 31, Techniques for evaluating and improving instruction* (pp. 39–46). San Francisco, CA: Jossey-Bass.

Braskamp, L.A., & Ory, J. C. (1994). *Assessing faculty work: Enhancing individual and institutional performance.* San Francisco: Jossey-Bass

Carr, J. W., & Padgett, T. C. (1992). Legal liability when designing or adopting student rating forms. In R. A. Arreola (Ed.), *Proceedings of the First Annual CEDA Conference on Practical Issues in Faculty Evaluation* (pp. 68–76). Memphis, TN: Center for Educational Development and Assessment.

Centra, J. A. (1993). *Reflective Faculty Evaluation: Enhancing Teaching and Determining Faculty Effectiveness.* San Francisco, CA: Jossey-Bass.

Clark, S. J. (2003). *Use of online student ratings at institutions of higher education: Results of a web search.* Provo, UT: Brigham Young University Faculty Center.

Franklin, J., & Theall, M. (1989, April). *Who reads ratings: Knowledge, attitudes, and practices of users of student ratings of instruction.* Paper presented at the annual meeting of the American Educational Research Association, San Francisco, CA. (ERIC Document Reproduction Services No. ED306241)

Hmieleski, K., & Champagne, M. V. (2000, September/October). Plugging into course evaluation. *The Technology Source.* Retrieved July 25, 2006, from: http://technologysource.org/article/plugging_in_to_course_evaluation/

Johnson, T. D. (2003). Online student ratings: Will students respond? In D. L. Sorenson & T. D. Johnson (Eds.), *New directions for teaching and learning: No. 96. Online student ratings of instruction* (pp. 49–60). San Francisco, CA: Jossey-Bass.

Kaplin, W. A. (1978). *The law of higher education: A comprehensive guide to legal implications of administrative decision making.* San Francisco, CA: Jossey-Bass.

Pascarella, E. T. (2001). Cognitive growth in college: Surprising and reassuring findings from The National Study of Student Learning. *Change, 33*(6), 21–27.

Sorenson, D.L., & Johnson, T.D. (Eds.). (2003). *New directions for teaching and learning: No. 96. Online student ratings of instruction.* San Francisco, CA: Jossey-Bass.

Theall, M. (2000, November/December) Electronic course evaluation is not necessarily the solution. *Technology Source.* Retrieved July 25, 2006, from: http://technologysource.org/article/electronic_course_evaluation_is_not_necessarily_the_solution/

14

Catalog of Student Rating Items

The following catalog of items may be used to develop a customized student rating form for your institution. These items are offered only as a beginning resource to aid in the construction of a student rating form. In using this catalog please refer to the section on designing a valid and reliable student rating form in Chapter 13. In considering these items please *do not* correct the grammar or replace colloquial terms with more precise language. As noted earlier, items for student rating forms must be written using language that the students themselves are likely to use. Changing the language of an item to that which a college professor might use will likely have the effect of decreasing its potential reliability in the student rating form.

The following is a brief overview of the procedures for developing a customized student rating form that are described more fully in Chapter 13.

- *Determine the issues or characteristics to be measured by the form* (e.g., teacher preparation and organization, clarity of communication, rapport with students, etc.).

- *Write or select the items.* Once the issues or characteristics to be measured have been determined, select at least eight items from the catalog that appear to measure each issue or characteristic determined earlier. For example, if you are planning on measuring four different characteristics, you should select a total of 32 items.

- *Develop/select appropriate response scales.* All items in this catalog have been constructed using the Strongly Agree–Strongly Disagree scale.

- *Conduct field trials to gather the data needed for subsequent validity and reliability determination.* You should

have approximately 40 or more items selected based on the work done earlier. Create experimental forms with subsets of items and administer them to all kinds of classes. Once you have at least 200 responses for each and every item (that is, each item will have appeared on one form or another so that at least 200 students had the opportunity to respond to it), you are ready to move to the next step.

- *Conduct a factor analytic study.* It is critical to determine the reliability and validity of the form as well as to determine the degree to which the items reliably measure each issue or characteristic of interest. Although the factor analytic study must be conducted by individuals proficient in statistics and psychometrics, the outcome of such an analysis should produce at least four items for each issue of interest. In order to adequately measure a specific perception or reaction to an issue of interest, at least four items measuring that perception or reaction must be used. From a technical perspective the factor loadings of these items on the dimension being measured should be .400 or higher.

- *Develop subscales based on the result of the factor analysis.* The form should produce separate scores for each of the dimensions or characteristics being measured. Such subscales provide more detailed diagnostic information for instructor use in improving or enhancing their performance, and they provide for fairer comparisons across time and across different courses.

- *Refine the form* based on the results of the factor analytic study to ensure reliability of each subscale and the form as a whole. Ideally, the reliability values should be .60 or higher.

- *Organize the items.* The final step in developing your student rating form is to decide how the items are to be grouped and labeled in the final design of the form: Determine how the items should be organized for easy reading and answering, and how and where the responses should be recorded. If there is a logical or chronological flow to the items, then their organization on the form should reflect that. If there are only a few negative items, then one or two should appear very early in the instrument to avoid positive response set mistakes (i.e., before students get in the habit of thinking the response to the extreme right is always the most positive). It is advisable to have a few negatively stated items in the instrument, but only if they can be stated negatively in a logical manner.

In accordance with the conceptual approach to defining the faculty role of teaching used in this book, the items have been divided into the following categories:

- Instructional design

- Instructional delivery

- Instructional assessment

- Course management

In considering these items please consult the discussions earlier in this book concerning the definitions of instructional design, instructional delivery, instructional assessment, and course management. Items have also been listed in two additional categories:

- Self-reported course impact on the student

- Alternate and supplementary teaching/learning environments

The "self-reported course impact on the student" category lists items that describe or report students' reactions to various aspects of the instruction and course in terms of the impact on their personal attitudes, beliefs, and capabilities. Care must be taken when using these items in that an agreement must be reached concerning what inference may be drawn from these perceptions and reactions concerning either the instructor or the course. The "alternate and supplementary teaching/learning environment" category lists items related to laboratories, seminars, discussion groups, field trips, and clinical instruction. Both of these latter two categories may contain items which, when coupled with items from other categories, might contribute to the measurement of the instructional design, delivery, assessment, and course management characteristics of specialized teaching/learning environments. In a few instances items may appear in more than one category if they appear to relate to more than one issue. However, the determination of what an item or set of items truly measures can be made only as a result of a factor analytic study of the specific items chosen to construct your form.

The category headings under which the items have been listed should *not* be considered as definitive identifiers since they were chosen primarily as an aid in finding items that appear to measure the issue in question. *No inference should be drawn that the items, as presented here, possess sufficient psychometric or statistical support (i.e., factor loadings) to define the category in which they are listed.* As noted earlier, only by conducting the appropriate factor analytic study of the particular items that you choose for your form can it be determined whether the items are reliably measuring a specific issue or dimension. Also, note that some of the items have been written with a blank space (_____) embedded in the text. For such items it is intended that a specific term or descriptor be placed in that space to create a customized item measuring a specific issue of interest.

All the items in this catalog have been written for the Strongly Agree–Strongly Disagree response format. Either the 5-response or the 4-response version of this scale should be used with these items. The use of any other scale could severely compromise the validity and reliability of your form.

5-point scale	4-point scale
SA = Strongly Agree	SA = Strongly Agree
A = Agree	A = Agree
N = Neither Agree	D = Disagree
nor Disagree	SD = Strongly Disagree
D = Disagree	
SD = Strongly Disagree	

Also note that some of the items are stated in a *negative* fashion. Such items will usually have the word "NOT" (in capitals) in the text. In developing a student rating form it is generally a good idea to include a few negative items that measure the same dimension or category as other positively stated items to provide a check on whether students have fallen into a response set. A response set is the habit students may fall into of marking all the choices down the middle or on one side of the rating scale. When using negatively stated items care must be taken to ensure that the computer analysis program correctly weights the responses to reflect the reversed scale.

Contents

■ Instructional Design

1) The instructor related the course material to my previous learning experiences.

2) The instructor incorporated current material into the course.

3) The instructor made me aware of the current problems in this field.

4) The instructor gave useful writing assignments.

5) The instructor adapted the course to a reasonable level of comprehension.

6) The instructor exposed students to diverse approaches to problem solutions.

7) The instructor provided information that supplemented assigned material.

8) The instructor provided essential material that was not in the text.

9) The instructor guided the preparation of student reports.

10) The instructor provided opportunities for self-directed learning.

11) The instructor did NOT provide a sufficient variety of topics.

12) The instructor required that students employ concepts to demonstrate comprehension.

13) The instructor related topics to other areas of knowledge.

14) The instructor did NOT combine theory and practical application.

15) The class demonstrations were effective in helping me learn.

16) The course content was up-to-date.

17) The catalog description of this course gave an accurate description of its content.

18) The course content included information from related fields.

19) The amount of time allotted for this class should be reduced.

20) Regular class attendance was necessary for understanding course material.

21) The instructor followed his/her stated course outline.

22) The instructor's class presentations were designed for easy note taking.

23) The course was well organized.

24) The course material appeared to be presented in logical content units.

25) There was continuity from one class to the next.

26) Course concepts were related in a systematic manner.

27) The course assignments were clearly specified.

28) I was informed of the direction the course was to take.

29) The objectives of the course were well explained.

30) The objectives of this course should be modified.

31) The content of this course was appropriate to the aims and objectives of the course.

32) Student responsibilities in this course were defined.

33) The instructor should rewrite the description of the course in the catalog.

34) It was not clear why I was being taught some things.

35) The instructor's expectations were NOT clearly defined.

36) The instructor defined realistic objectives for the students.

37) Objectives were stated for each unit in the course.

38) The course objectives were clear.

39) I understood what was expected of me in this course.

40) The course objectives allowed me to know when I was making progress.

41) In general, too little work was required in this class.

42) In general, too much work was required in this class.

43) This was a good course.

44) Too much material was covered in this course.

45) Prerequisites in addition to those stated in the catalog are necessary for understanding the material in this course.

46) The course was too easy for me.

47) The course was too difficult for me.

48) The amount of material covered in the course was reasonable.

49) The exams were of instructional value.

50) The assignments were challenging.

51) The non-text assignments were helpful in acquiring a better understanding of course materials.

52) I found the coverage of topics in the assigned readings too difficult.

53) The course required a reasonable amount of outside reading.

54) The instructor should have required more outside reading.

55) The text used in this course was helpful.

56) The instructor helped the students avoid duplication of content in selecting topics.

57) The instructor supplemented student summaries with additional material when necessary.

58) The amount of work was appropriate for the credit received.

59) The textbook was easy to understand.

60) The textbook presented various sides of issues.

61) The instructor should have given additional sources where supplementary information might be found.

62) The course should require more time in the lab.

63) The course should include a field trip.

64) The course assignments required too much time.

65) The assignments were related to the goals of the course.

66) The assignments were of definite instructional value.

67) Homework assignments were given too frequently.

68) The assigned readings were well integrated into the course.

69) The _____ assignments were relevant to what was presented in class.

70) The _____ assignments provided background for the lectures.

71) The _____ assignments were too time consuming relative to their contribution to my understanding of the course material.

72) The _____ assignments were interesting.

73) The _____ assignments appeared to be chosen carefully.

74) The _____ assignments were stimulating.

75) The _____ assignments made students think.

76) More _____ should have been assigned.

77) There was too much _____ required for this course.

78) Directions for _____ assignments were clear.

79) Directions for _____ assignments were specific.

80) The _____ assignments were helpful in understanding the course.

81) The _____ assignments covered both sides of issues.

82) The _____ assignments required a reasonable amount of effort.

■ INSTRUCTIONAL DELIVERY

83) The instructor gave clear explanations to clarify concepts.

84) The instructor's lectures broadened my knowledge of the area beyond the information presented in the readings.

85) The instructor demonstrated how the course was related to practical situations.

86) The instructor demonstrated that the course material was worthwhile.

87) The instructor's use of examples helped to get points across in class.

88) The instructor stresses important points in lectures/discussions.

89) The instructor was enthusiastic about the course material.

90) The instructor seemed to enjoy teaching.

91) The instructor's use of personal experiences helped to get points across in class.

92) The instructor clarified complex sections of the text.

93) The instructor accepted other viewpoints that could possibly be valid.

94) The instructor puts material across in an interesting way.

95) The instructor used his/her knowledge of other fields to help my understanding of the field being studied.

96) The instructor's explanations were clear.

97) The instructor encouraged independent thought.

98) The instructor stressed important points in lectures.

99) The instructor taught near the class level.

100) The instructor did NOT appear receptive to new ideas.

101) The instructor was an excellent resource person.

102) The instructor did NOT invite questions.

103) The instructor presented contrasting points of view.

104) The instructor did NOT encourage discussion of a topic.

105) The instructor answered all questions to the best of his/her ability.

106) The instructor carefully answered questions raised by students.

107) The instructor stimulated class discussion.

108) The instructor did NOT cover the reading assignments in sufficient depth in class.

109) The instructor was too involved with lecturing to be aware of the class.

110) The instructor clarified lecture material.

111) The instructor appeared to have a thorough knowledge of the subject.

112) The instructor seemed knowledgeable in many areas.

113) The instructor provided adequate individual remedial attention.

114) The instructor stressed important points in discussion.

115) The instructor overemphasized minor points.

116) The instructor showed mastery of the subject matter.

117) The instructor gave me a great deal which I would not get by independent study.

118) The instructor's lack of facility with the English language was a hindrance to the communication of ideas.

119) The instructor seems to keep current with developments in the field.

120) The instructor's teaching methods are effective.

121) The instructor uses novel teaching methods to help students learn.

122) The instructor uses different teaching methods to help students learn.

123) The instructor allows students to proceed at their own pace.

124) The instructor provides extra discussion sessions for interested students.

125) The instructor adequately helped me prepare for exams.

126) The instructor is careful and precise when answering questions.

127) The instructor helps me apply theory for solving homework problems.

128) The instructor demonstrated formal knowledge of the topic.

129) The instructor accepts suggestions from students.

130) The instructor shows enthusiasm when teaching.

131) The instructor was receptive to the expression of student views.

132) The instructor was concerned with whether or not the students learned the material.

133) The instructor intimidated the students.

134) The instructor embarrassed the students.

135) The instructor developed a good rapport with me.

136) A warm atmosphere was maintained in this class.

137) The instructor recognized individual differences in students' abilities.

138) The instructor seemed to dislike students.

139) The instructor often made me feel as if I was wasting his/her time.

140) The instructor treated students as inferiors.

141) The instructor seemed genuinely interested in me as a person.

142) The instructor maintained an atmosphere of good feeling in the class.

143) The instructor treated students with respect.

144) The instructor encouraged class discussion.

145) Students in this course were free to disagree.

146) The instructor was friendly.

147) The instructor could be relied upon for support in stressful situations.

148) The instructor criticized students in the presence of others.

149) The instructor treated students fairly.

150) The instructor promoted a feeling of self-worth in students.

151) Students were encouraged to express their own opinions.

152) The instructor helped students to feel free to ask questions.

153) The instructor treated students with respect.

154) The instructor was skillful in observing student reactions.

155) The instructor was permissive.

156) The instructor was friendly.

157) The instructor gave individual attention to students in this course.

158) The instructor demonstrated sensitivity to students' needs.

159) The instructor was aloof rather than sociable.

160) The instructor was flexible in dealing with students.

161) The instructor encourages students to talk about their problems.

162) The instructor meets informally with students out of class.

163) The instructor stimulates my thinking.

164) The instructor deals fairly and impartially with students.

165) The instructor makes me feel I am an important member of this class.

166) The instructor relates to students as individuals.

167) The instructor tells students when they have done particularly well.

168) The instructor motivates me to do my best work.

169) The instructor provided me with an effective range of challenges.

170) The instructor stimulates intellectual curiosity.

171) The instructor should do more to restrain students who monopolize class time.

172) The instructor should spend less time in class discussions.

173) The instructor should encourage students to participate more actively in class discussions.

174) More opportunity should be allowed for answering questions in class.

175) Students had an opportunity to ask questions.

176) The instructor used student questions as a source of discovering points of confusion.

177) The instructor overemphasized minor points.

178) The instructor was NOT willing to deviate from his/her course plans to meet the needs of the students.

179) The instructor used class time well.

180) The instructor provided time for discussion.

181) The instructor encourages students to ask questions.

182) The instructor encourages class participation.

183) The instructor encourages contributions concerning the conduct of this class.

184) The instructor makes me feel free to ask questions.

185) The instructor presented material in a clear manner.

186) The instructor presented a systematic approach to the course material.

187) Instructor presentations were well organized.

188) The instructor was well prepared for each class.

189) The instructor was well prepared for lectures.

190) The instructor frequently digressed too far from the subject matter of the course.

191) The instructor rarely digressed from a given topic to the detriment of the course.

192) Lectures often seemed disjointed and fragmented.

193) Class discussions were well organized.

194) The instructor was prepared for topics brought up during impromptu class discussions.

195) The instructor provided a good mixture of lecture and discussion.

196) The instructor wrote legibly on the blackboard, papers, etc.

197) The instructor's voice was audible.

198) The instructor's voice was understandable.

199) The instructor's vocabulary made understanding of the material difficult.

200) At times it was difficult to hear what the instructor was saying.

201) The instructor expressed ideas clearly.

202) The instructor could communicate his/her subject matter to the students.

203) The instructor should define the words he/she uses.

204) The instructor's tendency to stammer or stutter was annoying.

205) The instructor often mumbled.

206) The instructor often talked with his/her back to the students.

207) The instructor recognizes when some students fail to comprehend course material.

208) The instructor emphasizes conceptual understanding of course material.

209) The instructor lectures at a pace suitable for students' comprehension.

210) The instructor should improve his/her personal appearance.

211) The instructor flustered easily.

212) The instructor seemed to be interested in teaching.

213) The instructor was enthusiastic when presenting course material.

214) The instructor was relaxed in front of class.

215) At times, the instructor displayed only a shallow knowledge of course materials.

216) The instructor seemed genuinely interested in what he/she was teaching.

217) At times the instructor seemed tense.

218) The instructor exhibited self-confidence.

219) The instructor displayed a know-it-all attitude.

220) The instructor was too cynical or sarcastic.

221) The instructor often appeared arrogant.

222) The instructor was very entertaining.

223) The instructor's jokes sometimes interfered with learning.

224) The instructor demonstrated role model qualities that were of use to me.

225) The instructor demonstrated an appropriate sense of humor.

226) The instructor seemed to enjoy teaching.

227) The instructor was confused by unexpected questions.

228) The instructor encouraged constructive criticism.

229) The instructor has an interesting style of presentation.

230) When lecturing, the instructor holds the attention of class.

231) The instructor senses when students are bored.

232) The instructor is a dynamic and energetic person.

233) The instructor seems to have a well-rounded education.

234) The instructor appears to grasp quickly what a student is saying.

235) The instructor knows about developments in other fields.

236) The instructor shows enthusiasm when teaching.

237) The instructor exhibited distracting mannerisms.

238) The instructor's accent prevented me from understanding what was being said.

239) The instructor should reduce the monotony of his/her speech.

240) The instructor made the subject matter interesting.

241) The instructor was boring.

242) The instructor's presentations were thought provoking.

243) The instructor's classroom sessions stimulated my interest in the subject.

244) The instructor was quite lifeless.

245) The instructor was an effective speaker.

246) The class presentations were too formal.

247) Students frequently volunteered their own opinions.

248) The instructor was excellent.

249) The instructor was inadequate.

250) Within the time limitations, the instructor covered the course content in sufficient depth.

251) For the time allotted, topic coverage was exhaustive enough.

252) The course material was presented at a satisfactory level of difficulty.

253) The instructor attempted to cover too much material.

254) The instructor presented the material too rapidly.

255) The instructor should present the material more slowly.

256) The instructor moved to new topics before students understood the previous topic.

257) The course seemed to drag at times.

258) The instructor used appropriate amounts of information to teach new concepts.

259) The instructor encouraged out-of-class consultations.

260) The instructor made it clear that he/she did not want to be bothered by students at times other than when the class met.

261) The instructor should use more audiovisual aids (charts, movies, models, etc.)

262) The audiovisual aids were a valuable part of this course.

263) The audiovisual aids confused me more than they aided my learning.

264) Some of the audiovisual aids did not seem relevant.

265) Audiovisual aids were used too much in this class.

266) Audiovisual aids used in this course were stimulating.

267) The audiovisual aids generally contained material different from the instructor's material.

268) The instructor generally used the audiovisual aids effectively.

269) The audiovisual aids presented material or situations that could not normally be seen in real life.

270) The audiovisual aids were generally effective.

271) Certain ideas were presented effectively through the use of audiovisual aids than otherwise could have been presented.

272) The audiovisual aids (charts, movies, slides, etc.) used were effective in helping me learn.

273) The instructor did not cover reading assignments in sufficient depth in class.

274) Questions were answered satisfactorily by the instructor.

275) The instructor had a tight rein on the conduct of the class.

276) The instructor knew the names of the students.

277) The instructor encouraged constructive criticism.

■ INSTRUCTIONAL ASSESSMENT

278) The instructor's methods of evaluating me were fair.

279) The instructor did NOT provide for students' self-evaluation of their learning.

280) The instructor's evaluation of students' performances was constructive.

281) The instructor provided very helpful critiques of student papers.

282) The instructor's quizzes stress important points.

283) The instructor offers specific suggestions for improving my weaknesses.

284) The instructor returns assignments quickly enough to benefit me.

285) The instructor informed students of their progress.

286) The types of test questions used were good.

287) The instructor should give more examinations.

288) Emphasis on memorizing for examinations should be reduced.

289) The instructor should cover the course material more adequately in the examinations.

290) The exams were worded clearly.

291) Examinations were given often enough to give the instructor a comprehensive picture of my understanding of the course material.

292) The exams covered the reading assignments well.

293) The exams concentrated on factual material.

294) The exams concentrated on reasoning ability.

295) The exams concentrated on important aspects of the course.

296) The exams and quizzes were given too frequently.

297) The exams were fair.

298) The instructor took reasonable precautions to prevent cheating.

299) Course objectives were reflected in the exams.

300) Exams adequately covered the text material.

301) Exams were mainly comprised of material presented in class.

302) The answers to exam questions were adequately explained after the exam was given.

303) Enough time was provided to complete the examinations.

304) Too much emphasis was placed on the final exam.

305) Examinations were NOT too difficult.

306) The exams did NOT challenge me enough.

307) The instructor should use essay examinations rather than multiple-choice.

308) The instructor should use multiple-choice examinations rather than essay.

309) Examinations should contain a better mixture of multiple-choice and essay questions.

310) The exams covered the lecture material well.

311) The exams were creative.

312) The exams required original thought.

313) The exams concentrated on the important aspects of the course.

314) The exams were too long.

315) The exams were returned promptly.

316) The exams were graded carefully.

317) The exams were graded fairly.

318) The exams were used to improve instruction as well as to assign grades.

319) The exams were used to help students find their strengths and weaknesses.

320) The exams stressed the important points of the lectures.

321) The exams required conceptual understanding of the material in order to be able to get a high score.

322) Feedback on the exams indicated my relative standing within the class.

323) Exams emphasized understanding rather than memorization.

324) Relative to other courses, the grading in this course was harder.

325) I expected to get a higher grade in this course than I received.

326) My fieldwork was given appropriate weight in the formulation of the final grade.

327) My grades accurately reflected my performance in the course.

328) I knew my relative standing in the course.

329) The instructor adequately explained the grading system.

330) The instructor adequately assessed how well students mastered the material.

331) The procedure for grading was fair.

332) I do not feel that my grades reflected how much I have learned.

333) The method of assigning grades seemed very arbitrary.

334) It was easy to get a good grade in this class.

335) The instructor had a realistic definition of good performance.

336) My papers had adequate comments on them.

337) The grades reflected an accurate assessment of my knowledge.

338) The exam scores accurately reflected my performance on the tests.

339) The questions on the laboratory/discussion quizzes were a good sample of what I was expected to know.

340) My laboratory/discussion work was given appropriate weight in the formulation of final grades.

341) The _____ assignments were graded fairly.

342) The _____ assignments were returned promptly.

▪ COURSE MANAGEMENT

343) The instructor provided discussion material that supplemented lecture content.

344) The instructor is available during office hours.

345) The instructor helps me realize my full ability.

346) The instructor provides me with incentives for learning.

347) The instructor rewards success.

348) One real strength of this course was the classroom discussion.

349) The office hours were scheduled at times that were convenient for me to attend.

350) Assistance from the instructor outside of class was readily available.

351) Talking to the instructor in his/her office was helpful.

352) The instructor was readily available for consultation with students.

353) The laboratory equipment was, on most occasions, effectively set up.

354) Generally, the equipment used in the lab was adequate and reliable.

▪ SELF-REPORTED COURSE IMPACT ON THE STUDENT

355) I now feel able to communicate course material to others.

356) This course has increased my capacity for analytic thinking.

357) This course was helpful in developing new skills.

358) I learned more in this course than in similar courses.

359) I understood the material presented in this course.

360) This course challenged me intellectually.

361) I have become more competent in this area because of this course.

362) My opinions about some of the course topics changed because of taking this course.

363) I learned more in this course than I expected to learn.

364) Some of the ideas discussed really made me think.

365) I am a better person because of taking this course.

366) The course helped me to become a more critical thinker.

367) The course helped me become a more creative thinker.

368) The course was intellectually exciting.

369) I learned a great deal of factual material in this course.

370) I developed the ability to communicate clearly about the subject.

371) I developed creative ability in this field.

372) I developed the ability to solve real problems in this field.

373) I learned how to identify formal characteristics of works of art.

374) I learned how to identify main points and central issues in this field.

375) I developed the ability to carry out original research in this field.

376) I developed an ability to evaluate new work in this field.

377) I was stimulated to discuss related topics outside of class.

378) I participated actively in class discussion.

379) I developed leadership skills in this class.

380) I developed greater awareness of societal problems.

381) I became interested in community projects related to the course.

382) I learned to value new viewpoints.

383) I gained a better understanding of myself through this course.

384) I gained an understanding of some of my personal problems.

385) I developed a greater sense of personal responsibility.

386) I increased my awareness of my own interests.

387) I increased my awareness of my own talents.

388) I feel that I performed up to my potential.

389) I read independently beyond the required readings in this course.

390) The course significantly changed my outlook on personal issues.

391) I felt free to ask for extra help from the instructor.

392) This course material will be useful in future courses.

393) The course provided me with a general background in the area.

394) The course material was of personal interest to me aside from its professional application.

395) I have learned the basic concepts from this course that I will be able to relate to other situations.

396) This course has stimulated me to take additional courses in this field.

397) The material covered in this course will be directly relevant to my future occupation.

398) The course gave me skills that will be directly applicable to my career.

399) The concepts in this course were pertinent to my major field.

400) The course was valuable only to majors in this field.

401) This course should be required for a major in this area.

402) The course was related to my personal goals.

403) The course did NOT prepare me to reach my personal goals.

404) The course had NO relevance outside of a grade and credit hours.

405) I was interested in the subject before I took this course.

406) The course stimulated me to read further in the area.

407) The course content was valuable.

408) I gained an excellent understanding of concepts in this field.

409) I learned to apply principles from this course to other situations.

410) I deepened my interest in the subject matter of this course.

411) I developed enthusiasm about the course material.

412) I developed skills needed by professionals in this field.

413) I learned about career opportunities.

414) I developed a clearer sense of professional identity.

415) I would take this course if it were not required.

416) I participated more in class discussions in this course than in similar courses.

417) The class discussions broadened by knowledge of the area beyond what I learned from the readings.

418) It was easy to remain attentive in class.

419) Remaining attentive in class was often quite difficult.

420) The course was quite interesting.

421) I have made careful preparations for this course.

422) I really had to think about some of the ideas discussed.

423) The time spent in this course was worthwhile.

424) My attendance in this course was better than for most other courses.

425) I usually delayed studying for this course as long as possible.

426) I spent more time than usual complaining about this course to others.

427) I would take this course again even if it were not required.

428) I would recommend this course to a fellow student.

429) I looked forward to this class.

430) I cut this class more frequently than I cut other classes.

431) I had a strong desire to take this course.

432) I enjoyed going to class.

433) In this course I used my study time effectively.

434) I spent more time studying for this course than for other courses with the same amount of credit.

435) I would rather NOT take another course from this instructor.

436) In comparison to all the other instructors I have had, he/she was one of the best.

437) I would recommend this instructor to a fellow student.

438) I would avoid courses taught by this instructor.

439) I was able to get personal help in this course if I needed it.

440) There was ample opportunity to ask questions in the laboratory/discussion section.

441) I participated more in class discussion in this course than in similar courses.

442) I had an opportunity to participate in discussions with the instructor.

443) I was hesitant to ask questions in this course.

444) I found the laboratory/discussion section interesting.

445) The laboratory increased my competence in manipulating laboratory materials.

446) My laboratory/discussion work was beneficial in terms of my personal goals.

447) I generally found the laboratory (recitations, clinical) sessions valuable.

ALTERNATE AND SUPPLEMENTARY TEACHING/LEARNING ENVIRONMENTS

Laboratory and Discussion

448) I found the laboratory/discussion section interesting.

449) The laboratory/discussion instructor adequately prepared me for the material covered in his/her section.

450) The laboratory/discussion instructor clarified lecture material.

451) The laboratory/discussion instructor carried on meaningful dialogue with the students.

452) The laboratory/discussion instructor provided adequate individual remedial attention.

453) The laboratory/discussion instructor knew my name.

454) The laboratory/discussion instructor discovered my trouble areas.

455) The laboratory/discussion instructor helped me find supplemental references.

456) The laboratory/discussion instructor was available during office hours.

457) The questions on the laboratory/discussion quizzes were a good sample of what I was expected to know.

458) The laboratory increased my competence in manipulating laboratory materials.

459) The laboratory equipment was, on most occasions, effectively set up.

460) The laboratory/discussion instructor presented materials supplemental to the lecture material.

461) The laboratory/discussion instructor has the potential for being a competent teacher.

462) The laboratory/discussion instructor graded my papers (exams, homework, etc.) fairly.

463) The laboratory/discussion instructor extended the coverage of topics presented in lecture.

464) The laboratory/discussion section appeared well integrated with the lecture.

465) My laboratory/discussion work was beneficial in terms of the goals of this course.

466) My laboratory/discussion work was beneficial in terms of my personal goals.

467) My laboratory/discussion work was given appropriate weight in the formulation of final grades.

468) The use of laboratory equipment was satisfactorily explained.

469) The laboratory/discussion section was a valuable part of this course.

470) The laboratory/discussion section was a great help in learning.

471) There was ample opportunity to ask questions in the laboratory/discussion section.

472) The laboratory/discussion section clarified lecture material.

473) Students received individual attention in the laboratory/discussion section.

474) The instructor gave every student a chance to practice.

475) The laboratories covered too much material to be absorbed in only one period.

476) The material in the laboratories was too easy.

477) I generally found the laboratory (recitations, clinical) sessions valuable.

478) The laboratory (recitations, clinical) instructor related lecture material to real life situations.

479) The laboratory/discussion instructor explained experiments and/or assignments.

480) The laboratory/discussion instructor adequately helps me prepare for examinations.

481) The laboratory/discussion instructor is precise when answering questions.

482) The laboratory/discussion instructor deals fairly with students.

483) The laboratory/discussion instructor is available through the lab/discussion period.

484) The laboratory/discussion instructor's quizzes stress important points.

485) The laboratory/discussion instructor helps me apply theory for solving problems.

486) The laboratory/discussion instructor demonstrates formal knowledge of the topic.

487) The laboratory/discussion instructor makes me feel I am an important member of the class.

488) The laboratory/discussion instructor accepts criticism from students well.

489) The laboratory/discussion instructor accepts suggestions from students well.

490) The laboratory/discussion instructor shows enthusiasm when teaching.

491) The laboratory/discussion instructor offers specific suggestions for improving my weaknesses.

492) The laboratory/discussion instructor evaluates my work quickly enough to benefit me.

493) The laboratory/discussion instructor plans the lab/discussion time effectively.

494) The laboratory/discussion instructor thoroughly understands the experiments and assignments.

495) The course would be improved by adding a laboratory/discussion section.

496) The lab had adequate facilities.

497) There was opportunity to do imaginative work in the labs.

498) Generally, the equipment used in the lab was adequate and reliable.

499) Most of the lab work was simply routine.

500) The course should require more time in the lab.

Clinical

501) The teaching done in clinical settings increased my learning.

502) The instructor provided relevant clinical experiences.

503) The instructor was NOT helpful when students had questions concerning patient care.

504) The instructor's questions in clinical discussions were thought provoking.

505) The instructor observed students' techniques of interviewing.

506) The instructor helped me develop good clinical techniques.

507) The instructor observed students' techniques of physical examination.

Seminars

508) The seminar approach was effectively implemented in the course.

509) The seminar method met my needs.

510) The seminar provided me with diverse insights into the course materials.

511) The seminar leader effectively included everyone's views into the discussion.

512) The seminar allowed me to learn from other students.

Team Teaching

513) The team teaching method provided me with a valuable learning experience.

514) Instruction was well coordinated among the team members.

515) The team teaching approach was effectively implemented in this course.

516) The team teaching approach met my needs.

517) Team teaching provided me with diverse insights into course materials.

518) Team teaching provided insights that a single instructor could not.

Field Trips

519) The field trips were of instructional value.

520) The field trips were well planned.

521) The course should include a field trip.

522) The field trips were useful learning experiences.

523) The field trips fit in with the course objectives.

524) The timing of the field trips was well planned relative to the progress of the course.

525) The field trips offered insights that the lectures and/or readings could not provide.

## 15

Commercially Available Student Rating Forms

Student rating forms constitute a critical element of virtually every faculty evaluation system. Because the data generated by student rating forms can play a major role in the evaluation of faculty performance, it is important that the forms used be reliable and valid and provide meaningful information that can be used for improvement purposes as well as personnel decision-making purposes. As has been noted earlier, the development of a valid and reliable student rating form is a process that requires the application of a host of professional measurement and statistical skills.

Because numerous student rating forms have been developed locally and may not possess the necessary psychometric qualities of reliability and validity, it is generally a good idea to consider adopting or adapting a professionally developed form rather than developing one from scratch. This chapter provides guidelines for selecting from among a number of available student rating forms. Included here is a checklist for selecting forms and technical reviews of well-known and commercially available forms, including the Aleamoni Course/Instructor Evaluation Questionnaire (CIEQ) system, Kansas State University's IDEA forms, and the Educational Testing Service's Student Instructor Rating (SIR II) form.

■ CHECKLIST FOR IDENTIFYING AND SELECTING PUBLISHED FORMS

In examining the field of published student rating forms for possible adoption or adaptation by your institution, it is best to follow a specific set of steps that give you the best possibility of identifying the better forms to consider. The following checklist is suggested as a guide for finding and testing such forms.

___ Use the Mental Measurement Yearbook (MMY; Buros Institute of Mental Measurements) and Tests in Print (Buros Institute of Mental Measurements) to learn what forms are available. The MMY and the Tests in Print should be available in your library and provide critical reviews by experts concerning each form.

___ Write to the publishers, universities, or private corporations identified in the MMY as producing or reviewing such forms. Request any manuals and announcements for references to forms, services, and technical data from the publishers.

___ Review the literature on student ratings of instruction. Professional publications such as the American Educational Research Association's Instructional Evaluation and Faculty Development or the National Council on Measurement in Education's quarterly newsletter or its Journal of Educational Measurement often contain announcements and/or reviews of new forms as well as general articles on the use and analysis of student rating forms. The bibliography at the end of this handbook provides an excellent starting point for reviewing the literature.

___ Send for a specimen set of the form or forms selected for consideration. Publishers will often provide such sets to institutions wishing to consider their purchase or use. Examine the specimen set to analyze in depth the questions used and material covered.

___ Try out the form. It is a good idea to simply try out the questionnaire or rating form in its original form. Check with the form's publisher to determine policies concerning trial administrations.

___ After trying out a number of possible forms, have the individuals responsible for the courses or course sections in which the forms might be used critically review their appropriateness.

___ As part of the process in selecting a form for possible adoption or adaptation, determine whether the form publisher provides any of the following services and how much these services cost:

- Form scanning and processing.

- Rapid turnaround in providing computer analyses of form results.

- Comparative norms for appropriate groupings of faculty and courses.

- Willing to sell the system to your institution including debugged computer software and the rights to print modified forms.

In many instances, it may be more cost effective to buy the entire processing system. Buying a complete service or adapting an existing operating student rating system saves time and effort in the overall development of your faculty evaluation system.

■ REVIEW OF SELECTED PUBLISHED OR COMMERCIALLY AVAILABLE STUDENT RATING FORMS

The following are reviews of the three major commercially available student-rating-of-instruction-and-instructor forms for use in higher education. Although the systems included for review here are considered among the best in the field, they are not the only commercially available student rating forms and systems. Care must be taken in selecting any commercial student rating form system. The purpose of this chapter is to provide a starting point for faculty and administrators who may be interested in adopting a commercially available student rating system. The information contained in the reviews may also be helpful to those designing local systems to meet unique needs. However, you are urged to familiarize yourself with the relevant original reports and descriptions of a system and to obtain the most recent technical descriptions of

products and services from the contact source listed with each review.

It is generally not recommended that an institution develop its own student rating form unless it is willing to conduct the appropriate psychometric studies required to do so correctly. If none of the commercially available forms meet the needs of your institution and you wish to design and develop your own student rating form, Chapter 13 outlines the recommended procedure and Chapter 14 provides a catalog of student rating items.

Each review of a student rating form system includes a technical critique, a description of the service, a sample of the basic student rating form, and an example of the report provided to the faculty member. More detailed information on the specifications of the forms, the services provided, costs, and other related issues are available at each agency's web site as indicated in the contact information section of each review.

■ ALEAMONI COURSE/INSTRUCTOR EVALUATION QUESTIONNAIRE (CIEQ)

Contact Information

Lawrence M. Aleamoni, Director
Comprehensive Data Evaluation Services, Inc.
6730 N. Camino Padre Isidoro
Tucson, AZ 85718
Phone: 520-621-7832
FAX: 520-297-9427
Web site: www.cieq.com

Format

The CIEQ rating form is available on a computer scorable answer sheet only. No online version of the CIEQ is currently available.

The CIEQ answer sheet is divided into five sections. The first section elicits student background information including student level, whether the student is taking the course pass/fail, whether the course is an elective, student gender, expected grade, whether the student is taking the course as a part of a major, and the semester in which the evaluation takes place. The second section consists of three general items that elicit student responses to the course content, the instructor, and the course in general. Ratings in this section are made on a 6-point scale ranging from Excellent to Very Poor. Section three includes 21 statements which represent 5 subscales or factors labeled General Course, Attitude, Method of Instruction, Course Content, Interest and Attention, and Instructor. A sixth scale, Total, provides scores for all items combined. Items are rated on a 4-point scale ranging from Agree Strongly to Disagree Strongly. The fourth section provides space for 42 optional items if the instructor wishes to include any additional items. These items may either be selected from an item catalog, which is part of the CIEQ system, or written by the instructor. The final section allows for open-ended responses to questions on course content, the instructor, course objectives, papers and homework, examinations, suggested improvements, and an evaluation of the course based upon student satisfaction with the course and student perceptions of its value as an educational experience.

Results

The results of the CIEQ are presented on computer output in four parts. The first part presents course and instructor identification. The second part presents student background information and results for the three general items. Given are the proportion and number responding to each item alternative and the proportion *not* responding. The mean and the standard deviation are also presented for each of the general items.

The third part lists the responses to the five subscales. Included are the:

- Percentage responding
- Mean response
- Standard deviation
- Reliability coefficient (based upon an internal consistency calculation)

Also provided are a variety of normative comparisons, including:

- The rank norm (a comparison of the course with all courses given by instructors at the same rank)
- The level norm (a comparison of the course with all courses at the same course level)
- The institution norm (a comparison of the course with all courses at the university)
- The college norm (a comparison of the course with all other courses in the appropriate college within the university)
- The nationwide norm (a comparison of the course to all the courses throughout the U.S. which have used the CIEQ)

- The department norm (a comparison of the course with all other courses in a particular department)

The final part lists each of 21 standard items and provides:

- The proportion and number responding to each alternative
- The most favorable response
- The mean response
- The standard deviation
- The college-wide norm decile (a comparison of the mean response with those obtained throughout the college or university) for each item
- An optional item listing (if any optional items are used)

Special Features

The optional item catalog (Aleamoni & Carynnk, 1977) contains 350 items divided into 20 categories. The results interpretation manual (Aleamoni & Laham, 1992) provides information on scale development and validation, recommended uses and administrative procedures, description and interpretation of results, and decile norm cutoff scores for seven various subscale databases.

Institutions wishing to use the CIEQ may select one of two options:

- *Option 1.* CIEQ forms may be purchased individually from Comprehensive Data Evaluation Services, Inc. (CODES) and returned for processing.
- *Option 2.* An institution may choose to purchase the computer analysis program and rights to print and use the CIEQ under a royalty arrangement. Institutions purchasing the program receive annual updates of the normative database derived from the hundreds of institutions that have used and/or are currently using the CIEQ. The computer program is written for Apple Macintosh computers and is designed to be used as a simple desktop system.

Development and Validation

The CIEQ was developed in 1975 through an analysis of the earlier versions of the Illinois Course Evaluation Questionnaire (CEQ). The original CEQ was based on an initial pool of more than 1,000 items collected in the early 1960s, reduced and refined by a variety of techniques, including factor analysis, to a form containing 50 items (Aleamoni & Spencer, 1973). The current version (Form

76) uses normative data from approximately 10,000 course sections at the University of Arizona and the University of Illinois at Urbana–Champaign and 150,000 course sections from other U.S. institutions gathered from 1972 through 1999. Internal consistency reliability coefficients for the five subscales range from 88 to .98 (Aleamoni & Laham, 1992). Test-retest reliability ranges from .92 to .98 for the subscales and the total and from .81 to .94 for individual items (Gillmore, 1973). Aleamoni (1978) reviews several studies of the CEQ that he claims are generalizable to the CIEQ. He reports that the CIEQ is not affected by gender, term, curriculum, class size, instructor rank, required/elective, major/minor, student status, pass/fail, expected grade, and final grade. In addition, the ratings of colleagues and trained judges appear to correlate with CIEQ student ratings (Aleamoni, 1978).

Research on the CIEQ has shown it to be a valid, reliable measure of student reactions to the course and instructor. The CIEQ provides meaningful information that may be successfully used in a program of instructional improvement or as part of a comprehensive faculty evaluation system designed to provide data for faculty personnel decisions.

Sample Form and Report

Figure 15.1 shows a copy of the CIEQ form (double-sided), the reverse side of which contains the free response section. Figure 15.2 presents an example of the report (analysis printout) for the CIEQ. Figure 15.3 shows a copy of the brief interpretation guide provided to faculty using the form.

Figure 15.1 CIEQ Form (front)

ALEAMONI COURSE/INSTRUCTOR EVALUATION QUESTIONNAIRE (CIEQ) (FORM 76)

COMPREHENSIVE DATA EVALUATION SERVICES, INC. © LAWRENCE M. ALEAMONI, 1975

MARKING INSTRUCTIONS

MARK:

AS — IF YOU AGREE STRONGLY WITH THE ITEM

A — IF YOU AGREE MODERATELY WITH THE ITEM

D — IF YOU DISAGREE MODERATELY WITH THE ITEM

DS — IF YOU DISAGREE STRONGLY WITH THE ITEM

MARK ONLY ONE RESPONSE PER ITEM USING PENCIL ONLY.

ERASE CHANGED ANSWERS CLEANLY AND COMPLETELY.

SAMPLE MARK
AS ▮ D DS

STUDENT INFORMATION

ARE YOU A: FRESHMAN, SOPHOMORE, JUNIOR, SENIOR, GRADUATE, OTHER

ARE YOU TAKING THIS COURSE FOR PASS/FAIL: YES NO

ARE YOU TAKING THIS COURSE AS A: REQUIRED, ELECTIVE

ARE YOU A: MALE, FEMALE

YOUR EXPECTED GRADE IN THIS COURSE IS: A B C D E

THIS COURSE IS WITHIN YOUR: MAJOR, MINOR, OTHER

SEMESTER: FALL, SPRING, SUMMER

COURSE INFORMATION

RATE EACH OF THE FOLLOWING

COURSE CONTENT: EXCELLENT, VERY GOOD, GOOD, FAIR, POOR, VERY POOR

MAJOR INSTRUCTOR: EXCELLENT, VERY GOOD, GOOD, FAIR, POOR, VERY POOR

COURSE IN GENERAL: EXCELLENT, VERY GOOD, GOOD, FAIR, POOR, VERY POOR

CODING INFORMATION

COURSE CODE: 0 1 2 3 4 5 6 7 8 9 (×5)

SPECIAL CODE: 0 1 2 3 4 5 6 7 8 9 (grid)

TECHNI/FORMS 0613

(Number)

(Name)

THE MAJOR INSTRUCTOR OF THIS COURSE IS

THE NAME AND NUMBER OF THIS COURSE IS

PLEASE PRINT.

PLEASE FILL OUT THE OTHER SIDE

STANDARD ITEM SECTION

#	Item		OPTIONAL ITEMS SECTION I		SECTION II
1	It was a very worthwhile course.	AS A D DS	22 AS A D DS	43 A B C D E	
2	I would take another course that was taught this way.	AS A D DS	23 AS A D DS	44 A B C D E	
3	The instructor seemed to be interested in students as individuals.	AS A D DS	24 AS A D DS	45 A B C D E	
4	The course material was too difficult.	AS A D DS	25 AS A D DS	46 A B C D E	
5	It was easy to remain attentive.	AS A D DS	26 AS A D DS	47 A B C D E	
6	NOT much was gained by taking this course.	AS A D DS	27 AS A D DS	48 A B C D E	
7	I would have preferred another method of teaching in this course.	AS A D DS	28 AS A D DS	49 A B C D E	
8	The course material seemed worthwhile.	AS A D DS	29 AS A D DS	50 A B C D E	
9	The instructor did NOT synthesize, integrate or summarize effectively.	AS A D DS	30 AS A D DS	51 A B C D E	
10	The course was quite interesting.	AS A D DS	31 AS A D DS	52 A B C D E	
11	The instructor encouraged development of new viewpoints and appreciations.	AS A D DS	32 AS A D DS	53 A B C D E	
12	I learn more when other teaching methods are used.	AS A D DS	33 AS A D DS	54 A B C D E	
13	Some things were NOT explained very well.	AS A D DS	34 AS A D DS	55 A B C D E	
14	The instructor demonstrated a thorough knowledge of the subject matter.	AS A D DS	35 AS A D DS	56 A B C D E	
15	This was one of my poorest courses.	AS A D DS	36 AS A D DS	57 A B C D E	
16	The course content was excellent.	AS A D DS	37 AS A D DS	58 A B C D E	
17	Some days I was NOT very interested in this course.	AS A D DS	38 AS A D DS	59 A B C D E	
18	I think that the course was taught quite well.	AS A D DS	39 AS A D DS	60 A B C D E	
19	The course was quite boring.	AS A D DS	40 AS A D DS	61 A B C D E	
20	The instructor seemed to consider teaching as a chore or routine activity.	AS A D DS	41 AS A D DS	62 A B C D E	
21	Overall, the course was good.	AS A D DS	42 AS A D DS	63 A B C D E	

Figure 15.1 (continued)   CIEQ Form (back)

C I E Q

PLEASE USE THIS SIDE OF THE FORM FOR YOUR PERSONAL COMMENTS ON TEACHER EFFECTIVENESS AND GENERAL COURSE VALUE. YOUR INSTRUCTOR WILL NOT SEE YOUR COMPLETED EVALUATION UNTIL AFTER FINAL GRADES ARE IN FOR YOUR COURSE.

COURSE CONTENT
PLEASE GIVE YOUR COMMENTS ON THE COURSE CONTENT, SUBJECT MATTER AND ANY PARTICULAR RELEVANCE THIS COURSE HAS HAD TO YOUR AREA OF STUDY.

INSTRUCTORS
WRITE THE NAME OF YOUR PRINCIPAL INSTRUCTOR _____ T.A. _____
WHAT ARE YOUR GENERAL COMMENTS ABOUT THE INSTRUCTOR(S) IN THIS COURSE?

COURSE/INSTRUCTIONAL OBJECTIVES
WERE THE OBJECTIVES CLEARLY STATED FOR THIS COURSE?   YES _____ NO _____   COMMENT:

PAPERS AND HOMEWORK
COMMENT ON THE VALUE OF BOOKS, HOMEWORK AND PAPERS (IF ANY) IN THIS COURSE.

EXAMINATIONS
COMMENT ON THE EXAMINATIONS AS TO DIFFICULTY, FAIRNESS, ETC.

GENERAL
1. WHAT IMPROVEMENTS WOULD YOU SUGGEST FOR THIS COURSE?

2. WHAT IS YOUR EVALUATION OF THIS COURSE BASED UPON (A) YOUR SATISFACTION WITH WHAT YOU GOT OUT OF THIS COURSE AND (B) WHETHER IT WAS A VALUABLE EDUCATIONAL EXPERIENCE OR A DISAPPOINTMENT? PLEASE COMMENT.

PLEASE FILL OUT THE OTHER SIDE

Figure 15.2 Example of CIEQ Analysis Printout

CIEQ Analysis — U of Arizona — Spring 2001

ALEAMONI COURSE/INSTRUCTOR EVALUATION QUESTIONNAIRE

Instructor: ALEAMONI   **Class: EDP 640 1**   **Sample size: 23**
Process Date: 6/19/01   **College Code: 20020**

Class Description Results

Class Information

	Fr	So	Jr	Sr	Grad	Oth	OMIT
%	0.00	0.00	0.00	0.00	0.65	0.00	0.35
#	0.00	0.00	0.00	0.00	15.00	0.00	8.00

Gender   Course Option

	M	F	OMIT		Req	Elec	OMIT
%	0.26	0.39	0.35	%	0.43	0.22	0.35
#	6.00	9.00	8.00	#	10.00	5.00	8.00

Pass-Fail Option   Major-Minor

	Yes	No	OMIT		Maj	Min	Oth	OMIT
%	0.00	0.61	0.39	%	0.610.00	0.04	0.35	
#	0.00	14.00	9.00	#	14.000.00	1.00	8.00	

Expected Grade

	A	B	C	D	E	OMIT
%	0.22	0.35	0.09	0.00	0.00	0.35
#	5.00	8.00	2.00	0.00	0.00	8.00

Content Rating

	V.P.	Poor	Fair	Good	V.G.	Ex	OMIT			
%	0.00	0.10	0.00	0.20	0.20	0.50	0.00	Mean	=	5.00
#	0	1	0	2	2	5	0	S.D.	=	1.33

Instructor Rating

	V.P.	Poor	Fair	Good	V.G.	Ex	OMIT			
%	0.00	0.10	0.10	0.10	0.20	0.50	0.00	Mean	=	4.90
#	0	1	1	1	2	5	0	S.D.	=	1.29

Course Rating

	V.P.	Poor	Fair	Good	V.G.	Ex	OMIT			
%	0.00	0.10	0.10	0.10	0.20	0.50	0.00	Mean	=	4.80
#	0	1	1	1	2	5	0	S.D.	=	1.69

Subscale Results

Subscale	Items	% Res	Mean	S.D.	Rel.	IR	CL	D	C	UA	N
Attitude	4	1.00	3.28	1.06	0.98	4	5	3	4	5	6
Method	4	1.00	3.13	1.09	0.94	6	7	6	6	6	7
Content	4	1.00	3.30	0.91	0.68	8	8	8	8	8	9
Interest	4	1.00	3.08	1.07	0.88	7	7	5	6	7	7
Instructor	5	0.98	3.27	0.93	0.91	4	5	2	4	5	5
Total	21	1.00	3.21	1.01	0.98	6	7	5	6	6	7

IR=Instructor Rank; CL=Class Level; D=Department;C=College; UA=University of Arizona; N=Nationwide. NA in a normative decile category indicates that normative data is not available for this category or that this category is not applicable to the current data.

Figure 15.2 (continued)   Example of CIEQ Analysis Printout

Instructor: ALEAMONI   **Class: EDP 646**   **Sample size: 10**
Process Date: 12/7/99   **College Code: 78933**

Individual Item Results

1. It was a very worthwhile course.

	AS	A	D	DS	OMIT	BEST	MEAN	S.D.	DEC
%	0.70	0.00	0.20	0.10	0.00	AS	3.30	1.16	5
#	7	0	2	1	0				

2. I would take another course that was taught this way.

	AS	A	D	DS	OMIT	BEST	MEAN	S.D.	DEC
%	0.70	0.00	0.20	0.10	0.00	AS	3.00	1.16	7
#	7	0	2	1	0				

3. The instructor seemed to be interested in students as individuals.

	AS	A	D	DS	OMIT	BEST	MEAN	S.D.	DEC
%	0.50	0.20	0.20	0.00	0.10	AS	3.33	0.87	4
#	5	2	2	0	1				

4. The course material was too difficult.

	AS	A	D	DS	OMIT	BEST	MEAN	S.D.	DEC
%	0.00	0.00	0.30	0.70	0.00	DS	3.70	0.48	10
#	0	0	3	7	0				

5. It was easy to remain attentive.

	AS	A	D	DS	OMIT	BEST	MEAN	S.D.	DEC
%	0.50	0.30	0.20	0.00	0.00	AS	3.30	0.82	8
#	5	3	2	0	0				

6. NOT much was gained by taking this course.

	AS	A	D	DS	OMIT	BEST	MEAN	S.D.	DEC
%	0.00	0.30	0.00	0.70	0.00	DS	3.40	0.97	5
#	0	3	0	7	0				

7. I would have preferred another method of teaching this course.

	AS	A	D	DS	OMIT	BEST	MEAN	S.D.	DEC
%	0.20	0.10	0.20	0.50	0.00	DS	3.00	1.25	6
#	2	1	2	5	0				

8. The course material seemed worthwhile.

	AS	A	D	DS	OMIT	BEST	MEAN	S.D.	DEC
%	0.50	0.30	0.20	0.00	0.00	AS	3.30	0.82	6
#	5	3	2	0	0				

9. The instructor did NOT synthesize, integrate or summarize effectively.

	AS	A	D	DS	OMIT	BEST	MEAN	S.D.	DEC
%	0.00	0.10	0.30	0.60	0.00	DS	3.50	0.71	8
#	0	1	3	6	0				

10. The course was quite interesting.

	AS	A	D	DS	OMIT	BEST	MEAN	S.D.	DEC
%	0.50	0.20	0.20	0.10	0.00	AS	3.10	1.10	5
#	5	2	2	1	0				

Figure 15.2 (continued)   Example of CIEQ Analysis Printout

11. The instructor encouraged development of new viewpoints and appreciations.

	AS	A	D	DS	OMIT	BEST	MEAN	S.D.	DEC
%	0.50	0.10	0.30	0.10	0.00	AS	3.00	1.15	4
#	5	1	3	1	0				

12. I learn more when other teaching methods are used.

	AS	A	D	DS	OMIT	BEST	MEAN	S.D.	DEC
%	0.00	0.20	0.40	0.40	0.00	DS	3.20	0.79	9
#	0	2	4	4	0				

13. Some things were not explained very well.

	AS	A	D	DS	OMIT	BEST	MEAN	S.D.	DEC
%	0.10	0.00	0.60	0.30	0.00	DS	3.10	0.88	8
#	1	0	6	3	0				

14. The instructor demonstrated a thorough knowledge of the subject matter.

	AS	A	D	DS	OMIT	BEST	MEAN	S.D.	DEC
%	0.60	0.30	0.10	0.00	0.00	AS	3.50	0.71	4
#	6	3	1	0	0				

15. This was one of my poorest courses.

	AS	A	D	DS	OMIT	BEST	MEAN	S.D.	DEC
%	0.10	0.20	0.10	0.60	0.00	DS	3.20	1.14	3
#	1	2	1	6	0				

16. The course content was excellent.

	AS	A	D	DS	OMIT	BEST	MEAN	S.D.	DEC
%	0.60	0.10	0.10	0.20	0.00	AS	3.10	1.29	6
#	6	1	1	2	0				

17. Some days I was NOT very interested in this course.

	AS	A	D	DS	OMIT	BEST	MEAN	S.D.	DEC
%	0.40	0.10	0.20	0.30	0.00	DS	2.40	1.35	5
#	4	1	2	3	0				

18. I think that the course was taught quite well.

	AS	A	D	DS	OMIT	BEST	MEAN	S.D.	DEC
%	0.50	0.20	0.10	0.20	0.00	AS	3.00	1.25	4
#	5	2	1	2	0				

19. The course was quite boring.

	AS	A	D	DS	OMIT	BEST	MEAN	S.D.	DEC
%	0.00	0.10	0.30	0.60	0.00	DS	3.50	0.71	8
#	0	1	3	6	0				

20. The instructor seemed to consider teaching as a chore or routine activity.

	AS	A	D	DS	OMIT	BEST	MEAN	S.D.	DEC
%	0.20	0.00	0.40	0.40	0.00	DS	3.00	1.15	2
#	2	0	4	4	0				

21. Overall, the course was good.

	AS	A	D	DS	OMIT	BEST	MEAN	S.D.	DEC
%	0.60	0.10	0.20	0.10	0.00	AS	3.20	1.14	4
#	6	1	2	1	0				

Figure 15.3 CIEQ Interpretation Guide

A BRIEF CIEQ INTERPRETATION GUIDE

The following outline is provided as an aid to the rapid interpretation of CIEQ results. This guide can be used as a checklist when examining the computerized analysis output of the CIEQ. CIEQ interpretation is discussed in complete detail in the Manual.

Step 1. Adequacy of Results

A. Refer to the top of the first page of the CIEQ output. Check the SAMPLE SIZE. If it or number of the students responding is less than one-half of the course enrollment, results may be biased and should be interpreted with caution.

B. At the bottom of the first page is the section entitled SUBSCALE RESULTS that contains a column of figures labeled REL. This column contains the obtained reliabilities for the six subscales of the CIEQ. Any subscale with a REL below .65 should be interpreted with caution. Consult the Manual for further details.

Step 2. Comparative Information

A. In all cases, comparative information is provided by decile rank (DEC). The decile rank describes the current course MEAN in relation to other courses that have administered the CIEQ. Decile ranks are always interpreted as follows:

   1 – 3   Substantial improvement needed
   4 – 7   Some improvement needed
   8 – 10   No improvement needed

Differences between adjacent pairs of decile ranks within each interval (e.g., 1 vs. 2, or 4 vs. 5) are not considered to be significantly different.

B. First refer to the SUBSCALE listing at the bottom of output on page 1. Each subscale represents a different aspect of the course as indicated by its title. Decile ranks for the current course/instructor are listed for each subscale in comparison to six normative groups:

   1. IR   all instructors of the same faculty rank
   2. CL   all courses at the same grade level (e.g., freshman, sophomore., etc.)
   3. D   all courses within the same department
   4. C   all courses within the same college
   5. UA   all course at the University of Arizona
   6. N   all courses that have used the CIEQ in the United States

C. On the following two pages under INDIVIDUAL ITEM RESULTS are listed each of the 21 individual items of the CIEQ along with the proportion (%), frequency (#), mean, and standard deviation (SD) of responses to each individual item of the CIEQ. Also listed are the text of each item and the most favorable response or BEST answer for each item. All means have been scaled such that 4.00 is the most favorable response and 1.00 is the least favorable response, regardless of the initial wording of the item. To the far right of each individual item are listed decile ranks that compare each item mean to the item means obtained in all courses within the same college.

Figure 15.3 (continued)   CIEQ Interpretation Guide

A Brief CIEQ Interpretation Guide (continued)

D. In interpreting results, refer first to the decile ranks for subscales. Low deciles for a subscale identify potential problem areas. Individual items can then be examined for more specific information. The subscales are composed of the following individual items:

Attitude	items 1, 6, 15, 21
Method	items 2, 7, 12, 18
Content	items 4, 8, 13, 16
Interest	items 5, 10, 17, 19
Instructor	items 3, 9, 11, 14, 20
Total	items 1 - 21

Step 3. Descriptive Information

A. Refer to the top of the first page of CIEQ output. Following the initial titles, information is listed on the composition of the responding sample under the heading Class Description Results. Both the proportion and frequency of responses are listed for each alternative of the following items: Class Information, Gender, Course Option, Pass-Fail Option, Major-Minor, and Expected Grade.

B. The next portion of the output lists the proportion (%), frequency (#), mean, and standard deviation (SD) of responses to three global ratings: Course Content, Instructor Rating, and the Course Rating. A mean value of 6.00 is the most favorable rating. These three items have NOT been validated and should therefore be used only for the purpose of feedback to the instructor.

■ IDEA Student Ratings of Instruction

Contact Information

The IDEA Center, Inc.
211 South Seth Child Road
Manhattan, KS 66502-3089
Phone: 800-255-2757
                785-532-5970
FAX: 785-532-5725
Email: idea@ksu.edu
Web site: www.idea.ksu.edu

Format

The IDEA student rating forms are available as either paper answer sheets or as an online service. Complete description of the online service is available at the IDEA Center web site at www.idea.ksu.edu.

The IDEA system requires instructors to describe their course objectives prior to administering the rating form. The instructor is asked to rate the importance, on a 3-point scale (essential, important, or minor importance), of each of 12 IDEA objectives. The importance the instructor assigns to each objective is taken into account in tabulating results. The optically scanned rating form is divided into seven parts.

The first section consists of 20 items, which deal with 5 dimensions of instruction: Student-Faculty Contact, Involving Students, Establishing Expectations, Clarity of Communication, and Assessment/Feedback. Items are scored on a 5-point scale ranging from Hardly Ever to Almost Always. The second section deals with the students' evaluation of their progress on 12 course objectives, including gaining factual knowledge, acquiring team skills, developing creative capacities, and clarifying/developing personal values. Students are asked to compare the progress made on each objective with the progress made in other courses. Each item is scored on a 5-point scale ranging from Low (Lowest 10% of Courses Taken) to High (Highest 10% of Courses Taken). The third section deals with three course characteristics: amount of reading, amount of work in other assignments, and difficulty of subject matter. Ratings are compared to other courses on a 5-point scale ranging from Much Less Than Most Courses to Much More Than Most Courses. The next section includes a self-rating of student attitudes and behaviors in the course. Each item is scored on a 5-point scale from definitely false to definitely true. The fifth section consists of five "experimental questions" which the IDEA Center is studying for possible inclusion in future revisions of the form. The sixth section is for optional instruc-

tor-designed, multiple-choice questions. Finally, the form provides a space for students to make open-ended comments. A "short form" version, appropriate for "summative" but not "formative" evaluation, is also available. It employs only Sections 2, 4, and 6 of the standard form.

Results

The IDEA report consists of seven parts plus identifying information (faculty and course name, number of students enrolled, percent providing ratings). The first two parts summarize evaluation results for overall measures (Part I) and for specific objectives (Part II). "Unadjusted" and "adjusted" averages are compared with results in a very large national database. Adjusted results take into account factors which influence ratings but which are beyond the control of the instructor (e.g., class size, course-related student motivation, academic habits/effort, etc.) The overall evaluation measures, presented numerically and graphically, include progress on instructor-chosen objectives, improved student attitude, overall excellence of the teacher, and overall excellence of the course. Part II provides similar information for the specific objectives selected as "important" or "essential" by the instructor. Part III (Methods) summarizes responses to the 20 items dealing with teaching procedures found on Section 1 of the standard form (but not included on the short form). Averages are reported graphically for each item and for scales designed to measure five instructional dimensions. Items are labeled as Strengths, Weaknesses, or In-Between depending on how their averages differ from classes of similar size and student motivation level. A second section of Part III is intended to facilitate improvement efforts by identifying Strengths and Weaknesses that research by the IDEA Center has shown to be most relevant to specific teaching objectives. Part IV summarizes student descriptions of course characteristics and also reports a course description provided by the instructor, including principal instructional methods; intended audience; special circumstances; and the amount of emphasis given to such matters as writing, computer applications, and quantitative skills. Section V provides statistical detail—frequencies, averages, and standard deviations for all items, including optional instructor-designed items.

Special Features

The IDEA system is a commercial rating package. Charges for forms and processing vary depending upon the number of forms ordered and classes processed. Forms must be ordered from the center and returned to them for processing. Institutions receive three copies of the IDEA computer report; interpretation aids are incorporated in the report. For an additional fee, participating institutions may receive Group Summary Reports, which combine results for all classes or for selected subgroups, and Faculty Summary Reports, which summarize all reports for a given faculty member over a specified period of time. The IDEA Center publishes *Exchange*, an occasional newsletter, and a series of technical and nontechnical publications on topics in faculty evaluation and development. National workshops on selected topics are offered annually, and consultative services can also be arranged.

Development and Validation

The development and initial validation of the IDEA system is described by Hoyt (1973) and Hoyt and Cashin (1977). Items on instructor objectives were originally formed from earlier taxonomic classifications, factor analytic work, and input from award-winning teachers, faculty-student committees, and users of IDEA. The 1998 revision employed the advice of users in eliminating three of these and adding five that reflect higher education's contemporary emphases on team skills, values, lifelong learning, and critical thinking. The 20 teaching method items (10 of which are new) were written to reflect Chickering and Gamson's (1987) seven principles and were selected on the basis of their unique contribution to the prediction of outcomes. Items on course management and student characteristics were included primarily to adjust outcome measures by taking into account factors that were

beyond the control of the instructor. The reliability of the five scales of teaching methods ranged from .76 to .91, averaging .86 for classes of 15–34 students. For individual items, reliabilities in similar classes ranged from .71 to .91, averaging .83. A principal indicator of validity was the finding that student ratings of progress on objectives were positively related to instructor ratings of importance of objectives. Also, relationships between teaching methods and progress on objectives were consistent with theoretical expectations. Multiple regression analyses showed that each of the 20 teaching methods made an independent contribution to the prediction of at least one progress rating, and that the relevance of specific instructor behaviors varied with class size. Factors that were used to adjust outcome measures included class size, student desire to take the course regardless of who taught it, the portion of "difficulty" ratings and of "effort" ratings that could not be attributed to the instructor, and a measure of "other student motivation." Later technical reports (e.g., Cashin & Perrin, 1978; Sixbury & Cashin, 1995a, 1995b; Hoyt, Chen, Pallett, & Gross, 1998) provide additional data on reliability and validity as well as a description of the computational procedures and comparative databases used in producing reports for the latest version of IDEA.

Sample Form and Report

The following pages contain a sample of the IDEA student rating form (front and back) as well as an example of a faculty report. The IDEA system also provides institutional summary reports.

Figure 15.4   IDEA Survey Form—Student Reactions to Instruction and Courses (front)

SURVEY FORM - STUDENT REACTIONS TO INSTRUCTION AND COURSES

IDEA CENTER

IMPORTANT!   USE NO. 2 PENCIL ONLY

Proper Marks ● ● ● ● ●
Improper Marks ⊙ ⊘ ⊗ ⊙ ◡ ⊕

Your thoughtful answers to these questions will provide helpful information to your instructor.

Describe the frequency of your instructor's teaching procedures, using the following code:

1=Hardly Ever   2=Occasionally   3=Sometimes   4=Frequently   5=Almost Always

The Instructor:

1. ① ② ③ ④ ⑤ Displayed a personal interest in students and their learning
2. ① ② ③ ④ ⑤ Found ways to help students answer their own questions
3. ① ② ③ ④ ⑤ Scheduled course work (class activities, tests, projects) in ways which encouraged students to stay up-to-date in their work
4. ① ② ③ ④ ⑤ Demonstrated the importance and significance of the subject matter
5. ① ② ③ ④ ⑤ Formed "teams" or "discussion groups" to facilitate learning
6. ① ② ③ ④ ⑤ Made it clear how each topic fit into the course
7. ① ② ③ ④ ⑤ Explained the reasons for criticisms of students' academic performance
8. ① ② ③ ④ ⑤ Stimulated students to intellectual effort beyond that required by most courses
9. ① ② ③ ④ ⑤ Encouraged students to use multiple resources (e.g. data banks, library holdings, outside experts) to improve understanding
10. ① ② ③ ④ ⑤ Explained course material clearly and concisely
11. ① ② ③ ④ ⑤ Related course material to real life situations
12. ① ② ③ ④ ⑤ Gave tests, projects, etc. that covered the most important points of the course
13. ① ② ③ ④ ⑤ Introduced stimulating ideas about the subject
14. ① ② ③ ④ ⑤ Involved students in "hands on" projects such as research, case studies, or "real life" activities
15. ① ② ③ ④ ⑤ Inspired students to set and achieve goals which really challenged them
16. ① ② ③ ④ ⑤ Asked students to share ideas and experiences with others whose backgrounds and viewpoints differ from their own
17. ① ② ③ ④ ⑤ Provided timely and frequent feedback on tests, reports, projects, etc. to help students improve
18. ① ② ③ ④ ⑤ Asked students to help each other understand ideas or concepts
19. ① ② ③ ④ ⑤ Gave projects, tests, or assignments that required original or creative thinking
20. ① ② ③ ④ ⑤ Encouraged student-faculty interaction outside of class (office visits, phone calls, e-mail, etc.)

Twelve possible learning objectives are listed below. For each, rate your progress in this course compared with your progress in other courses you have taken at this college or university. (Of course, ratings on objectives which were not addressed by the course will usually be low.)

In this course, my progress was:
1-Low (lowest 10 percent of courses I have taken here)
2-Low Average (next 20 percent of courses I have taken here)
3-Average (middle 40 percent of courses I have taken here)
4-High Average (next 20 percent of courses I have taken here)
5-High (highest 10 percent of courses I have taken here)

Progress on:

21. ① ② ③ ④ ⑤ Gaining factual knowledge (terminology, classifications, methods, trends)
22. ① ② ③ ④ ⑤ Learning fundamental principles, generalizations, or theories
23. ① ② ③ ④ ⑤ Learning to *apply* course material (to improve thinking, problem solving, and decisions)
24. ① ② ③ ④ ⑤ Developing specific skills, competencies, and points of view needed by professionals in the field most closely related to this course
25. ① ② ③ ④ ⑤ Acquiring skills in working with others as a member of a team
26. ① ② ③ ④ ⑤ Developing creative capacities (writing, inventing, designing, performing in art, music, drama, etc.)
27. ① ② ③ ④ ⑤ Gaining a broader understanding and appreciation of intellectual/cultural activity (music, science, literature, etc.)
28. ① ② ③ ④ ⑤ Developing skill in expressing myself orally or in writing
29. ① ② ③ ④ ⑤ Learning how to find and use resources for answering questions or solving problems
30. ① ② ③ ④ ⑤ Developing a clearer understanding of, and commitment to, personal values
31. ① ② ③ ④ ⑤ Learning to *analyze* and *critically evaluate* ideas, arguments, and points of view
32. ① ② ③ ④ ⑤ Acquiring an interest in learning more by asking my own questions and seeking answers

Printed in the U.S.A.   (C3.F3)   CP98-1300   Continue on back page

On the next three items, compare this course with others you have taken at this institution, using the following code:

| 1=Much Less than | 2=Less than | 3=About Average | 4=More than | 5=Much More |
| Most Courses | Most Courses | | Most Courses | than Most Courses |

The Course:

33. ① ② ③ ④ ⑤ Amount of reading
34. ① ② ③ ④ ⑤ Amount of work in other (non-reading) assignments
35. ① ② ③ ④ ⑤ Difficulty of subject matter

Describe your attitudes and behavior in this course, using the following code:

| 1=Definitely | 2=More False | 3=In Between | 4=More True | 5=Definitely |
| False | Than True | | Than False | True |

Self Rating:

36. ① ② ③ ④ ⑤ I had a strong desire to take this course.
37. ① ② ③ ④ ⑤ I worked harder on this course than on most courses I have taken.
38. ① ② ③ ④ ⑤ I really wanted to take a course from this instructor.
39. ① ② ③ ④ ⑤ I really wanted to take this course regardless of who taught it.
40. ① ② ③ ④ ⑤ As a result of taking this course, I have more positive feelings toward this field of study.
41. ① ② ③ ④ ⑤ Overall, I rate this instructor an excellent teacher.
42. ① ② ③ ④ ⑤ Overall, I rate this course as excellent.

For the following items, blacken the space which best corresponds to your judgment:

| 1=Definitely | 2=More False | 3=In Between | 4=More True | 5=Definitely |
| False | Than True | | Than False | True |

43. ① ② ③ ④ ⑤ As a rule, I put forth more effort than other students on academic work.
44. ① ② ③ ④ ⑤ The instructor used a variety of methods--not only tests--to evaluate student progress on course objectives.
45. ① ② ③ ④ ⑤ The instructor expected students to take their share of responsibility for learning.
46. ① ② ③ ④ ⑤ The instructor had high achievement standards in this class.
47. ① ② ③ ④ ⑤ The instructor used educational technology (e.g., Internet, e-mail, computer exercises, multi-media presentations, etc.) to promote learning.

EXTRA QUESTIONS

If your instructor has extra questions, answer them in the space designated below (questions 48-66):

48. ① ② ③ ④ ⑤   58. ① ② ③ ④ ⑤
49. ① ② ③ ④ ⑤   59. ① ② ③ ④ ⑤
50. ① ② ③ ④ ⑤   60. ① ② ③ ④ ⑤
51. ① ② ③ ④ ⑤   61. ① ② ③ ④ ⑤
52. ① ② ③ ④ ⑤   62. ① ② ③ ④ ⑤
53. ① ② ③ ④ ⑤   63. ① ② ③ ④ ⑤
54. ① ② ③ ④ ⑤   64. ① ② ③ ④ ⑤
55. ① ② ③ ④ ⑤   65. ① ② ③ ④ ⑤
56. ① ② ③ ④ ⑤   66. ① ② ③ ④ ⑤
57. ① ② ③ ④ ⑤

Your comments are invited on how the instructor might improve this course or teaching procedures. Use the space below for comments (unless otherwise directed). *Note: Your written comments may be returned to the instructor. You may want to PRINT to protect your anonymity.*

Institution: _____   Instructor: _____

Course Number: _____   Time and Days Class Meets: _____

Comments: _____
_____
_____
_____
_____
_____
_____

Figure 15.5 Sample IDEA Report

The IDEA Report
Communications 0000 (MWF 11:30)
IDEA Center
www.idea.ksu.edu

Faculty Name: SAMPLE, AX   Number Enrolled: 18   Term: Fall 1998-1999
Institution: ALPHA UNIVERSITY   Number Responding: 15   % Responding: 83.3

Your results are considered fairly reliable; it is unlikely that re-rating by the same students would produce more than a moderate change in your report. The percentage of enrollees who provided ratings is high; results can be considered representative of the class as a whole.

Sections and Purposes of the Report

Page	Section	Purpose
2	I. Overall Measures of Teaching Effectiveness	Primarily for **administrative use** in helping to make personnel recommendations. *Only this page and Page 6 are essential if this is the only use you plan to make of the report.*
3	II. Student Ratings of Progress on Specific Objectives	Primarily to identify the **teaching objectives** where improvement is most needed
4-5	III. Teaching Methods or Style Related to Student Ratings of Progress	Primarily to help develop a **strategy for improving teaching** methods
6	IV. Course Description/Context	Primarily to **assist in interpreting** the results by considering the context in which the course was taught
7-8	V. Statistical Detail	Primarily to provide details which may help you or your consultants to **understand or interpret** the report accurately
8	VI. Processing Error Messages	Identifies errors resulting from incomplete information provided on the Faculty Information Form

---

Definitions

Raw Score: Results obtained by using students' numerical ratings, all of which are based on a scale of 1 (low) to 5 (high).

Adjusted Score: Ratings which have been statistically adjusted to take into account factors which affect ratings but which are beyond the instructor's control (size of class; student desire to take course regardless of who taught it; course difficulty not attributable to instructor; student effort not attributable to instructor; and other student motivational influences)

T Score: A statistically derived score which makes it easy to compare various measures. Unlike raw scores which have different averages and standard deviations (variabilities), T Scores all have an <u>average of 50</u> and a <u>standard deviation of 10</u>. This means that 40% of all T Scores will be in the range of 45-55, while less than 2% will be below 30 or above 70.

Similar Classes: On Page 4, ratings of specific teaching methods are compared with national averages for classes of "similar size and level of student motivation." Your ratings are compared with those from one of 20 groups defined by considering both class size (less than 15; 15-34; 35-99; or 100 or more) and average student response to "I had a strong desire to take this course" (under 3.0; 3.0-3.4; 3.5-3.9; 4.0-4.4; or 4.5 or above).

Understanding the Graphs

Most results are presented on graphs. Unadjusted T Scores are shown by the symbol ✕; adjusted T Scores are shown by the symbol ◆. In most cases, we use a line on both sides of a symbol to indicate that ratings have a "margin of error"; the line represents ± one standard error of measurement, a statistical indication of the reliability of the measure.

A Few Words of Caution

1. New items on the IDEA form are marked by an asterisk (*) because they have been tested on only 3,668 classes. Comparisons with the national database on these items will be less stable than for the items retained from the original IDEA form which are based on over 35,000 classes rated during the 1993-94 and 1994-95 academic years.

2. Student ratings can make a useful contribution to the appraisal of teaching effectiveness and to the development of improvement strategies. However, they have distinct limitations which need to be acknowledged before appropriate use can be made of them. Please read the enclosed *Overview of Student Ratings: Value and Limitations.*

Figure 15.5 (continued)   Sample IDEA Report

Section II Overall Measures of Teaching Effectiveness

This section compares your results with those for other instructors and courses in the national database on four OVERALL MEASURES OF TEACHING EFFECTIVENESS. **The primary value of this information is to aid in making administrative recommendations; if this is the only use you will make of the report, you need to consult only these results and the context provided by Part IV, page 6.** Please remember that most of the classes included in the database have been taught in a reasonably successful manner; therefore, a rating which is "below average" does not necessarily mean that the quality of instruction was unacceptable.

Overall Measures of Effectiveness	T-Score Unadj. Adj.	2% of all classes	28% of all classes	40% of all classes (Avg. range)	28% of all classes	2% of all classes	Your Average (5-Point Scale)	
							Raw	Adjusted
1. Progress on Relevant (Essential and Important) Objectives	58 55						NA₁	NA₁
2. Improved Student Attitude	50 46						3.9	3.6
3. Overall Excellence of Teacher	51 52						4.2	4.3
4. Overall Excellence of Course	51 44						3.9	3.5

20   30   40   45   50   55   60   70   80
T Score--Comparison with all Classes in National Database

⊢✕⊣   Unadjusted T Score ± one standard error of measurement
⊢◆⊣   Adjusted T Score ± one standard error of measurement (adjusted for class size; student desire to take course regardless of who taught it; course difficulty not attributable to instructor; student effort not attributable to instructor; and other student motivational influences)

You may wish to assign these ratings to categories like those which have been used historically with the IDEA system. Simply assign T Scores to categories as follows: **Low** (lowest 10%)=T Score below 37; **Low Average** (next 20%)=T Score 37-44; **Average** (middle 40%)=T Score 45-55; **High Average** (next 20%)=T Score 56-63; and **High** (highest 10%)=T Score above 63.

1. Progress on Relevant (Essential and Important) Objectives. Because student learning is the central purpose of teaching, and because you chose the objectives considered by this measure, this is probably the most vital measure of effectiveness. A double weight is given to student ratings of progress on objectives you chose as *Essential*, and a single weight to those chosen as *Important*; objectives identified as being of *Minor or No Importance* were ignored in developing this measure.

2. Improved Student Attitude. The graph shows the average response of students to item 40, "As a result of taking this course, I have more positive feelings toward this field of study." This rating is most meaningful for courses which are taken by many non-majors. Most teachers hope that such students will develop a respect and appreciation for the discipline even if they choose to take no additional courses in it.

3. Overall Excellence of Teacher. This shows the average response to item 41, "Overall, I rate this instructor an excellent teacher." Overall impressions of a teacher affect student attitudes, effort, and learning.

4. Overall Excellence of Course. This shows the average response to item 42, "Overall, I rate this course as excellent." This evaluation is likely determined by a number of factors (e.g., teaching style, student satisfaction with course outcomes, and characteristics such as organization, selection of readings and^or other influences).

NA₁: Based on a combination of ratings where an average on a 5-point scale is not comparable.

Figure 15.5 (continued) Sample IDEA Report

Section II. Student Ratings of Progress on Specific Objectives

This graph shows student progress ratings on the objectives you chose as *Essential* (Part A) and those you chose as *Important* (Part B). To the degree that students make progress on the objectives you stress, your teaching has been effective.

Part A. Essential Objectives	T-Score Unadj. Adj.	2% of all classes	28% of all classes	40% of all classes (Avg. range)	28% of all classes	2% of all classes	Your Average (5-Point Scale)	
							Raw	Adjusted
24. Professional skills, viewpoints	52 / 45			⊢◆⊣ ⊢×⊣			4.1	3.7
28. Oral and written communication skills	61 / 61				⊢×⊣ ⊢◆⊣		4.5	4.6

Part B. Important Objectives								
26. Creative capacities	61 / 56			⊢◆ ⊢×⊣			4.5	4.3
*31. Analysis and critical evaluation of ideas	62 / 61			⊢×⊣ ⊢◆⊣			4.1	4.1

```
        20      30      40  45  50  55   60      70      80
      T Score--Comparison with all Classes in National Database where the
              Objective was Selected as "Essential" or "Important"
```

⊢×⊣ Unadjusted T Score ± one standard error of measurement

⊢◆⊣ Adjusted T Score ± one standard error of measurement (adjusted for class size; student desire to take course regardless of who taught it; course difficulty not attributable to instructor; student effort not attributable to instructor; and other student motivational influences)

Similar to Section I, you may wish to assign ratings to categories. Simply assign T Scores to categories as follows: **Low** (lowest 10%)=T Score below 37; **Low Average** (next 20%)=T Score 37-44; **Average** (middle 40%)=T Score 45-55; **High Average** (next 20%)=T Score 56-63; and **High** (highest 10%)=T Score above 63.

It is recommended that priority attention be given to *Essential* objectives with progress ratings which are *below average*. The second priority might be directed to *Important* objectives for which progress ratings are *below average*. A third priority might be *Essential* or *Important* objectives for which progress ratings are in the *average* range. If all progress ratings are *above the average* range, it is suggested that your present methods of teaching are effective and changes in your teaching style or approaches do not appear to be needed in order to ensure that your teaching promotes student learning. If improvement is needed, strategies can be formulated by examining "Strengths" and "Weaknesses" associated with progress ratings on the objectives chosen for priority attention. These are identified in **Section III** of this report.

Note: Students in your class also rated their progress on the objectives which you classified as being of *Minor or No Importance*. These ratings are considered irrelevant in judging your teaching effectiveness. However, a review of student ratings on these objectives, found in **Section V** (Statistical Detail), may provide you with insights about some "unintended" or "additional" effects of your instruction.

*New Item

Figure 15.5 (continued)   Sample IDEA Report

Faculty Name: SAMPLE, AX
Course: Communications 0000

Term: Fall 1998-1999
Page 4

Section III. Teaching Methods or Style Related to Student Ratings of Progress

This section focuses on specific teaching methods. Results are given in two parts. **Part One** graphically compares ratings of your teaching methods with those of others who teach classes similar to this one in terms of size and level of student motivation. **Part Two** identifies the teaching methods most closely related to attaining your *Important* and *Essential* objectives, providing a basis for developing improvement strategies. **Part Three** highlights potential areas to emphasize for improvement efforts and teaching strengths that should be retained.

Part One: The graphs below classify methods as "strengths" if your rating was at least 0.3 above average for classes of similar size and level of student motivation and as "weaknesses" if your rating was at least 0.3 below the average for such classes. Although effectiveness generally improves when weaknesses are overcome while maintaining strengths, not all teaching methods promote progress on every teaching objective. The methods which are especially relevant to each of your *Essential* and *Important* objectives are identified in **Part Two** (page 5).

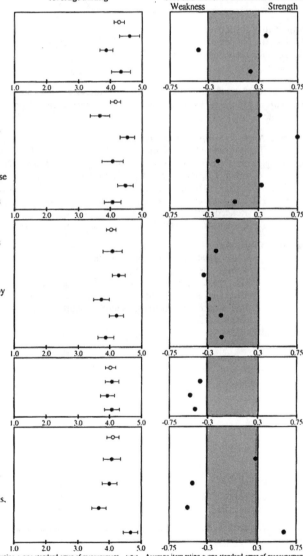

Teaching Methods and Styles

A. Student-Faculty Contact (Average of 1, 2, 20)
  *1. Displayed a personal interest in students and their learning
  2. Found ways to help students answer their own questions
  *20. Encouraged student-faculty interaction outside of class (office visits, phone calls, e-mail, etc.)

B. Involving Students (Average of 5, 9, 14, 16, 18)
  *5. Formed "teams" or "discussion groups" to facilitate learning
  *9. Encouraged students to use multiple resources (e.g. data banks, library holdings, outside experts) to improve understanding
  *14. Involved students in "hands on" projects such as research, case studies, or "real life" activities
  *16. Asked students to share ideas and experiences with others whose backgrounds and viewpoints differ from their own
  *18. Asked students to help each other understand ideas or concepts

C. Establishing Expectations (Average of 3, 4, 8, 13, 15)
  *3. Scheduled course work (class activities, tests, projects) in ways which encouraged students to stay up to date in their work
  4. Demonstrated the importance and significance of the subject matter
  8. Stimulated students to intellectual effort beyond that required by most courses
  13. Introduced stimulating ideas about the subject
  *15. Inspired students to set and achieve goals which really challenged them

D. Clarity of Communication (Average of 6, 10, 11)
  6. Made it clear how each topic fit into the course
  10. Explained course material clearly and concisely
  11. Related course material to real life situations

E. Assessment/Feedback (Average of 7, 12, 17, 19)
  7. Explained the reasons for criticisms of students' academic performance
  12. Gave tests, projects, etc. that covered the most important points of the course
  *17. Provided timely and frequent feedback on tests, reports, projects, etc. to help students improve
  19. Gave projects, tests or assignments that required original or creative thinking

*New Item   ⊢o⊣ Average Category rating ± one standard error of measurement   ⊢●⊣ Average item rating ± one standard error of measurement

Figure 15.5 (continued)   Sample IDEA Report

Section III. Teaching Methods or Style Related to Student Ratings of Progress (continued)

Part Two: Column 1 below again lists those objectives you listed as *Essential* or *Important*. Column 2 lists those teaching methods which in combination are most closely related to progress ratings on your chosen objectives. Column 3 separates out those teaching methods rated as "strengths" and those rated as "weaknesses" in comparison to the national average. (The numbers in Columns 2 and 3 refer to the teaching methods numbered 1-20 on the graphical presentations in **Part One, page 4**.)

Column 1 Chosen Objectives	Column 2 Most Relevant Teaching Methods	Column 3 Most Relevant Strengths/Weaknesses Strengths	Weaknesses
Essential Objectives			
24. Professional skills, viewpoints	3,4,6,7,8,11,12,14,18		4,6,11,12
28. Oral and written communication skills	1,3,5,7,8,9,10,19	1,5,9,19	10
Important Objectives			
26. Creative capacities	1,5,6,7,13,19,20	1,5,19	6
*31. Analysis and critical evaluation of ideas	3,5,8,13,18,19,20	5,19	

Part Three: This section summarizes teaching methods to consider for improvement strategies and methods which are effective and should be retained.

Potential Areas for Improvement Efforts

Generally, improvement efforts are most successful if they focus on no more than three teaching strategies at a time. These results suggest that your improvement strategies might best be chosen from the following teaching methods:

   6. Made it clear how each topic fit into the course
   4. Demonstrated the importance and significance of the subject matter
  10. Explained course material clearly and concisely
  11. Related course material to real life situations
  12. Gave tests, projects, etc. that covered the most important points of the course

Strengths to Retain

In doing so, you should take care to retain the methods which are currently effective, including:

   *5. Formed "teams" or "discussion groups" to facilitate learning
  19. Gave projects, tests or assignments that required original or creative thinking
   *1. Displayed a personal interest in students and their learning
   *9. Encouraged students to use multiple resources (e.g. data banks, library holdings, outside experts) to improve understanding

*New Item

Figure 15.5 (continued)   Sample IDEA Report

Faculty Name: SAMPLE, AX
Course: Communications 0000

Term: Fall   1998-1999
Page 6

Section IV. Course Description/Context

This section describes several aspects of your course. Some of the description summarizes information you supplied when you administered the IDEA form, and some of the information comes from student responses. Information on this page provides the context in which the class was taught and in which interpretation of the ratings should be made. The IDEA Center will conduct additional research on these data to determine more precisely how they can improve interpretation of the report.

Course Description:

Primary Instructional Type:	*Discussion/recitation*	Team Taught:	*Not reported*
Secondary Instructional Type:	*Other/Not Indicated*	Distance Learning:	*Not reported*
Principal Type of Student:	*Underclassmen, general*		

Instructor's Ratings of Special Circumstances:

Positive Impact on Learning	Neither Positive nor Negative Impact	Negative Impact on Learning
Previous experience teaching course	*Physical facilities and/or equipment*	*Adequacy of students' background/preparation*
Desire to teach course	*Changes in teaching approach*	
	Control over course management decisions	
	Student enthusiasm	
	Student effort	
	Technical/instructional support	

Instructor's Ratings of Course Requirements:

Much Required	Some Required	None (or little) Required
Writing		*Computer applications*
Oral communication		*Group work*
Critical thinking		*Mathematical/quantitative work*
Creative/artistic/design endeavor		

Student Ratings of the Course:

	Number of Students Saying:*					Average	T Score
	1	2	3	4	5		
33. Amount of reading	2	3	7	1	0	2.5	43
34. Amount of work in other (non-reading) assignments	0	1	3	7	2	3.8	57
35. Difficulty of subject matter	0	0	7	4	2	3.6	56

*1 = Much less than most courses   2 = Less than most courses   3 = About average   4 = More than most courses   5 = Much more than most courses

Similar to Sections I and II, you may wish to assign ratings to categories. Simply assign T Scores to categories as follows: **Low** (lowest 10%)=T Score below 37; **Low Average** (next 20%)=T Score 37-44; **Average** (middle 40%)=T Score 45-55; **High Average** (next 20%)=T Score 56-63; and **High** (highest 10%)=T Score above 63.

Figure 15.5 (continued)   Sample IDEA Report

Section V. Statistical Detail: Item Frequencies, Averages, and Standard Deviations

Items 1-20: Teaching Methods

Key: 1=Hardly Ever   2=Occasionally   3=Sometimes
     4=Frequently   5=Almost Always

	1	2	3	4	5	Omit	Avg.	s.d.
1.	0	0	0	6	9	0	4.6	0.5
2.	0	1	5	4	5	0	3.9	1.0
3.	0	1	3	5	6	0	4.1	1.0
4.	0	1	2	4	8	0	4.3	1.0
5.	2	0	5	2	6	0	3.7	1.4
6.	0	1	4	3	7	0	4.1	1.0
7.	1	1	1	4	7	1	4.1	1.3
8.	0	2	5	3	5	0	3.7	1.1
9.	0	0	1	5	9	0	4.5	0.6
10.	0	1	5	3	6	0	3.9	1.0
11.	1	1	1	5	7	0	4.1	1.2
12.	0	2	2	5	6	0	4.0	1.1
13.	0	0	4	4	7	0	4.2	0.9
14.	0	2	4	0	9	0	4.1	1.2
15.	0	1	5	4	5	0	3.9	1.0
16.	0	0	3	2	10	0	4.5	0.8
17.	1	2	4	2	6	0	3.7	1.3
18.	0	3	1	3	8	0	4.1	1.2
19.	0	0	0	5	10	0	4.7	0.5
20.	0	0	4	2	9	0	4.3	0.9

Items 21-32: Progress on Objectives

Key: 1=Low   2=Low Average   3=Average
     4=High Average   5=High

	1	2	3	4	5	Omit	Avg.	s.d.
21.	0	1	2	4	8	0	4.3	1.0
22.	1	2	1	5	6	0	3.9	1.3
23.	1	0	4	3	7	0	4.0	1.2
24.	**0**	**2**	**2**	**4**	**7**	**0**	**4.1**	**1.1**
25.	1	0	3	5	6	0	4.0	1.1
26.	**0**	**1**	**1**	**2**	**11**	**0**	**4.5**	**0.9**
27.	2	0	3	3	7	0	3.9	1.4
28.	**0**	**0**	**2**	**3**	**10**	**0**	**4.5**	**0.7**
29.	0	0	3	4	8	0	4.3	0.8
30.	2	1	3	4	5	0	3.6	1.4
31.	**0**	**0**	**5**	**3**	**7**	**0**	**4.1**	**0.9**
32.	0	1	5	2	7	0	4.0	1.1

Bold items were selected as *Essential* or *Important*.

Items 33-35: The Course

Key: 1=Much Less than Most Courses   2=Less than Most Courses
     3=About Average   4=More than Most Courses
     5=Much More than Most Courses

	1	2	3	4	5	Omit	Avg.	s.d.
33.	2	3	7	1	0	2	2.5	0.9
34.	0	1	3	7	2	2	3.8	0.8
35.	0	0	7	4	2	2	3.6	0.8

Items 43-47: Experimental

Key: 1=Definitely False   2=More False Than True
     3=In Between   4=More True Than False
     5=Definitely True

	1	2	3	4	5	Omit	Avg.	s.d.
43.	1	4	1	5	3	1	3.4	1.3
44.	0	2	2	6	4	1	3.9	1.0
45.	0	0	1	9	4	1	4.2	0.6
46.	0	1	2	7	4	1	4.0	0.9
47.	1	1	6	5	1	1	3.3	1.0

Items 36-42: Self-Ratings

Key: 1=Definitely False   2=More False Than True
     3=In Between   4=More True Than False
     5=Definitely True

	1	2	3	4	5	Omit	Avg.	s.d.
36.	1	0	1	1	11	1	4.5	1.2
37.	0	2	4	6	2	1	3.6	0.9
38.	1	2	6	0	5	1	3.4	1.3
39.	1	0	3	4	6	1	4.0	1.2
40.	2	1	0	4	7	1	3.9	1.5
41.	0	1	2	4	7	1	4.2	1.0
42.	0	1	4	4	5	1	3.9	1.0

Figure 15.5 (continued)   Sample IDEA Report

Faculty Name: SAMPLE, AX
Course: Communications 0000

Term: Fall   1998-1999
Page 8

Section V. Statistical Detail: Continued

Items 48-66: Extra Questions

	1	2	3	4	5	Omit	Avg.	s.d.
48.	0	0	4	18	6	0	4.1	0.6
49.	1	3	11	13	0	0	3.3	0.8
50.	3	7	14	4	0	0	2.7	0.9
51.	0	11	7	10	0	0	3.0	0.9
52.	23	0	2	0	3	0	1.6	1.3
53.	4	12	10	2	0	0	2.4	0.8
54.	5	4	9	6	4	0	3.0	1.3
55.	0	0	0	0	0	28	N/A	N/A
56.	0	0	0	0	0	28	N/A	N/A
57.	0	0	0	0	0	28	N/A	N/A

	1	2	3	4	5	Omit	Avg.	s.d.
58.	0	0	0	0	0	28	N/A	N/A
59.	0	0	0	0	0	28	N/A	N/A
60.	0	0	0	0	0	28	N/A	N/A
61.	0	0	0	0	0	28	N/A	N/A
62.	0	0	0	0	0	28	N/A	N/A
63.	0	0	0	0	0	28	N/A	N/A
64.	0	0	0	0	0	28	N/A	N/A
65.	0	0	0	0	0	28	N/A	N/A
66.	0	0	0	0	0	28	N/A	N/A

Section VI. Processing Error Messages

■ STUDENT INSTRUCTIONAL REPORT II (SIR II)

Contact Information

Educational Testing Service (ETS)
Rosedale Road
Princeton, NJ 08541-0001
Phone: 609-921-9000
FAX: 609-734-5410
Web site: www.ets.org (For specific information about purchasing the SIR II visit the ETS web site, click on the "Products" tab, and scroll down to "SIR II".)

Format

The SIR II is available as a paper version and as an online service. The SIR II rating form consists of 45 core items that are divided into 10 sections with space for up to 10 instructor-prepared supplementary questions. The form is printed on both sides of a scannable answer sheet. The first five sections focus on instructor characteristics, including Course Organization and Planning, Communication, Faculty/Student Interaction, Assignments, Exams and Grading, and Supplementary Instructional Methods.

Each of these sections contains five or six questions. Items are scored on a 5-point scale, plus the option of Not Applicable. The 5-point scale is: 5=Very Effective, 4=Effective, 3=Moderately Effective, 2=Somewhat Ineffective, and 1=Ineffective. Questions in the first five sections include such teaching and learning factors as instructor's use of class time, ability to make clear presentations, responsiveness to students, comments on assignments and exams, and the use of practices and tools such as journals, portfolios, computers, case studies, and team learning.

The sixth and seventh sections of the SIR II provide the student with a different 5-point scale, asking them to rate the relationship between the course and their self-assessment of their contributions. The choices are: 5=Much More (than most courses), 4=More Than (most courses), 3=About the Same (as other courses), 2=Less (than most courses), and 5=Much Less (than most courses). In the Course Outcomes section, the questions are about a student's increase in interest in the subject, progress toward achieving course objectives, and involvement in learning. In the Student Effort and Involvement section, the questions ask for how much effort was put into the course, degree of preparation through homework, and how challenged the student felt.

The eighth section asks three questions about course difficulty, workload, and pace. The ninth section contains one question asking for an overall evaluation of the quality of instruction using the same 5-point scale as the first five sections. The final section of the SIR II questionnaire asks for student information such as class level, reason for taking the course, English language proficiency, gender, and expected grade. After space for up to 10 instructor-supplied questions, a final paragraph suggests that students make additional comments in writing on a separate sheet of paper.

Results

Three copies of a two-page report are provided for each class evaluated. For each of the questions, the percentages of the total number of completed questionnaires for each of the five ratings is displayed together with the mean score. An overall mean for each section is also printed, and for most of the sections, a comparative mean from either two-year or four-year institutions is also displayed. These means are based on a comparison of the instructor's average score on each item with means from a wide variety of two-year, technical, and four-year institutions that use the SIR II. Item means are flagged with a "+" if they are reliably at or above the 90th percentile of comparative data and with a "−" if they are reliably at or below the 10th percentile of comparative data. When class size is small and/or the percentage of students responding is low, responses may be flagged or not tabulated, reducing the probability of interpreting unreliable data. Separate comparative data guides for two-year and four-year institutions are provided with each set of reports. Each guide contains data analyzed for specific institution types, class size, class level, class type, and subject area. In addition to class reports, institutions may request a summary report and/or special combined reports.

Special Features

SIR II is a commercial rating system; the questionnaire must be purchased from Educational Testing Service. Sales of questionnaires are separate from processing charges, providing institutions the option of processing the questionnaires themselves. Costs vary with quantity ordered.

Development and Validation

The SIR II is a 1995 revision of the original 1972 SIR (Student Instructional Report). Two new forms were developed and pretested in spring 1994. These forms included five of the scales from the original SIR with questions added or deleted. Three new scales or dimensions were added. These new scales reflected recent emphases on measuring learning outcomes and promoting students' time on task and effort in their learning. Each of the two pretested forms included a different response format to the same set of items and scales. By having random halves of students in 50 classes respond to the two forms, it was possible to determine which response format was better. Pretesting was carried out at 10 two- and four-year colleges. Traditional item and scale analyses of the two forms included computing means, standard deviations, coefficient alphas, item-to-scale correlations, and factor analyses. A Rasch analysis also compared the response categories for the two forms to determine which provided better variation in student responses. Pilot-testing of the final form occurred at a variety of colleges from spring 1995 through spring 1996. Course means and standard deviations were computed for each item and scale. A sample of the data from the pilot-testing was used to determine the reliability and construct validity of SIR II. The three kinds of reliability computed established the internal consistency of the items within the scales (coefficient alpha), the number of students needed for consistency of course results (intraclass correlations), and the stability of responses over brief periods of time (test-retest). The factor analysis indicated that the resulting factors matched perfectly with the expected or a priori scales for SIR II.

Research Reports of the SIR also support the SIR II, given their similar research basis. John Centra, professor of education at Syracuse University, performed many studies of the SIR and was also instrumental in developing the SIR II (Centra, 1972a, 1972b, 1973, 1976, 1998; Centra & Gaubatz, 2000). He continues to write research reports from SIR II data. Six research reports based on SIR data covering such topics as comparisons with alumni data, research productivity and teaching effectiveness, relationships with the use of portfolio evaluation, and comparisons with self-ratings are available from Educational Testing Service.

Sample Form and Report

The following is a sample of the SIR II form as well as an example of the faculty report provided.

Figure 15.6 Student Instructional Report II (front)

sir II — STUDENT INSTRUCTIONAL REPORT II (SIR II)

SIR II Report Number

This questionnaire gives you the chance to comment anonymously about this course and the way it was taught. Using the rating scale below, mark the one response for each statement that is closest to your view. Fill in the appropriate circle to the right of the statement.

- (5) Very Effective
- (4) Effective
- (3) Moderately Effective
- (2) Somewhat Ineffective
- (1) Ineffective
- (0) Not applicable, not used in the course, or you don't know. In short, the statement does not apply to the course or instructor.

As you respond to each statement, think about each practice as it contributed to your learning in this course.

A. Course Organization and Planning

1. The instructor's explanation of course requirements
2. The instructor's preparation for each class period
3. The instructor's command of the subject matter
4. The instructor's use of class time
5. The instructor's way of summarizing or emphasizing important points in class

B. Communication

6. The instuctor's ability to make clear and understandable presentations
7. The instructor's command of spoken English (or the language used in the course)
8. The instructor's use of examples or illustrations to clarify course material
9. The instructor's use of challenging questions or problems
10. The instructor's enthusiasm for the course material

C. Faculty/Student Interaction

11. The instructor's helpfulness and responsiveness to students
12. The instructor's respect for students
13. The instructor's concern for student progress
14. The availability of extra help for this class (taking into account the size of the class)
15. The instructor's willingness to listen to student questions and opinions

D. Assignments, Exams, and Grading

16. The information given to students about how they would be graded
17. The clarity of exam questions
18. The exams' coverage of important aspects of the course
19. The instructor's comments on assignments and exams
20. The overall quality of the textbook(s)
21. The helpfulness of assignments in understanding course material

E. Supplementary Instructional Methods

Many different teaching practices can be used during a course. In this section (E), **rate only those practices that the instructor included** as part of this course.

Rate the effectiveness of each practice used as it contributed to your learning.

22. Problems or questions presented by the instructor for small group discussions
23. Term paper(s) or project(s)
24. Laboratory exercises for understanding important course concepts
25. Assigned projects in which students worked together
26. Case studies, simulations, or role playing
27. Course journals or logs required of students
28. Instructor's use of computers as aids in instruction

Questionnaire continued on the other side. ➡

Commercially Available Student Rating Forms

Figure 15.6 (continued)   Student Instructional Report II (back)

For the next **two** sections (F and G), use the rating scale below. Mark the one response for each statement that is closest to your view. Fill in the appropriate circle to the right of each statement.

(5)   **Much More** than most courses
(4)   **More Than** most courses
(3)   About the **Same** as others
(2)   **Less** than most courses
(1)   **Much Less** than most courses
(0)   **Not Applicable**, not used in the course, or you don't know. In short, the statement does not apply to the course or instructor.

F. Course Outcomes

29. My learning increased in this course ....
30. I made progress toward achieving course objectives ....
31. My interest in the subject area has increased ....
32. This course helped me to think independently about the subject matter ....
33. This course actively involved me in what I was learning ....

G. Student Effort and Involvement

34. I studied and put effort into the course ....
35. I was prepared for each class [writing and reading assignments] ....
36. I was challenged by this course ....

H. Course Difficulty, Work Load, and Pace

37. For my preparation and ability, the level of difficulty of this course was:

(5) Very difficult   (4) Somewhat difficult   (3) About right   (2) Somewhat elementary   (1) Very elementary

38. The work load for this course in relation to other courses of equal credit was:

(5) Much heavier   (4) Heavier   (3) About the same   (2) Lighter   (1) Much lighter

39. For me, the pace at which the instructor covered the material during the term was:

(5) Very fast   (4) Somewhat fast   (3) Just about right   (2) Somewhat slow   (1) Very slow

I. Overall Evaluation

40. Rate the quality of instruction in this course as it contributed to your learning (try to set aside your feelings about the course content):

(5) Very effective   (4) Effective   (3) Moderately effective   (2) Somewhat Ineffective   (1) Ineffective

J. Student Information

41. Which one of the following best describes this course for you?

(1) A major/minor requirement   (2) A college requirement   (3) An elective   (4) Other

42. What is your class level?

(1) Freshman/1st year   (2) Sophomore/2nd year   (3) Junior/3rd year   (4) Senior/4th year   (5) Graduate   (6) Other

43. Do you communicate better in English or in another language?

(1) Better in English   (2) Better in another language   (3) Equally well in English and another language

44. Sex   (1) Female   (2) Male

45. What grade do you expect to receive in this course?

(1) A   (2) A-   (3) B+   (4) B   (5) B-   (6) C   (7) Below C

K. Supplementary Questions   If the instructor provided supplementary questions and response options, mark your answers in this section. Mark only one response for each question.

46. (5)(4)(3)(2)(1)(NA)   48. (5)(4)(3)(2)(1)(NA)   50. (5)(4)(3)(2)(1)(NA)   52. (5)(4)(3)(2)(1)(NA)   54. (5)(4)(3)(2)(1)(NA)
47. (5)(4)(3)(2)(1)(NA)   49. (5)(4)(3)(2)(1)(NA)   51. (5)(4)(3)(2)(1)(NA)   53. (5)(4)(3)(2)(1)(NA)   55. (5)(4)(3)(2)(1)(NA)

L. Student Comments   If you would like to make additional comments about the course or instruction, use a separate sheet of paper. You might elaborate on the particular aspects you liked most as well as those you liked least. Also, how can the course or the way it was taught be improved? An additional form may be provided for your comments. **Please give these comments to the instructor.**

If you have any comments about this questionnaire, please send them to:
Student Instructional Report II, Educational Testing Service, Princeton, NJ 08541-0001.

Figure 15.7 SIR II Sample Class Report

STUDENT INSTRUCTIONAL REPORT II

Enrollment	Admin. Date	Report No.	Batch No.
33	00/00	00000	0000

CLASS REPORT

SAMPLE

Assessing Courses and Instruction

PERCENTAGES reported below are based on the total number responding, which is: **33**

A. Course Organization and Planning *Think about each practice as it contributed to your learning in this course.*	Omit	Not Applicable	5 Very Effective	4 Effective	3 Moderately Effective	2 Somewhat Ineffective	1 Ineffective	Mean
1. The instructor's explanation of course requirements ...			39	42	18			4.21
2. The instructor's preparation for each class period ...			42	42	9	6		4.21
3. The instructor's command of the subject matter ...			39	42	12	6		4.15
4. The instructor's use of class time ...			42	30	18	6	3	4.03
5. The instructor's way of summarizing or emphasizing important points in class ...			27	45	6	18	3	3.76

Overall mean for COURSE ORGANIZATION AND PLANNING is: **4.07**   The comparative mean for X-year institutions is: x.xx.

B. Communication *Think about each practice as it contributed to your learning in this course.*	Omit	Not Applicable	5 Very Effective	4 Effective	3 Moderately Effective	2 Somewhat Ineffective	1 Ineffective	Mean
6. The instructor's ability to make clear and understandable presentations ...			30	36	27	6		3.91
7. The instructor's command of spoken English (or the language used in the course) ...			61	36	3			4.58
8. The instructor's use of examples or illustrations to clarify course material ...			33	33	30	3		3.97
9. The instructor's use of challenging questions or problems ...			30	39	27	3		3.97
10. The instructor's enthusiasm for the course material ...			21	45	30	3		3.85

Overall mean for COMMUNICATION is: **4.06**   The comparative mean for X-year institutions is: x.xx.

C. Faculty/Student Interaction *Think about each practice as it contributed to your learning in this course.*	Omit	Not Applicable	5 Very Effective	4 Effective	3 Moderately Effective	2 Somewhat Ineffective	1 Ineffective	Mean
11. The instructor's helpfulness and responsiveness to students ...			39	33	15	12		4.00
12. The instructor's respect for students ...			45	24	18	9	3	4.00
13. The instructor's concern for student progress ...			36	33	15	15		3.91
14. The availability of extra help for this class (taking into account the size of the class) ...			36	33	21	9		3.97
15. The instructor's willingness to listen to student questions and opinions ...			39	36	12	6	6	3.97

Overall mean for FACULTY/STUDENT INTERACTION is: **3.97**   The comparative mean for X-year institutions is: x.xx.

+ This mean is higher than the comparative mean. See page 4.

− This mean is lower than the comparative mean. See page 4.   For explanation of flagging (*), see "Number of Students Responding," page 4.

Figure 15.7 (continued)   SIR II Sample Class Report

STUDENT INSTRUCTIONAL REPORT II

D. Assignments, Exams, and Grading
Think about each practice as it contributed to your learning in this course

	Omit	Not Applicable	5 Very Effective	4 Effective	3 Moderately Effective	2 Somewhat Ineffective	1 Ineffective	Mean
16. The information given to students about how they would be graded . . .			45	39	15			4.30
17. The clarity of exam questions . . .			36	33	21	9		3.97
18. The exams' coverage of important aspects of the course . . .			33	42	18	6		4.03
19. The instructor's comments on assignments and exams . . .			27	39	21	12		3.82
20. The overall quality of the textbook(s) . . .		6	12	45	15	15	6	3.45
21. The helpfulness of assignments in understanding course material . . .			27	48	21	3		4.00

Overall mean for ASSIGNMENTS, EXAMS, AND GRADING is: 3.93   The comparative mean for X-year institutions is: x.xx.

E. Supplementary Instructional Methods
Rate the effectiveness of each practice used as it contributed to your learning

	Omit	Not Used	5 Very Effective	4 Effective	3 Moderately Effective	2 Somewhat Ineffective	1 Ineffective	Mean
22. Problems or questions presented by the instructor for small group discussions . . .	3	3	21	64	9			***
23. Term paper(s) or project(s) . . .			30	58	12			***
24. Laboratory exercises for understanding important course concepts . . .	12	52	18	9	9			***
25. Assigned projects in which students worked together . . .			33	48	12		6	***
26. Case studies, simulations, or role playing . . .			33	55	12			***
27. Course journals or logs required of students . . .	9	64	9	9	6	3		***
28. Instructor's use of computers as aids in instruction . .	9	70	9	12				***

Means are not reported (***) for SUPPLEMENTARY INSTRUCTIONAL METHODS.

F. Course Outcomes
Mark the response that is closest to your view

	Omit	Not Applicable	5 Much More Than Most Courses	4 More Than Most Courses	3 About the Same as Others	2 Less Than Most Courses	1 Much Less Than Most Courses	Mean
29. My learning increased in this course . . .	3		15	33	33	12	3	3.47
30. I made progress toward achieving course objectives . . .	3		18	30	45	3		3.66
31. My interest in the subject area has increased . . .	3		15	24	33	15	9	3.22
32. This course helped me to think independently about the subject matter . . .	3		24	18	45	9		3.59
33. This course actively involved me in what I was learning . . .	3		27	33	30	6		3.84

Overall mean for COURSE OUTCOMES is: 3.56   The comparative mean for X-year institutions is: x.xx.

G. Student Effort and Involvement
Mark the response that is closest to your view

	Omit	Not Applicable	5 Much More Than Most Courses	4 More Than Most Courses	3 About the Same as Others	2 Less Than Most Courses	1 Much Less Than Most Courses	Mean
34. I studied and put effort into this course . . .	3		45	12	36	3		4.03
35. I was prepared for each class (writing and reading assignments) . . .	3		33	27	30	3	3	3.88
36. I was challenged by this course . . .	3		33	12	36	9	6	3.59

Overall mean for STUDENT EFFORT AND INVOLVEMENT is: 3.83   The comparative mean for X-year institutions is: x.xx.

+ This mean is higher than the comparative mean. See page 4.

− This mean is lower than the comparative mean. See page 4.   For explanation of flagging (*), see "Number of Students Responding," page 4.

Figure 15.7 (continued) SIR II Sample Class Report

ASSESSING COURSES and INSTRUCTION

H. Course Difficulty, Workload, and Pace
Mark the response that is closest to your view.

	Omit	Very Difficult	Somewhat Difficult	About Right	Somewhat Elementary	Very Elementary
37. For my preparation and ability, the level of difficulty of this course was . . .	3	6	42	42	3	3

	Omit	Much Heavier	Heavier	About the Same	Lighter	Much Lighter
38. The work load for this course in relation to other courses of equal credit was . . .	3	55	24	15	3	

	Omit	Very Fast	Somewhat Fast	Just About Right	Somewhat Slow	Very Slow
39. For me, the pace at which the instructor covered the material during the term was . . .	3	6	33	55	3	

Means are not appropriate for COURSE DIFFICULTY, WORKLOAD, and PACE.   Review the distribution of students' responses.

I. Overall Evaluation

	Omit	5 Very Effective	4 Effective	3 Moderately Effective	2 Somewhat Ineffective	1 Ineffective	Mean
40. Rate the quality of instruction in this course as it contributed to your learning. (Try to set aside your feelings about the course content.)	3	18	52	21	6		3.84

OVERALL EVALUATION mean is: 3.84

J. Student Information

	Omit	Requirement in Major	College Requirement	Elective	Other
41. Which one of the following best describes this course for you?	3	76	18	3	

42. What is your class level?	Omit	Freshman/ 1st Year	Sophomore/ 2nd Year	Junior/ 3rd Year	Senior/ 4th Year	Graduate	Other
	3			3	85	6	3

43. Do you communicate better in English or in another language?	Omit	Better in English		Better in Another Language		Equally well in English and Another Language	
	3	91		3		3	

44. Sex	Omit	Female			Male		
	3	52			45		

45. What grade do you expect to receive in this course?	Omit	A	A-	B+	B	B-	C	Below C
	100							

K. Supplementary Questions

	Omit	NA	5	4	3	2	1
46.							
47.							
48.							
49.							
50.							
51.							
52.							
53.							
54.							
55.							

+ This mean is higher than the comparative mean. See page 4.

− This mean is lower than the comparative mean. See page 4.   For explanation of flagging (*), see "Number of Students Responding," page 4.

Figure 15.7 (continued)   SIR II Sample Class Report

INTERPRETING SIR II

The SIR II is designed to:

- Identify areas of strength and/or areas for improvement.
- Provide information on new teaching methods or techniques used in class.
- Provide feedback from students about their courses.

NUMBER OF STUDENTS RESPONDING

The number of students responding can affect the results when the class is very small (fewer than 10 students are enrolled), or when fewer than two-thirds of the students enrolled in the class actually respond. For this reason, a Class Report **will not be produced** when fewer than five students responded, that is, fewer than five completed answer sheets were received for a class.

The degree of accuracy for each item mean increases as the number of students responding increases. For example, the estimated reliability for the Overall Evaluation item is .78 if 10 students respond; .88 if 20 students respond; and .90 if 25 students respond. (A full discussion of the reliability of student evaluation items can be found in *SIR Report No. 3*.) To call attention to possible reliability concerns, a report will be flagged (*) for one or more of the following.

* The number responding **will be flagged** when: 10 or fewer students responded or less than 60 percent of the class responded (this calculation is based on information from the *Instructor's Cover Sheet*).

* An item mean **will not be reported** when: 50 percent or more of the students did not respond, or marked an item "Not Applicable," or fewer than five students responded to an item.

* An overall mean **is not reported** when one or more item means are not reported.

COMPARATIVE DATA (NOT AVAILABLE FOR SIR II PILOT)

The comparative means used throughout this report are based on user data from a sample of two and four year colleges and universities. An institution is identified by type — two-year or four-year — on the Processing Request Form that is returned with the questionnaires for scoring. Either two-year or four-year comparative data are used, based on that identification.

These data are **comparative** rather than normative. That is, they are prepared by combining class reports from institutions at which the questionnaire was administered. The data are updated periodically and are developed and published separately for two-year and for four-year institutions in the *Comparative Data Guides*.

The *Comparative Data Guides* for both two- and four-year colleges contain data analyzed for: size of class, level of class (freshman/sophomore and junior/senior), type of class (lecture, discussion, lab), and several different subject areas. A copy of the appropriate *Guide* is sent to Institutional Coordinators with the SIR II reports.

Local Comparative Data: Equally important and useful are an institution's own comparative data. Such local comparative data — e.g., an Institutional Summary, departmental summaries, program summaries — are available to any user institution. Forms for ordering these reports are included in the *Institutional Coordinator's Manual*.

Understanding Mean Ratings

Ratings can vary by class size and discipline. The *Comparative Data Guides* provide data by various categories to assist users in interpreting the SIR II reports. Please refer to the *Guide* and to the SIR II Guidelines for further information. Since student ratings typically tend to be favorable, it is important to have comparative data to interpret a report fully. For example, while a 3.6 is numerically above average on a 5-point scale, it may be average or even slightly below average in comparison to other means for items in SIR II.

What Makes a Score Difference Significant?

The mean scores on all of the items and scales in this report have been compared against the scores obtained by all of the classes in one of the appropriate comparative data groups (two-year or four-year institutions). Specifically, the scores have been compared against the score values corresponding to the 10th percentile and 90th percentile in the comparative group. If the results indicate a score is sufficiently reliable and is below the 10th percentile or above the 90th percentile, it will be flagged in the report as follows:

+ This class mean is reliably at or above the 90th percentile.

− This class mean is reliably at or below the 10th percentile.

Scores above the 90th percentile or below the 10th percentile are flagged when there is appropriate statistical confidence that the "true scores" (i.e., the scores that would be obtained if there were no measurement error) fall within these ranges. If a score is flagged with a +, there is less than one chance in 20 that the "true score" is below the 90th percentile; if a score is flagged with a −, there is less than one chance in 20 that the "true score" is above the 10th percentile. (One chance in 20 is the commonly accepted measurement standard for a 95% confidence level.)

Because measurement error varies from class to class, instructors with identical means on the SIR II items may not have the same items flagged. In particular, measurement error tends to be larger when the number of respondents is low and when disagreement among the respondents is high. For example, instructors in small classes are likely to have fewer items flagged than those in large classes because there is less confidence of the reliability of means in small classes.

■ REFERENCES

Aleamoni, L. M. (1978). Development and factorial validation of the Arizona Course/Instructor Evaluation Questionnaire. *Educational and Psychological Measurement, 38*(6), 1063–1067.

Aleamoni, L. M., & Carynnk, D. B. (1977). *Optional item catalog (revised).* (Information Memorandum No. 6). Tucson, AZ: University of Arizona, Office of Instructional Research and Development.

Aleamoni, L. M., & Laham, D. (1992). *Arizona course/instructor evaluation questionnaire: Results interpretation manual.* Tucson, AZ: University of Arizona, Office of Instructional Research and Development.

Aleamoni, L. M., & Spencer, R. E. (1973). The Illinois Course Evaluation Questionnaire: A description of its development and a report of some of its results. *Educational and Psychological Measurement, 33,* 669–684.

Cashin, W. E., & Perrin, B. M. (1978). *Description of standard form data base* (IDEA Technical Report No. 4). Manhattan, KS: Kansas State University, Center for Faculty Evaluation and Development.

Centra, J. A. (1972a). *The Student Instructional Report: Its Development and Uses* (SIR Report No. 1). Princeton, NJ: Educational Testing Service.

Centra, J. A. (1972b). *The effectiveness of student feedback in modifying college instruction. Two studies on the utility of student ratings for instructional improvement* (SIR Report No. 2). Princeton, NJ: Educational Testing Service.

Centra, J. A. (1973). *Comparisons with alumni ratings, reliability of items, and factor structure* (SIR Report No. 3). Princeton, NJ: Educational Testing Service.

Centra, J. A. (1976). *Two studies on the validity of the Student Instructional Report: I. Student ratings of instruction and their relationship to student learning. II. The relationship between student, teacher, and course characteristics and student ratings of teacher effectiveness* (SIR Report No. 4). Princeton, NJ: Educational Testing Service.

Centra, J. A. (1998). *The development of the Student Instructional Report II.* Princeton, NJ: Educational Testing Service.

Centra, J. A., & Gaubatz, N. B. (2000). Is there gender bias in student evaluations of teaching? *The Journal of Higher Education, 70*(1), 17–23.

Chickering, A. W., & Gamson, Z. F. (1987, March). Seven principles for good practice in undergraduate education. *AAHE Bulletin, 39*(7), 3–7.

Gillmore, G. M. (1973). *Estimates of reliability coefficients for items and subscales of the Illinois Course Evaluation Questionnaire* (Research Report No. 341). Urbana, IL: University of Illinois Office of Instructional Resources, Measurement, and Research Division.

Hoyt, D. P. (1973). Measurement of instructional effectiveness. *Research in Higher Education, 1,* 367–378.

Hoyt, D. P., & Cashin, W. E. (1977). *Development of the IDEA system* (IDEA Technical Report No. 1). Manhattan, KS: Kansas State University, Center for Faculty Evaluation and Development.

Hoyt, D. P., Chen, Y., Pallett, W. H., & Gross, A. B. (1998) *Revising the IDEA system for obtaining student ratings of instructors and courses* (IDEA Technical Report No. 11). Manhattan, KS: Kansas State University, the IDEA Center.

Sixbury, G. R., & Cashin, W. E. (1995a). *Description of database for the IDEA diagnostic form.* (IDEA Technical Report No. 9). Manhattan, KS: Kansas State University, Center for Faculty Evaluation and Development.

Sixbury, G. R., & Cashin, W. E. (1995b). *Comparative data by academic field* (IDEA Technical Report No. 10). Manhattan, KS: Kansas State University, Center for Faculty Evaluation and Development.

16

Case Studies and Sample Faculty Evaluation Manuals

Anumber of colleges and universities have developed comprehensive faculty evaluation systems employing the eight-step process described in this book. This chapter presents the results from three of these institutions. The eight-step process described in Chapters 1 through 8 contains a number of decision points that can lead in different directions in the development of a comprehensive faculty evaluation system. Thus, no two institutions using this approach will develop precisely the same system.

The first section of this chapter presents the case study of Frostburg State University in constructing its faculty evaluation system using the principles outlined in this book. This section was prepared specifically for this chapter by Thomas F. Hawk, Ph.D., professor of management at Frostburg State University. Dr. Hawk offers important insights and details concerning the practical and political aspects of developing a comprehensive faculty evaluation system using the steps described in Chapters 1 through 8.

Following the Frostburg State University case study is an excerpt from the Georgia Perimeter College *Faculty Evaluation, Promotion, and Tenure Handbook* (1998–1999). Although not presented as a case study, the Georgia Perimeter College faculty evaluation manual demonstrates another variation of system developed by the application of the procedures described in this book.

The third section presents a case study of the work done by the School of Business at Fairmont State University in constructing its automated, online, faculty evaluation system using the eight-step process described in this book. The case study, written by Dr. Rebecca Schaupp, dean of the School of Business, and Dr. Tracie Dobson, provides an excellent example of using computer technol-

ogy in developing and implementing a comprehensive faculty evaluation system.

In all three cases a coordinating task force or committee was appointed and charged with the task of guiding the institution through the eight steps described in Chapters 1 through 8.

The materials shown in this chapter represent separate expressions of the concepts of defining the faculty role model, identifying sources, defining roles, and weighting role and source impact in designing a comprehensive faculty evaluation system. These materials are not presented as idealized models but simply three institutions' interpretations of how to use the process described in this book to design and develop a faculty evaluation system that works for them. The system your institution develops may differ considerably. However, the faculty evaluation systems shown in this chapter contain various forms and procedures that may be of interest as you develop your own faculty evaluation system.

■ FROSTBURG STATE UNIVERSITY CASE STUDY: DEVELOPING A MANAGED SUBJECTIVITY PROCESS OF FACULTY EVALUATION AT FROSTBURG STATE UNIVERSITY

by Thomas F. Hawk, Ph.D.

In May 1998 the 25 members of the Frostburg State University Faculty Senate passed the fourth faculty evaluation process in the history of the university, with passage of the first three occurring in 1973, 1981, and 1989. The passage of the new evaluation process was a culmination of four years of subcommittee and committee work triggered by dissatisfaction with the existing departmentally based evaluation process initiated in 1989. The managed subjectivity model for faculty evaluation developed by Raoul A. Arreola was the basis for the 1998 evaluation process.

This case study describes the context for faculty evaluation at Frostburg State University as well as the three-year work of the Faculty Evaluation Subcommittee and the subsequent one-year work of the Faculty Concerns Committee, both operating under the umbrella of the university's faculty senate. It highlights the characteristics of the development process, including the major milestones, difficulties, and political considerations.

The Context

Frostburg State University (FSU) is one of the constituent institutions of the University System of Maryland (USM), a system of two research units and 11 universities and colleges operated under a System Board of Regents appointed by the governor. The USM Regents have published policies on appointment, retention, and tenure and on posttenure review that specify the general guidelines under which the constituent institutions must design and operate their respective faculty evaluation systems.

The university's initial faculty evaluation process based on Richard I. Miller's (1972) seminal work, *Evaluating Faculty Performance*, was passed in 1973. It was standard across all departments and divided evaluation into five categories: teaching, professional development and service, professional characteristics, department service, and college service. Department heads held primary responsibility for evaluation of each faculty member in all five categories. The teaching component was based in part upon a single summative rating item at the end of a common 23-item student questionnaire. There was no merit pay attached to the evaluation.

The 1981 evaluation process, also standard across all departments, combined the five 1973 categories into three general categories of teaching, professional development and service, and college/department service, with evaluation performed by either the department chair or a Departmental Evaluation Committee. Teaching carried 60% of the overall evaluation weight, with the other two carrying 20% each. Student ratings constituted 50% of the teaching category weight. The student rating form was a common questionnaire with seven questions, of which four gave a pedagogical rating and three a rapport rating. High merit pay was at the recommendation of the department chair but limited to only 20% of each department's

full-time, tenure-track faculty. The academic administrators determined the merit pay amount.

The 1989 evaluation process allowed each department to construct its own process within a general framework of the three evaluation categories of teaching, professional development, and service. Departments were encouraged to use a Departmental Evaluation Committee but could choose to use the department chair if that was the wish of the department faculty. The Department Evaluation Committee or the chair was the sole rater in the Professional Development and Service categories and shared that task with students for the teaching category. The faculty handbook stipulated that each department was to create its own student rating questionnaire to address criteria under the teaching category. It also specified examples of performance that met the criteria for a rating of Outstanding, Meets Expectations, or Needs Improvement in each of the three major categories. One merit pay unit was available for achieving Meets Expectations in teaching, professional development, and service. An additional merit pay unit was available for achieving Outstanding in teaching and an additional half unit was granted for Outstanding performance in each of the professional development and service categories. In effect, the teaching category received a 50% weight and the other two categories a weight of 25% each. Each school received a merit pay pool equivalent to its percentage of full-time, tenure-track faculty at the university. The value of a merit pay unit was determined by dividing the school's merit pay pool by the number of merit units awarded to its faculty.

Beginning the Process

In fall 1994 the faculty senate established a Faculty Evaluation Subcommittee under the Faculty Concerns Committee to address a number of faculty evaluation issues. The primary issues were: 1) the absence of an articulated evaluation process and evaluation criteria in some departments, 2) the wide range of quality of processes, criteria, and student rating forms in departments that did have an articulated process and criteria, 3) the near-total reliance on the student ratings for the teaching category evaluation in most of the departments, and 4) the difficulty of comparing ratings across departments. The Faculty Concerns Committee of the University's Faculty Senate had been unable to address these issues due to the large number and wide range of issues that came before it for consideration. Therefore, the Faculty Concerns Committee requested that the senate establish a Faculty Evaluation Subcommittee to address the faculty evaluation portion of its work. At the first meeting the subcommittee established its primary agenda item to be the overhaul of the existing faculty evaluation system and that this effort be in partnership with the four school deans.

We were fortunate in that, at a department chairs retreat in the summer of 1993, the provost had invited Dr. Raoul Arreola to present a half-day seminar on the managed subjectivity evaluation model that he had developed. The chairs received it very positively. Subsequent to that retreat, the provost sent one chair from the School of Natural and Social Sciences, one faculty member from the School of Education, the dean of the School of Natural and Social Sciences, and the associate provost (all four were tenured faculty members) to the full two-day seminar on the Arreola model conducted in Florida.

At the next meeting the four made a presentation of the model and answered questions. After a lengthy discussion that explored what we had learned about the model, as well as what other possible models we might use, it was decided to tentatively adopt the model—pending a more thorough understanding of the model after receiving copies of Dr. Arreola's workbook (an earlier edition of *Developing a Comprehensive Faculty Evaluation System*). We also agreed that the four who had attended the two-day seminar should become invited working members of the subcommittee. This provided a representative from the provost's office, a second representative from the School of Education, a third representative from the School of Natural and Social Sciences, and the dean of natural and social sciences who was already an invited member. The final configuration of the 1995 subcommittee consisted of the following:

- Subcommittee chair—associate professor of management (department chair)

- Appointed member—associate professor of economics (department chair)

- Appointed member—professor of English

- Appointed member—associate professor of communication

- Appointed member—professor of mathematics

- Appointed member—associate professor of chemistry

- Appointed member—associate professor of physical education

- Invited member—associate professor of education

- Invited member—professor of biology (department chair)

- Invited member—associate provost (Professor of English)

- Invited member—dean, School of Natural and Social Sciences

- Ex Officio—dean, School of Arts and Humanities

- Ex Officio—dean, School of Education

- Ex Officio—dean, School of Business

The Work of the Subcommittee

After the initial organizing meetings in November and December of 1994 and the arrival of Dr. Arreola's books (which were purchased for the committee by the provost) in January 1995, the subcommittee began its work in earnest at the start of the spring 1995 semester in early February. The subcommittee met on a regular monthly schedule until April 1997 when it passed its completed document to the Faculty Concerns Committee for its consideration before presentation to the senate.

Throughout the 27-month period, the character of our work went from the general to the specific, with the more global characteristics of the new faculty evaluation process emerging first and leading to consideration of more specific detail in different segments of the system. There was a clear iterative character to the work; however, we struggled to understand each other's concerns and develop the detail needed to provide an effective and useable system. Preliminary resolution of the detail in one area frequently generated more questions in other areas as well as the more global characteristics and frequently led to a reexamination of the global framework and/or the detail of an area agreed upon earlier.

The first struggle for the members was to develop a strong working understanding of the managed subjectivity model. Almost everyone was diligent in studying Dr. Arreola's book, although we had to do a lot a verbal reinforcement and explanation of concepts in the book to get everyone at a relatively equal level of comprehension of the model. This took several months as we attempted to define the main categories and their weight ranges as well as the elements of each category.

During that process, we confronted what we believed to be a major issue: To what degree were we going to depart from the explicit category definitions of teaching, professional achievement and development, and service of the 1989 system that were published in the faculty handbook. After considerable discussion it was noted that the committee was going to be asking the faculty to accept a large number of changes in the faculty evaluation system. These changes included 1) negotiating individual role percentages, 2) keeping negotiated weights within established weight ranges, 3) accepting fixed role component weights, 4) accepting the use of data from multiple sources, 5) weighting data from different sources in different amounts, and 6) facing the likely change in the way merit pay was calculated. The committee agreed to attempt to maintain as much of the existing category descriptions as possible in order to give the faculty familiar ground on which to overlay the new process. In the final analysis, however, during the open comment period the faculty indicated that they were more open to changes in the category and element descriptions than we had assumed.

Throughout 1995 we made slow but deliberate progress, surviving the departure of one natural and social science and one arts and humanities faculty appointees and bringing their replacements up to speed with the work. By the end of 1995, however, we were having difficulty dealing with several complex issues, such as the new student rating form and the need for a new merit pay concept. The associate provost was observant enough to recognize the need for some all-day sessions and actively pushed for them during the intersession period of January 1996. Those sessions proved to be crucial in getting us over the hump in developing the basic elements of our new process.

In April 1995 the chair of the faculty senate had asked me to make a short status presentation to the faculty senate. At that meeting, I had informed the senators that we would not send any proposal to the Faculty Concerns Committee without first holding an open comment and feedback period for all of the academic departments and individual faculty. Therefore, late in the spring 1996 semester we sent out the preliminary proposal and gave all departments until the end of September to respond.

We continued to meet through the summer and fall of 1996 as we worked with the feedback we were receiving. Critical feedback focused on 1) improving the category definitions, with a lot of encouragement to depart from the existing category definitions in the faculty handbook, 2) incorporating into the teaching category ways to encourage experimentation and innovation in teaching, 3) improving the student rating form, 4) finding ways to reduce the paperwork required by the process without sacrificing the documentation of performance, and 5) giving the deans oversight and appeal responsibility but keeping primary control of the evaluation process with the De-

partmental Evaluation Committees, the department chair, and the Faculty Concerns Committee.

By the middle of the spring 1997 semester, we had finished revising our spring 1996 proposal. The timing of completing the revision was fortunate as it was becoming obvious that most of the members of the subcommittee were experiencing burnout with the process. As a result, we formally submitted the revised faculty evaluation process to the Faculty Concerns Committee, stating that we felt we had taken it as far we could. Any further changes would have to originate with the Faculty Concerns Committee. As chair of the Faculty Evaluation Subcommittee, I would function in an advisory role to the Faculty Concerns Committee. Additionally, a major overhaul of the faculty governance structure that had passed that spring had resulted in the dissolution of the subcommittee once it finished its work on building the evaluation process. Everyone on the subcommittee opposed that dissolution due to our expectation of a continued high level of activity for the Faculty Concerns Committee on faculty evaluation issues.

The Work of the Faculty Concerns Committee

During the 1997–1998 academic year, the members of the Faculty Concerns Committee worked with the Department Chairs Council and through the members of the senate to further improve the proposal. Their efforts did not alter the basic structure of the process. Rather, there was an easing of the stringency of the professional achievement and development category, the addition of standards in a number of elements where none had existed, and clarification of several administrative provisions, particularly in the area of moving evaluation weights to accommodate assigned time activities in service or professional development activities that substituted for some teaching responsibilities.

In March 1998 the Faculty Concerns Committee distributed the final version of the evaluation process to the members of the senate and to the entire university faculty. The senate gave its first reading at the April meeting and passed it with one dissenting vote at the May meeting, stipulating that implementation would begin with the spring 1999 semester. It also asked the Faculty Concerns Committee to look for ways to bring greater clarity to the process.

Summary of Changes

In the final analysis, the members of the Faculty Evaluation Subcommittee felt that five characteristics of the new system were major improvements in the process of faculty evaluation at Frostburg State University (see Table 16.1 for a summary). The first was the incorporation of a negotiated range for each of the three evaluation categories, allowing faculty members to address workload and personal preferences in their yearly category weights. The second was the specification of the appropriate sources of rating and rating weights for each element of each major evaluation category. This change was particularly welcomed where students were the appropriate rating source. The third was the combination of the symmetrical rating scale of 1.0 to 5.0 and the stepped merit pay scale beginning at the midpoint of 3.0 (See Table 16.2). The fourth was the inclusion of a specific element within the teaching category to encourage innovation, experimentation, and creative instructional development. And the fifth was the documentation of justifications for the ratings in each element of all categories so that there would be an annual check on the progress toward tenure for all untenured faculty. This justification includes a statement assessing the professional behavior of the untenured faculty member for the year.

As a postscript, the Faculty Concerns Committee continued to work with the new evaluation process during the fall 1998 semester, finding several additional improvements and clarifications to make. And, at the request of the Faculty Concerns Committee, the Senate established an Ad Hoc Task Force on Faculty Evaluation to coordinate the new evaluation process and relieve the Faculty Concerns Committee of the detail work on the process.

Table 16.1   1998 Frostburg State University Faculty Evaluation System

Evaluation Category	Category Weight	Evidence	Sub-Weight	Sources (Weight)
Teaching	50%–80%	Course materials and course syllabus ratings	25%	Chair rating (.30) DEC rating (.70)
		Teaching performance and feedback to students ratings	50%	Student rating (.65) Chair rating (.20) DEC rating (.15)
		Instructional development ratings	25%	Chair rating (.70) DEC rating (.30)
Professional Development and Achievement	10%–30%	Examples of performance to be rated 3.0, 4.0, & 5.0 on a scale of 1.0–5.0 are given	100%	Chair rating (.25) DEC rating (.75)
Service	5%–25%	Examples of performance to be rated 3.0, 4.0, & 5.0 on a scale of 1.0–5.0 are given	100%	Chair rating (.75) DEC rating (.25)

Developing a Comprehensive Faculty Evaluation System

Table 16.2 Faculty Merit Pay Calculation

The merit pay system is a stepped system in increments of 0.1, with merit pay awarded for those faculty who achieve an overall rating of at least 2.95. The rating scale is a 5-point scale, where:

5.0 = Outstanding Performance
4.0 = Above Expectations
3.0 = Meets Expectations
2.0 = Below Expectations
1.0 = Unacceptable Performance

To calculate the merit unit level for each faculty member, round the overall rating to the nearest tenth (e.g., under the convention that 1–4 round down and 5–9 round up; a rating between 3.05 to 3.14 would be rounded to 3.1) and subtract 2.9 from the overall rating (merit pay begins at the 3.0 level).

To calculate the merit unit amount (the dollar value associated with each full merit unit), divide the total merit pay pool by the total number of merit units awarded across the university. For example, assume that the total merit pay pool is $120,000 and the total number of merit unit levels awarded across the university is 220. The merit unit amount would be $545.45 ($120,000/220).

To calculate the merit pay amount for any faculty member, multiply the merit unit amount by the merit unit level for the faculty member. For example, assume that there are seven faculty in a department who end up with the overall ratings below. The merit pay amount for each of the seven faculty members would be:

Faculty	Overall Rating	Merit Unit Level	Merit Pay Amount
Dr. Alfred	3.09	3.1 - 2.9 = 0.2	0.2 x $545.45 = $109.09
Dr. Bowens	3.48	3.5 - 2.9 = 0.6	0.6 x $545.45 = $327.27
Dr. Hiller	3.92	3.9 - 2.9 = 1.0	1.0 x $545.45 = $545.45
Dr. James	4.09	4.1 - 2.9 = 1.2	1.2 x $545.45 = $654.54
Dr. Malloy	4.33	4.3 - 2.9 = 1.4	1.4 x $545.45 = $763.63
Dr. Peters	4.47	4.2 - 2.9 = 1.6	1.6 x $545.45 = $872.72
Dr. Thomas	4.70	4.7 - 2.9 = 1.8	1.8 x $545.45 = $981.81

The same process would be used to calculate the merit pay amount for each of the remaining faculty members at the university. The total merit pay awarded would equal $120,000.

◼ FROSTBURG STATE UNIVERSITY FACULTY EVALUATION SYSTEM

Passed by Faculty Senate, May 1998

Introduction

Academic departments carry out faculty evaluation for four purposes:

1) To inform faculty members regarding the degree to which their performance matches department/school/university expectations

2) To supply information and guidance to faculty with respect to professional improvement and development

3) To establish a base of information for future personnel decisions including contact renewal, tenure, and promotions

4) To determine annual merit pay increases

Components of the System

The faculty evaluation system follows a comprehensive approach to reviewing and evaluating the activities of faculty members within their three major roles. The evaluation process allows faculty members the opportunity to place greater emphasis on one or another of the three major roles in a given year:

- Teaching

- Professional development and achievement

- Service

While it is not possible or desirable to identify and review all the roles of a faculty member for evaluation purposes, the roles incorporated within this system for Frostburg State University include those identified as being the most important to all faculty and those that could be reviewed efficiently and effectively. For each major role there are institutional minimum and maximum values (weights) that are derived from the faculty workload guidelines established by the University System of Maryland, giving faculty the opportunity to negotiate a weight for each role. These weights reflect the philosophy and mission of Frostburg State University as to the importance of each role within the faculty member's total set of professional responsibilities.

Data gathered for review and evaluation come from students and from the faculty member. Each rating source—department peers, department chair, and students, as appropriate—has a pre-established weight to reflect the impact each source has on the evaluation of each faculty role. Each faculty member will enter into an evaluation agreement for category weights with the department chair by December 1 for the subsequent year. Those faculty who choose to enter the evaluation process every three years need to negotiate weights yearly, and those weights will be applied at each three-year evaluation.

The minimum and maximum weights allowed in the evaluation system are as follows:

Minimum		*Maximum*
50%	Teaching	80%
10%	Professional development and achievement	30%
5%	Service	25%

Procedures

The evaluation process is standard across all of the university's academic departments, including the use of the same student rating form in all courses, except internships. The process results in a score, or Overall Rating, which summarizes the faculty member's performance.

Evaluation Cycle

Yearly evaluation will occur for all untenured, tenure-track faculty; all tenured faculty evaluated in the previous year below a 3.0 rating in any category; and all tenured faculty seeking ratings above 3.0.

Tenured faculty have the option to be evaluated once every three years. When evaluated in the third year, the faculty member must provide information for the current year and for each of the previous two years; however, only the current year's Overall Rating will be calculated for the merit pool. In addition, tenured faculty should request a complete evaluation in the two years preceding a request for a sabbatical or a request for a promotion. Departments employing contractual (full-time and part-time) faculty may design particular evaluation procedures depending on the faculty member's responsibilities in the department and the terms of the contract.

Negotiated Category Weights

Faculty negotiate with department chairs differences in individual annual category weights, within the allowable ranges, to reflect differences in faculty interests and workload. The negotiations with the department chair for a given evaluation cycle must take place prior to December 1 in the semester before the evaluated year. In the event of substantive changes in the actual workload, a faculty member may renegotiate the distribution of category weights with the department chair. Faculty with non-standard assignments (reassigned times for department chair, departmental projects, research, etc.) will adjust category rates in the following manner: For each course of reassigned time, the weight typically assigned to teaching will be reduced by 1/4, which will then be added to the appropriate category (service or professional development and achievement). In such cases, sources, source weights, and elements may also change to reflect the altered faculty role.

While tenured faculty are not required to submit an evaluation package every year, they are required to set weights for each evaluation cycle. If a faculty member fails to formally negotiate weights with the chair, default weights will be applied at midpoints: 65% teaching, 20% professional development and achievement; and 15% service.

Element Ratings

Faculty receive ratings from each rating source within each element based on the following 5-point scale:

5.0 = Outstanding Performances
4.0 = Above Expectations
3.0 = Meets Expectations
2.0 = Below Expectations
1.0 = Unacceptable Performance

Element Ratings are derived by multiplying each source rating of an element by its assigned source weight and adding the weighted source scores totaling the weighted Element Rating.

Category Ratings

The Category Rating is derived by multiplying the Element Rating by the element weight to get the Weighted Element Rating and adding all of the Weighted Element Ratings for the category.

Overall Rating

The Overall Rating is the result of multiplying each Category Rating by the category weight chosen by the faculty member for that year and adding the three weighted Category Ratings.

Merit Pay Scale

The Merit Pay scale is a 21-step scale in increments of 0.1, from 3.0 to 5.0. Merit pay begins at the 3.0 level and increases as a faculty member's Overall Rating rises to 5.0. There is no merit pay increase for an Overall Rating below 3.0. Faculty members must score 3.0 or above to be eligible for merit increases.

Responsibilities of the Evaluators

Responsibilities of the Department Evaluation Committee

Each department may establish a Department Evaluation Committee of three to five individuals on which all faculty will eventually serve through rotation if the Department is large enough; otherwise, the faculty may establish a standing committee or invite faculty from other departments to serve on the committee. The chair may not serve both as a member of the Department Evaluation Committee and as an independent evaluator. In rare circumstances a department may elect to have the chair as sole evaluator in a given cycle. When necessary to do so, the Faculty Concerns Committee must approve the chair as sole evaluator each year.

When the chair is evaluated (separate from the department evaluation of chair's duties) the department will appoint an alternative faculty member to perform the chair's function as evaluator.

The specific duties of the Department Evaluation Committee include:

1) Review the faculty member's self-statement and materials submitted for the three elements of the teaching category, including student free responses, the professional development and achievement category, and the service category, rating the faculty member on the numerical scale of 1–5 in the elements of each category.

2) Prepare a brief written justification supporting each element rating for the faculty member

3) Prepare a written assessment of the professional behavior of the faculty member for the year (praiseworthy collegial conduct should be noted as well as problematic professional conduct).

4) Forward the completed Department Evaluation Committee Faculty Evaluation Report to the department chair.

Responsibilities of Faculty Concerns Committee

The Faculty Concerns Committee will have the responsibility for the Faculty Evaluation Procedures. It will annually review and recommend to the Faculty Senate needed changes in the Faculty Evaluation Procedures. In addition, Faculty Concerns will review and approve exceptions and amendments to University Evaluation procedures.

Responsibilities of Individual Faculty

Faculty are responsible for providing the information and materials needed for the Department Evaluation Committee and the chair to carry out their respective rating responsibilities. Faculty are also responsible for writing self-statements to address, as appropriate, the following issues:

1) Express concern over difficulties in planning assignments and activities for courses.

2) Briefly describe how readings, conferences attended, etc., enhanced his/her instructional development.

3) Respond to student perceptions of course content and/or faculty performance in those courses, based, in part, on the Common Student Rating form and free responses.

4) Send letters of rebuttal to the appropriate school dean and to the provost if she/he does not agree with the chair and/or DEC evaluations/recommendation.

Responsibilities of Students

Students will rate faculty using the Common Student Rating Form. Departments may add questions to the student rating form for use by the department evaluation committee and the chair within the department. Those questions, however, will not count in the student rating component of the Performance/Feedback Element. Students will be encouraged to provide Free Responses when they complete the Rating Form.

Responsibilities of the Department Chair

1) Insure that the administration of the student ratings during the last two weeks of class includes standard instructions to be given to students prior to each rating.

2) Meet with the Department Evaluations Committee before the evaluation period to establish and articulate a common set of criteria to be used for evaluating department members.

3) Review the faculty member's self-statement and materials submitted for the three elements of the teaching category, the professional development and achievement category, and the service category and give the faculty member a numerical rating on a scale of 1–5 in the element of each category.

4) Prepare a brief written justification supporting each element rating for each faculty member.

5) Prepare a written assessment of the professional behavior of the faculty member for the year (praiseworthy collegial conduct should be noted as well as problematic professional conduct).

6) Complete the Department Chair Faculty Evaluation Report.

7) Forward the Department Faculty Evaluation Summary, the DEC Faculty Evaluation Report, and the Department Chair Faculty Evaluation Report for each faculty member to the dean, with a copy to the faculty member.

8) Communicate the results of the departmental evaluation process to each faculty member, preferably in a face-to-face interview and assist the faculty member in development in needed areas.

9) Maintain permanent departmental files, including student rating results, student comments, the faculty member's self-statement, the Department Evaluation Committee Faculty Evaluation Report, the departmental merit pay recommendation, and the final contract letter for each full-time faculty member of the department.

Responsibilities of the Dean

1) Share responsibility with the department chair for establishing and maintaining appropriate professional standards for faculty evaluation, including the option of establishing school-wide standards in one or more categories when appropriate.

2) Be responsible for reviewing the Overall Element Ratings, the Category Rating, the Overall Rating, and the rating justifications for each full-time faculty member.

3) Forward his/her endorsement of the departmental recommendation for merit level of each faculty member to the provost.

4) Should the dean not concur with the departmental recommendation for merit level, or should a faculty member challenge the evaluation of the Departmental Evaluation Committee and/or the chair, or if the dean's Overall Rating is different from the departmental rating, the dean will forward his/her rating recommendation and the departmental rating recommendation to the provost.

Responsibilities of the Provost

1) Receive and review the recommendations from the department and the dean.

2) Be responsible for preparing faculty merit pay recommendations, which he/she will forward to the president.

3) Report a summary of faculty merit pay recommendations to the Faculty Concerns Committee for publication to the faculty. The summary should include: the distribution of faculty Overall Ratings by department and school as well as for the entire university; the average Overall Rating for each department, each school, and the university; and the number of recommendations, by school, that differed from those provided by the department.

Description of the Faculty Role Model

Each of the three categories below contains the descriptions of activities (Elements) that constitute expectations of all faculty members. Similarly, each Element contains specific dimensions that describe the expected activities of all faculty members.

Evaluators will judge the faculty member's performance on using the previously defined 5-point scale within each of the Elements as described below. An element rating of 3.0 will be appropriate to performance that does not have any substantive areas of weakness and meets the minimal requirements of the Element. To qualify for a 5.0 rating (Outstanding), the faculty member must demonstrate achievement substantially beyond what is expected for Meets Expectations. In all three categories the Department Evaluation Committee may justify as equivalent other faculty achievement activities.

Teaching Category (Minimum = 50%; Maximum = 80%)

Course Materials and Course Syllabus (Weight = 25%). Course syllabus should conform to requirements described in the Faculty Handbook. Course materials should be appropriate, current, and supportive of course goals and objectives. These materials may include:

1) Examinations, quizzes, assignments allowing students to demonstrate achievement of course objectives

2) Appropriate texts, audiovisual aids, handouts, and other significant materials or equipment used reflect current technology

3) Evidence that the course content is current and appropriate for the classes

Teaching Performance and Feedback to Students (Weight = 50%).

1) Those rated at the 3.0 level (Meets Expectations) should meet the following minimal requirements:

- Specified course objectives and provided a reasonable opportunity for students' achievement of those objectives

- Demonstrated evidence of planning and ability to carry through

- Demonstrated knowledge of and respect for the subject matter

- Presented course assignments and materials clearly

- Encouraged students' questions and expressions of ideas

- Demonstrated respect for the student as an individual

- Reasonably adhered to the syllabus or to a change in the syllabus that was provided in a timely manner

- Posted and maintained those office hours which are expected of all faculty members, or if office hours were preempted, provided adequate notice

- Demonstrated evidence of accurate and timely advising to assigned advisees

2) Faculty should provide timely and sufficient feedback to the student concerning performance in the class. Examples of feedback, which meet minimum expectations include:

- Returning tests and papers in a reasonable amount of time

- Providing students with periodic summaries of performance

- Issuing mid-semester warnings to students performing at the D or F quality level

- Providing evaluation remarks on the content, logic, organization, clarity, and grammatical correctness of all written papers, such as essays, research papers, projects, and case analyses

3) Faculty rated at the 4.0 or 5.0 levels demonstrate characteristics, attitude, and behavior in those categories substantially beyond what is expected of 3.0 rating in teaching performance and feedback to students. Such a faculty member:

- Is self-critical; for example, asks for and values the opinions of peers regarding teaching methods

- Recognizes that classes represent a learning experience for both students and faculty

- Demonstrates enthusiasm toward students, the profession, and the subject matter

- Sets a high standard for other faculty, for example by setting high standards for students in courses

- Provides students with a high quality of constructive comments on papers and other written work

- Is a motivator of students, resulting in students pursuing study beyond normal course expectations

- Has classes which are rated as challenging by students, in which grades are awarded competitively, but which continue to be sought out by students

- Mentors students through activities that facilitate individual student's academic and professional development by providing out-of-class time to students above and beyond what is expected (e.g., study sessions, review session, extracurricular field trips, work with student groups, etc.)

4) In addition, those rated at the 4.0 or 5.0 levels are consistently recognized for providing additional time and commentary to students, for example, in conferences, through extensive commentary, or other appropriate and effective means.

Instructional Development (Weight = 25%). The Departmental Evaluation Committee may add and/or substitute professional activities that are not applied to the professional development and achievement category and that are appropriate to the advancement of instruction within its discipline. Examples of instructional development activities rated as 3.0 (Meets Expectations) include:

1) Presenting evidence of experimentation in instructional methods that enhance student learning

2) Presenting evidence that scholarly activities in the discipline have led to integration of new materials into a course or courses taught by the faculty member

3) Presenting evidences that those scholarly activities (e.g., attending workshops, seminars, and the like) in pedagogy have led to the enhancement of teaching methods by the faculty member

Faculty rated at the 4.0 or 5.0 levels demonstrate achievement in one or more of these categories substantially beyond what is expected for 3.0 (Meets Expectations). *Note: Internship instruction will be evaluated according to approved departmental guidelines and evaluation mechanisms.*

Professional Development and Achievement Category (Minimum = 10%, Maximum = 30%)

Below are examples of performance in the areas of professional development and achievement. Some examples of activities that rate 3.0 (Meets Expectations) are:

1) Proof of active membership in professional organization (e.g., conference attendance, etc.)

2) Serving in capacities such as adjudicator, review, or session moderator, to a local professional organization

3) Participating in a publisher's text review

4) Sharing expertise within the discipline (locally or regionally)

5) Acting as a journal reviewer

6) Reading in field and presenting evidence of ongoing scholarship in preparation for professional presentation (e.g., workshop, conference paper, and the like)

7) Continuing certification in discipline

8) Contributing to the development of instructional materials for K–16 programs

9) Managing a web page; acting as a newsgroup facilitator

The Department Evaluation Committee may add and/or substitute professional activities appropriate to the advancement of the discipline or the development of the faculty member. A faculty member may receive a 4.0 rating for accomplishing more than three of the above activities. Examples of individual activities that rate a 4.0 (Above Expectations):

10) Regional conference leadership role (e.g., paper presentation, discussant, panel organizer, session chair, etc.)

11) Published book review

12) Poster presentations at major conferences

Some examples of activities that rate a 5.0:

13) Production of a publication, performance, workshop, or artistic creation that has received some form of favorable peer review and has received at least regional recognition

14) Organization of a major regional or national conference

15) Significant participation in a national or international conference (e.g., paper presentation, workshop)

Service Category (Minimum = 5%, maximum = 25%)

Minimum service occurs at department and school level, earning the faculty member a rating of 3.0. Standard service includes:

1) Regular attendance at, and participation in department and school meetings

2) Fulfillment of normal committee assignment

3) Participation in regular departmental and school activities, as deemed appropriate

Additional service (beyond regular department duties) may earn faculty a 4.0 or 5.0 rating depending on level of contribution to department/school/university/community. Some examples include:

4) Service on faculty senate, ad hoc committees, or task forces

5) Involvement in major governance activities

6) Steering major curricular initiatives

7) Making a substantive contribution to the community in a manner that clearly impacts positively on the community, in a role that requires a high level of involvement and time, and in a manner that is clearly related to the faculty member's professional role

Department chairs, program coordinators, and other reassigned time assignments appropriate to service are automatically rated a 4.0 with a possibility of a 5.0 rating with demonstration of outstanding performance in that activity.

Summary of the Process

The faculty member is responsible for maintaining records of his/her performance, achievements, etc. for each evaluation period (currently, the calendar year). At the end of each year in which the faculty member is to be evaluated he/she must develop an Evaluation Packet which presents evidence of his/her performance, achievements, etc., in each of the three categories (teaching, professional development and achievement, and service) as well as professional behavior. The university will provide the faculty member with the numerical results from the Common Student Rating Form for his or her courses. In addition to the numerical score generated by the rating

form, the faculty member is encouraged to use information from student free responses in developing his/her Evaluation Packet.

The numerical score for the faculty member on the Common Student Rating Form will be generated by the university and provided to the faculty member and the department chair. The faculty member will submit his/her evaluation packet to both the Department Evaluation Committee (DEC) and his/her department chair.

The DEC will review the faculty member's evaluation packet, complete the Department Evaluation Committee Faculty Evaluation Report, which includes a rating of the faculty member's performance in each category (including each element within the teaching category) and a justification for each rating, and submit the report to the chair.

The chair will review the faculty member's evaluation packet and complete the Department Chair Faculty Evaluation Report, which includes a rating of the faculty member's performance in each category (including each element within the teaching category) and a justification for each rating. The chair, based on his/her rating of the faculty member's evaluation packet and the rating awarded by the DEC, will complete the Department Faculty Evaluation Summary.

The chair will forward the Department Faculty Evaluation Summary Form, the DEC Faculty Evaluation Report, and the Department Chair Faculty Evaluation Report for each faculty member to the school dean, with a copy to the faculty member.

The dean will review the ratings made by the department chair and the DEC and forward the departmental rating recommendation to the provost. If the dean does not concur with the departmental recommendation for merit level or the faculty member challenges the DEC's or the chair's rating, the dean will forward his/her own rating recommendation and the departmental rating recommendation to the provost.

The provost will review the recommendations from the dean and the department and forward faculty merit pay recommendations to the president.

FROSTBURG STATE UNIVERSITY
DEPARTMENT FACULTY EVALUATION SUMMARY FORM

Faculty Member_____ Department_____ Evaluation Period_____

Faculty Member Status (check one)
___ untenured/tenure track faculty
___ tenured faculty, required three-year evaluation
___ tenured faculty, preceding evaluation was below expectations
___ tenured faculty, requesting merit evaluation for year
___ full-time contractual

	Rating	Dept. Avg.
A. Teaching (Negotiated Weight = _____%)		
1. Course Materials and Course Syllabus		
DEC ___ (.70) + Chair ___ (.30) = ____(.25) =	_____	_____
2. Teaching Perform and Feedback to Students		
DEC ___ (.15) + Chair ___ (.20) + Students (.65) = ____(.50) =	_____	_____
3. Instructional Development		
DEC ___ (.30) + Chair ___ (.70) = ____(.25) =	_____	_____
Teaching Category Rating	_____	_____
B. Prof. Development and Achievement (Negotiated Weight = ____%)		
DEC ___ (.75) + Chair ___ (.25) = ____(1.0) =	_____	_____
Development and Achievement Category Rating	_____	_____
C. Service (Negotiated Weight = _____%)		
DEC ___ (.25) + Chair ___ (.75) = ____(1.0) =	_____	_____
Service Category Rating	_____	_____

	Rating	×	Weight		Rating	Dept. Avg.
Teaching Category	_____	×	_____	=	_____	_____
Prof. Achievement Category	_____	×	_____	=	_____	_____
Service Category	_____	×	_____	=	_____	_____
Overall Rating					_____	_____

Rating Source and Faculty Signatures

Dept. Chair _____ Date_____ DEC Chair _____ Date_____

I have read and discussed with my department chair my faculty evaluation for the evaluation year.

Signature _____ Date_____

▪ GEORGIA PERIMETER COLLEGE FACULTY EVALUATION SYSTEM

The following is not a case study but, rather, a presentation of the final faculty evaluation procedure developed by Georgia Perimeter College following the process described in this book. This section has been excerpted, with permission, from the Georgia Perimeter College *Faculty Evaluation, Promotion, and Tenure Handbook* (1998–1999). The development of the Georgia Perimeter College system was accomplished by the Process Renewal Team on Faculty Evaluation chaired by professors Margo L. Eden-Camann and Virginia Parks. The manual refers to the Board of Regents' Policy on Faculty Evaluation, which is found as an addendum at the end of this section.

Georgia Perimeter College's Policy on Faculty Evaluation

In keeping with Board of Regents' Policy, Georgia Perimeter College has adopted the Annual Performance Review of Faculty described herein. The primary purpose of faculty evaluation at Georgia Perimeter College is to promote individual and institutional self-improvement. To ensure that faculty are aware of the expectations of their supervisor and are informed of their progress as members of Georgia Perimeter College faculty, evaluations are completed on an annual basis. This evaluation, which serves as an evaluation of progress and a discussion of expectations for the future, focuses on the objectives and goals of the individual and of the college. Because the results of this evaluation will be the sole determiner of the annual merit pay award made to each faculty member as well as the bases for promotion, tenure, pre-tenure, and post-tenure decisions made by the institution, the College recognizes the need for a consistent system for evaluating its faculty. (Any academic year in which a leave is taken cannot count as a year's service for purposes of promotion and/or tenure. Merit pay will not be awarded for time on leave.) However, the college also recognizes the diversity among its faculty and has, therefore, adopted a system of evaluation that values that diversity, asserts that progress may occur in many directions, and recognizes that many types of activities make valuable contributions to the college's success and growth.

All faculty members with teaching responsibilities will be evaluated annually on three components of their performance: teaching effectiveness, service, and professional activities. Faculty members at different points in their academic careers often find that they want or need to direct more effort to one component or another of their responsibilities. The Annual Performance Review allows each faculty member to determine the emphasis that he or she will place on each component of the evaluation and to select, within prescribed ranges, the weight of each component in the overall evaluation.

Because of the great diversity in possible approaches to the act of teaching, the Annual Performance Review, while maintaining a consistent process of evaluation, allows some flexibility to the faculty member. The process supports a multi-source faculty evaluation system that includes self-evaluation, peer evaluation, student evaluation, and department chair evaluation. The system allows the faculty member to determine, within established ranges, the weights of these evaluations in determining the faculty member's teaching effectiveness rating.

This need for flexibility is also reflected in the evaluation of service and the evaluation of professional activities. Faculty members may select from a wide range of activities in which to participate each year.

The department chair is responsible for assembling the various parts of the evaluation system and calculating the Faculty Member's Performance Review Summary. The evaluation should be submitted to the dean of academic services and then to the provost on the appropriate campus.

Faculty Evaluation Committee

Purpose. The Faculty Evaluation Committee reviews and revises the evaluation system and promotion and tenure system and recommends improvements in content and procedure. The committee's recommendations are submitted by the vice president for academic affairs to the Academic Affairs Policy Council, which advises and makes recommendations for changes to the College Advisory Board, which advises and makes recommendations to the president. The president may accept or reject the recommendations and must approve all changes.

Memberships. Membership consists of faculty from each campus and is representative of the various disciplines. The members are appointed to three-year terms on a rotating basis by the vice president for academic affairs. At least one-third of the membership changes each year.

Meetings. Meetings may be held at any time during the year as need arises as determined by the chairperson.

Chairperson. The chairperson is appointed by the vice president for academic affairs.

Faculty Portfolio for Annual Evaluation

The Faculty Portfolio for Annual Evaluation requires each faculty member to provide documentation for the Annual

Performance Review in the areas of teaching effectiveness, service, and professional activities. It also allows the faculty member to select the weights of the three components of the overall evaluation as well as the weights of the sources in the evaluation of teaching effectiveness. In addition, the guidelines define and limit the types and quantities of information that should be submitted by the faculty member. (The faculty portfolio should include the items listed here.)

Declaration of Weights. In the spring term of each academic year, each faculty member must submit the Declaration of Weights—Part I: Overall Evaluation to his or her department chair. In conference with the department chair, each faculty member will choose the percentage that he/she wants each area to weigh in the overall evaluation, thereby determining how the evaluation in each area will affect his/her merit pay award for the evaluation period (each selected percentage must be a multiple of ten, and no area may have a weight of zero percent). The declaration of weights form will be provided by the department chair. The faculty member should return both copies to the department chair by the announced deadline. The department chair will sign the form, keep the original, and return the copy to the faculty member.

As part of the faculty portfolio submitted in the fall term each year, each faculty member must include the Declaration of Weights Part II: Evaluation of Teaching Effectiveness. Each faculty member will choose the percentage that he or she wants each source to weigh in the evaluation of teaching effectiveness. (Each selected percentage must be a multiple of 10, and no area may have a weight of zero percent.) The faculty member should include the original form in the Faculty Portfolio and keep a copy for his/her records.

Faculty Member's Report on Teaching Effectiveness: A Focused Narrative. The Focused Narrative should present evidence of successful practices the faculty member has used *during this evaluation period,* which characterize his/her teaching effectiveness. This narrative should include a discussion of the faculty member's knowledge, course organization and planning, communication and delivery, and policy/procedure practices.

Only if it is essential that the evaluator see the materials described, faculty members may choose to attach an addendum to the focused narrative including labeled materials to which they have made direct reference in the narrative. The purpose of the addendum is to provide documentation for the narrative. It is separate from the Course Materials Review and will not be reviewed by the Peer Review Panel.

Faculty Member's Course Materials. The Course Materials Packet should include materials used by the faculty member during the evaluation period. These materials may have been created by the faculty member, selected from other sources, or created in collaboration with others but materials not developed by an instructor should acknowledge the original source or the collaborator. While these instructions require all faculty members to submit course syllabi (which adhere to the guidelines in the Faculty Syllabus Checklist) and assessment tools, they also allow instructors to choose to submit materials that best reflect their teaching ability from the following areas: innovative instruction, writing activities, revision of course materials, grading/feedback to students, instructional support materials, and instructional technology. These materials will be reviewed by both the department chair and the Peer Review Panel, a panel of peers elected from the faculty members department.

Service Report. In the Service Report, faculty will list their activities completed during the evaluation period in the following areas: service to the campus, discipline, and department, and service to the college and community. Faculty members should list their activities under the appropriate item in each category. If a service activity does not fit one of the items listed, it may be listed under other activities. The department chair will award points for each activity using the Evaluation of Service form. The service rating will be determined using the point scale at the end of that document.

Professional Activities Report. In the Professional Activities Report, faculty will list their activities completed during the evaluation period in the following areas: professional organizations; further education and degrees; scholarly and/or creative activities; awards, grants, artistic commissions, and/or fellowships. Faculty members should list their activities under the appropriate item in each category. If a professional activity does not fit one of the items listed, it may be listed under Other Activities. The department chair will award points for each activity using the Evaluation of Professional Activities form. The Professional Activities Rating will be determined using the point scale at the end of that document.

Goals. Each faculty member should submit a Review of Goals from the Previous Year form and establish Goals for the Coming Year. All faculty must indicate a plan in the area of teaching effectiveness and in at least one of the other areas.

Self-Evaluation. In keeping with the Board of Regents policy that requires that evaluation provide an opportunity to assess strengths and weaknesses of faculty performance, the self-evaluation offers the opportunity for personal assessment of one's teaching effectiveness. Based on the information provided in the focused narrative, each faculty member must use the self-evaluation form to rate his or her own performance in the area of teaching and provide justification when required.

Peer Review of Course Materials

The Board of Regents requires that a faculty member's teaching performance be evaluated by his or her peers. Each faculty member has submitted, as part of the Faculty Portfolio for Annual Evaluation, a packet of course materials used during the evaluation period. These materials will be reviewed and evaluated by a panel of faculty peers elected according to the following procedures:

Course Materials Review Panel. The Course Materials Review Panels will be composed of three department members, elected annually, who have, at the time of the election, at least one complete year of teaching experience at Georgia Perimeter College. No faculty member serving on a Promotion and Tenure Panel will be eligible for membership. The election of the faculty to these panels will be carried out by the appropriate department chair mid-spring term, by secret ballot, from a list of all faculty members in the department with at least one year of teaching experience at Georgia Perimeter College. Each faculty member will vote for three candidates. The department chair will vote, but his or her name will not appear on the ballot. The three faculty members with the highest vote totals within the department will be elected. Each department will create at least one panel. Departments with more than 20 faculty members may create two panels using the same process.

Following discussion of each packet, each panel member will complete an individual review of the course materials of every department member. Course materials review for a faculty member serving on a panel will be done by the other two panel members. Each panel member will forward the completed Peer Review of Course Materials forms to the department chair. The department chair will tabulate the rating from each panel member for every department member. The department chair will then calculate the appropriate mean rating for each faculty member's course materials and report it on the Peer Course Materials Evaluation Summary. The mean will be used for annual evaluation.

The course materials review for a department chair will be completed by the panel in his/her department. The dean of academic services will calculate the appropriate mean rating for each department chair's course materials and report it on the Peer Course Materials Evaluation Summary.

Chairperson

1) The chairperson will be elected from the faculty membership of the panel.

2) Duties of the chairperson:

- Ensure that all reviews are conducted within the time frame outlined in the Implementation Timetables

- Ensure the integrity and confidentiality of the process

- Ensure the security of the Course Materials Review files at all times

- Submit the documents to the department chair

- Serve as the representative of the panel if a faculty member requests further information about the ratings

Course Materials Packet. The following is a list of items to be included in the Course Materials Packet. These materials will be reviewed by the department chair and the Peer Review Panel. Categories one and two *must* be included in your packet:

1) Syllabus for at least one (1) and not more than three (3) courses. (Refer to the Faculty Syllabus Checklist for a description of required and suggested components for all Georgia Perimeter College syllabi.)

2) At least one (1) and not more than three (3) samples of materials demonstrating how you assess student achievement on expected learning outcomes identified in the common course outline. (These materials may include tests but are not limited to tests.)

Choose exactly three categories from the list below, and submit no more than three items for each selected category:

3) Sample of materials demonstrating innovative instruction

4) Sample of materials demonstrating the use of writing in a course

5) Sample of materials demonstrating a revision of course materials

6) Sample of materials demonstrating grading techniques and comments to students

7) Sample of instructional support material designed to help students master concepts and content (i.e., study

guides, original problem-solving sets, concept maps, annotated bibliographies, etc.)

8) Sample of materials demonstrating efforts to incorporate technology into course content

Faculty Rating by Students

Beginning in fall 1997 the Student Instructional Report II (SIR II), published by Educational Testing Service, will be used to elicit student input concerning each faculty member's teaching performance. The report requires students to rate instructors on items organized into ten areas. Six of these areas—course organization and planning; communication; faculty/student interaction; assignments, exams, and grading; course outcomes; and overall evaluation—will provide mean ratings used to calculate the Composite Student Rating, a part of the overall evaluation. The other areas—supplementary instructional methods; student effort and involvement; course difficulty, workload, and pace; and student information—will provide information to instructors which may help them to improve their teaching effectiveness. The SIR II will be administered annually in the fall term. In some unique circumstances, a spring administration may be necessary. The faculty member and the department chair will receive a copy of the results of this evaluation.

Department Chairs Evaluation of Faculty Performance

Each year the department chair will evaluate each faculty member in his/her department in three areas of performance: teaching effectiveness, service, and professional activities. Using the information provided in the Faculty Portfolio for Annual Evaluation, the Peer Evaluation of Course Materials Summary, the Faculty Rating by Students, and other pertinent information, the department chair will evaluate the faculty members' teaching effectiveness. Using the information provided in the Service Report and the Professional Activities Report, the department chair will assign points as indicated in the Evaluation of Service and Evaluation of Professional Activities instruments.

Faculty Member Performance Review Summary

To complete the Faculty Member Performance Review Summary, the department chair will calculate the Overall Teaching Effectiveness Rating of each faculty member using the Declaration of Weights and the ratings of teaching effectiveness from the Self-Evaluation, Student Rating Summary, Peer Review of Course Materials, and Department Chair's Evaluation of Faculty Performance. After including the Service Rating of Faculty Member and the Professional Activities Rating of Faculty Member, the department chair will calculate the Overall Faculty Evaluation Rating. The department chair will hold a conference with each faculty member to discuss the evaluation. The faculty member will be asked to sign the summary.

Evaluation of First-Year Faculty

Because the faculty portfolio is submitted in the fall term, reporting activities completed during the previous academic year, faculty joining the institution that fall will not have worked during that evaluation period and, therefore, will have no report. However, the department chair must evaluate the performance of new faculty to support a recommendation for contract renewal, New faculty will be required to turn in a portfolio of activities completed during fall term. The First Term Progress Report will provide evaluative information for the department chair. Additionally, new faculty should submit, at the beginning of the fall term, a set of goals that should guide their professional growth during the first year of employment. These goals should be submitted on the Goals for the Coming Year form from the faculty portfolio.

Rebuttal of Annual Performance Review of Faculty

The only component of the Annual Performance Review that may be rebutted is the Department Chair's Evaluation of Faculty Performance, including the evaluation of teaching effectiveness, service, and professional activities.

Faculty evaluations by department chairs must be signed and dated by the faculty member and the department chair at the time of evaluation. The faculty member's signature indicates review of the evaluation only. However, failure to sign the evaluation by the faculty member could become grounds for disciplinary action. A faculty member who wishes to rebut an evaluation by a department chair should follow the procedure outlined here:

1) The faculty member should review and discuss the evaluation with the department chair before the evaluation is placed in the personnel file.

2) If the faculty member disagrees with the evaluation, the faculty member may write a memorandum of rebuttal or explanation of any parts of the evaluation with which there is disagreement. Within *five working days* of the evaluation conference, he/she should send the memorandum to the department chair with

copies to the dean of academic services and the campus provost.

3) Upon receipt of a memorandum of rebuttal from a faculty member, the department chair will acknowledge receipt in writing.

4) Any changes in the annual evaluation made as a result of either the conference or the faculty member's written rebuttal must be noted in writing by the department chair. This written acknowledgment of change will be appended to the original evaluation and all copies become a part of the evaluation record along with the memorandum of rebuttal.

5) If the faculty member is dissatisfied with the outcome of the rebuttal, then the faculty member may discuss the evaluation, the memorandum of rebuttal, and any changes that have been noted with the dean of academic services.

6) The evaluation, the memorandum of rebuttal, the department chair's response, and a summary of the conference with the dean of academic services, if any, and

any changes to the evaluation which have been noted will become a part of the faculty member's permanent file.

7) In addition to signing and dating the evaluation form, the faculty member is required to sign and date any attachments and return the signed evaluation and any attachments to the department chair.

8) The department chair will provide the faculty member with a copy of the evaluation, including any changes which have been noted. The department chair will keep a copy of the evaluation and submit the original files through the dean of academic services to the provost.

9) The provost will submit all completed annual evaluations of faculty to the human resources department, where they will become a part of the faculty member's permanent file.

GEORGIA PERIMETER COLLEGE FACULTY PORTFOLIO FOR EVALUATION

Evaluation Period: July 1, _____ –June 30, _____

_____   _____
Faculty Member   Department Chair

_____   _____
Department   Campus

Table of Contents

Faculty Member's Report on Teaching Effectiveness: A Focused Narrative

Addendum to the Faculty Member's Report

Declaration of Weights to Be Used in Faculty Evaluation

> Part I

> Part II

Goals

Review of Goals from the Previous Year

> Goals for the Coming Year

Faculty Member's Self-Evaluation of Teaching Effectiveness

Faculty Member's Course Materials

> Course Materials Description

> Course Materials Evaluation Criteria

Service Report

Professional Activities Report

To the best of my knowledge, the information included in my Faculty Portfolio is accurate. (See Board of Regents' Policy 803.9P6.)

_____   _____
Faculty Member's Signature   Date

FACULTY MEMBER'S REPORT ON TEACHING EFFECTIVENESS: A FOCUSED NARRATIVE

In no more than two typewritten pages present evidence of successful practices you have used *in this evaluation period* which characterize your teaching effectiveness in the areas below. Under each area are criteria to consider. These are not necessarily equal components of teaching effectiveness.

1) Knowledge

- Faculty member demonstrates knowledge of discipline.

- Faculty member demonstrates competence with course content that is relevant and thorough.

- Faculty member increases knowledge of discipline and/or pedagogy.

2) Course organization and planning

- Faculty member prepares assignments handouts, exams, and/or activities to promote student interest and enhance learning.

- Faculty member demonstrates evidence of attention to active learning, writing, and critical thinking skills as appropriate.

- Faculty member implements course objectives appropriately.

3) Communication and delivery

- Faculty member uses class time effectively.

- Faculty member uses effective instructional techniques and tools (including lecture, discussion, audio/visuals, group activities, or technology).

- Faculty member demonstrates efforts to stimulate student interest and achievement.

4) Policy/procedure practices

- Faculty member adheres to established college, discipline, and department policies and procedures.

- Faculty member performs assigned duties for the conduct of business of the department.

- Faculty member is available to students outside class.

ADDENDUM TO THE FACULTY MEMBER'S REPORT

Attach and label materials to which you make direct reference in your report on teaching effectiveness.

DECLARATION OF WEIGHTS TO BE USED IN FACULTY EVALUATION

Evaluation Period: July 1, _____ –June 30, _____

Part I—Overall Evaluation

Instructions: Complete Part I during April 1–May 1 of the academic year prior to the evaluation period. The faculty member should return both copies to the department chair by the announced deadline. The department chair will sign the form, keep the original, and return the copy to the faculty member. The department chair should include this document in the annual evaluation of the faculty member. All selected percentages should be within the indicated ranges, in multiples of 10 (i.e., 10%, 20%, 30%, etc.), and must total 100%.

TEACHING EFFECTIVENESS   _____%
(Choose from 50%–70%)

SERVICE   _____%
(Choose from 10%–30%)

PROFESSIONAL ACTIVITIES   _____%
(Choose from 10%–30%)

SIGNATURES:

_____   _____
Faculty Member   Date

_____   _____
Department Chair   Date

Part II—Evaluation of Teaching Effectiveness

Instructions: Complete Part II and submit with the faculty Portfolio. All selected percentages should be within the indicated ranges, in multiples of 10 (i.e., 10%, 20%, 30%, etc.), and must total 100%.

SELF   _____%
(Choose from 10%–20%)

PEER   _____%
(Choose from 10%–20%)

STUDENTS   _____%
(Choose from 10%–20%)

DEPARTMENT CHAIR   _____%
(Choose from 40%–60%)

TOTAL   _____%
                                                             (100%)

REVIEW OF GOALS FROM THE PREVIOUS YEAR

Report on your efforts to meet the goals you submitted last year. Please check those areas for which you are supplying a review, and attach a copy of your goals from last year.

    __X__ TEACHING EFFECTIVENESS

    _____ SERVICE

    _____ PROFESSIONAL ACTIVITIES

GOALS FOR THE COMING YEAR

Describe your goals for the coming year. In each area describe the goal you plan to attain, the activities that you will undertake to achieve that goal, the methods you will use to evaluate your efforts, and the resources that you require to achieve the goals. Check the areas for which you are providing a plan. All faculty must indicate a plan in the area of TEACHING EFFECTIVENESS and in at least one of the other areas. Your declaration of weights for faculty evaluation may reflect the goals for the evaluation period.

    __X__ TEACHING EFFECTIVENESS

    _____ SERVICE

    _____ PROFESSIONAL ACTIVITIES

FACULTY MEMBER'S SELF-EVALUATION OF TEACHING EFFECTIVENESS

Rating Scale:

EP — Exemplary Professional Performance
Consistently exceeds accepted standards of professional performance
(JUSTIFICATION MUST BE INCLUDED)

HP — High Professional Performance
Frequently exceeds accepted standards of professional performance

SP — Standard Professional Performance
Consistently meets accepted standards of professional performance

MP — Minimal Performance
Does not consistently meet accepted standards of professional performance
(JUSTIFICATION MUST BE INCLUDED)

UP — Unsatisfactory Performance
Does not meet minimal standards of professional performance
(JUSTIFICATION MUST BE INCLUDED.)

Justification from the Faculty Member's Report on Teaching Effectiveness (for ratings of EP, MP, or UP) must be included on the following page.

1) Knowledge   RATING:_____

2) Course organization and planning   RATING:_____

3) Communication and delivery   RATING:_____

4) Policy/procedure practices   RATING:_____

To compute your Teaching Effectiveness Self-Rating, assign the following values:

EP = 5   HP = 4   SP = 3   MP = 2   UP = 1

Directions: Add the four values assigned to the ratings, and divide by four to calculate the teaching effectiveness rating by the faculty member. Do not round.

TEACHING EFFECTIVENESS SELF-RATING: _____

Justification of ratings of EP, MP, or UP from the previous page should follow. Ratings of HP or SP require no response.

1) Knowledge:

2) Course Organization and Planning:

3) Communication and Delivery:

4) Policy/Procedure Practices:

COURSE MATERIALS DESCRIPTION

The following is a list of categories of course materials that may be included in your packet. Keep in mind that these materials will be reviewed by your department chair and Peer Review Panel. To facilitate their review, clearly identify each component of your materials packet. The faculty evaluation system recognizes that instructors select course materials from a variety of sources; however, materials not developed by an instructor should acknowledge the original source

Categories one and two *must* be included in your packet:

1) Syllabus for at least one (1) and not more than three (3) courses (Refer to the Faculty Syllabus Checklist for a description of required and suggested components for all Georgia Perimeter College syllabi.)

2) At least one (1) and not more than three (3) samples of materials demonstrating how you assess student achievement on expected learning outcomes identified in the common course outlines (These materials may include tests but are not limited to tests.)

Choose exactly *three* categories from the list below, and submit no more than three items for each selected category:

3) Sample of materials demonstrating innovative instruction

4) Sample of materials demonstrating the use of writing in a course

5) Sample demonstrating a revision of course materials

6) Sample of materials demonstrating grading techniques and comments to students

7) Sample of instructional support materials from one course designed to help students master concepts and content (i.e., study guides, original problem-solving sets, concept maps, annotated bibliographies, etc.)

8) Sample of materials demonstrating efforts to incorporate technology into course content

COURSE MATERIALS EVALUATION CRITERIA

1) **Syllabus**
   - Syllabus follows guidelines identified in the Georgia Perimeter College Faculty Syllabus Checklist.
   - Syllabus clearly explains instructor's expectations (i.e., grading, attendance, assignments, deadlines, projects).
   - Syllabus identifies learning resources for the course and their locations.
   - Syllabus is free of grammatical errors and communicates in simple, clear, positive language.

2) **Assessment of Achievement of Expected Learning Outcomes**
   - Assignments, projects, and exams are related to the outcome(s) identified for the course

3) **Innovative Instruction**
   - Instructional activity is clearly related to the outcome(s) identified for the course.
   - Instructional activity is appropriate for the target student population.
   - Instructional activity promotes mastery of concept(s) or content of the course.
   - Instructional activity involves students' participation.

4) **Writing Activity**
   - Writing activity is clearly related to the outcome(s) identified for the course.
   - Writing activity is appropriate for the target population.
   - Writing activity promotes mastery of concept(s) or content of the course.

5) **Revision of Course Materials**
   - Revision of course materials is clearly related to course outcome(s).
   - Revision of course materials is appropriate to target student population.
   - Revision of course materials promotes mastery of concept(s) and content of course.

6) **Grading/Feedback to Students**
   - Grading policy agrees with Georgia Perimeter College policy.
   - Grading techniques are fair and appropriate for course.
   - Written feedback to students offers constructive criticism and suggestions for improvement.

7) **Instructional Support Materials**
   - Instructional support materials are clearly related to the outcome(s) identified for the course.
   - Instructional support materials are appropriate for the target student population.
   - Instructional support materials promote mastery of concept(s) or content of the course.
   - Instructional support materials are free of grammatical errors and are written in simple, clear, positive language.

8) **Instructional Technology**
   - Instructional technology use is clearly related to the outcome(s) identified for the course.
   - Instructional technology use is appropriate for the target student population.
   - Instructional technology use promotes mastery of concept(s) or content of the course.

SERVICE REPORT

Instructions: Under the appropriate items below, list all service activities completed during the period under evaluation.

A) **Service to the Campus, Discipline, and Department**

- Membership on campus, discipline, or department committee
- Chair of campus, discipline, or department committee
- Leader of campus, discipline, or department workshop or presentation
- Mentor of new faculty member
- Mentor of part-time faculty

B) **Service to College and Community**

- Membership on college-wide councils or committees
- Chair of college-wide council or committee
- Leader of college-wide or community workshops, courses, or presentations
- Organizer of lecture series
- Advisor to student organization recognized by SGA
- Advisor/editor of college publication
- Application of your recognized area of expertise in the community without pay
- Participation in college-sponsored outreach activities

C) **Other Activities**

List those activities, other than the ones noted above, which directly contributed to either the academic or administrative functioning of the college.

Developing a Comprehensive Faculty Evaluation System

PROFESSIONAL ACTIVITIES REPORT

Instructions: Under the appropriate items below, list all professional activities completed during the period under evaluation.

A) **Professional Organizations**
- Held current membership in professional organization
- Served on a committee of a professional organization
- Held an elective or appointed office or chaired a committee of a state or local professional organization
- Held an elective or appointed office or chaired a committee of a regional or national professional organization

B) **Further Education and Degrees**
- Received credit for a graduate course (other than dissertation or thesis hours)
- Participated in scholarly, pedagogical, or technological workshops or presentations at Georgia Perimeter College (excluding those that were required)
- Participated in workshops, summer institutes, short courses, audited a graduate-level course, etc. (excluding Georgia Perimeter College Activities)
- Completed a graduate degree from an accredited institution

C) **Scholarly and/or Creative Activities**
- Attended a professional conference
- Gave a presentation at a professional conference (indicate national/regional or state/local conference)
- Served on a discussion roundtable/panel
- Published an article, short story, or poem in a scholarly publication
- Published a book
- Published a new edition of a book
- Published a book review in an appropriate scholarly publication
- Served as an editor of a scholarly publication
- Served as a referee for a scholarly publication
- Reviewed a manuscript for publication
- Published a comment, note, or letter to the editor in a scholarly publication
- Published an article, short story, or poem in a non-scholarly publication

D) **Awards, Grants, Artistic Commissions, and/or Fellowships**
- Received an award, grant, artistic commission, or fellowship (excluding tuition grants for graduate study)
- Served on a grant review panel

E) **Other Activities**
List those activities, other than the ones noted above, which directly contributed to either the academic or administrative functioning of the college.

F) **Fine Arts and Humanities Faculty Only**
- Performed in a musical, dramatic, or media production
- Created a musical, dramatic, or media work which was performed, published, exhibited, and/or broadcast
- Directed or produced a musical, dramatic, or media event/performance/broadcast recording/exhibition
- Designed and/or implemented the technical work (scene, costume, lighting, sound, etc.) for a musical, dramatic, or media production

FACULTY SYLLABUS CHECKLIST

This checklist includes required and suggested components of syllabi at Georgia Perimeter College as indicated in the *Georgia Perimeter College Policy Manual*. It may be used by faculty at the college as a convenience in composing syllabi.

REQUIRED COMPONENTS:

Information About the Instructor

_____ Name

_____ Office number

_____ Office hours

_____ Times when students may contact you

_____ Office phone number

Course Information

_____ Heading (college name)

_____ Course title and location

_____ Course description

_____ Attendance Policy

_____ Course ID (e.g., PADL 101 400)

_____ Required texts—titles, authors, editions

_____ Course objectives reflecting expected educational results

Schedule Information

_____ Dates of major assignments, papers, field trips, projects, etc.

_____ Dates of midterm and/or other important tests

_____ Disclaimer stating dates may change

_____ Date and time of final exam

Grading Information

_____ Course requirements: exams, quizzes, classroom participation, projects, and papers, including the percentage each counts toward the final grade

_____ Policies on missed exams and late work

_____ Grading scale and standards

Other Statements*

_____ Americans with Disabilities Act

_____ Equal Opportunity

_____ Academic Honesty

_____ Affirmative Action

This information may be included in departmental handouts distributed with the syllabus.

SUGGESTED COMPONENTS:

_____ Recommended supplemental course materials

_____ Schedule of class meetings, including subject matter and topics to be covered as well as pre-class readings and other assignments

_____ Unique class procedure/structures, such as cooperative learning, peer review, panel presentations, portfolios, case studies, journals or learning logs, and others

_____ Special components: science and computer labs, tutorials, computer classroom, instructional support services lab, and others

Developing a Comprehensive Faculty Evaluation System

PEER EVALUATION OF COURSE MATERIALS

_____

Faculty Member

Evaluation Period: July 1, _____ –June 30,_____

For the purposes of peer evaluation of course materials, professional performance is defined as the faculty member's ability to select, create, and use course materials.

Rating Scale:

EP — Exemplary Professional Performance
Consistently exceeds accepted standards of professional performance
(JUSTIFICATION MUST BE INCLUDED)

HP — High Professional Performance
Frequently exceeds accepted standards of professional performance

SP — Standard Professional Performance
Consistently meets accepted standards of professional performance

MP — Minimal Performance
Does not consistently meet accepted standards of professional performance
(JUSTIFICATION MUST BE INCLUDED)

UP — Unsatisfactory Performance
Does not meet minimal standards of professional performance
(JUSTIFICATION MUST BE INCLUDED.)

Directions: Using the criteria identified for each category as a guideline, assign a rating to each applicable category using the rating scale above.

I) Faculty member was required to include items from categories one and two below. Rate both categories.
   1) Syllabus Rating:_____
   2) Assessment of Achievement of Learning Outcomes   Rating:_____

II) Faculty member selected three of the following categories. For those categories not chosen, write "NS"
   (*not selected)* in the rating blank. Rate the other categories.
   3) Innovative Instruction   Rating:_____
   4) Writing Activity   Rating:_____
   5) Revision of Course Materials   Rating:_____
   6) Grading/Feedback   Rating:_____
   7) Instructional Support Materials   Rating:_____
   8) Instructional Technology   Rating:_____

To compute your Teaching Effectiveness Self-Rating, assign the following values:
   EP = 5   HP = 4   SP = 3   MP = 2 UP = 1

Directions: Add the five values assigned to the ratings, and divide by five to calculate the Course Materials Rating by the faculty member. Do not round.

COURSE MATERIALS RATING: _____

_____   _____
Peer Reviewer Signature   Date

Peer Evaluation of Course Materials Summary

Record the course materials rating from each of the Peer Evaluation of Course Materials for the indicated faculty member.

Faculty Member:_____   Date: _____

1) Peer Reviewer #1   Rating: _____

2) Peer Reviewer #2   Rating: _____

3) Peer Reviewer #3   Rating: _____

For faculty members who are not members of the Course Materials Review Panel, compute the Peer Rating of Course Materials as follows: Add the ratings, and divide by three. Round to two decimals.

Faculty members who are members of the Course Materials Review Panel will not rate their own materials. To compute the Peer Rating of Course Materials for members of the Course Materials Peer Review Panel, add the ratings, and divide by two. Round to two decimals.

PEER RATING OF COURSE MATERIALS: _____

GEORGIA PERIMETER COLLEGE ANNUAL PERFORMANCE REVIEW OF FACULTY MEMBER

Evaluation Period: July 1, _____ –June 30, _____

_____   _____

Faculty Member   Department Chair

_____   _____

Department   Campus

Table of Contents

Faculty Member's Acknowledgment: I have reviewed the attached evaluations with my department chair. If I wish to submit a written response, I will do so within five working days of the evaluation conference, The response must be signed, dated, attached to the original evaluation form, and submitted to the campus academic dean.

SIGNATURES:

_____   _____

Faculty Member   Date

_____   _____

Department Chair   Date

_____   _____

Campus Academic Dean   Date

STUDENT RATING SUMMARY

1) Identify each class by name and section number (e.g., ECON2OI–140).

Class 1_____   Class 2_____

Class 3_____   Class 4_____

Class 5_____   Class 6_____

Class 7_____   Class 8_____

2) For areas A, B, C, D, F, and I, record the mean from the STUDENT INSTRUCTOR RATING II (SIR II) report for each class. Calculate a mean for each area by adding the means for each class in that area and dividing by the number of classes reported. Round to two decimals.

A) Course Organization and Planning

Class 1 _____   Class 2 _____   Class 3 _____   Class 4 _____

Class 5 _____   Class 6 _____   Class 7 _____   Class 8 _____

Area Mean_____

B) Communication

Class 1 _____   Class 2 _____   Class 3 _____   Class 4 _____

Class 5 _____   Class 6 _____   Class 7 _____   Class 8 _____

Area Mean_____

C) Faculty/Student Interaction

Class 1 _____   Class 2 _____   Class 3 _____   Class 4 _____

Class 5 _____   Class 6 _____   Class 7 _____   Class 8 _____

Area Mean_____

D) Assignments, Exams, and Grading

Class 1 _____   Class 2 _____   Class 3 _____   Class 4 _____

Class 5 _____   Class 6 _____   Class 7 _____   Class 8 _____

Area Mean_____

F) Course Outcomes

Class 1 _____   Class 2 _____   Class 3 _____   Class 4 _____

Class 5 _____   Class 6 _____   Class 7 _____   Class 8 _____

Area Mean_____

I) Overall Evaluation

Class 1 _____   Class 2 _____   Class 3 _____   Class 4 _____

Class 5 _____   Class 6 _____   Class 7 _____   Class 8 _____

Area Mean_____

3) To calculate the Composite Student Rating, add the area means for A, B, C, D, F, and I, and divide by six. Round to two decimals.

COMPOSITE STUDENT RATING: _____

EVALUATION OF TEACHING EFFECTIVENESS OF FACULTY MEMBER BY DEPARTMENT CHAIR

Under each area are criteria to consider. These are not necessarily equal components of teaching effectiveness.

1) Knowledge

- Faculty member demonstrates knowledge of discipline.

- Faculty member demonstrates competence with course content that is relevant and thorough.

2) Course Organization and Planning

- Faculty member prepares assignments, handouts, exams, and/or activities to promote student interest and enhance learning.

- Faculty member demonstrates evidence of attention to active learning, writing, and critical thinking skills as appropriate.

- Faculty member implements course objectives appropriately.

3) Communication and Delivery

- Faculty member uses class time effectively.

- Faculty member uses effective instructional techniques and tools (including lecture, discussion, audio/visuals, group activities, or technology).

- Faculty member demonstrates efforts to stimulate student interest and achievement.

4) Policy/Procedure Practices

- Faculty member adheres to established college, discipline, and department policies and procedures.

- Faculty member performs assigned duties for the conduct of business of the department.

- Faculty member is available to students outside class.

EVALUATION OF TEACHING EFFECTIVENESS OF FACULTY MEMBER BY DEPARTMENT CHAIR
(Continued)

Rating Scale:

EP — Exemplary Professional Performance
Consistently exceeds accepted standards of professional performance
(JUSTIFICATION MUST BE INCLUDED)

HP — High Professional Performance
Frequently exceeds accepted standards of professional performance

SP — Standard Professional Performance
Consistently meets accepted standards of professional performance

MP — Minimal Performance
Does not consistently meet accepted standards of professional performance
(JUSTIFICATION MUST BE INCLUDED)

UP — Unsatisfactory Performance
Does not meet minimal standards of professional performance
(JUSTIFICATION MUST BE INCLUDED.)

Justification for ratings of EP, MP, or UP must be included on the following page.

1) Knowledge   Rating: _____

2) Course organization and planning   Rating: _____

3) Communication and delivery   Rating: _____

4) Policy/procedure practices   Rating: _____

To compute the Teaching Effectiveness rating of faculty member by department chair, assign the following values:

$$EP = 5 \qquad HP = 4 \qquad SP = 3 \qquad MP = 2 \qquad UP = 1$$

Directions: Add the four values assigned to the ratings, and divide by four to calculate the Teaching Effectiveness Rating of the faculty member. Do not round.

TEACHING EFFECTIVENESS RATING
OF FACULTY MEMBER BY DEPARTMENT CHAIR: _____

Justification of ratings of EP, MP, or UP from the previous page should follow. Ratings of HP or SP require no response.

1) Knowledge:

2) Course Organization and Planning:

3) Communication and Delivery:

4) Policy/Procedure Practices:

EVALUATION OF SERVICE

Instructions: After reviewing the Service Report in the Faculty Portfolio for Annual Evaluation, determine points for each of the appropriate items below.

A) Service to the Campus, Discipline, and Department

_____ Membership on campus, discipline, or department committee
(4 points per committee, maximum 12 points)

_____ Chair of campus, discipline, or department committee
(2 points in addition to membership points, maximum 4 points)

_____ Leader of campus, discipline, or department workshop or presentation
(2–4 points each, maximum 8 points)
(4 points for the preparation and original offering of the presentation, 2 points for repeating a previous presentation)

_____ Mentor of new faculty member
(4 points)

_____ Mentor of part-time faculty
(2 points)

B) Service to the College and Community

_____ Membership on college-wide councils or committees
(6 points per committee or council, maximum 12 points)

_____ Chair of college-wide council or committee
(4 points in addition to membership points)

_____ Leader of college-wide or community workshops, courses, or presentations
(2–4 points each, maximum 8 points)
(4 points for the preparation and original offering of the presentation, 2 points for repeating a previous presentation)

_____ Organizer of lecture series
(2 points, maximum 2 points)

_____ Advisor to student organization recognized by SGA
(4 points, maximum 4 points)

_____ Advisor/editor of college publication
(4 points)

_____ Application of recognized area of expertise in the community without pay
(2 points per activity, maximum 4 points)

_____ Participation in college-sponsored outreach activities
(2 points, maximum 2 points)

C) Other activities: Those activities, other than the ones noted on the preceding page, which directly contributed to either the academic or administrative functioning of the college

_____ (1–8 points; points should be assigned based upon the significance of the activity and the amount of effort involved and should be in line with other listed activities of comparable scope)

Total Service Points_____

Service Points	Rating Scale
27 and above	Exemplary Performance
18–26	High Performance
9–17	Standard Performance
5–8	Minimal Performance
0–4	Unsatisfactory Performance

To assign the Service Rating of Faculty Member, use the following values:

EP = 5   HP = 4   SP = 3   MP = 2   UP = 1

SERVICE RATING OF FACULTY MEMBER: _____

Report the Service Rating on Faculty Member Performance Review Summary.

EVALUATION OF PROFESSIONAL ACTIVITIES

Instructions: After reviewing the Professional Activities Report in the Faculty Portfolio for Annual Evaluation, determine points for each of the appropriate items below.

A) Professional Organizations

_____ Held current membership in professional organization
(2 points each, maximum 6 points)

_____ Served on a committee of a professional organization
(2 points each, maximum 4 points)

_____ Held an elective or appointed office or chaired a committee of a state or local professional organization
(4 points each, maximum 8 points)

_____ Held an elective or appointed office or chaired a committee of a regional or national professional organization
(6 points each, maximum 12 points)

B) Further Education and Degrees

_____ Received credit for a graduate course (other than dissertation or thesis hours)
(4 points per course, maximum 8 points)

_____ Participated in scholarly, pedagogical, or technological workshops or presentations at Georgia Perimeter College (excluding those that were required)
(2 points each, maximum 4 points)

_____ Participated in workshops, summer institutes, short courses, audited a graduate-level course, etc. (excluding Georgia Perimeter College activities)
(2 points each, maximum 4 points)

_____ Completed a graduate degree from an accredited institution
(6 points each)

C) Scholarly and/or Creative Activities

_____ Attended a professional conference
(2 points each, maximum 6 points)

_____ Gave a presentation at a professional conference
(4 points per presentation at a state or local conference, 6 points per presentation at a regional or national conference, maximum 10 points)

_____ Served on a discussion roundtable/panel
(2 points each, maximum 4 points)

_____ Published an article, short story, or poem in a scholarly publication
(6 points each, maximum 12 points)

_____ Published a new edition of a book
(4 points each, maximum 8 points)

C) Scholarly and/or Creative Activities (continued)

_____ Published a book review in an appropriate scholarly publication
(4 points per review, maximum 8 points)

_____ Served as an editor of a scholarly publication
(4 points each, maximum 8 points)

_____ Served as a referee for a scholarly publication
(1 point per submission refereed, maximum 2 points)

_____ Reviewed a manuscript for publication
(1 point per manuscript, maximum 2 points)

_____ Published a comment, note, or letter to the editor in a scholarly publication
(1 point each, maximum 2 points)

_____ Published an article, short story, or poem in a non-scholarly publication
(2 points each, maximum 4 points)

D) Awards, Grants, Artistic Commissions, and/or Fellowships

_____ Received an award, grant, artistic commission, or fellowship (excluding tuition grants for graduate study)
(2 points for a local award, grant, commission, or fellowship)
(4 points for a statewide award, grant, commission, or fellowship)
(6 points for a regional award, grant, commission, or fellowship)
(8 points for a national or international award, grant, commission, or fellowship)

_____ Served on a grant review panel
(2 points, maximum 2 points)

E) Other Activities: Those activities, other than the ones noted above, which directly contributed to either the academic or administrative functioning of the college

_____ (1–8 points; points should be assigned based upon the significance of the accomplishment and the amount of effort involved and should be in line with other listed activities of comparable scope)

F) Fine Arts and Humanities Faculty only

_____ Performed in a musical, dramatic, or media production
(6 points each, maximum of 12 points)

_____ Created a musical, dramatic, or media work which was performed, published, exhibited, and/or broadcast (8 points each, maximum of 12 points)

_____ Directed or produced a musical, dramatic, or media event, performance, broadcast, recording, exhibition (6 points each, maximum of 12 points)

_____ Designed and/or implemented the technical work (scenery, costume, lighting, sound etc.) for a musical, dramatic, or media production (4 points each, maximum of 8 points)

Total Professional Activities Points_____

Professional Activities Points	Rating Scale
27 and above	Exemplary Performance
18–26	High Performance
9–17	Standard Performance
5–8	Minimal Performance
0–4	Unsatisfactory Performance

To assign the Service Rating of Faculty Member, use the following values:

EP = 5   HP = 4   SP = 3   MP = 2   UP = 1

PROFESSIONAL ACTIVITIES RATING OF FACULTY MEMBER: _____

Report the Professional Activities Rating on Faculty Member Performance Review Summary.

SUMMARY OF WEIGHTS TO BE USED IN FACULTY EVALUATION
(From the Faculty Portfolio)

Evaluation Period: July 1, _____ –June 30, _____

Part I—Overall Evaluation

Instructions: Part I was completed at the end of the academic year prior to the evaluation period. The faculty member should have a copy, and the department chair should include the document in the annual evaluation of the faculty member. All selected percentages should be within the indicated ranges, in multiples of 10 (i.e., 10%, 20%, 30%, etc.), and must total 100%.

TEACHING EFFECTIVENESS
(Choose from 50%–70%)
_____%

SERVICE
(Choose from 10%–30%)
_____%

PROFESSIONAL ACTIVITIES
(Choose from 10%–30%)
_____%

Part II—Evaluation of Teaching Effectiveness

Instructions: Report weights submitted with the Faculty Portfolio.

SELF
(Choose from 10%–20%)
_____%

PEER
(Choose from 10%–20%)
_____%

STUDENTS
(Choose from 10%–20%)
_____%

DEPARTMENT CHAIR
(Choose from 40%–60%)
_____%

TOTAL
_____%
(100%)

INSTRUCTIONS

Step 1: Calculate the Overall Teaching Effectiveness Rating, using the Declaration of Weights and the ratings of Teaching Effectiveness from the Self-Evaluation, Student Rating Summary, and Evaluation of Teaching Effectiveness of Faculty Member by Department Chair.

Example:

1) Suppose the percentages from a faculty member's declaration of weights were as follows:

TEACHING EFFECTIVENESS

SELF (Choose from 10%–20%)	20%
PEER (Choose from 10%–20%)	20%
STUDENTS (Choose from 10%–20%)	10%
DEPARTMENT CHAIR (Choose from 40%–60%)	50%

TOTAL 100%

2) Suppose the faculty member's ratings were as follows:

TEACHING EFFECTIVENESS

SELF-RATING	4.25
PEER RATING OF COURSE MATERIALS	3.75
STUDENT RATING	4.00
DEPARTMENT CHAIR RATING	3.75

Calculate the Overall Teaching Effectiveness Rating using the following formula:
20%(Self Rating) + 20%(Peer Rating) + 10%(Student Rating) + 50%(Department Chair Rating)
.2(4.25) + .2(3.75) + .1 (4.00) + .5(3.75) = 3.875

The faculty member's overall Teaching Effectiveness rating is 3.875.

Step 2: Report the Service Rating of Faculty Member.

Step 3: Report the Professional Activities Rating of Faculty Member.

Step 4: Calculate the Overall Faculty Evaluation Rating using the Declaration of Weights and ratings for Teaching Effectiveness (50%–70%), Service (10%–30%), and Professional Activities (10%–30%).

FACULTY MEMBER PERFORMANCE REVIEW SUMMARY

_____   _____
Faculty Member   Department Chair

_____   _____
Department   Campus

Calculation of the Teaching Effectiveness Rating:

Declared Weights:

    SELF
    (10%–20%)   _____

    PEER
    (10%–20%)   _____

    STUDENTS
    (10%–20%)   _____

    DEPARTMENT CHAIR (DC)
    (40%–60%)   _____

(Self %)(Self-Rating) + (Peer %)(Peer Rating) + (Student %)(Student Rating) + (DC %)(DC Rating)

    (_____)(_____) + (_____)(_____) + (_____)(_____) + (_____)(_____) = _____

Round to two decimals.

    TEACHING EFFECTIVENESS RATING   _____

    SERVICE RATING   _____

    PROFESSIONAL ACTIVITIES RATING   _____

CALCULATION OF THE OVERALL FACULTY EVALUATION RATING

Declared Weights:

    TEACHING EFFECTIVENESS
    (50%–70%)   _____

    SERVICE
    (10%–30%)   _____

    PROFESSIONAL ACTIVITIES
    (10%–30%)   _____

(Teaching Effectiveness %)(Teaching Effectiveness Rating) + (Service %)(Service Rating) +
(Professional Activities %)(Professional Activities Rating)

    (_____)(_____) + (_____)(_____) + (_____)(_____) = _____
    Round to two decimals.

OVERALL FACULTY EVALUATION RATING: _____

ADDENDUM

Georgia Perimeter College Faculty Evaluation Handbook

Board of Regents' Policy on Faculty Evaluation (Policy 803.07)

In 1996, the Board of Regents of the University System of Georgia accepted the report of the Task Force on Faculty and Staff Development and adopted many of that group's recommendations. Included in those adopted measures are policies concerning faculty evaluation.

Purpose

The purpose of faculty evaluation is to provide regular feedback to faculty members regarding their performance so that they can provide high quality service to institutions in the University System of Georgia. Regular evaluations can provide an opportunity to assess strengths and weaknesses of faculty performance. Faculty evaluation should encourage and reward superior performance and offer the opportunity for career development when the process identifies ways to improve the performance. Each institution must establish procedures for evaluation of faculty. These procedures must include the following:

Annual Evaluation of Faculty

1) Evaluation of faculty members must take place each year.

2) Each institution must establish the criteria for evaluation consistent with Board of Regents' policy and the statutes and mission of the institution.

3) Each institution must specify who is responsible for the annual evaluation of faculty members and provide appropriate training for those who undertake this responsibility.

4) Faculty members with teaching responsibilities must be evaluated on the criterion of teaching effectiveness. As defined by the institution, the measures of teaching effectiveness must include at a minimum a combination of written student evaluations and peer evaluations. The procedures for conducting these evaluations must be specified in writing by the institution.

5) Each institution must require that the faculty member's participation in faculty development during the current year and the faculty member's plans for the coming year be included in the annual evaluation. The person responsible for the annual evaluation should participate as appropriate in evaluating past and planned faculty development activities.

6) Faculty members must receive a written report of the evaluation. The faculty member, if he or she desires, shall have the opportunity to add a written response to the written report of the evaluation. The person responsible for the annual evaluation may then comment on this response if he or she desires. At that point, the written evaluation, together with any written response to it by the evaluated faculty member and any comment upon that response by the person responsible for preparing it, should be sent to the administrative office at least one level above the faculty member's administrative unit, as specified by the institution. *(Changing the Results of Higher Education—Faculty and Staff Development 1996, pp. 41–42).*

FAIRMONT STATE UNIVERSITY CASE STUDY: SCHOOL OF BUSINESS AUTOMATED FACULTY EVALUATION SYSTEM

by Rebecca Schaupp, Ed.D., & Tracie Dodson, Ed.D.

The Mandate for a New Faculty Evaluation System

The West Virginia Higher Education System has undergone significant changes since 2001. Fairmont State is a prime example of the rapid changes that have occurred. During the 2001 legislative session, a bill was passed mandating that a merit-based pay structure be used in public institutions of higher education in West Virginia. Institutional compliance with this legislative mandate required Fairmont State to analyze its existing evaluation instrument and develop an objective performance evaluation instrument that would more accurately measure performance. This case study details the process the faculty and dean used to overcome obstacles and successfully develop, automate, and implement the Fairmont State University School of Business's Faculty Evaluation System.

The University's Response to the Mandate

The institution decided to develop its new faculty evaluation system using Raoul Arreola's eight-step process for developing a comprehensive faculty evaluation system. Dr. Arreola was invited to campus to conduct a workshop on the process with the administration and members of the Faculty Evaluation Task Group and presented a keynote address at a general faculty meeting.

The Faculty Evaluation Task Group was a system-wide committee consisting of division heads, faculty members, and administrators led by the provost and vice president for academic affairs and the then-vice president of the community and technical college that works in collaboration with and shares the geographical location of Fairmont State University. The task group was given the charge to develop a comprehensive faculty evaluation system that would be better suited to merit-based pay raises. This committee established guidelines that were used as the basis of the individual unit's system of evaluation.

Discussions of the need for change began with the administrative leaders of each academic unit discussing the matter with their respective faculty. At this stage departments began to shape their own plans and, to some extent, also shared what they had developed with each other. While that was an excellent beginning to our development, the School of Business decided to bring in another outside consultant, Dr. Thomas Hawk from Frostburg State University in Maryland, to review the actual content-related activities as well as the developing instrument. Dr. Hawk came with considerable experience in implementing Dr. Arreola's eight-step process, having chaired the task force at Frostburg State University responsible for developing their comprehensive faculty evaluation system.

Several mandates were made at the institutional level, including the frequency of meetings and evaluations and the timing of the evaluations. At the beginning of each calendar year, faculty meet with their dean or chair to establish goals and objectives for the year. The three roles, which are the three traditional roles of teaching and advising, scholarship, and service, as well as their weight ranges, are specified at the institutional level. All ratings are to be based on a 4-point scale. At their initial meeting, faculty, in consultation with their dean or chair, establish exact weights within the institution-set range for the upcoming year. The remaining recommendations, including the activities that comprised the three faculty roles, further limitations of the weight ranges, specific evaluation sources, evaluation methods, rating scale, exact forms and their development, the contents of faculty portfolios, and any appeals process are left to the discretion of the department or school (with the administration's approval after development).

The School of Business Response to the Mandate

The dean's perspective. From the dean's perspective it was evident that the president and members of his cabinet had a very sincere desire to develop an evaluation system that would be much more objective than the previous system. For years there had been much skepticism on the part of faculty with regard to the validity of the evaluation process and the lack of money earmarked for merit raises. It was recognized early on as a necessary evil on the part of the faculty; however, it was also something that was required for both probationary and tenured professors. It was considered very important that the dean communicate with the faculty members in the School of Business every step of the way. The institution had to have something in place in a short amount of time in order to meet the mandate that, henceforth, raises would be based solely on merit.

The faculty perspective. From the School of Business faculty's perspective, it was clear that the university administration was committed to developing a revised faculty evaluation system. It was a mandate. What also appeared clear was the fact that the faculty was, at best, apprehensive and, at worst, hostile about the thought of a new system. There had been no money for raises in the previous years, and the thought of committing a significant amount of work to a new system was not well received. The thought was "Why spend a lot of time developing a system for merit raises when there is no money to fund the raises? No matter how well we develop the system or how well we perform as academics, we will not have any more money than we do right now."

Nonetheless, the legislature made the decision for the faculty and certain responses and decisions were expected. Although the institution had made the decision to use Dr. Arreola's model to develop the revised system, each academic unit was given autonomy within that framework. Initially, the School of Business decided to use its resident faculty as sources of expertise. The school was quite fortunate to have on staff faculty members who had industry experience in human resources, employment law, industrial and labor relations, and information systems. Throughout 2001–2004 several School of Business faculty and ad hoc committee meetings were held to determine the components and the corresponding weights for each role.

Building the System

The School of Business had a growing information systems department that had skill in developing databases and programming for front-end database interaction. Thus, the decision was made to build an automated system. Because this project required a focus and a significant amount of time on the part of the developer, a recent graduate was contracted to build the program. Working closely with the dean and two faculty members (one who was an assistant professor and coordinator of information systems and the other an assistant professor of human resources management), the programmer began to produce a prototype system for evaluation. The School of Business faculty was immediately in favor of the process, because it would enable a faster completion of the evaluation process.

Since the information systems department taught advanced courses in Visual Basic 6.0, and since this package was under site license and was well known, it was selected as the language chosen for the development of the School of Business faculty evaluation system program. After the program was completed it was tested and updated for approximately two months until it was considered ready to go live, at which time it was placed on the university's intranet and made available online to the faculty.

Implementing the System

As with any new process or procedure, training is a major component in successful implementation. Throughout the development stages, input was sought from faculty and other members of the campus community on a continuous basis; however, this input did not preclude the need for training workshops and one-on-one mentoring in the use of the program on the part of the faculty and the dean. Part of the contract with the programmer specified the development and presentation of faculty workshops and seminars. In addition, a detailed help menu was established in the program that could be accessed via the standard menus and the F1 key on a computer.

During this initial use, the need for changes became apparent to better ensure smooth operations. The following is a partial list of changes made to improve the efficiency of the program:

1) Change evaluation year from academic year to calendar year

2) Ability for the faculty to submit Parts I, II, and III of self-evaluation at different times; in the original program design faculty had to submit all self-evaluation parts (teaching and advising, service, and scholarship) at the same time

3) Record of final score on a 4.00 scale and on a percentage basis

4) Ability to delete evaluation for faculty information

5) Integration of IDEA scale system for student ratings

6) Ability to change, modify, or adjust the IDEA scoring scale without having to recode

7) Ability to change or modify all evaluation criteria without having to recode; evaluation criteria are stored independently in the database

8) Ability for the school head to change or modify student rating scores entered by the faculty; IDEA scores

are entered by each faculty member; if for any reason the wrong score is entered, the school head can make appropriate corrections

9) Change in terminology: from *school chair* to *school head; instructor area* to *faculty area*

10) Development of a user's manual to be used in conjunction with the computer-based version

11) Ability to modify self-selected weight any time before evaluation activities start

12) Ability for the school head to modify the evaluation scoring scheme, which allows changing the way evaluation scores are computed

13) Graph view of evaluation final scores

14) Ability for the program to perform independently and maintain system back-up locally or remotely

Using the System

When faculty enter the online program at the beginning of the calendar year, they login and enter their desired weights for the upcoming year (Figure 16.1). To ensure that weights have been selected, faculty will not be allowed to proceed until they enter this information. Figure 16.2 shows the screen presented to faculty for role weight selection. Once weights are entered, the main Faculty Evaluation System screen opens (Figure 16.3), and the faculty member can navigate to any area of the program. The main faculty screen has a menu bar, a large icon toolbar, a welcome message, and buttons for entering evaluation data. Faculty can easily review their prior evaluations by selecting "Search Past Evaluations" and then the year from the Tool menu.

The communication center screen (Figure 16.4) allows faculty, department heads, and system administrators to communicate within the system. There are some automatic messages that are sent upon completion of actions. For example, once a faculty member has completed his or her evaluation for the year, a message is sent indicating all peer and department evaluations are entered and his or her final reports are ready to be printed. In addition, the dean or chair can enter the faculty area (Figure 16.5) to view information entered for a particular faculty member, edit information, or remove the account.

As data is entered into the system by the various approved sources, summary screens are generated which provide information concerning the faculty member's evaluation (Figures 16.6, 16.7, and 16.8). The dean and department chair also have access to this information through their respective administrator screens.

Figure 16.1 Faculty Login Screen

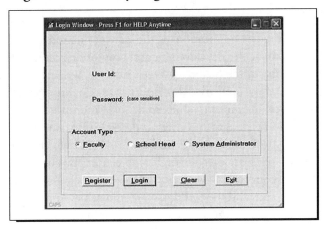

Figure 16.2 Role Weight Selection Dialog Box

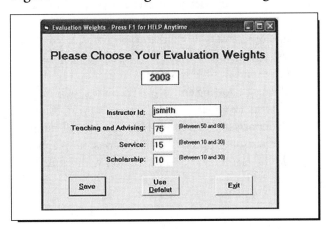

Figure 16.3 Main Faculty Evaluation Screen

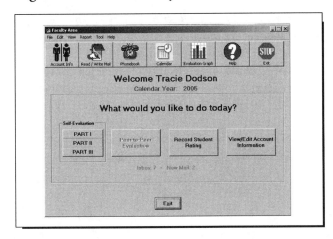

Figure 16.4 Communication Center Screen

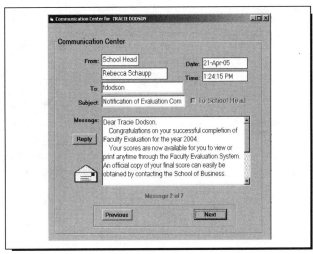

Figure 16.5 Administrator's Welcome Screen

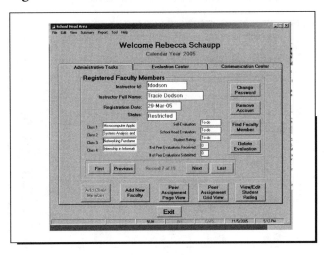

Figure 16.6 Role Summary Report for Teaching and Advising

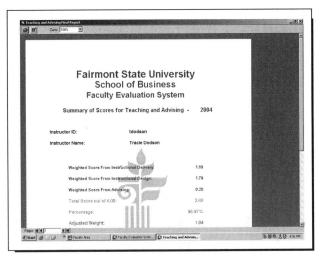

Figure 16.7 Faculty Activity Summary

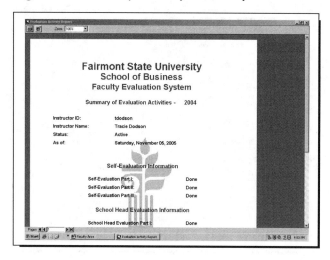

Figure 16.8 Final Faculty Evaluation Report

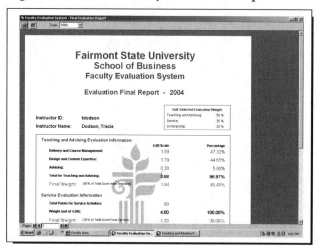

CONCLUSIONS

Currently, there is great discussion at the institutional level regarding the application of the new evaluation instruments to faculty development and promotion and tenure decisions. In the School of Business's case, because items were clearly identified for point values, many faculty achieved maximum values in scholarship and service. Questions arose from other academic units concerning the rigor of the activities and the ease with which each faculty member met his or her objectives. Business faculty responded by saying they knew what their goals were for the year, and they worked hard and achieved them.

As noted earlier, the current system in operation was written in Visual Basic 6.0. Because the software limits the program's web interface capabilities, a new updated version of the software is in the works. In addition, updates allowing the export of data to an Excel spreadsheet and the import of data from external sources (including employed faculty, login and user information, IDEA ratings, and other available data) are being considered. A new database schema is also being developed with a more comprehensive and flexible system for storage and retrieval of annual data—allowing end-of-year activities to be ongoing as new items are entered for the upcoming year. Many additional reports including multiyear reports and summary and comparison reports. Other revisions are planned to provide the faculty and administration with more useful information.

REFERENCES

Georgia Perimeter College. (1998–1999). *Faculty evaluation, promotion, and tenure handbook.* DeKalb, GA: Author.

Miller, R. I. (1972). *Evaluating faculty performance.* San Francisco, CA: Jossey-Bass.

Bibliography

Since the publication of the first edition of this book in 1995, electronic communications technology, notably the Internet with its vast document-searching capability, has nearly obviated the need for a bibliography in a static published document such as this. A quick Google search on such terms as *faculty evaluation, student ratings,* or *faculty development* will instantaneously generate a list of hundreds, if not thousands, of documents. As of this writing, entering the term *faculty evaluation* in the ERIC search engine (see www.eric.ed.gov) alone generates 6,860 hits. Many professional organizations, including the American Educational Research Association (see www.aera.net) now offer searchable, online access to full-text archives of articles published in its journals, many of which are the primary outlet for much of the literature on faculty evaluation. So, why include a bibliography here? The purpose of the bibliography that follows is *not* to provide an exhaustive listing of all publications in the field of faculty evaluation, but, rather, to provide an entry resource for those wishing to pursue either a review of the literature or focus on a specific issue. In most cases the publications listed are less than 30 years old—although certain older "classic" publications have been retained. Also, publications that may have achieved some historical notoriety, but that subsequent rigorous research has proven to be flawed and erroneous, have been omitted. My intent has been to list only those documents that provide a meaningful contribution to either a theoretical/technical discussion, or a historical perspective on the development, of the concepts and practices surrounding faculty evaluation, faculty development, student ratings, and the characteristics of effective teaching. The chief criterion for including a publication in this list is that it be reasonably accessible. For this reason references to many otherwise notable conference papers, newsletters, and in-house reports that may be referenced in other publications, but are very difficult to find, have been omitted. However, some of the significant papers and in-house published reports pertaining to the evaluation of teaching and the general issues of faculty evaluation and faculty development can be found at the following web sites:

- For papers (and reports of panel discussions) related to faculty evaluation, student ratings, faculty development, and other related topics presented at the American Educational Research Association conventions, go to www.umanitoba.ca/uts/sigfted.

- For in-house publications on the IDEA student rating form and related issues, especially those authored by Bill Cashin, go to www.idea.ksu.edu/resources/Papers.html.

- For in-house reports on the SIR II student rating form published by the Educational Testing Service, especially those authored by John Centra, go to www.ets.org.

- For papers by Raoul Arreola, Michael Theall, and Lawrence Aleamoni related to the meta-profession model, go to www.cedanet.com/meta.

Abbott, R. D., Wulff, D. H., Nyquist, J. D., Ropp, V. A., & Hess, C. W. (1990). Satisfaction with processes of collecting student opinions about instruction: The student perspective. *Journal of Educational Psychology, 82*(2), 201–206.

Abrami, P. C. (1984). Using meta-analytic techniques to review the instructional evaluation literature. *Postsecondary Education Newsletter, 6,* 8.

Abrami, P. C. (1985). Dimensions of effective college instruction. *Review of Higher Education, 8*(3), 211–228.

Abrami, P. C. (1988). SEEQ and ye shall find. A review of Marsh's students' evaluations of university teaching. *Instructional Evaluation, 9*(2), 19–27.

Abrami, P. C. (1989). How should we use student ratings to evaluate teaching? *Research in Higher Education, 30*(2), 221–227.

Abrami, P. C. (1989). Seeking the truth about student ratings of instruction. *Educational Researcher 18,* 43–45.

Abrami, P. C. (1993). Using student rating norm groups for summative evaluation. *Evaluation and Faculty Development 13,* 5–9.

Abrami, P. C. (2001). Improving judgments about teaching effectiveness: How to lie without statistics. In M. Theall, P. C. Abrami, & L. A. Metes (Eds.), *New directions for institutional research: No. 109. The student ratings debate: Are they valid? How can we best use them?* (pp. 97–102). San Francisco, CA: Jossey-Bass.

Abrami, P. C. (2001). Improving judgments about teaching effectiveness using teacher rating forms. In M. Theall, P. C. Abrami, & L. A. Metes (Eds.), *New directions for institutional research: No. 109. The student ratings debate: Are they valid? How can we best use them?* (pp. 59–87). San Francisco, CA: Jossey-Bass.

Abrami, P. C., & d'Apollonia, S. (1990). The dimensionality of ratings and their use in personnel decisions. In M. Theall & J. Franklin (Eds.), *New directions for teaching and learning: No. 43. Student ratings of instruction: Issues for improving practice* (pp. 97–111). San Francisco, CA: Jossey-Bass.

Abrami, P. C., & d'Apollonia, S. (1991). Multidimensional students' evaluations of teaching effectiveness—Generalizability of N = 1 research: Comment on Marsh (1991). *Journal of Educational Psychology, 83*(3), 411–415.

Abrami, P. C., & d'Apollonia, S. (1999). Current concerns are past concerns. *American Psychologist, 54*(7), 519–520.

Abrami, P. C., & Mizener, D. A. (1983). Does the attitude similarity of college professors and their students produce 'bias' in course evaluations? *American Educational Research Journal, 20*(1), 123–136.

Abrami, P. C., & Mizener, D. A. (1985). Student/instructor attitude similarity, student ratings, and course performance. *Journal of Educational Psychology, 77,* 693–702.

Abrami, P. C., & Murphy, V. (1980). *A catalogue of systems for student evaluation of instruction.* Montreal, Canada: McGill University Centre for Teaching and Learning.

Abrami, P. C., d'Apollonia, S., & Cohen, P. A. (1990). Validity of student ratings of instruction: What we know and what we do not know. *Journal of Educational Psychology, 82*(2), 285–296.

Abrami, P. C., d'Apollonia, S., & Rosenfield, S. (1996). The dimensionality of student ratings of instruction: What we know and what we do not. In J. C. Smart (Ed.), *Higher Education: Handbook of theory and research* (pp. 213–264). New York, NY: Agathon Press.

Abrami, P. C., d'Apollonia, S., & Rosenfield, S. (1997). The dimensionality of student ratings of instruction: What we know and what we do not. In. R. P. Perry & J. C. Smart (Eds.), *Effective teaching in higher education: Research and practice* (pp.321–367). New York, NY: Agathon Press.

Abrami, P. C., Dickens, W. J., Perry, R. P., & Leventhal, L. (1980). Do teacher standards for assigning grades affect student evaluations of instruction? *Journal of Educational Psychology, 72,* 107–118.

Abrami, P. C., Leventhal, L., & Perry, R. (1976). Do teacher evaluation forms reveal as much about students as about teachers? *Journal of Educational Psychology, 68*(4), 441–445.

Abrami, P. C., Leventhal, L., & Perry, R. P. (1982). Educational seduction. *Review of Educational Research, 52*(3), 446–464.

Abrami, P. C., Perry, R. P., & Leventhal, L. (1982). The relationship between student personality characteristics, teacher ratings, and student achievement. *Journal of Educational Psychology, 74,* 111–125.

Aleamoni, L. M. (1972). Response to Professor W. Edwards Deming's 'memorandum on teaching'. *The American Statistician, 26*(4), 54.

Aleamoni, L. M. (1973). Course evaluation questionnaire at the University of Illinois. *Evaluation, 1*(2), 73–74.

Aleamoni, L. M. (1976). On the invalidity of student ratings for administrative personnel decisions. *Journal of Higher Education, 47*(5), 607–610.

Aleamoni, L. M. (1976). Proposed system for rewarding and improving instructional effectiveness. *College University, 51*(3), 330–338.

Aleamoni, L. M. (1976). Typical faculty concerns about student evaluation of instruction. *National Association of Colleges and Teachers of Agriculture Journal, 20*(1), 16–21.

Aleamoni, L. M. (1977). How can an institution improve and reward instructional effectiveness? *Faculty Development and Evaluation in Higher Education, 3*(4), 4–9.

Aleamoni, L. M. (1978). Development and factorial validation of the Arizona Course/Instructor Evaluation Questionnaire. *Educational and Psychological Measurement, 38*(6), 1063–1067.

Aleamoni, L. M. (1978). The usefulness of student evaluations in improving college teaching. *Instructional Science, 7*(1), 95–105.

Aleamoni, L. M. (1980). Students can evaluate teaching effectiveness. *National Forum, 60*(4), 41.

Aleamoni, L. M. (1980). The use of student evaluations in the improvement of instruction. *National Association of Colleges and Teachers of Agriculture Journal, 24*(3), 18–21.

Aleamoni, L. M. (1981). Student ratings of instruction. In J. Millman (Ed.), *Handbook of Teacher Evaluation* (pp. 110–145). Beverly Hills, CA: Sage.

Aleamoni, L. M. (1984). The dynamics of faculty evaluation. In P. Seldin (Ed.), *Changing practices in faculty evaluation.* San Francisco, CA: Jossey-Bass.

Aleamoni, L. M. (1987). Evaluating instructional effectiveness can be a rewarding experience. *Journal of Plant Disease, 71*(4), 377–379.

Aleamoni, L. M. (1987). Some practical approaches for faculty and administrators. In L. M. Aleamoni (Ed.), *Techniques for instructional improvement and evaluation.* San Francisco, CA: Jossey-Bass.

Aleamoni, L. M. (1987). Student rating myths versus research facts. *Journal of Personnel Evaluation in Education, 1,* 111–119.

Aleamoni, L. M. (1987). Typical faculty concerns about student evaluation of teaching. In L. M. Aleamoni (Ed.), *New directions for teaching and learning: No. 31. Techniques for evaluating and improving instruction* (pp. 25–31). San Francisco, CA: Jossey-Bass.

Aleamoni, L. M. (1990). Faculty development research in colleges, universities, and professional schools: The challenge. *Journal of Personnel Evaluation in Education, 3,* 193–195.

Aleamoni, L. M. (1996). Why do we need norms of student ratings to evaluate faculty: Reaction to McKeachie. *Evaluation and Faculty Development, 14,* 18–19.

Aleamoni, L. M. (1999). Student rating myths versus research facts from 1924 to 1998. *Journal of Personnel Evaluation in Education, 13*(2), 153–166.

Aleamoni, L. M., & Graham, M. H. (1974). The relationship between CEQ ratings and instructor's rank, class size, and course level. *Journal of Educational Measurement, 11*(3), 189–202.

Aleamoni, L. M., & Hexner, P. Z. (1980). A review of the research on student evaluation and a report on the effect of different sets of instructions on student course and instructor evaluation. *Instructional Science, 9*(1), 67–84.

Aleamoni, L. M., & Spencer, R. E. (1973). The Illinois Course Evaluation Questionnaire: A description of its development and a report of some of its results. *Educational and Psychological Measurement, 33,* 669–684.

Aleamoni, L. M., & Stevens, J. J. (1984). The effectiveness of consultation in support of student evaluation feedback: A ten-year follow-up. *The Pen, 7.*

Aleamoni, L. M., & Thomas, G. S. (1980). Differential relationships of student, instructor, and course characteristics to general and specific items on a course questionnaire. *Teaching of Psychology, 7*(4), 233–235.

Aleamoni, L. M., & Yimer, M. (1973). An investigation of the relationship between colleague rating, student rating, research productivity, and academic rank in rating instructional effectiveness. *Journal of Educational Psychology, 64*(3), 274–277.

Aleamoni, L. M., Yimer, M., & Mahan, M. M. (1972). Teacher folklore and sensitivity of a course evaluation questionnaire. *Psychological Reports, 31,* 607–614.

Ambady, N., & Rosenthal, R. (1993, March). Half a minute: Predicting teacher evaluations from thin slices of nonverbal behavior and physical attractiveness. *Journal of Personality and Social Psychology, 64,* 431–441.

American Association of University Professors. (1998). *Post-tenure review: An AAUP response.* Washington, DC: Author.

Amey, M. J. (2004). Evaluating outreach performance. In C. Colbeck (Ed.), *New directions for institutional research: No. 113. Evaluating faculty performance.* San Francisco, CA: Jossey-Bass.

Anderson, L. W., & Krathwohl, D. (2001). *A taxonomy for learning, teaching, and assessing: A revision of Bloom's taxonomy of educational objectives.* New York, NY: Longman.

Andreson, L. W., Powell, J., & Smith, E. (1987). Competent teaching and its appraisal. *Assessment and Evaluation in Higher Education, 12*(1), 66–72.

Andrews, H. A. (1985). *Evaluating for excellence.* Stillwater, OK: New Forums Press.

Angelo, T. A., & Cross, P. (1993). *Classroom assessment techniques: A handbook for college teachers* (2nd ed.). San Francisco, CA: Jossey-Bass.

Anikeef, A. M. (1953). Factors affecting student evaluation of college faculty members. *Journal of Applied Psychology, 37,* 458–460.

Armstrong, J. S. (1998). Are student ratings of instruction useful? *American Psychologist, 53*(11), 1223–1224.

Arreola, R. A. (1979). Strategy for Developing a Comprehensive Faculty Evaluation System. *Engineering Education, 70*(3), 239–244.

Arreola, R. A. (1983). Establishing successful faculty evaluation and development programs. In A. Smith (Ed.), *New directions for community colleges: No. 41: Evaluating faculty and staff* (pp. 83–90). San Francisco, CA: Jossey-Bass.

Arreola, R. A. (1983). Students can distinguish between personality and content/organization in rating teachers. *Phi Delta Kappan, 65*(3), 222–223.

Arreola, R. A. (1984). Evaluation of faculty performance: Key issues. In P. Seldin (Ed.), *Changing practices in faculty evaluation* (pp. 79–85). San Francisco, CA: Jossey-Bass.

Arreola, R. A. (1986). Evaluating the Dimensions of Teaching. *Instructional Evaluation, 8*(2), 4–14.

Arreola, R. A. (1987). A faculty evaluation model for community and junior colleges. In L. Aleamoni (Ed.), *New directions for teaching and learning: No. 31. Faculty development and faculty evaluation practices in community and junior colleges* (pp. 65–74). San Francisco, CA: Jossey-Bass.

Arreola, R. A. (1987). The role of student government in faculty evaluation. In L. M. Aleamoni (Ed.), *New directions for teaching and learning: No. 31. Techniques for evaluating and improving instruction* (pp. 39–46). San Francisco, CA: Jossey-Bass.

Arreola, R. A. (1989). Defining and evaluating the elements of teaching. In W. Cashin (Ed.), *Proceedings of the sixth annual academic chairperson's conference.* Manhattan, KS: Center for Faculty Evaluation and Development, Kansas State University.

Arreola, R. A. (1997.). On the tightrope: The department chair as faculty evaluator and developer. *The Department Chair, 8*(1), 3–5.

Arreola, R. A. (1998). Evaluating faculty performance: An administrative perspective. *Administrator, 17*(8), 6.

Arreola, R. A. (1998). Facilitating faculty use of technology in teaching. *The Department Chair, 9*(1), 1, 14–15.

Arreola, R. A. (1999). Issues in Developing a Faculty Evaluation System. *American Journal of Occupational Therapy, 53*(1), 56–63.

Arreola, R. A. (2000). Higher education's meta-profession [Interview]. *The Department Chair, 11*(2), 4–5.

Arreola, R. A. (2005). Monster at the foot of the bed: Surviving the challenge of marketplace forces on higher education. In S. Chadwick-Blossey & D. R. Robertson (Eds.), *To Improve the Academy: Vol 24. Resources for faculty, instructional, and organizational development* (pp. 15–28). Bolton, MA: Anker.

Arreola, R. A., & Aleamoni, L. M. (1990). Practical decisions in developing and operating a faculty evaluation system. In M. Theall & J. Franklin (Eds.), *New directions for teaching and learning: No. 43. Student ratings of instruction: Issues for improving practice* (pp. 37–55). San Francisco, CA: Jossey-Bass.

Arubayi, E. (1986). Students' evaluation of instruction in higher education: A review. *Assessment and Evaluation in Higher Education, 11*(1), 1–10.

Austin, A. (1996). Institutional and departmental cultures: The relationship between teaching and research. In J. Braxton (Ed.), *New directions for institutional research: No. 90. Faculty teaching and research: Is there a conflict?* San Francisco, CA: Jossey-Bass.

Avi-Itzhak, T., & Kremer, L. (1983). The effects of organizational factors on student ratings and perceived instructions. *Higher Education, 12*(4), 411–418.

Avi-Itzhak, T., & Kremer, L. (1985). An investigation into the relationship between university faculty attitudes toward student rating and organizational and background factors. *Educational Research Quarterly, 10*(2), 31–38.

Baird, J. S., Jr. (1987). Perceived learning in relation to student evaluation of university instruction. *Journal of Educational Psychology, 79*(1), 90–91.

Ballard, M. J., Reardon, J., & Nelson, L. (1976). Student and peer rating of faculty. *Teaching of Psychology, 3*, 115–119.

Bannister, B. D., Kinicki, A. J., & Denisi, A. J. (1987). A new method for the statistical control of rating error in performance ratings. *Educational and Psychological Measurement, 47*(3), 583–596.

Banz, M. L., & Rodgers, J. L. (1985). Dimensions underlying student ratings of instruction: A multidimensional scaling analysis. *American Educational Research Journal, 22*(2), 267–272.

Barke, C. R., Tollefson, N., & Tracy, D. B. (1983). Relationship between course entry attitudes and end-of-course ratings. *Journal of Educational Psychology, 75*(1), 75–85.

Barnes, L. L., & Barnes, M. W. (1993). Academic discipline and generalizability of student evaluations of instruction. *Research in Higher Education, 34*(2), 135–149.

Basow, S. A., & Distenfeld, M. S. (1985). Teacher expressiveness: More important for males than females? *Journal of Educational Psychology, 77*, 45–52.

Basow, S. A., & Howe, K. G. (1987). Evaluations of college professors: Effects of professors' sex-type, and sex, and students' sex. *Psychological Reports, 60*, 671–678.

Basow, S. A., & Silberg, N. T. (1987). Student evaluations of college professors: Are female and male professors rated differently? *Journal of Educational Psychology, 79*(3), 308–314.

Bass, R. J. (2000). Technology, evaluation, and the visibility of teaching and learning. In K. E. Ryan (Ed.), *New directions for teaching and learning: No. 83. Evaluating teaching in higher education: A vision of the future.* San Francisco, CA: Jossey-Bass.

Batista, E. (1976). The place of colleague evaluation in the appraisal of college teaching: A review of the literature. *Research in Higher Education, 4*(3), 257–271.

Beaty, L. (2001). Broadening the context for teaching evaluation. In P. Abrami & C. Knapper (Eds.), *New directions for teaching and learning: No. 88. Fresh approaches to the evaluation of teaching.* San Francisco, CA: Jossey-Bass.

Bednash, G. (1991). Tenure review: Process and outcomes. *Review of Higher Education, 15*(1), 47–63.

Behrendt, R. L., & Parsons, M. H. (1983). Evaluation of part-time faculty. In R. J. Ernst (Ed.), *New directions for community colleges: No. 11. Adjusting to collective bargaining* (pp. 33–43). San Francisco, CA: Jossey-Bass.

Bejar, I. I. (1975). A survey of selected administrative practices supporting student evaluation of instructional programs. *Research in Higher Education, 3,* 77–86.

Bell, M. E. (1977). Peer evaluation as a method of faculty development. *Journal of the College and University Personnel Association, 28*(4), 15–17.

Bendig, A. W. (1952). A preliminary study of the effect of academic level, sex, and course variables on student rating of psychology instructors. *Journal of Psychology, 34,* 2–126.

Bendig, A. W. (1953). Relation of level of course achievement of students, instructor, and course ratings in introductory psychology. *Educational and Psychological Measurement, 13,* 437–488.

Bennet, J. B. (1985). Periodic evaluation of tenured faculty performance. In J. S. Stark (Ed.), *New directions for higher education: No. 13. Promoting consumer protection for students* (pp. 65–73). San Francisco, CA: Jossey-Bass.

Bennett, S. K. (1982). Student perceptions of and expectations for male and female instructors: Evidence relating to the question of gender bias in teaching evaluation. *Journal of Educational Psychology, 74,* 170–179.

Bergman, J. (1980). Peer evaluation of university faculty: A monograph. *College Student Journal, 14*(3, Pt. 2), 1–21.

Bergquist, W. H., & Phillips, S. R. (1975). Components of an effective faculty development program. *Journal of Higher Education, 46*(2), 177–211.

Bernstein, D. (1996). A departmental system for balancing the development and evaluation of college teaching. *Innovative Higher Education, 20,* 241–247.

Blackburn, R. T., & Clark, M. J. (1975). An assessment of faculty performance: Some correlates between administrators, colleague, student, and self-ratings. *Sociology of Education, 48,* 242–256.

Blunt, A. (1991). The effects of anonymity and manipulated grades on student ratings of instructors. *Community College Review, 18,* 48–54.

Bogue, E. G. (1967). Student appraisal of teaching effectiveness in higher education: Summary of the literature. *Education Quest, 11,* 6–10.

Boice, R. (1984). Reexamination of traditional emphases in traditional faculty development. *Research in Higher Education, 21*(2), 195–209.

Border, L. L. (1997). The creative art of effective consultation. In K. T. Brinko & R. J. Menges (Eds.), *Practically speaking: A sourcebook for instruction consultants in higher education* (pp. 17–21). Stillwater, OK: New Forums Press

Borgatta, E. F. (1970). Student ratings of faculty. *American Association of University Professors Bulletin, 56,* 6–7.

Borich, G. D., & Madden, S. K. (1977). *Evaluating classroom instruction: A sourcebook of instruments.* Reading, MA: Addison-Wesley.

Bowen, H. R., & Schuster, J. H. (1986). *American professors: A national resource imperiled.* New York, NY: Oxford University Press.

Boyer, E. L. (1990). *Scholarship reconsidered: Priorities of the professoriate.* Princeton, NJ: The Carnegie Foundation for the Advancement of Teaching.

Braskamp, L. A. (1982). Evaluation systems are more than information systems. In N. R. Berte (Ed.), *New directions for higher education: No. 10. Individualizing education by learning contracts* (pp. 55–66). San Francisco, CA: Jossey-Bass.

Braskamp, L. A. (2000). Toward a more holistic approach to assessing faculty as teachers. In K. E. Ryan (Ed.), *New directions for teaching and learning: No. 83. Evaluating teaching in higher education: A vision of the future.* San Francisco, CA: Jossey-Bass.

Braskamp, L.A., & Ory, J. C. (1994). *Assessing faculty work: Enhancing individual and institutional performance.* San Francisco, CA: Jossey-Bass.

Braskamp, L. A., Brandenburg, D. C., & Ory, J. C. (1984). *Evaluating teaching effectiveness: A practical guide.* Beverly Hills, CA: Sage.

Braskamp, L. A., Ory, J. C., & Pieper, D. M. (1980). Congruency of student evaluative information collected by three methods. *Journal of Educational Psychology, 72*(2), 181–185.

Braskamp, L. A., Ory, J. C., & Pieper, D. M. (1981). Student written comments: Dimensions of instructional quality. *Journal of Educational Psychology, 73*(1), 65–70.

Braunstein, D. N., Klein, G. A., & Pachla, M. (1973). Feedback, expectancy, and shifts in student ratings of college faculty. *Journal of Applied Psychology, 58*(2), 254–258.

Braxton, J. M., & Bayer, A. E. (1986). Assessing faculty scholarly performance. In J. W. Creswell (Ed.), *New directions for institutional research: No. 50. Measuring faculty research performance.* San Francisco, CA: Jossey-Bass.

Braxton, J. M., & Del Favero, M. (2002). Evaluating scholarship performance: traditional and emergent assessment techniques. In C. Colbeck (Ed.), *New directions for institutional research: No. 114. Evaluating faculty performance.* San Francisco, CA: Jossey-Bass.

Braxton, J. M., Bayer, A. F., & Finkelstein, M. J. (1992). Teaching performance norms in academia. *Research in Higher Education, 33*(5), 533–569.

Brinko, K. T. (1990). Instructional consultation with feedback in higher education. *Journal of Higher Education, 61*(1), 65–83.

Brinko, K. T. (1993). The practice of giving feedback to improve teaching: What is effective? *Journal of Higher Education, 64,* 574–593.

Brown, D. L. (1976). Faculty ratings and student grades: A university-wide multiple regression analysis. *Journal of Educational Psychology, 68,* 573–578.

Bruton, B. T., & Crull, S. R. (1981). Causes and consequences of student evaluation of instruction. *Research in Higher Education, 17*(3), 195–206.

Bryant, J., Comisky, P. W., Crane, J. S., & Zillman, D. (1980). Relationship between college teachers' use of humor in the classroom and students' evaluations of their teachers. *Journal of Educational Psychology, 72,* 511–519.

Buck, D. (1998). Student evaluations of teaching measure the intervention, not the effect. *American Psychologist, 53,* 1224–1226.

Burdsal. C. A., & Bardo, J. W. (1986). Measuring students' perceptions of teaching: Dimensions of evaluation. *Educational and Psychological Measurement, 56,* 63–79.

Cadwell, J., & Jenkins, J. (1985). Effects of the semantic similarity of items on student ratings of instructors. *Journal of Educational Psychology, 77,* 383–393.

Cahn, D. D. (1983). Relative importance of perceived understanding in students' evaluation of teachers. *Perceptual and Motor Skills, 59,* 610.

Camp, R. C., Gibbs, M. C., Jr., & Masters, R. J., II (1988). The finite increment faculty merit pay allocation model. *Journal of Higher Education, 59*(6), 652–667.

Carusetta, E. (2002). Evaluating teaching through teaching awards. In C. Knapper & P. Cranton (Eds.), *New directions for teaching and learning: No. 88. Fresh approaches to the evaluation of teaching.* San Francisco, CA: Jossey-Bass.

Cashin, W. E. (1983). Concerns about using student ratings in community colleges. In R. J. Ernst (Ed.), *New directions for community colleges: No. 11. Adjusting to collective bargaining* (pp. 57–65). San Francisco, CA: Jossey-Bass.

Cashin, W. E. (1990). Students do rate different academic fields differently. In M. Theall & J. Franklin (Eds.), *New directions for teaching and learning: No. 43. Student ratings of instruction: Issues for improving practice.* San Francisco, CA: Jossey-Bass.

Cashin, W. E. (1992). Student ratings: The need for comparative data. *Instructional Evaluation and Faculty Development, 12*(2), 1–6.

Cashin, W. E. (1997). Should student ratings be interpreted absolutely or relatively? Reaction to McKeachie. *Instructional Evaluation and Faculty Development, 16*(2), 14–19.

Cashin, W. E. (1999). Student ratings of teaching: Uses and misuses. In. P. Seldin & Associates, *Changing practices in evaluating teaching: A practical guide to improved faculty performance and promotion/tenure decisions* (pp. 25–44). Bolton, MA: Anker.

Cashin, W. E., & Downey, R. G. (1992). Using global student rating items for summative evaluation. *Journal of Educational Psychology, 84*(4), 563–572.

Cashin, W. E., & Downey, R. G. (1995). Disciplinary differences in what is taught and in students' perceptions of what they learn and of how they are taught. In N. Hativa & M. Marincovich (Eds.), *New directions for teaching and learning: No. 64. Disciplinary differences in teaching and learning: Implications for practice* (pp. 81–92). San Francisco, CA: Jossey-Bass.

Cashin, W. E., & Perrin, B. M. (1983). Do college teachers who voluntarily have courses evaluated receive higher ratings? *Journal of Educational Psychology, 75*(4), 595–602.

Cashin, W. E., Downey, R. G., & Sixbury, G. R. (1994). Global and specific ratings of teaching effectiveness and their relation to course objectives: A reply to Marsh. *Journal of Educational Psychology, 86,* 649–657.

Cavanagh, R. R. (1996). Summative and formative evaluation in the faculty peer review of teaching. *Innovative Higher Education, 20*(4), 235–240.

Ceci, S., & Peters, D. (1982). Peer review: A study of reliability. *Change, 14*(6), 44–48.

Centra, J. A. (1973). Effectiveness of student feedback in modifying college instruction. *Journal of Educational Psychology, 65*(3), 395–401.

Centra, J. A. (1974). The relationship between student and alumni ratings of teachers. *Educational and Psychological Measurement, 34,* 321–326.

Centra, J. A. (1975). Colleagues as raters of classroom instruction. *Journal of Higher Education, 46*(3), 327–337.

Centra, J. A. (1977). Student ratings of instruction and their relationship to student learning. *American Educational Research Journal, 14*(1), 17–24.

Centra, J. A. (1978). Types of faculty development programs. *Journal of Higher Education, 49*(2), 151–162.

Centra, J. A. (1979). *Determining faculty effectiveness: Assessing teaching, research, and service for personnel decisions and improvement.* San Francisco, CA: Jossey-Bass.

Centra, J. A. (1981). *Determining faculty effectiveness.* San Francisco, CA: Jossey-Bass.

Centra, J. A. (1983). Research productivity and teaching effectiveness. *Research in Higher Education, 18*(2), 379–388.

Centra, J. A. (1989). Faculty evaluation and faculty development in higher education. In J. C. Smart (Ed.), *Higher education: Handbook of theory and research*. New York, NY: Agathon Press.

Centra, J. A. (1993). *Reflective faculty evaluation: Enhancing teaching and determining faculty effectiveness*. San Francisco, CA: Jossey-Bass.

Centra, J. A. (1994). The use of the teaching portfolio and student evaluations for summative evaluation. *The Journal of Higher Education, 65*(5), 555–570.

Centra, J. A. (1999). *Reflective faculty evaluation: Enhancing teaching and determining faculty effectiveness*. San Francisco, CA: Jossey-Bass.

Centra, J. A. (2000). Evaluating the teaching portfolio: A role for colleagues. In K. E. Ryan (Ed.), *New directions for teaching and learning: No. 83. Toward a more holistic approach to assessing faculty as teachers. Evaluating teaching in higher education: A vision of the future*. San Francisco, CA: Jossey-Bass.

Centra, J. A., & Bonesteel, P. (1990). College teaching: An art or a science? In M. Theall & J. Franklin (Eds.), *New directions for teaching and learning: No. 43. Student ratings of instruction: Issues for improving practice*. San Francisco, CA: Jossey-Bass.

Centra, J. A., & Gaubatz, N. B. (2000). Is there gender bias in student evaluations of teaching? *The Journal of Higher Education, 70*(1), 17–23.

Chacko, T. I. (1983). Student ratings of instruction: A function of grading standards. *Educational Research Quarterly, 8*(2), 19–25.

Charkins, R. J., O'Toole, D. M., & Wetzel, J. N. (1985). Linking teacher and student learning styles with student achievement and attitudes. *Journal of Economic Education, 16*(2), 111–120.

Chickering, A. W., & Gamson, Z. F. (1987, March). Seven principles for good practice in undergraduate education. *AAHE Bulletin, 39*(7), 3–7.

Chism, N. V. N. (1999). *Peer review of reaching: A sourcebook*. Bolton, MA: Anker.

Chiu, C., & Alliger, G. M. (1990). A proposed method to combine ranking and graphic rating in performance appraisal: The quantitative ranking scale. *Educational and Psychological Measurement, 50*(3), 493–503.

Ciscell, R. E. (1987). Student ratings of instruction: Change the timetable to improve instruction. *Community College Review, 15*(1), 34–38.

Clark, B. R. (1997). The modern integration of research activities with teaching and learning. *Journal of Higher Education, 68*, 241–255.

Clark, D. J., & Bekey, J. (1979). Use of small groups in instructional evaluation. *The Journal of the Professional and Organizational Development Network in Higher Education, 1*, 87–95.

Clift, J. O. (1989). Establishing the validity of a set of summative teaching performance scales. *Assessment and Evaluation in Higher Education, 14*(3), 193–206.

Cohen, P. A. (1980). Effectiveness of student-rating feedback for improving college instruction: A meta-analysis. *Research in Higher Education, 13*, 321–341.

Cohen, P. A. (1981). Student ratings of instruction and student achievement: A meta-analysis of multi-section validity studies. *Review of Educational Research, 51*(3), 281–309.

Cohen, P. A. (1982). Validity of student ratings in psychology courses: A research synthesis. *Teaching of Psychology, 9*(2), 78–82.

Cohen, P. A. (1983). Comment on a selective review of the validity of student ratings of teaching. *Journal of Higher Education, 54*, 448–458.

Cohen, P. A. (1990). Bringing research into practice. In M. Theall, & J. Franklin (Eds.), *New directions for teaching and learning: No. 43. Student ratings of instruction: Issues for improving practice*. San Francisco, CA: Jossey-Bass.

Cohen, P. A. (1991). Effectiveness of student ratings feedback and consultation for improving instruction in dental school. *Journal of Dental Education, 55*(2), 145–150.

Cohen, P. A., & Herr, G. (1979). A procedure for diagnostic instructional feedback: The formative assessment of college teaching (FACT). *Educational Technology, 19*, 18–23.

Cohen, P. A., & Herr, G. (1982). Using an interactive feedback procedure to improve college teaching. *Teaching of Psychology, 9*(3), 138–140.

Cohen, P. A., & McKeachie, W. J. (1980). The role of colleagues in the evaluation of college teaching. *Improving College and University Teaching, 28*(4), 147–154.

Colbeck, C. L. (Ed.). (2002). *New directions for institutional research: No. 114. Evaluating faculty performance*. San Francisco, CA: Jossey-Bass.

Coleman, J., & McKeachie, W. J. (1980). Effects of instructor/course evaluations on student course selections. *Journal of Educational Psychology, 73*, 224–226.

Comer, J. C. (1980). The influence of mood on student evaluations of teaching. *Journal of Educational Research, 73*, 229–232.

Conway, R., Kember, D., Sivan, A., & Wu, M. (1993). Peer assessment of an individual's contribution to a group project. *Assessment and Evaluation in Higher Education, 18*(1), 45–56.

Cook, S. S. (1989). Improving the quality of student ratings of instruction: A look at two strategies. *Research in Higher Education, 30*(1), 31–45.

Cooper, P. J., Steward, L. P., & Gudykunst, W. B. (1982). Relationship with instructor and other variables influencing student evaluations of instruction. *Communication Quarterly, 30*(4), 308–315.

Costin, F., Greenough, W. T., & Menges, R. J. (1971). Student ratings of college teaching: Reliability, validity, and usefulness. *Review of Educational Research, 41*(5), 511–535.

Cowan, D. L. (1976). Peer review in medical education. *Journal of Medical Education, 51*(2), 130–131.

Cranton, P. A., & Hillgartner, W. (1981). The relationships between student ratings and instructor behavior: Implications for improving teaching. *Canadian Journal of Higher Education, 11,* 73–81.

Cranton, P. A., & Smith, R. A. (1986). A new look at the effect of course characteristics on student ratings of instruction. *American Educational Research Journal, 23,* 117–128.

Cranton, P. A., & Smith, R. A. (1990). Reconsidering the unit of analysis: A model of student ratings of instruction. *Journal of Educational Psychology, 82*(2), 207–212.

Cundy, D. T. (1982). Teacher effectiveness and course popularity: Patterns in student evaluations. *Teaching Political Science, 9*(4), 164–173.

d'Apollonia, S., & Abrami, P. C. (1997). Making students' evaluations of teaching effectiveness effective: The critical issues of validity, bias, and utility. *American Psychologist, 52,* 1187–1197.

d'Apollonia, S., & Abrami, P. C. (1997). Navigating student ratings of instruction. *American Psychologist, 52*(11), 1198–1208.

d'Apollonia, S., & Abrami, P. C. (1997). Scaling the ivory tower, pt. II: Student ratings of instruction in North America. *Psychology Teaching Review, 6,* 60–77.

Darling-Hammond, L., Wise, A. E., & Pease, S. R. (1983). Teacher evaluation in the organizational context: A review of the literature. *Review of Educational Research, 53*(3), 285–328.

Davis, S. M., & Botkin, J. W. (1994). *The monster under the bed: How business is mastering the opportunity of knowledge for profit.* New York, NY: Simon & Schuster.

DeCette, J., & Kenney, J. (1982). Do grading standards affect student evaluations of teaching? Some new evidence on an old question. *Journal of Educational Psychology, 74,* 308–314.

DeJung, J. E. (1964). Effects of rater frames of reference on peer ratings. *Journal of Experimental Education, 33*(2), 121–131.

DeNeve, H. M. F., & Janssen, P. J. (1982). Validity of student evaluation of instruction. *Higher Education, 11*(5), 543–552.

DeZure, D. (1999). Evaluating teaching through peer classroom observation. In P. Seldin (Ed.), *Changing practices in evaluating teaching: A practical guide to improved faculty performance and promotion/tenure decisions* (pp. 70–96). Bolton, MA: Anker.

Diamond, R. M. (1993). Instituting change in the faculty reward system. In R. M. Diamond & B. E. Adam (Eds.), *New directions for higher education: No. 81. Recognizing faculty work: Reward systems for the year 2000.* San Francisco, CA: Jossey-Bass.

Diamond, R. M. (1999). *Aligning faculty rewards with institutional mission: Statements, policies, and guidelines.* Bolton, MA: Anker.

Diamond, R. M., & Adam, B. E. (1993). *New directions for higher education: No. 81. Recognizing faculty work: Reward systems for the year 2000.* San Francisco, CA: Jossey-Bass.

Dick, W. (1982). Evaluation in diverse educational settings. *Viewpoints in Teaching and Learning, 58*(3), 84–89.

Donald, J. G. (1984). Quality indices for faculty evaluation. *Assessment and Evaluation in Higher Education, 9*(1), 41–52.

Dooris, M. J. (2002). Institutional research to enhance faculty performance. In C. Colbeck (Ed.), *New directions for institutional research: No. 114. Evaluating faculty performance.* San Francisco, CA: Jossey-Bass.

Dowell, D. A., & Neal, J. A. (1982). A selective review of the validity of student ratings of teaching. *Journal of Higher Education, 53,* 51–62.

Doyle, K. O., Jr. (1975). *Student evaluation of instruction.* Lexington, MA: Lexington Books.

Doyle, K. O., Jr. (1983). *Evaluating teaching.* Lexington, MA: Lexington Books.

Doyle, K. O., & Crighton, L. I. (1978). Student, peer, and self evaluations of college instructors. *Journal of Educational Psychology, 70*(5), 815–826.

Doyle, K. O., & Whitely, S. E. (1974). Student ratings as criteria for effective teaching. *American Educational Research Journal, 11*(3), 259–274.

Drucker, A. J., & Remmers, H. H. (1951). Do alumni and students differ in their attitudes toward instructors? *Journal of Educational Psychology, 42*(3), 129–143.

Earl, S. E. (1986). Staff and peer assessment—measuring an individual's contribution to group performance. *Assessment and Evaluation in Higher Education, 11*(1), 60–69.

Ebel, K. E. (1972). *Professors as teachers.* San Francisco, CA: Jossey-Bass.

Ebel, K. E. (1983). *The aims of college teaching.* San Francisco, CA: Jossey-Bass.

Edgerton, R. (1993). The Re-examination of faculty priorities. *Change, 25*(4), 10–26.

Elbow, P. (1980). One-to-one faculty development. In J. Noonan (Ed.), *Learning about teaching* (Vol. 4). San Francisco, CA: Jossey-Bass.

Elmore, P. B., & LaPointe, K. A. (1974). Effects of teacher sex and student sex on the evaluation of college instructors. *Journal of Educational Psychology, 66,* 386–389.

Elton, L. (1984). Evaluating teaching and assessing teachers in universities. *Assessment and Evaluation in Higher Education, 9*(2), 115.

Erdle, S., & Murray, H. G. (1986). Interfaculty differences in classroom teaching behaviors and their relationship to student instructional ratings. *Research in Higher Education, 24,* 115–127.

Erdle, S., Murray, H. G., & Rushton, J. P. (1985). Personality, classroom behavior, and student ratings of college teaching effectiveness: A path analysis. *Journal of Educational Psychology, 77*(4), 394–407.

Erickson, G. (1986). A survey of faculty development practices. In M Svinicki, J. Kerfiss, & J. Stone (Eds.). *To improve the Academy: Vol. 5. Resources for faculty, instructional, and organizational development* (182–196). Stillwater, OK: New Forums Press.

Erickson, G. R., & Erickson, B. L. (1979). Improving college teaching: An evaluation of a teaching consultation procedure. *Journal of Higher Education, 50*(5), 670–683.

Evertson, C. M., & Holley, F. M. (1981). Classroom observation. In J. Millman (Ed.), *Handbook of teacher evaluation.* Beverly Hills, CA: Sage.

Fairweather, J. S. (1996). *Faculty work and public trust: Restoring the value of teaching and public service in American academic life.* Boston, MA: Allyn & Bacon.

Fairweather, J. S. (2002). The ultimate faculty evaluation: promotion and tenure decisions. In C. Colbeck (Ed.), *New directions for institutional research: No. 114. Evaluating faculty performance.* San Francisco, CA: Jossey-Bass

Fear, F. A., & Sandmann, L. R. (1997). Unpacking the service category: Reconceptualizing university outreach for the 21st century. *Continuing Higher Education Review, 59*(3), 117–122.

Feldman, K. A. (1976). Grades and college students' evaluations of their courses and teachers. *Research in Higher Education, 4,* 69–111.

Feldman, K. A. (1976). The superior college teacher from the student's view. *Research in Higher Education, 5,* 243–288.

Feldman, K. A. (1977). Consistency and variability among college students in rating their teachers and courses: A review and analysis. *Research in Higher Education, 6*(3), 223–274.

Feldman, K. A. (1978). Course characteristics and college students' ratings of their teachers: What we know and what we don't. *Research in Higher Education, 9,* 199–242.

Feldman, K. A. (1979). The significance of circumstances for college students' ratings of their teachers and courses. *Research in Higher Education, 10,* 149–172.

Feldman, K. A. (1983). Seniority and instructional experience of college teachers are related to evaluations they receive from their students. *Research in Higher Education, 18*(1), 3–124.

Feldman, K. A. (1984). Class size and college students' evaluations of teachers and courses: A closer look. *Research in Higher Education, 21,* 45–116.

Feldman, K. A. (1986). The perceived instructional effectiveness of college teachers as related to their personality and attitudinal characteristics: A review and synthesis. *Research in Higher Education, 24,* 139–213.

Feldman, K. A. (1987). Research productivity and scholarly accomplishment of college teachers as related to their instructional effectiveness. *Research in Higher Education, 26,* 227–298.

Feldman, K. A. (1988). Effective college teaching from the students' and faculty view: Matched or mismatched priorities? *Research in Higher Education, 28*(4), 291–344.

Feldman, K. A. (1989). Instructional effectiveness of college teachers as judged by teachers themselves, current and former students, colleagues, administrators, and external (neutral) observers. *Research in Higher Education, 30*(2), 137–94.

Feldman, K. A. (1989). The association between student ratings of specific instructional dimensions and student achievement: Refining and extending the synthesis of data from multisection validity studies. *Research in Higher Education, 30*(6), 583–645.

Feldman, K. A. (1990). An afterword for the association between student ratings of specific instructional dimensions and student achievement: Refining and extending the synthesis of data from multisection validity studies. *Research in Higher Education, 31,* 315–318.

Feldman, K. A. (1992). College students' views of male and female college teachers. Part I—Evidence from the social laboratory and experiments. *Research in Higher Education, 33*(3), 317–375.

Feldman, K. A. (1993). College students' views of male and female college teachers: Part II—Evidence from students' evaluations of their classroom teachers. *Research in Higher Education, 34*(2), 151–211.

Feldman, K. A. (1997). Identifying exemplary teachers and teaching: Evidence from student ratings. In R. P. Perry & J. C. Smart (Eds.), *Effective teaching in higher education: Research and practice* (pp. 368–395). New York, NY: Agathon Press.

Feldman, K. A. (1998). Identifying exemplary teachers and teaching: Evidence from student ratings. In K. A. Feldman & M. B. Paulsen (Eds.), *Teaching and learning in the college classroom* (pp. 391–414). Needham Heights, MA: Simon & Schuster.

Feldman, K. A. (1998). Reflections on the study of effective college teaching and student ratings: One continuing quest and two unresolved issues. In J. C. Smart (Ed.), *Higher education: Handbook of theory and research* (Vol. 13). New York, NY: Agathon Press.

Fenwick, T. J. (2001). Using student outcomes to evaluate teaching: a cautious exploration. In C. Knapper & P. Abrami (Eds.), *New directions for teaching and learning: No. 88. Fresh approaches to the evaluation of teaching.* San Francisco, CA: Jossey-Bass.

Fiddler, M., McGury, S., Marienau, C. Rogers, R., & Scheideman, W. (1996). Broadening the scope of scholarship: A suggested framework. *Innovative Higher Education, 21*(2), 127–139.

Fitzgerald, M. J., & Grafton, C. L. (1981). Comparisons and implications of peer and student evaluation for a community college faculty. *Community and Junior College Research Quarterly, 5*(4), 331–337.

Fox, M. F. (1992). Research, teaching, and publication productivity: Mutuality versus competition in academia. *Sociology of Education, 65,* 293–305.

Frankhouser, W. M. J. (1984). The effects of different oral directions as to disposition of results on student ratings of college instruction. *Research in Higher Education, 20*(3), 367–374.

Franklin, J. (2001). Interpreting the numbers: Using a narrative to help others read student evaluations of your teaching accurately. In K. G. Lewis (Ed.), *New directions for teaching and learning: No. 87. Techniques and strategies for interpreting student evaluations.* San Francisco, CA: Jossey-Bass.

Franklin, J., & Theall, M. (1990). Communicating student ratings to decision makers: Design for good practice. In M. Theall & J. Franklin (Eds.), *New directions for teaching and learning: No. 43. Student ratings of instruction: Issues for improving practice* (pp. 75–93). San Francisco, CA: Jossey-Bass.

Franklin, J., & Theall, M. (1995). The relationship of disciplinary differences and the value of class preparation time to student ratings of instruction. In N. Hativa & M. Marincovich (Eds.), *New directions for teaching and learning: No. 64. Disciplinary differences in teaching and learning in higher education.* San Francisco, CA: Jossey-Bass.

Franklin, J. & Theall, M. (2002). Thinking about faculty thinking about the design and evaluation of instruction. In N. Hativa & P. Goodyear (Eds.), *Teacher thinking, beliefs, and knowledge in higher education.* New York, NY: Kluwer Academic.

Freedman, R. D., Stumpf, S. A., & Aguanno, J. C. (1979). Validity of the course-faculty instrument (CFI), Intrinsic and extrinsic variables. *Educational and Psychological Measurement, 39,* 153–158.

French-Lazovik, G. (1981). Peer review: Documentary evidence in the evaluation of teaching. In J. Millman (Ed.), *Handbook of teacher evaluation.* Beverly Hills, CA: Sage.

French-Lazovik, G. E. (Ed.). (1982). *New directions for Teaching and learning: No. 11. Practices that improve teaching evaluation.* San Francisco, CA: Jossey-Bass.

Fresko, B. (2002). Faculty views of student evaluation of college teaching. *Assessment and Evaluation in Higher Education, 27*(2), 187.

Frey, P. W. (1973). Student ratings of teaching: Validity of several rating factors. *Science, 182,* 83–85.

Frey, P. W. (1974). The ongoing debate: Student evaluation of teaching. *Change,* 47–49.

Frey, P. W. (1976). Validity of student instructional ratings: Does timing matter? *Journal of Higher Education, 47,* 327–336.

Frey, P. W. (1978). A two-dimensional analysis of student ratings of instruction. *Research in Higher Education, 9*(1), 69–91.

Frey, P. W., Leonard, D. W., & Beatty, W. W. (1975). Student rating of instruction: Validation research. *American Educational Research Journal, 12,* 435–447.

Friedrich, J. (1998). Teaching evaluations: Concerns for psychologists? *American Psychologist, 53,* 1226–1227.

Froh, R. C., Gray, P. J., & Lambert, L. M. (1993). Representing faculty work: The professional portfolio. In R. M. Diamond & B. E. Adam (Eds.), *New directions for higher education: No. 8. Recognizing faculty work: Rewards systems for the year 2000.* San Francisco, CA: Jossey-Bass.

Fuhrmann, B. B., & Grasha, A. F. (1983). *A Practical Handbook for College Teachers.* Boston, MA: Little, Brown and Co.

Gage, N. L. (1961). The appraisal of college teaching: An analysis of ends and means. *Journal of Higher Education, 32,* 17–22.

Gaski, J. F. (1987). On construct validity of measures of college teaching effectiveness. *Journal of Educational Psychology, 79,* 326–330.

Gessner, P. K. (1973). Evaluation of instruction. *Science, 180,* 566–569.

Gigliotti, R. J. (1987). Expectations, observations, and violations: Comparing their effects on course ratings. *Research in Higher Education, 26*(4), 401–415.

Gigliotti, R. J., & Buchtel, F. S. (1990). Attributional bias and course evaluations. *Journal of Educational Psychology, 82*(2), 341–351.

Gillmore, G. M. (1983–1984). Student ratings as a factor in faculty employment decisions and periodic review. *Journal of College and University Law, 10,* 557–576.

Gillmore, G. M. (1996). Chair's corner: Like devils, the instructor you know is better than the one you do not know. *Instructional Evaluation and Faculty Development, 16*(1), 10.

Gillmore, G. M., & Greenwald, A. G. (1999). Using statistical adjustment to reduce bias in student ratings. *American Psychologist, 54*(7), 518–519.

Gillmore, G. M., Kane, M. T., & Naccarato, R. W. (1978). The generalizability of student ratings of instruction: Estimates of teacher and course components. *Journal of Educational Measurement, 15,* 1–13.

Gillmore, G. M., Kane, M. T., & Smith, P. L. (1983). The dependability of student evaluations of teaching effectiveness: Matching the conclusions to the design. *Educational and Psychological Measurement, 43*(4), 1015–1018.

Glassick, C. E., Huber, M. T., & Maeroff, G. I. (1997). *Scholarship assessed: Evaluation of the professoriate.* San Francisco, CA: Jossey-Bass.

Goldfinch, J., & Raeside, R. (1990). Development of a peer assessment technique for obtaining individual marks on a group project. *Assessment and Evaluation in Higher Education, 15*(3), 210–231.

Goodman, M. J. (1990). The review of tenured faculty: A collegial model. *Journal of Higher Education, 61*(4), 408–424.

Goodwin, L. D., & Stevens, E. A. (1993). The influence of gender on university faculty members' perceptions of "good" teaching. *Journal of Higher Education, 64*(2), 166–185.

Grasha, A. F. (1977). *Assessing and developing faculty performance.* Cincinnati, OH: Communication and Education Associates.

Gray, D. M., & Brandenburg, D. C. (1985). Following student ratings over time with a catalog-based system. *Research in Higher Education, 22*(2), 155–168.

Greenwald, A. G. (1997). Current issues: Student ratings of professors. *American Psychologist, 52,* 1186–1225.

Greenwald, A. G. (1997). Validity concerns and usefulness of student ratings of instruction. *American Psychologist, 52,* 1182–1186.

Greenwald, A. G., & Gillmore, G. M. (1997). Grading leniency is a removable contaminant of student ratings. *American Psychologist, 52*(11), 1209–1217.

Greenwald, A. G., & Gillmore, G. M. (1997). No pain, no gain? The importance of measuring course workload in student ratings of instruction. *Journal of Educational Psychology, 89*(4), 743–751.

Greenwood, G. E., & Ramagli, H. J. (1980). Alternatives to student ratings of college teaching. *Journal of Higher Education, 51*(6), 673–684.

Griffin, B. W. (2001). Instructor reputation and student ratings of instruction. *Contemporary Educational Psychology, 26,* 534–552.

Guthrie, E. R. (1949). The evaluation of teaching. *Educational Record, 30,* 109–115.

Hammons, J. (1983). Faculty development: A necessary corollary to faculty evaluation. In R. J. Ernst (Ed.), *New directions for community colleges: No. 11. Adjusting to collective bargaining* (pp. 75–82). San Francisco, CA: Jossey-Bass.

Handal, G. (1999). Consultation using critical friends. In C. Knapper & S. Piccinin (Eds.), *New directions for teaching and learning: No. 79. Using consultants to improve teaching* (pp. 59–70). San Francisco, CA: Jossey-Bass.

Hanna, G. S., Hoyt, D. P., & Aubrecht, J. D. (1983). Identifying and adjusting for biases in student evaluations of instruction: Implications for validity. *Educational and Psychological Measurement, 43*(4), 1175–1185.

Harris, E. L. (1982). Student ratings of faculty performance: Should departmental committees construct the instruments. *Journal of Educational Research, 76*(2), 100–106.

Harris, M. B. (1975). Sex role stereotypes and teacher evaluations. *Journal of Educational Psychology, 67,* 751–756.

Harrison, P. D., Douglas, D. K., & Burdsal, C. A. (2004). The relative merits of different types of overall evaluations of teaching effectiveness. *Research in Higher Education, 45*(3), 311–323.

Harrison, P. D., Ryan, J. M., & Moore, P. S. (1996). College students' self-insight and common implicit theories in ratings of teaching effectiveness. *Journal of Educational Psychology, 88*(4), 775–782.

Harry, J., & Goldner, N. S. (1972). The null relationship between teaching and research. *Sociology of Education, 45*(1), 47–60.

Haskell, R. E. (1997). Academic freedom, tenure, and student evaluations of faculty: Galloping polls in the 21st century. *Educational Policy Analysis Archives, 5*(6).

Hativa, N. (1993). Student ratings: A non-comparative interpretation. *Evaluation and Faculty Development, 13,* 1–4.

Hativa, N., & Raviv, A. (1993). Using a single score for summative evaluation by students. *Research in Higher Education, 34*(5), 625–646.

Hattie, J., & Marsh, H. W. (1996). The relationship between research and teaching—A meta-analysis. *Review of Educational Research, 66*(4), 507–542.

Healy, P. (1999, March 26). Mass. governor seeks to free some colleges from tenure and most regulations. *The Chronicle of Higher Education,* p. A43.

Hebron, C. D. W. (1984). An aid for evaluating teaching in higher education. *Assessment and Evaluation in Higher Education, 9*(2), 145–163.

Heilman, J. D., & Armentrout, W. D. (1936). The rating of college teachers on ten traits by their students. *Journal of Educational Psychology, 27,* 197–216.

Helling, B. B. (1988). Looking for good teaching: A guide to peer observation. *Journal of Staff, Program, and Organizational Development, 6,* 147–158.

Helmstadter, G. C., & Krus, D. J. (1982). The factorial validity of student ratings in faculty promotions. *Educational and Psychological Measurement, 42*(4), 1135–1139.

Hersh, R. H., & Merrow, J. (2005). *Declining by degrees: Higher education at risk.* New York, NY: Palgrave Macmillan.

Hicks, O. (1999). A conceptual framework for instructional consultation. In C. Knapper & S. Piccinin (Eds.), *New directions for teaching and learning: No. 79. Using consultation to improve teaching* (pp. 9–18). San Francisco, CA: Jossey-Bass.

Hoffman, R. A. (1984). An assessment of the teaching, research, and service function of a college faculty. *Journal of Research and Development in Education, 17,* 51–54.

Hogan, T. P. (1973). Similarity of student ratings across instructors, courses, and time. *Research in Higher Education, 1*(2), 149–154.

Holmes, D. S. (1972). Effects of grades and disconfirmed grade expectancies on students' evaluations of their instruction. *Journal of Educational Psychology, 63,* 130–133.

Howard, G. S., & Maxwell, S. E. (1980). The correlation between student satisfaction and grades: A case of mistaken causation? *Journal of Educational Psychology, 72,* 810–820.

Howard, G. S., & Maxwell, S. E. (1982). Do grades contaminate student evaluations of instruction? *Research in Higher Education, 16,* 175–188.

Howard, G. S., Conway, C. G., & Maxwell, S. E. (1985). Construct validity of measures of college teaching effectiveness. *Journal of Educational Psychology, 77,* 187–196.

Hoyt, D. P., & Howard, G. S. (1978). The evaluation of faculty development programs. *Research in Higher Education, 8,* 25–38.

Huber, M. T. (2002). Faculty evaluation and the development of academic careers. In C. Colbeck (Ed.), *New directions for institutional research: No. 114. Evaluating faculty performance.* San Francisco, CA: Jossey-Bass.

Hunnicutt, G. G., Lesher-Taylor, R. L., & Keeffe, M. J. (1991). An exploratory examination of faculty evaluation and merit compensation systems in Texas colleges and universities. *CUPA Journal, 42*(1), 13–21.

Husbands, C. T., & Fosh, P. (1993). Students' evaluation of teaching in higher education: Experience from four European countries and some implications of the practice. *Assessment and Evaluation in Higher Education, 18*(2), 95–114.

Hutchings, P. (1994). Peer review of teaching: From idea to prototype. *AAHE Bulletin, 47*(3), 3–7.

Hutchings, P. (1996). The peer review of teaching: Progress, issues, prospects. *Innovative Higher Education, 20,* 221–234.

Hutchings, P., & Shulman, L. (1999). The scholarship of teaching: New elaborations, new developments. *Change, 31*(5), 11–15.

Isaacs, G. (1989). Changes in ratings for staff who evaluated their teaching more than once. *Assessment and Evaluation in Higher Education, 14*(1), 1–10.

Issacson, R. L., McKeachie, W. J., & Milholland, J. M. (1963). Correlation of teacher personality variables and student ratings. *Journal of Educational Psychology, 54,* 110–117.

Isaacson, R. L., McKeachie, W. J., Milholland, J. E., Lin, Y. G., Hofeller, M., Baerwaldt, J. W., & Zinn, K. L. (1964). Dimensions of student evaluations of teaching. *Journal of Educational Psychology, 55,* 344–351.

Jackson, D. L., Teal, C. R., Raines, S. J., Nansel, T. R., Force, R. C., & Burdsal, C. A. (1999). The dimensions of students' perceptions of teaching effectiveness. *Educational and Psychological Measurement, 59*(4), 580–596.

Jauch, L. R. (1976). Relationships of research and teaching: Implications for faculty evaluation. *Research in Higher Education, 5,* 1–13.

Jenkins, A., Blackman, T., Lindasay, R., & Paton-Saltzberg, R. (1998). Teaching and research: Student perspectives and policy implications. *Studies in Higher Education, 23,* 127–141.

Johnson, T., & Ryan, K. E. (2000). A comprehensive approach to the evaluation of college teaching: Toward a more holistic approach to assessing faculty as teachers. In K. E. Ryan (Ed.), *New directions for teaching and learning: No. 83. Evaluating teaching in higher education: A vision of the future.* San Francisco, CA: Jossey-Bass.

Johnson, T., & Sorenson, L. (Eds.). (2004). *New directions for teaching and learning: No. 96. Online student ratings of instruction.* San Francisco, CA: Jossey-Bass.

Jolly, B., & Macdonald, M. M. (1987). More effective evaluation of clinical teaching. *Assessment and Evaluation in Higher Education, 12*(3), 175–190.

Kane, J., & Lawler, E. (1978). Methods of peer assessment. *Psychological Bulletin, 85,* 555–586.

Kane, M. T., Gillmore, G. M., & Crooks, T. J. (1976). Student evaluations of teaching: The generalizability of class means. *Journal of Educational Measurement, 13,* 171–184.

Kaschak, E. (1978). Sex bias in student evaluations of college professors. *Psychology of Women Quarterly, 2*(3), 235–243.

Kaschak, E. (1981). Another look at sex bias in students' evaluations of professors: Do winners get the recognition that they have been given? *Psychology of Women Quarterly, 5,* 767–772.

Kierstead, D., D'Agostino, P., & Dill, H. (1988). Sex role stereotyping of college professors: Bias in students' ratings of instructors. *Journal of Educational Psychology, 80*(3), 342–344.

Kimlicka, T. M. (1982). Student evaluation of course content, teaching effectiveness, and personal growth in an experimental course. *College Student Journal, 16*(2), 198–200.

Kingsbury, M. (1982). How library schools evaluate faculty performance. *Journal of Education for Librarianship, 22*(4), 219–238.

Kinney, D. P., & Smith, S. P. (1992). Age and teaching performance. *Journal of Higher Education, 63*(3), 282–302.

Knapper, C., & Cranton, P. A. (2001). *New directions for teaching and learning: No. 88. Fresh Approaches to the Evaluation of Teaching.* San Francisco, CA: Jossey-Bass.

Knapper, C., & Piccinin, S. (1999). Consulting about teaching: An overview. In C. Knapper & S. Piccinin (Eds.), *New directions for teaching and learning: No. 79. Using consultants to improve teaching* (pp. 3–7). San Francisco, CA: Jossey-Bass.

Koehler, W. F. (1983). From evaluations to an equitable selection of merit-pay recipients and increments. *Research in Higher Education, 25*(3), 253–263.

Kohlan, R. G. (1973). A comparison of faculty evaluations early and late in the course. *Journal of Higher Education, 44,* 587–597.

Koon, J., & Murray, H. G. (1995). Using multiple outcomes to validate student ratings of overall teacher effectiveness. *Journal of Higher Education, 66*(1), 61–81.

Krahenbuhl, G. S. (1998). Faculty Work: Integrating responsibilities and institutional needs. *Change, 30*(6), 18–25.

Kreber, C. E. (2001). *New directions for teaching and learning: No. 86. Scholarship revisited: Defining and implementing the scholarship of teaching.* San Francisco, CA: Jossey-Bass.

Kreber, C., & Cranton, P. (2000). Exploring the scholarship of teaching. *Journal of Higher Education, 71*(4), 476–495.

Kremer, J. (1991). Identifying faculty types using peer ratings of teaching, research, and service. *Research in Higher Education, 32*(4), 351–361.

Kremer, J. F. (1990). Construct validity of multiple measures in teaching, research, and service and reliability of peer ratings. *Journal of Educational Psychology, 82*(2), 213–218.

Kuhn, T. S. (1970). *The structure of scientific revolution.* Chicago, IL: University of Chicago Press.

Kulik, J. A. (2001). Student ratings: Validity, utility, and controversy. In M. Theall, P. C. Abrami, & L. A. Mets (Eds.), *New directions for institutional research: No. 109. The student ratings debate: Are they valid? How can we best use them?* (pp. 9–26).San Francisco, CA: Jossey-Bass.

Kulik, J. A., & Kulik, C. L. C. (1974). Student ratings of instruction. *Teaching of Psychology, 1,* 51–57.

Kulik, J. A., & McKeachie, W. J. (1975). The evaluation of teachers in higher education. *Review of Research in Education, 3,* 210–240.

Kurz, R. S., Meuller, J. J., Gibbons, J. L., & DiCataldo, F. (1989). Faculty performance: Suggestions for the refinement of the concept and its measurement. *Journal of Higher Education, 60*(1), 43–58.

Lacefield, W. E. (1986). Faculty enrichment and the assessment of teaching. *Review of Higher Education, 9*(4), 361–379.

Land, M. L., & Smith, L. R. (1980). Student perception of teacher clarity in mathematics. *Journal of Research in Mathematics Education, 11,* 137–146.

Langsam, D. M., & Dubois, P. L. (1996). Can nightmares become sweet dreams? Peer review in the wake of a system wide administrative mandate. *Innovative Higher Education, 20*(4), 249–259.

Leatherman, C. (1999, April 9). Growth in positions off the tenure track is a trend that's here to stay, study finds. *The Chronicle of Higher Education,* p. A14.

Lee, B. A. (1983). Balancing confidentiality and disclosure in faculty peer review: Impact of Title VII legislation. *Journal of College and University Law, 9*(3), 279–314.

Lee, B. A. (1985). Federal court involvement in academic personnel decisions: Impact on peer review. *Journal of Higher Education, 56*(1), 38–54.

Lester, D. (1982). Students' evaluation of teaching and course performance. *Psychological Reports, 50,* 1126.

Leventhal, L., Abrami, P. C., & Perry, R. P. (1976). Do teacher ratings forms reveal as much about students as about teachers? *Journal of Educational Psychology, 68,* 441–445.

Leventhal, L., Abrami, P. C., Perry, R. P., & Breen, L. J. (1975). Section selection in multi-section courses: Implications for the validation and use of teacher rating forms. *Educational and Psychological Measurement, 35,* 885–895.

Leventhal, L., Perry, R. P., & Abrami, P. C. (1977). Effects of lecturer quality and student perception of lecturer's experience on teacher ratings and student achievement. *Journal of Educational Psychology, 69*(4), 360–374.

Leventhal, L., Turcotte, S. J. C., Abrami, P. C., & Perry, R. P. (1983). Primacy/recency effects in student ratings of instruction: A reinterpretation of gain-loss effects. *Journal of Educational Psychology, 75*(5), 692–704.

Lewis, K. G. (2001). *New directions for teaching and learning: No. 87. Techniques and strategies for interpreting student evaluations.* San Francisco, CA: Jossey-Bass.

L'Hommedieu, R., Menges, R. J., & Brinko, K. T. (1990). Methodological explanations for the modes effects of feedback from student ratings. *Journal of Educational Psychology, 82*(2), 232–241.

Lin, Y. G., McKeachie, W. J., & Tucker, D. G. (1984). The use of student ratings in promotion decisions. *Journal of Higher Education, 55*(5), 583–589.

Linn, R. L., Centra, J. A., & Tucker, L. (1975). Between, within, and total group factor analysis of student ratings of instruction. *Multivariate Behavioral Research, 10,* 277–288.

Linsky, A. S., & Straus, M. A. (1975). Student evaluations, research productivity, and eminence of college faculty. *Journal of Higher Education, 46*(1), 89–102.

Malik, D. (1996). Peer review of teaching: External review of course content. *Innovative Higher Education, 20,* 277–285.

Marincovich, M. (1999). Using student feedback to improve teaching. In P. Seldin (Ed.), *Changing practices in evaluating teaching: A practical guide to improved faculty performance and promotion/tenure decisions* (pp. 45–69). Bolton, MA: Anker.

Marine, R. J. (2002). A systems framework for evaluating faculty web work. In C. Colbeck (Ed.), *New directions for institutional research: No. 114. Evaluating faculty performance.* San Francisco, CA: Jossey-Bass.

Marlin, J. W., Jr. (1987). Student perception of end-of-course evaluations. *Journal of Higher Education, 58*(6), 704–716.

Marques, T. E., Lane, D. M., & Dorfman, P. W. (1979). Toward the development of a system for instructional evaluation: Is there consensus regarding what constitutes effective teaching? *Journal of Educational Psychology, 71,* 840–849.

Marsh, H. W. (1980). The influence of student, course, and instructor characteristics on evaluations of university teaching. *American Educational Research Journal, 17,* 219–237.

Marsh, H. W. (1982). Factors affecting students' evaluations of the same course by the same instructor on different occasions. *American Educational Research Journal, 19*(4), 485–497.

Marsh, H. W. (1982). Validity of students' evaluations of college teaching: A multitrait-multimethod analysis. *Journal of Educational Psychology, 74*(2), 264–279.

Marsh, H. W. (1983). Multidimensional ratings of teaching effectiveness by students from different academic settings and their relation to student/course/instructor characteristics. *Journal of Educational Psychology, 75*(1), 150–166.

Marsh, H. W. (1984). Students' evaluations of university teaching: Dimensionality, reliability, validity, potential biases, and utility. *Journal of Educational Psychology, 76*(5), 707–754.

Marsh, H. W. (1986). Applicability paradigm: Students' evaluations of teaching effectiveness in different countries. *Journal of Educational Psychology, 78*(6), 465–473.

Marsh, H. W. (1987). *Students' evaluations of university teaching: Research findings, methodological issues, and directions for future research.* Elmsford, NY: Pergamon Press.

Marsh, H. W. (1987). Students' evaluations of university teaching: Research findings, methodological issues, and directions for future research. *International Journal of Education Research, 11*(3), 253–388.

Marsh, H. W. (1991). A multidimensional perspective on students' evaluations of teaching effectiveness: A reply to Abrami and d'Apollonia. *Journal of Educational Psychology, 83*(3), 416–421.

Marsh, H. W. (1991). Multidimensional students' evaluations of teaching effectiveness: A test of alternative higher-order structures. *Journal of Educational Psychology, 83*(2), 285–296.

Marsh, H. W. (1994). Comments to 'review of the dimensionality of student ratings of instruction' at the 1994 annual American Educational Research Association meeting by d'Apollonia, Abrami, and Rosenfield. *Instructional Evaluation and Faculty Development, 14,* 13–19.

Marsh, H. W. (1994). Weighting for the right criteria to validate student evaluations of teaching in the IDEA system. *Journal of Educational Psychology, 86*(4), 631–648.

Marsh, H. W. (1995). Still weighting for the right criteria to validate student evaluations of teaching in the IDEA system. *Journal of Educational Psychology, 87,* 666–679.

Marsh, H. W. (2001). Distinguishing between good (useful) and bad workloads on student evaluations of teaching. *American Educational Research Journal, 38,* 183–212.

Marsh, H. W., & Bailey, M. (1993). Multidimensionality of students' evaluations of teaching effectiveness: A profile analysis. *Journal of Higher Education, 64*(1), 1–18.

Marsh, H. W., & Cooper, T. L. (1981). Prior subject interest, students' evaluations and instructional effectiveness. *Multivariate Behavioral Research, 16,* 81–104.

Marsh, H. W., & Dunkin, M. J. (1992). Students' evaluations of university teaching: A multidimensional perspective. In J. C. Smart (Ed.), *Higher Education: Handbook of Theory and Research, 8,* 143–233. New York, NY: Agathon Press.

Marsh, H. W., & Dunkin, M. J. (1997). Students' evaluations of university teaching: A multidimensional perspective. In R. Perry & J. Smart (Eds.), *Effective teaching in higher education: Research and practice.* New York, NY: Agathon Press.

Marsh, H. W., & Hocevar, D. (1984). The factorial invariance of student evaluations of college teaching. *American Educational Research Journal, 21*(2), 341–366.

Marsh, H. W., & Hocevar, D. (1991). Students' evaluations of teaching effectiveness: The stability of mean ratings of the same teachers over a 13-year period. *Teaching and Teacher Education, 7,* 303–314.

Marsh, H. W., & Hocevar, D. (1991). The multidimensionality of students' evaluations of teaching effectiveness: The generality of factor structures across academic discipline, instructor level, and course level. *Teaching and Teacher Education, 7*(1), 9–18.

Marsh, H. W., & Overall, J. U. (1979). Long-term stability of students' evaluations: A note on Feldman's consistency and variability among college students in rating their teachers and courses. *Research in Higher Education, 10*(2), 139–147.

Marsh, H. W., & Overall, J. U. (1980). Validity of students' evaluations of teaching effectiveness: Cognitive and affective criteria. *Journal of Educational Psychology, 72,* 468–475.

Marsh, H. W., & Overall, J. U. (1981). The relative influence of course level, course type, and instructor on students' evaluations of college teaching. *American Educational Research Journal, 18,* 103–112.

Marsh, H. W., & Roche, L. A. (1992). The use of student evaluations of university instructors in different settings. *Australian Journal of Education, 36,* 278–300.

Marsh, H. W., & Roche, L. A. (1993). The use of students' evaluations and an individually structured intervention to enhance university teaching effectiveness. *American Educational Research Journal, 30*(1), 217–251.

Marsh, H. W., & Roche, L. A. (1997). Making students' evaluations of teaching effectiveness effective: The critical issues of validity, bias, and utility. *American Psychologist, 52*(11), 1187–1197.

Marsh, H. W., & Roche, L. A. (1999). Rely upon SET research. *American Psychologist, 54*(7), 517–518.

Marsh, H. W., & Roche, L. A. (2000). Effects of grading leniency and low workload on students' evaluations of teaching: Popular myth, bias, validity, and innocent bystanders. *Journal of Educational Psychology, 92,* 202–228.

Marsh, H. W., & Solomon, D. (1958). Student ratings of instructors: A validity study. *Journal of Educational Research, 51,* 379–382.

Marsh, H. W., & Ware, J. E., Jr. (1982). Effects of expressiveness, content coverage, and incentive on multidimensional student rating scales: New interpretations of the Dr. Fox effect, *Journal of Educational Psychology, 74*(1), 126–134.

Marsh, H. W., Fleiner, H., & Thomas, C. S. (1975). Validity and usefulness of student evaluations of instructional quality. *Journal of Educational Psychology, 67*(6), 883–889.

Marsh, H. W., Overall, J. U., & Kesler, S. P. (1979). Class size, students' evaluations, and instructional effectiveness. *American Educational Research Journal, 16*(1), 57–69.

Marsh, H. W., Overall, J. U., & Kesler, S. P. (1979). Validity of student evaluations of instructional effectiveness: A comparison of faculty self-evaluations and evaluation by their students. *Journal of Educational Psychology, 71,* 149–160.

Martin, R. E., et al. (1983). A planned program for evaluation and development of clinical pharmacy faculty. *American Journal of Pharmaceutical Education, 47*(2), 102–107.

Maslow, A. H., & Zimmerman, W. (1956). College teaching ability, scholarly activity, and personality. *Journal of Educational Psychology, 47,* 185–189.

Mathias, H. (1984). The evaluation of university teaching: Context, values, and innovation. *Assessment and Evaluation in Higher Education, 9*(2), 79–96.

Mathias, H., & Rutherford, D. (1982). Lecturers as evaluators: The Birmingham experience. *Studies in Higher Education, 7*(1), 47–56.

McBean, E. A., & Al-Nassir, S. (1982). Questionnaire design for student measurement of teaching effectiveness. *Higher Education, 11*(3), 273–288.

McBean, E. A., & Lennox, W. C. (1982). Issues of teaching effectiveness as observed via course critiques. *Higher Education, 11*(6), 645–655.

McBean, E. A., & Lennox, W. C. (1985). Effect of survey size on student ratings of teaching. *Higher Education, 14*(2), 117–125.

McCallum, L. W. (1984). A meta-analysis of course evaluation data and its use in tenure decisions. *Research in Higher Education, 21*(2), 150–158

McCarthy, P. R., & Shmeck, R. R. (1982). Effects of teacher self-disclosure on student learning and perceptions of teacher. *College Student Journal, 16*(1), 45–49.

McConnell, D., & Hodgson, V. (1985). The development of student constructed lecture feedback questionnaires. *Assessment and Evaluation in Higher Education, 9*(3), 2–27.

McGrath, E. J. (1962). Characteristics of outstanding college teachers. *Journal of Higher Education, 33,* 148–152.

McInnis, C. (2002). The impact of technology on faculty performance and its evaluation. In C. Colbeck (Ed.), *New directions for institutional research: No. 114. Evaluating faculty performance.* San Francisco, CA: Jossey-Bass.

McKeachie, W. J. (1979). Student ratings of faculty: A reprise. *Academe, 65*(6), 384–397.

McKeachie, W. J. (1980). Class size, large classes, and multiple sections. *Academe, 66,* 24–27.

McKeachie, W. J. (1983). The role of faculty evaluation in enhancing college teaching. *Phi Kappa Journal, 63*(2), 37–39.

McKeachie, W. J. (1990). Research on college teaching: The historical background. *Journal of Educational Psychology, 82*(2), 189–200.

McKeachie, W. J. (1996). Do we need norms of student ratings to evaluate faculty? *Instructional Evaluation and Faculty Development, 16*(1), 14–17.

McKeachie, W. J. (1997). Student ratings: The validity of use. *American Psychologist, 52*(11), 1218–1225.

McKeachie, W. J. (1999). Teaching, learning, and thinking about teaching and learning. In J. C. Smart (Ed.), *Higher education: Handbook of theory and research* (Vol. 14). New York, NY: Agathon Press.

McKeachie, W. J., & Lin, Y. G. (1976). Multiple discriminate analysis of student ratings of college teachers. *Journal of Educational Research, 68,* 300–305.

McKeachie, W. J., & Lin, Y. G. (1979). A note on validity of student ratings of teaching. *Educational Research Quarterly, 4*(3), 45–47.

McKeachie, W. J., & Svinicki, M. (2006). *McKeachie's teaching tips: Strategies, research, and theory for college and university teachers* (12th ed.). Boston, MA: Houghton Mifflin.

McKeachie, W. J., Lin, Y. G., & Mann, W. (1971). Student ratings of teaching effectiveness: Validity studies. *American Educational Research Journal, 8,* 435–445.

McMahon, J. D., & Caret, R. K. (1997). Redesigning the faculty roles and rewards structure. *Metropolitan Universities Journal, 7*(4), 11–22.

Meier, R. S., & Feldhusen, J. F. (1979). Another look at Dr. Fox: Effect of stated purpose for evaluation, lecturer expressiveness, and density of lecture content on student ratings, *Journal of Educational Psychology, 71*(3), 339–345.

Menges, R. J. (1973). The new reporters: Students rate instruction. In C. R. Pace (Ed.), *New directions in higher education: No. 4. Evaluating learning and teaching* (pp. 59–75). San Francisco, CA: Jossey-Bass.

Menges, R. J. (1979). Evaluating teaching effectiveness: What is the proper role for students? *Liberal Education, 65,* 356–370.

Menges, R. J. (1988). Research on teaching and learning: The relevant and the redundant. *Review of Higher Education, 11*(3), 259–268.

Menges, R. J. (2000). Shortcomings of research on evaluating and improving teaching in higher education. In K. E. Ryan (Ed.), *New directions for teaching and learning: No. 83. Evaluating teaching in higher education: A vision of the future.* San Francisco, CA: Jossey-Bass.

Menges, R., & Svinicki, M. (Eds.). (1995). *New directions for teaching and learning: No. 65. Honoring exemplary teaching.* San Francisco, CA: Jossey-Bass.

Meredith, G. M. (1980). Impact of lecture size on student-based ratings of instruction. *Psychological Reports, 46,* 21–22.

Meredith, G. M. (1982). Grade-related attitude correlates of instructor/course satisfaction among college students. *Psychological Reports, 50,* 1142.

Meredith, G. M. (1983). Factor-specific items for appraisal of laboratory and seminar/discussion group experiences among college students. *Perceptual and Motor Skills, 56*(1), 133–134.

Meredith, G. M., & Ogasawara, T. H. (1981). Lecture size and students' ratings of instructional effectiveness. *Perceptual and Motor Skills, 52,* 353–354.

Miller, A. H. (1988). Student assessment of teaching in higher education. *Higher Education, 17,* 3–15.

Miller, M. D. (1982). Factorial validity of a clinical teaching scale. *Educational and Psychological Measurement, 42*(4), 1141–1147.

Miller, M. T. (1971). Instructor attitudes toward, and their use of, student ratings of teachers. *Journal of Educational Psychology, 62,* 235–239.

Miller, R. I. (1972). *Evaluating faculty performance.* San Francisco, CA: Jossey-Bass.

Miller, R. I. (1987). *Evaluating faculty for promotion and tenure.* San Francisco, CA: Jossey-Bass.

Miller, S. (1984). Student rating scales for tenure and promotion. *Improving College and University Teaching, 32*(2), 87–90.

Millis, B. J. (1992). Conducting effective peer classroom observations. In D. H. Wulff & J. D. Nyquist (Eds.), *To improve the academy: Vol. 11. Resources for faculty, instructional, and organizational development* (pp. 189–206). Stillwater, OK: New Forums Press.

Millman, J. (1981). *Handbook of teacher evaluation.* Beverly Hills, CA: Sage.

Mintzes, J. J. (1982). Relationship between student perceptions of teaching behavior and learning outcomes in college biology. *Journal of Research in Science Teaching, 19*(9), 789–794.

Morrow, J. (1977). Some statistics regarding the reliability and validity of student ratings of teachers. *Research Quarterly, 48,* 372–375.

Moses, I. (1986). Self and student evaluation of academic staff. *Assessment and Evaluation in Higher Education, 11*(1), 76–86.

Muchinsky, P. (1995). Peer review of teaching: Lessons learned from military and industrial research on peer assessment. *Journal on Excellence in College Teaching, 6*(3), 17–30.

Murphy, K. R., & Cleveland, J. N. (1991). *Performance appraisal: An organizational perspective.* Boston, MA: Allyn and Bacon.

Murphy, K. R., Balzer, W. K., Kellam, K. L., & Armstrong, J. G. (1984). Effects of the purpose of rating on accuracy in observing teacher behavior and evaluating teacher performance. *Journal of Educational Psychology, 76*, 45–54.

Murray, H. G. (1975). Predicting student ratings of college teaching from peer ratings of personality types. *Teaching of Psychology, 2*(2), 66–69.

Murray, H. G. (1983). Low-inference classroom teaching behaviors and student ratings of college teaching effectiveness. *Journal of Educational Psychology, 75*(1), 138–149.

Murray, H. G. (1984). The impact of formative and summative evaluation of teaching in North American universities. *Assessment and Evaluation in Higher Education, 9*(2), 117–132.

Murray, H. G. (1985). Classroom teaching behaviors related to college teaching effectiveness. In J. G. Donald & A. M. Sullivan (Eds.), *New directions for teaching and learning: No. 23. Using research to improve teaching* (pp. 21–34). San Francisco, CA: Jossey-Bass.

Murray, H. G. (1991). Effective teaching behaviors in the college classroom. In J. C. Smart (Ed.), *Higher education: Handbook of theory and research* (Vol. 7). New York, NY: Agathon Press.

Murray, H. G. (1997). Does evaluation of teaching lead to improvement of teaching? *International Journal of Academic Development, 2*(1), 8–23.

Murray, H. G. (2001). Low-inference teaching behaviors and college teaching effectiveness: Recent developments and controversies. In J. C. Smart (Ed.), *Higher education: Handbook of theory and research* (Vol. 16). New York, NY: Agathon Press.

Murray, H. G., & Renaud, R. (1995). Disciplinary differences in classroom teaching behaviors. In N. Hativa & M. Marincovich (Eds.), *New directions for teaching and learning: No. 64. Disciplinary differences in teaching and learning: Implications for practice.* San Francisco, CA: Jossey-Bass.

Murray, H. G., Rushton, J. P., & Paunonen, S. V. (1990). Teacher personality traits and student instructional ratings in six types of university courses. *Journal of Educational Psychology, 82*(2), 250–261.

Naftulin, D. H., Ware, J. E. and Donnelly, F. A. (1973). The Dr. Fox lecture: A paradigm of educational seduction. *Journal of Medical Education, 48*, 630–635.

Neumann, L., & Neumann, Y. (1985). Determinants of students' instructional evaluation: A comparison of four levels of academic areas. *Journal of Educational Psychology, 78*, 152–158.

Neumann, R. (2001). Disciplinary differences and university teaching. *Studies in Higher Education, 26*(2), 135–146.

Newman, R., Couturier, L., & Scurry, J. (2004). *The future of higher education: Rhetoric, reality, and the risks of the market.* San Francisco, CA: Jossey-Bass.

Newstead, S. E., & Arnold, J. (1989). The effect of response format on ratings of teaching. *Educational and Psychological Measurement, 49*(1), 33–43.

Newton, R. R. (1982). Performance evaluation in education. *Journal of the College and University Personnel Association, 33*(2), 39–43.

Nimmer, J. G., & Stone, E. F. (1991). Effects of grading practices and time of rating on student evaluations of faculty performance and student learning. *Research in Higher Education, 32*(2), 195–215.

Nordstron, K. (1995). Multiple-purpose use of a peer review of course instruction program in a multidisciplinary university department. *Journal on Excellence in College Teaching, 6*(3), 125–144.

North, J. D. (1999). Administrative courage to evaluate the complexities of teaching. In P. Seldin (Ed.), *Changing practices in evaluating teaching: A practical guide to improve faculty performance and promotion/tenure decisions* (pp. 183–193). Bolton, MA: Anker.

Null, E. J., & Nicholson, E. W. (1972). Personal variables of students and their perception of university instructors. *College Student Journal, 6*, 6–9.

Obenchain, K. M., Abernathy, T. V., & Wiest, L. R. (2001). The reliability of students' ratings of faculty teaching effectiveness. *College Teaching, 49*(3), 100–104.

O'Hanlon, J. O., & Mortensen, L. (1980). Making teacher evaluation work. *Journal of Higher Education, 51*, 664–672.

Ohler, S. & Theall, M. (2004). An exploratory study of teacher opinions about teaching and learning on-line and face-to-face: The instructional choices of a sample of faculty in computer science. *Instructional Evaluation and Faculty Development, 24*(1).

Orpen, C. (1980). Student evaluation of lecturers as an indicator of instructional quality: A validity study. *Journal of Educational Research, 74*, 5–7.

Ory, J. C. (1980). Evaluative criteria: How important and to whom? *Center on Evaluation Development and Research Quarterly, 13*, 14–16.

Ory, J. C. (1982). Item placement and wording effects on overall ratings. *Educational and Psychological Measurement, 42*(3), 767–775.

Ory, J. C. (2000). Teaching evaluation: Past, present, and future. In K. E. Ryan (Ed.), *New directions for teaching and learning: No. 83. Evaluating teaching in higher education: A vision for the future* (pp. 13–18). San Francisco, CA: Jossey-Bass.

Ory, J. C., & Braskamp, L. A. (1981). Faculty perceptions of the quality and usefulness of three types of evaluative information. *Research in Higher Education, 15*(3), 271–282.

Ory, J. C., & Braskamp, L. A. (2001). Faculty thoughts and concerns about student ratings. In K. G. Lewis (Ed.), *New directions for teaching and learning: No. 87. Techniques and strategies for interpreting student evaluations.* San Francisco, CA: Jossey-Bass.

Ory, J. C., & Parker, S. A. (1989). Assessment activities at large, research universities. *Research in Higher Education, 30*(4), 375–385.

Ory, J. C., & Ryan, K. (2001). How do student ratings measure up to a new validity framework? In M. Theall, P. C. Abrami, & L. A. Mets (Eds.), *New directions for institutional research: No. 109. The student ratings debate: Are they valid?* San Francisco, CA: Jossey-Bass.

Ory, J. C., Brandenburg, D. C., & Pieper, D. M. (1980). Selection of course evaluation items by high and low rated faculty. *Research in Higher Education, 12,* 245–253.

Ory, J. C., Braskamp, L. A., & Pieper, D. M. (1980). Congruency of student evaluative information collected by three methods. *Journal of Educational Psychology, 72*(1), 321–325.

Overall, J. U., & Marsh, H. W. (1979). Midterm feedback from students: Its relationship to instructional improvement and students' cognitive and affective outcomes. *Journal of Educational Psychology, 71,* 856–865.

Overall, J. U., & Marsh, H. W. (1980). Students' evaluations of instruction: A longitudinal study of their stability. *Journal of Educational Psychology, 72*(2), 321–325.

Overall, J. U. & Marsh, H. W. (1982). Students' evaluations of teaching: An update. *AAHE Bulletin, 35*(4), 9–13.

Palmer, J. (1983). Sources and information: Faculty and administrator evaluation. In R. J. Ernst (Ed.), *New directions for community colleges: No. 11. Adjusting to collective bargaining* (pp. 109–118). San Francisco, CA: Jossey-Bass.

Pambookian, H. S. (1974). Initial level of student evaluation of instruction as a source of influence on change after feedback. *Journal of Educational Psychology, 66,* 52–56.

Pasen, R. M., Frey, P. W., Menges, R. J., & Rath, G. J. (1978). Different administrative directions and student ratings on instruction: Cognitive versus affective states. *Research in Higher Education, 9,* 161–168.

Paulsen, M. B. (2001). The relation between research and the scholarship of teaching. In C. Kreber (Ed.), *New directions for teaching and learning: No. 86. Scholarship revisited: Defining and implementing the scholarship of teaching.* San Francisco, CA: Jossey-Bass.

Paulsen, M. B. (2002). Evaluating teaching performance. In C. Colbeck (Ed.), *New directions for institutional research: No. 114. Evaluating faculty performance.* San Francisco, CA: Jossey-Bass.

Paulsen, M. B., & Feldman, K. A. (1995). Toward a reconceptualization of scholarship: A human action system with functional imperatives. *The Journal of Higher Education, 66*(6), 615–640.

Payne, D. A., & Hobbs, A. M. (1979). The effect of college course evaluation feedback on instructor and student perceptions of instructional climate and effectiveness. *Higher Education, 8,* 525–533.

Pellino, G. R., Blackburn, R. T., & Boberg, A. L. (1984). The dimensions of academic scholarship: Faculty and administrator views. *Research in Higher Education, 20*(1), 103–115.

Perkins, D., & Abbott, R. (1982). Validity of student ratings for two affective outcomes of introductory psychology. *Educational and Psychological Measurement, 42*(1), 317–323.

Perry, R. P. (1985). Instructor expressiveness: Implications for improved teaching. In J. G. Donald & A. M. Sullivan (Eds.)., *New directions for teaching and learning: No. 23. Using research to improve teaching* (pp. 35–49). San Francisco, CA: Jossey-Bass.

Perry, R. P., Abrami, P. C., & Leventhal, L. (1979). Educational seduction: The effect of instructor expressiveness and lecture content on student ratings and achievement. *Journal of Educational Psychology, 71*(1), 107–116.

Perry, R. P., & Smart, J. C. (1997). *Effective teaching in higher education: Research and practice.* New York, NY: Agathon Press.

Peterson, C., & Cooper, S. (1980). Teacher evaluation by graded and ungraded students. *Journal of Educational Psychology, 72,* 682–685.

Peterson, K., Gunne, G. M., Miller, P., & Rivera, O. (1984). Multiple audience rating form strategies for student evaluation of college teaching. *Research in Higher Education, 20*(3), 309–321.

Piccinin, S. (1999). How individual consultation affects teaching. In C. Knapper & S. Piccinin (Eds.), *New directions for teaching and learning: No. 79. Using consultants to improve teaching* (pp. 71–84). San Francisco, CA: Jossey-Bass.

Piccinin, S., Cristi, C., & McCoy, M. (1999). The impact of individual consultation on student ratings of teaching. *International Journal of Academic Development, 4*(2), 75–88.

Pittman, R. B. (1985). Perceived instructional effectiveness and associated teaching dimensions. *Journal of Experimental Education, 54*(1), 34–39.

Poole, L. H., & Dellow, D. A. (1983). Evaluation of full-time faculty. In R. J. Ernst (Ed.), *New directions for community colleges: No. 11. Adjusting to collective bargaining* (pp. 19–31). San Francisco, CA: Jossey-Bass.

Powell, R. W. (1977). Grades, learning, and student evaluation of instruction. *Research in Higher Education, 7,* 193–205.

Quinlan, K. (1996). Involving peers in the evaluation and improvement of teaching: A menu of strategies. *Innovative Higher Education, 20,* 299–307.

Rayder, N. F. (1968). College student ratings of instructors. *Journal of Experimental Education, 37,* 76–81.

Redding, R. E. (1998). Students' evaluations of teaching fuel grade inflation. *American Psychologist, 53,* 1228–1229.

Remmers, H. H. (1928). The relationships between students' marks and students' attitudes toward instructors. *School and Society, 28,* 759–760.

Remmers, H. H., Martin, F. D., & Elliot, D. N. (1949). Are student ratings of their instructors related to their grades? *Purdue University Studies in Higher Education, 44,* 17–26.

Renner, R. R., & Greenwood, G. E. (1985). Professor 'X': How experts rated his student ratings. *Assessment and Evaluation in Higher Education, 10*(3), 203–212.

Renner, R. R., & Others. (1986). Responsible behaviour as effective teaching: A new look at student ratings of professors. *Assessment and Evaluation in Higher Education, 11*(2), 138–145.

Reynolds, A. (1992). What is competent beginning teaching? A review of the literature. *Review of Educational Research, 62*(1), 1–35.

Richlin, L., & Manning, B. (1995). Evaluating college and university teaching: Principles and decisions for designing a workable system. *Journal on Excellence in College Teaching, 6*(3), 3–15.

Richlin, L., & Manning, B. (1995). *Improving a college-university teaching evaluation system: A comprehensive, developmental curriculum for faculty and administrators.* Pittsburgh, PA: Alliance Publishers.

Roche, L. A., & Marsh, H. W. (2000). Multiple dimensions of university teacher self-concept. *Instructional Science, 28,* 439–468.

Romberg, E. (1984). A factor analysis of students' ratings of clinical teaching. *Journal of Dental Education, 48,* 258–262.

Root, L. S. (1987). Faculty evaluation: reliability of peer assessments of research, teaching, and service. *Research in Higher Education, 26*(1), 71–84.

Rotem, A., & Glasman, N. S. (1979). On the effectiveness of students' evaluative feedback to university instructors. *Review of Educational Research, 49,* 497–511.

Rozeman, J. E., & Kerwin, M.A. (1991). Evaluating the effectiveness of a teaching consultation program on changing student ratings of teaching behaviours. *Journal of Staff, Program, and Organizational Development, 9*(4), 223–230.

Ryan, J. M., & Harrison, P. D. (1995). The relationship between individual instructional characteristics and the overall assessment of teaching effectiveness across different instructional contexts. *Research in Higher Education, 36*(5), 213–228.

Ryan, K. E. (Ed.). (2001). *New directions for teaching and learning: No. 83. Evaluating teaching in higher education: A vision of the future.* San Francisco, CA: Jossey-Bass.

Saaty, T. L., & Ramanujam, V. (1983). An objective approach to faculty promotion and tenure by the analytical hierarchy process. *Research in Higher Education, 18*(3), 311–331.

Sacken, D. M. (1990). Taking teaching seriously: Institutional and individual dilemmas. *Journal of Higher Education, 61*(5), 548–564.

Sagen, H. B. (1974). Student, faculty, and department chairmen ratings of instructors: Who agrees with whom? *Research in Higher Education, 2,* 265–272.

Salsberg, H. E., & Schiller, B. (1982). A decade of student evaluations. *College Student Journal, 16*(1), 84–88.

Sauter, R. C., & Walker, J. K. (1976). A theoretical model for faculty 'peer' evaluation. *American Journal of Pharmaceutical Education, 40*(2), 165–166.

Schein, M. W. (1985). Student achievement as a measure of teaching effectiveness. *Journal of College Science Teaching, 14*(6), 471–474.

Scheurich, V., Graham, B., & Drolette, M. (1983). Expected grades versus specific evaluations of the teacher as predictors of students' overall evaluation of the teacher. *Research in Higher Education, 19*(2), 159–173.

Scriven, M. (1988). The validity of student ratings. *Instructional Evaluation, 9,* 5–18.

Scriven, M. (1994). Duties of the teacher. *Journal of Personnel Evaluation in Education, 8,* 151–184.

Scwier, R. A. (1982). Design and use of student evaluation instruments in instructional development. *Journal of Instructional Development, 5*(4), 28–34.

Seldin, P. (1980). *Successful faculty evaluation programs: A practical guide to improve faculty performance and promotion/tenure decisions.* Cruger, NY: Coventry Press.

Seldin, P. (1982). Improving faculty evaluation systems. *Peabody Journal of Education, 59*(2), 93–99.

Seldin, P. (1982). Self-assessment of college teaching. *Improving College and University Teaching, 30*(2), 70–74.

Seldin, P. (1984). *Changing practices in faculty evaluation.* San Francisco, CA: Jossey-Bass.

Seldin, P. (1988). *Evaluating and developing administrative performance.* San Francisco, CA: Jossey-Bass.

Seldin, P. (1993). How colleges evaluate professors: 1983 vs. 1993. *AAHE Bulletin, 45*(2), 6–12.

Seldin, P. (1993). *Successful use of teaching portfolios.* Bolton, MA: Anker.

Seldin, P. (1998). How colleges evaluate teaching: 1988 vs. 1998. *AAHE Bulletin, 50*(7), 3–7.

Seldin, P. (2004). *The teaching portfolio: A practical guide to improved performance and promotion/tenure decisions* (3rd ed.). Bolton, MA: Anker.

Seldin, P., & Associates. (1995). *Improving college teaching.* Bolton, MA: Anker.

Seldin, P., & Associates. (1999). *Changing practices in evaluating teaching: A practical guide to improved faculty performance and promotion/tenure decisions.* Bolton, MA: Anker.

Selmes, C. (1989). Evaluation of teaching. *Assessment and Evaluation in Higher Education, 14*(3), 167–178.

Shapiro, E. G. (1990). Effect of instructor and class characteristics on students' class evaluations. *Research in Higher Education, 31*(2), 135–148.

Shea, M. A. (1997). Variability among faculty. In K. T. Brinko & R. J. Menges (Eds.)., *Practically speaking: A sourcebook for instructional consultants in higher education* (pp. 181–186). Stillwater, OK: New Forums Press.

Sherman, T. M. (1978). The effects of student formative evaluation of instruction on teacher behavior. *Journal of Educational Technology Systems, 6,* 209–217.

Shevlin, M., Banyard, P., Davies, M., & Griffiths, M. (2000). The validity of student evaluation of teaching in higher education: Love me, love my lectures? *Assessment and Evaluation in Higher Education, 25*(4), 397.

Shore, B., Pinker, S., & Bates, M. (1990). Research as a model for university teaching. *Higher Education, 19,* 21–38.

Shulman, L. S. (1993). Teaching as community property: Putting an end to pedagogical solitude. *Change, 25*(6), 6–7.

Shulman, L. S. (1999). Taking teaching seriously. *Change, 31*(4), 10–17.

Silvernail, D. L., & Johnson, J. L. (1992). The impact of interactive televised instruction on student evaluations of their instructors. *Educational Technology, 32*(6), 47–50.

Skoog, G. (1980). Improving college teaching through peer observation. *Journal of Teacher Education, 31*(2), 23–25.

Small, A. C., Hollenbeck, A. R., & Haley, R. L. (1982). The effect of emotional state on student ratings of instructors. *Teaching of Psychology, 9*(4), 205–208.

Smelby, J. C. (1998). Knowledge production and knowledge transmission: the interaction between research and teaching at universities. *Teaching in Higher Education, 3,* 5–20.

Smith, A. (1983). A conceptual framework for staff evaluation. In R. J. Ernst (Ed.), *New directions for community colleges: No. 11. Adjusting to collective bargaining* (pp. 3–18). San Francisco, CA: Jossey-Bass.

Smith, M. (1982). Protecting confidentiality of faculty peer review records: Department of Labor vs. the University of California. *Journal of College and University Law, 8*(1), 20–53.

Smith, P. L. (1979). The generalizability of student ratings of courses: Asking the right questions. *Journal of Educational Measurement, 16,* 77–87.

Smith, R. A. (2001). Formative evaluation and the scholarship of teaching and learning. In C. Knapper & P. A. Cranton, (Eds.), *New directions for teaching and learning: No. 88. Fresh approaches to the evaluation of teaching.* San Francisco, CA: Jossey-Bass.

Smith, R. A., & Cranton, P. A. (1992). Students' perceptions of teaching skills and overall effectiveness across instructional settings. *Research in Higher Education, 33*(6), 747–764.

Snyder, C. R., & Clair, M. (1976). Effects of expected and obtained grades on teacher evaluations and attribution of performance. *Journal of Educational Psychology, 68,* 75–82.

Solomon, D. (1966). Teacher behavior dimensions, course characteristics, and student evaluations of teachers. *American Educational Research Journal, 3,* 35–47.

Sorcinelli, M. (1984). An approach to colleague evaluation of classroom instruction. *Journal of Instructional Development, 7*(4), 11–17.

Sorcinelli, M. D. (1994). Dealing with troublesome behaviors in the classroom. In K. W. Prichard & R. Sawyer (Eds.), *Handbook of college teaching: Theory and application.* Westport, CT: Greenwood Press.

Sorcinelli, M. D. (1997). The teaching improvement process. In K. T. Brinko & R. J. Menges (Eds.), *Practically speaking: A sourcebook for instructional consultants in higher education* (pp. 157–158). Stillwater, OK: New Forums Press.

Spence, L., & Lenze, L. F. (2001). Taking student criticism seriously: Using student quality teams to guide critical reflection. In K. G. Lewis (Ed.), *New directions for teaching and learning: No. 87. Techniques and strategies for interpreting student evaluations.* San Francisco, CA: Jossey-Bass.

Spencer, R. E., & Aleamoni, L. M. (1970). A student course evaluation questionnaire. *Journal of Educational Measurement, 7*(3), 209–210.

Stanley, C. A., Porter, M. E., & Szabo, B. L. (1997). An exploratory study of the faculty developer-client relationship. *Journal of Staff, Program, and Organizational Development, 14*(3), 115–126.

Stapleton, R. J., & Murkison, G. (2001). Optimizing the fairness of student evaluations: A study of correlations between instructor excellence, study production, learning production, and expected grades. *Journal of Management Education, 25*(3), 269–291.

Stedman, C. H. (1983). The reliability of teaching effectiveness rating scale for assessing faculty performance. *Tennessee Education, 12*(3), 25–32.

Stevens, J. J., & Aleamoni, L. M. (1985). Issues in the development of peer evaluation systems. *Instructional Evaluation, 8*(1), 4–9.

Stevens, J. J., & Aleamoni, L. M. (1985). The use of evaluative feedback for instructional improvement: A longitudinal perspective. *Instructional Science, 13*, 285–304.

Strenski, E. (1995). Two cheers for peer review: Problems of definition, interpretation, and appropriate function. *Journal on Excellence in College Teaching, 6*(3), 31–49.

Stumpf, S. A. (1979). Assessing academic program and department effectiveness using student evaluation data. *Research in Higher Education, 11*, 353–364.

Stumpf, S. A., & Freedman, R. D. (1979). Expected grade co-variation with student ratings of instruction: Individual versus class effects. *Journal of Educational Psychology, 71*, 293–302.

Stumpf, S. A., Freedman, R. D., & Aguanno, J. A. (1979). Validity of the Course-Faculty Instrument (CFI): Intrinsic and extrinsic variables. *Educational and Psychological Measurement, 39*, 153–158.

Stumpf, S. A., Freedman, R. D., & Aguanno, J. A. (1990). A path analysis of extrinsic factors related to student ratings of teaching effectiveness. *Research in Higher Education, 11*, 111–123.

Sullivan, A. M., & Skanes, G. R. (1974). Validity of student evaluations of teaching and the characteristics of successful instructors. *Journal of Educational Psychology, 66*(4), 584–590.

Sullivan, A. V. S. (1996). Teaching norms and publication productivity. In J. M. Braxton (Ed.), *New directions for institutional research: No. 90. Faculty teaching and research: Is there a conflict?* (pp. 15–21). San Francisco, CA: Jossey-Bass.

Svinicki, M. D. (2001). Encouraging your students to give feedback. In K. G. Lewis (Ed.), *New directions for teaching and learning: No. 87. Techniques and strategies for interpreting student evaluations.* San Francisco, CA: Jossey-Bass.

Theall, M. (1993). Disciplinary differences in higher education: A symposium report. *Instructional Evaluation and Faculty Development, 13*(1), 13–20.

Theall, M. (1994). What's wrong with faculty evaluation?: A debate on the state of the practice. *Instructional Evaluation and Faculty Development, 14*(1–2), 27–33.

Theall. M. (1995). When meta-analysis isn't enough: A report of a symposium on critical issues and unresolved problems in faculty evaluation practice. *Instructional Evaluation and Faculty Development, 15*(1), 1–13.

Theall, M. (1999). Why student ratings? *Advocate, 1*(3), 5–8.

Theall, M. (2000). New directions for research and theory in teaching: A look at the last twenty years. In M. Svinicki (Ed.), *New directions for teaching and learning: No. 80. Teaching and learning at the edge of the millennium: Building on what we have learned.* San Francisco, CA: Jossey-Bass.

Theall, M. (2001). Thinking about motivation: Some issues for instructional consultants In K. Lewis & J. P. Lunde (Eds.), *Face to face: A sourcebook of individual consultation techniques for faculty/instructional developers* (2nd ed.). Stillwater, OK: New Forums Press.

Theall, M. (2002). Faculty evaluation and leadership. In R. Diamond (Ed.), *A field guide to academic leadership.* San Francisco, CA: Jossey-Bass.

Theall, M. (2002). Leadership in faculty evaluation and development: some thoughts on why and how the meta-profession can control its own destiny. *Instructional Evaluation and Faculty Development, 22*(1).

Theall, M. (2005). Valid faculty evaluation data: Are there any? *Instructional Evaluation and Faculty Development, 23*(1), 6–10.

Theall, M., Abrami, P. C., & Mets, L. A. (Eds.). (2001). *New directions for institutional research: No. 109. The student ratings debate: Are they valid? How can we best use them?* San Francisco, CA: Jossey-Bass.

Theall, M., & Arreola, R. A. (2002). Planning and assessing large classes. In C. A. Stanley & M. E. Porter (Eds.), *Engaging large classes: Strategies and techniques for college faculty* (pp. 28–43). Bolton, MA: Anker.

Theall, M., & Arreola, R. A. (2006). The 'meta-profession' of college teaching. *Thriving in Academe, 22*(5), 5–8.

Theall, M., & Centra, J. A. (2001). Assessing the scholarship of teaching: Valid decisions from valid evidence. In C. Kreber (Ed.), *New directions for teaching and learning: No. 86. Scholarship revisited: Perspectives on the scholarship of teaching.* San Francisco, CA: Jossey-Bass.

Theall, M., & Franklin, J. (1989). Two different worlds: Research and practice in faculty evaluation. *Instructional Evaluation, 10*(2), 10–21.

Theall, M., & Franklin, J. (1997). Collecting information using student ratings. In K. T. Brinko & R. J. Menges (Eds.), *Practically speaking: A source book for instructional consultants in higher education.* Stillwater, OK: New Forums Press.

Theall, M., & Franklin, J. (2000). Creating responsive student ratings systems to improve evaluation practice. In K. Ryan (Ed.), *New directions for teaching and learning: No. 83. Evaluating faculty performance.* San Francisco, CA: Jossey-Bass.

Theall, M., & Franklin, J. (2002). Using technology to facilitate evaluation. In P. Cranton & C. Knapper (Eds.), *New directions for teaching and learning: No. 88. Fresh approaches to teaching evaluation.* San Francisco, CA: Jossey-Bass.

Theall, M., & Franklin, J. (Eds.). (1990). *New directions for teaching and learning: No. 43. Student ratings of instruction: Issues for improving practice.* San Francisco, CA: Jossey-Bass.

Theall, M., & Franklin, J. (Eds.). (1991). *New directions for teaching and learning: No. 48. Effective practices for teaching improvement.* San Francisco, CA: Jossey-Bass.

Theall, M., Franklin, J., & Ludlow, L. (1990). Attributions and retributions: Student ratings and the perceived causes of performance. *Instructional Evaluation, 11*(1), 12–17.

Theall, M., Powers, K., & Franklin, J. (2000). A case study in faculty evaluation and development. *Journal of Staff, Professional, and Organizational Development, 17*(4), 215–226.

Theall, M., Scriven, M., Abrami, P. C., Nuhfer, E., Franklin, J., & Arreola, R. A. (2006). Valid faculty evaluation data: A symposium report. *Instructional Evaluation and Faculty Development, 23*(2), 11–35.

Thomas, D., Ribich, F., & Freie, J. (1982). The relationship between psychological identification with instructors and student ratings of college courses. *Instructional Science, 11*(2), 139–154.

Thompson, G. E. (1988). Difficulties in interpreting course evaluations: Some Bayesian insights. *Research in Higher Education, 28*(3), 217–222.

Tiberius, R. (2001). Making sense and making use of feedback from focus groups. In K. G. Lewis (Ed.), *New directions for teaching and learning: No. 87. Techniques and strategies for interpreting student evaluations.* San Francisco, CA: Jossey-Bass.

Tiberius, R. G., Sackin, H. D., Slingerland, J. M., Jubas, K., Bell, M., & Matlow, A. (1989). The influence of student evaluative feedback on the improvement of clinical teaching. *Journal of Higher Education, 60*(6), 665–681.

Tollefson, H. (1983). Course ratings as measures of instructional effectiveness. *Instructional Science, 12*(4), 389–395.

Tollefson, H., & Tracy, D. B. (1983). Comparison of self-reported teaching behaviors of award-winning and non-award winning university faculty. *Perceptual and Motor Skills, 56*(1), 39–44.

Tollefson, N., Chen, J. S., & Kleinsasser, A. (1989). The relationship of students' attitudes about effective teaching to students' ratings of effective teaching. *Educational and Psychological Measurement, 49*(3), 529–536.

Trice, A. J. (1992, June 17). The tensions between teaching and scholarship. *Chronicle of Higher Education,* p. B4.

Turcotte, S. J. C., & Leventhal, L. (1984). Gain-loss versus reinforcement-affect ordering of student rating of teaching: Effect of rating instructions. *Journal of Educational Psychology, 76*(5), 782–791.

Van Allen, G. H. (1982). Students rate community college faculty as slightly above average. *Community College Review, 10*(1), 41–43.

Vasta, R., & Sarmiento, R. F. (1979). Liberal grading improves evaluations but not performance. *Journal of Educational Psychology, 71,* 207–211.

Wachtel, H. K. (1998). Student evaluation of college teaching effectiveness: A brief review. *Assessment and Evaluation in Higher Education, 23*(2), 191.

Ware, J. E., Jr., & Williams, R. G. (1975). The Dr. Fox effect: A study of lecturer effectiveness and ratings of instruction. *Journal of Medical Education, 50*(2), 149–156.

Ware, J. E., Jr., & Williams, R. G. (1977). Discriminant analysis of student ratings as a means of identifying lecturers who differ in enthusiasm or information giving. *Educational and Psychological Measurement, 37*(3), 627–639.

Waters, M., Kemp, E., & Pucci, A. (1988). High and low faculty evaluations: Descriptions by students. *Teaching of Psychology, 15,* 203–204.

Watkins, D. (1990). Student ratings of tertiary courses for 'alternative calendar' purposes. *Assessment and Evaluation in Higher Education, 15*(1), 12–21.

Watkins, D. (1994). Student evaluations of teaching effectiveness: A cross-cultural perspective. *Research in Higher Education, 35,* 251–266.

Watkins, D., & Thomas, B. (1991). Assessing teaching effectiveness: An Indian perspective. *Assessment and Evaluation in Higher Education, 16*(3), 185–198.

Weber, L. J., & Frary, R. B. (1982). Profile uniqueness in student ratings of instruction. *Journal of Experimental Education, 51*(1), 42–45.

Webster, D. (1985). Does research productivity enhance teaching? *Educational Record, 66,* 60–62.

Webster, D. (1986). Research productivity and classroom teaching effectiveness. *Instructional Evaluation, 9,* 14–20.

Webster, D. S. (1985). Institutional effectiveness using scholarly peer assessments as major criteria. *Review of Higher Education, 9*(1), 67–82.

Weeks, K. M. (1990). The peer review process: Confidentiality and disclosure. *Journal of Higher Education, 61,* 2.

Weimer, M. (1990). *Improving college teaching: Strategies for developing instructional effectiveness.* San Francisco, CA: Jossey-Bass.

Whitely, S. E., & Doyle, K. O. (1976). Implicity theories in student ratings. *American Educational Research Journal, 13,* 241–253.

Whitely, S. E., & Doyle, K. O. (1979). Validity and generalizability of student ratings between-classes and within-class data. *Journal of Educational Psychology, 71,* 117–124.

Whitley, J. S. (1984). Are student evaluations constructive criticism? *Community and Junior College Journal, 54*(7), 41–42.

Whitmore, J., & Gillespie, P. P. (1983). Resolved: That directing plays and readers theater productions should be evaluated more as a part of teaching than as research and creative work. *Association for Communication Administration Bulletin, 44,* 21–24.

Wigington, H., Tollefson, N., & Rodriquez, E. (1989). Students' ratings of instructors revisited: Interactions among class and instructor variables. *Research in Higher Education, 30*(3), 331–344.

Williams, R. G., & Ware, J. E. (1976). Validity of student ratings of instruction under different incentive conditions: A further study of the Dr. Fox effect. *Journal of Educational Psychology, 68*(1), 48–56.

Williams, W. M., & Ceci, S. J. (1997). How'm I doing?: Problems with student ratings of instructors and courses. *Change, 29*(5), 13–23.

Wilson, R. C. (1986). Improving faculty teaching: Effective use of student evaluations and consultants. *Journal of Higher Education, 57*(2), 196–211.

Wilson, R. C. (1990). Commentary: The education of a faculty developer. *Journal of Educational Psychology, 82*(2), 272–274.

Wilson, T. C. (1988). Student evaluation-of-teaching forms: A critical perspective. *Review of Higher Education 12*(1), 79–95.

Wilson, W. R. (1999, September/October). Students rating teachers. *Journal of Higher Education, 70*(5), 562–571. (Original work published 1932)

Wood, K., Linsky, A. S., & Straus, M. A. (1974). Class size and student evaluation of faculty. *Journal of Higher Education, 45*(7), 524–534.

Worthington, A. G., & Wong, P. T. P. (1979). Effects of earned and assigned grades on student evaluations of an instructor. *Journal of Educational Psychology, 71,* 764–775.

Wotruba, T. R., & Wright, P. L. (1975). How to develop a teacher-rating instrument: A research approach. *Journal of Higher Education, 46,* 653–663.

Wright, W. A., & Associates. (1995). *Teaching improvement practices: Successful strategies for higher education.* Bolton, MA: Anker.

Wright, W. A., & O'Neil, M. C. (1992). Improving summative student ratings of instruction practices. *Journal of Staff, Program, and Organizational Development, 10*(2), 75–85.

Wulff, D. H., Staton-Spicer, A., Hess, C., & Nyquist, J. (1985). The student perspective on evaluating teaching effectiveness. *ACA Bulletin, 53,* 39–47.

Young, R. J., & Gwalamubisi, Y. (1986). Perceptions about current and ideal methods and purposes of faculty evaluation. *Community College Review, 13*(4), 27–33.

Index